Ordnance Survey
The Cotswolds
Landranger Guidebook

Compiled by Peter and Helen Titchmarsh

JARROLD

How to use this Guide

Space has not allowed us to include every place on the relevant Landranger Maps in the **Places of Special Interest** section (pages 21-121). The items have been selected, however, to provide you with a varied and interesting companion during your travels around the Cotswolds and some of the towns and places of interest nearby. Places of exceptional interest have been highlighted by being printed in blue, and any place which has a separate entry in the **Places of Special Interest** section is identified in the text by a star symbol: ★.

Each entry is identified first by the number of the Landranger map or maps on which it appears (e.g. 163, 164, etc). This is followed by two letters (e.g. SP) and by a four-figure reference number (e.g. 07-37). The first two figures of this number are those which appear in blue along the north and south edges of Landranger maps; the other two appear in blue along the east and west edges.

Therefore, to locate any place or feature referred to in this guide book on the relevant Landranger map, first read the two figures along the north or south edges of the map, then the two figures along the east or west edges. Trace the lines adjacent to each of the two sets of figures across the map face and the point where they intersect will be the south-west corner of the grid square in which the place or feature lies. Thus Taynton falls in the grid square 23-13 on Landranger map 163.

The Key Maps on pages 4-7 identify the suggested starting points of our five tours and twelve walks, and in the **Tours** and **Walks** sections, all places which also have a separate entry in the **Places of Special Interest** section are in bold type. Each tour and walk is accompanied by a map, and there are cross-references between Tours and Walks on both the maps and in the text. Also to be found in the **Places of Special Interest** section are sixteen maps, on each of which is marked a suggested **mini-walk**. These **mini-walks** are listed on page 22.

Acknowledgements

We would like to thank the staff of all the Tourist Information Centres in the area for their help and advice. Our special thanks also to Mr Ted Fryer of the Cotswold Warden Service, who provided much vital information on the routing of a number of the walks.

Ordnance Survey ISBN 0-319-00180-6
Jarrold Publishing ISBN 0-7117-0564-X

First published 1989 by Ordnance Survey and Jarrold Publishing
Reprinted 1991

Ordnance Survey
Romsey Road
Maybush
Southampton SO9 4DH

Jarrold Publishing
Barrack Street
Norwich NR3 1TR

Contents

KEY MAP INDEX

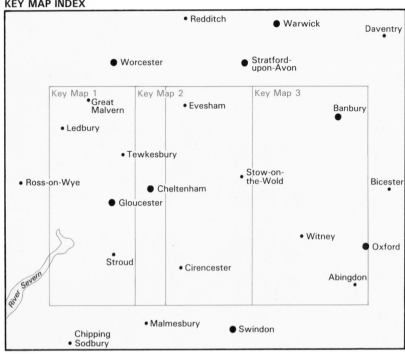

Motor and Cycle Tour Start

Walk Start

Mini-Walk Start

LANDRANGER MAPS OF THE COTSWOLDS

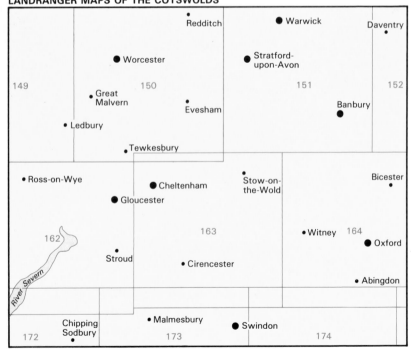

Key Map 1

SCALE 1:250 000 or 4 MILES to 1 INCH

0 1 km = 0·6214 mile   5   10   Kilometres 15

0 1 mile = 1·61 kms   5   Miles   10

Key Map 2

Key Map 3

SCALE 1:250 000 or 4 MILES to 1 INCH

0   1 km = 0·6214 mile   5   10   Kilometres   15

0   1 mile = 1·61 kms   5   Miles   10

The landscape of the Cotswolds

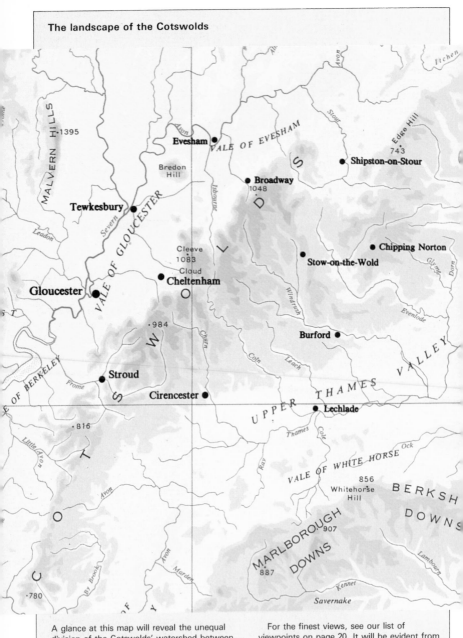

A glance at this map will reveal the unequal division of the Cotswolds' watershed between the Thames and the Severn/Avon. From the steep north-western scarp flow the Stour, the Isbourne and the Frome, while a series of longer, more leisurely streams flow south and east to the Thames. These include the headwaters of the Thames itself, the Churn, the Coln, the Leach, the Windrush and the Evenlode. Many of the choicest Cotswold villages will be found in the valleys of these clear-watered streams, and each valley can be explored, either on foot or by road.

For the finest views, see our list of viewpoints on page 20. It will be evident from this map that most of these will be westwards, out over the Vales of Berkeley, Gloucester or Evesham to the Malverns, the Forest of Dean and the mountains of mid-Wales. However, there are also many less dramatic prospects southwards across the broad valley of the Upper Thames to the distant line of the Marlborough and Berkshire Downs.

Introduction

This guide covers the whole of the classic Cotswold country, from Chipping Norton in the east, to Dursley and Tetbury in the south-west. It also takes in many places of particular interest lying outside these confines, including Cheltenham, Gloucester, Tewkesbury, Berkeley, Woodstock and Witney. Although not necessary for its enjoyment, Landranger Maps 150, 151, 162, 163 and 164 could go hand in hand with the book, to provide a companion without equal in the exploration of this exceptionally beautiful area.

Regrettably perhaps, the Cotswolds are no longer characterised by the 'high wild hills and rough uneven ways' of Shakespeare's *Richard II*. The centuries following Shakespeare's days have, however, been very gentle with this countryside and today it offers a compelling variety of natural and man-made features. Without the more dramatic appeal of the mountains and moorlands of the north and west, the Cotswolds attracted only a handful of visitors before the latter part of the 19th century. It was from this time onwards that a number of factors contributed to the gradual awakening of the Cotswolds — their 'discovery' by William Morris and his Pre-Raphaelite friends, the publication of Arthur Gibbs's *A Cotswold Village* (see Ablington), and the activities of various artists and

A guide to distant horizons at Dover's Hill

craftsmen who settled in the hills in the early years of the 20th century. It was, however, the arrival of the motor car on their then still dusty upland roads that really established the Cotswolds as a tourist area, in the 1920s and '30s.

What are the features which drew these early visitors to the Cotswolds, and which continue to enchant us today? The physical divisions are reasonably clear and may be outlined as follows. A long, relatively steep scarp face extends south-westwards from Mickleton, near Stratford-upon-Avon, to Wotton-under-Edge and the countryside north of Bath. This scarp, with its splendid views out over the Avon and Severn Valleys, has always provided fine walking country, and for many years it has been possible to traverse it by using the well-signed Cotswold Way.

Behind this edge, the hills to its east consist largely of open wold country — the Cotswolds' best-known feature. Here were the great sheep runs of the Middle Ages, later divided up by long dry-stone walls erected largely during the 18th and 19th centuries, the time of the enclosures, and also relieved by the scattered beech plantations of the great enclosing landlords. These walls and woodlands still endure — both essential elements of the present-day Cotswold scene. The northern half of this area, between Chipping Campden and Winchcombe, consists of wide, rolling country with many distant views and broad open skies. It lies largely within the Thames watershed, and few streams of any consequence flow north or west to join the Avon or Severn.

Further south, beyond Cheltenham, the character of much of the hill country changes considerably. Here are deep, often densely wooded valleys, some carrying streams flowing south to the Thames, and others feeding the Severn, largely via the deeply intruding valley of the River Frome. This was the country which gave birth to the great cloth industry of the 17th, 18th and early 19th centuries, an industry which has just survived until the present day.

To the east of these wooded valleys, beyond Tetbury and Cirencester, and further eastwards to Bibury and Burford, the character of the countryside is closer to that of the northern Cotswolds, with its open wold country here intersected by a series of delightful clear-watered streams flowing southwards to the Thames. The area's southern extremities merge with the flat gravel country of the Upper Thames Valley, and beyond Burford, to the east, lie the remains of the great forest of Wychwood.

These are the natural divisions of the Cotswolds — an area of infinite beauty even without further adornment. But happily the towns and villages amongst these hills are also enriched by some of the loveliest medieval churches and domestic buildings to be found anywhere in Britain, and it is this architectural flowering in such a perfect series of settings that endows the Cotswolds with a quite unique flavour.

To guide you to the very best of these features, we have devised a series of five **tours**. They are, like the guide as a whole, self-contained, but if you purchase the relevant Landranger map or maps you will be able to vary these tours to suit your own requirements. They have been designed primarily for motorists, but most are also suitable for cyclists.

We have also provided a series of twelve **walks** in widely varied countryside, and each of these links on to at least one of the tours. There are also sixteen **mini-walks** depicted on the maps in the **Places of Special Interest** section. We cannot stress too strongly that whilst your car is an ideal means to 'arrive' at an area, to gain real enjoyment and satisfaction it is infinitely preferable to explore it on foot once you have arrived. So, if you do decide to use the **Tours** section, please do so with discretion, and take your walking gear with you.

We do hope that you enjoy the Cotswolds as much as we have over the last forty years or so. With good fortune we hope to continue our explorations well into the future. We shall look out for you!

Peter & Helen Titchmarsh.

History Revealed . . .
A Short Survey of the
Area's Past

Being comparatively easy to cultivate, Cotswold limestone, like downland chalk, provided Neolithic (or Stone Age) man with ideal farming country. Having arrived from continental Europe, these early settlers moved inland, and by 2500 BC they had firmly established themselves on the upland ridges of the Cotswolds. Relics of this era include the fine burial mounds (or long barrows) of **Hetty Pegler's Tump**, **Belas Knap** and **Notgrove**.

About 2000 BC the so-called Beaker Folk moved westward from the Continent, heralding the Bronze Age, a culture that was to spread even further westwards than its Neolithic predecessor. This culture was characterised by burials made in round barrows, few very dramatic examples of which are to be found in the Cotswolds. Bronze Age man worshipped at stone circles or henges, the most famous of which are at Stonehenge and Avebury in Wiltshire. However, the only circle of any significance in our area is to be found above Long Compton — the interesting but more modest **Rollright Stones**, which are situated close to the line of one of Britain's great prehistoric trade routes, **The Jurassic Way**.

Belas Knap Long Barrow . . . over 4000 years old

A third wave of settlers, the Belgic, Iron Age peoples, moved westward from the Continent between about 550 BC and AD 50. They organised themselves into larger and more cohesive groups, eventually banding together in this area to form a tribe known as the Dobunni. This formidable tribe's capital was established at **Bagendon** near Cirencester, with great earthworks enclosing an area of about 200 acres. Other defensive dykes or earthworks dating from this period are still to be seen — the Bulwarks on **Minchinhampton Common** and the long **Grim's Ditch** — but the series of great hill forts along the Cotswold Edge including **Uleybury, Haresfield Beacon, Crickley, Beckbury Camp** and Shenberrow above **Stanton** are the most dramatic reminders of the organised power of these Iron Age tribesmen. They also started a process, to be continued later by the Romans and Anglo-Saxons, of extending their farming into the lower and more difficult valley country. They were also a relatively cultured people, capable of producing such great art treasures as the 'Birdlip Mirror', which may be seen at Gloucester Museum.

The Romans landed in Britain in AD 43, and they had soon advanced as far as a line which was later to become the Foss Way. Control over the area behind it, to its south and east, was rapidly consolidated, and by AD 47 the legions were able to move on to the task of pacifying the wilder parts of Britain, far away to the west and north. A provincial capital was established at **Cirencester**, and the tribesmen of the Dobunni were moved out of their fortress at **Bagendon** into the new city. At the same time improved techniques allowed for the agricultural development of not only the uplands but also the valleys below. The more prosperous Roman and Romano-British farmers built large villas such as those at **Chedworth, Witcombe** and **North Leigh**, and they had good communications with the provincial capital via a splendid network of roads, including the **Foss Way**, the **Ermin Way**, the **Akeman Street**, and the more rural **White Way**. These villas give a clear picture of the high level of civilisation that must have been maintained in the Cotswolds for almost four centuries.

It is not surprising that the next period of history has become known as the Dark Ages, as our knowledge of what really took place in the centuries following the departure of the legions is still extremely scanty. However, it seems certain that the largely Celtic Romano-British inhabitants were quickly conquered by Anglo-Saxons coming from the east, Gloucester and Cirencester being in their hands by AD 577, and that the vanquished tribesmen either moved further westwards, or were subjugated by their conquerors. Anglo-

Font in Southrop Church . . . a superb example of 12th-century craftsmanship

Saxon remains in the area are not very plentiful, but the quality of the sculpture to be found at **Daglingworth, Langford, Deerhurst** and **Notgrove** gives some indication of the vitality of Christian culture in the years before the coming of the Normans.

The defeat of the Anglo-Saxon army at Hastings in 1066 led to the rapid occupation of almost the whole of England, and Norman influence was felt in the Cotswolds in a comparatively short time. The area is particularly rich in its Norman churches, and outstanding examples include **Avening** and **Elkstone**, both with vaulted chancels; **Quenington** and **Windrush**, with fine doorways; and **Hook Norton, Rendcomb** and **Southrop** with beautifully carved fonts.

The round-headed Norman arch gradually gave way to the pointed but still simple 'Early English' equivalent, with narrow lancet windows often in evidence, and this style predominated throughout most of the 13th century. Surviving examples in the Cotswolds include **Wyck Rissington, Meysey Hampton, Bibury** and **Icomb**. From this early form developed the 'Decorated' style, which dates approximately from 1290 to 1350. This period coincided with hard times for Cotswold sheep farmers and the churches at **Badgeworth, Eastleach Martin, Taynton, Todenham** and **Longborough** are the best of a very small number of examples to be found in the area.

On the other hand, the period from the late 14th to the early 16th century was an age of great prosperity, with sheep graziers, wool merchants and clothiers amassing considerable wealth. It was fortunate indeed that this prosperity coincided so closely with the final flowering of English Gothic, the style now known as 'Perpendicular'. The wool merchants spent generously and we are indebted

William Morris and the Cotswolds

Born in Walthamstow in 1834, William was the eldest son of a prosperous London businessman. He was educated at Marlborough and Exeter College, Oxford. Soon after going up to the latter in 1853 he became a close friend of Edward Burne-Jones, and the two of them soon became the centre of a small group of undergraduates fired with enthusiasm for poetry, Gothic architecture, and the ideals of the Middle Ages, and a corresponding dislike of industrialisation and materialism, and in fact almost every aspect of 19th-century 'progress'.

On going down from Oxford in 1856, Morris entered the office of the prolific architect, G.E.Street, whose work incidentally is still to be seen in many Cotswolds churches today. However, it was in that year that Burne-Jones and Morris met Dante Gabriel Rossetti, who soon persuaded Morris to give up his architecture and to take up painting. Rossetti was one of the founding members of the Pre-Raphaelite Brotherhood, which he had established in 1848 together with William Holman Hunt and John Everett Millais. By the time Burne-Jones and Morris joined them, the Pre-Raphaelites had already had a stormy reception from both critics and fellow artists, but from this time onwards their work gradually came to be more widely accepted, thanks in no small part to the support of John Ruskin.

By 1860 Morris, Burne-Jones and Rossetti were all married. Morris had soon realised that painting was not to be his strong point (only one of his paintings has survived — an indifferent portrait of his wife-to-be, which now hangs in the Tate Gallery) and he turned to poetry, the revival of handicrafts, the art of house decoration and furnishing. In 1861 he and a number of Pre-Raphaelite friends, inevitably including Burne-Jones and Rossetti, founded a small company devoted to church decoration, metalwork, stained glass, furniture, wallpaper, chintzes and carpets. Some of the results of their fine craftsmanship may be seen at **Selsley Church**, which was built in 1862. Their firm lasted until 1875, when it was dissolved and then reconstituted with Morris as sole manager and proprietor. A few of its early ideals may have been lost, but its success was great and its influence, especially on fabric and wallpaper design, is still felt today. Morris also had a far-reaching influence upon the whole Arts and Crafts Movement, and this was first to manifest itself in the Cotswolds in Charles Ashbee's work at **Chipping Campden** and in Gimson's and the Barnsleys' at Pinbury and **Daneway**. The tradition lived on in the furniture design of Gordon Russell at **Broadway**, and survives today, both here and in the silversmithing of the Harts at **Chipping Campden**.

In 1871 Morris and Rossetti took a joint tenancy of **Kelmscot Manor** near Lechlade,

to them, not only for the great 'wool churches' of **Cirencester**, **Chipping Campden**, **Northleach**, **Fairford**, and **Wotton-under-Edge**, but also for the rebuilding or enrichment of a host of smaller churches, including such fine examples as **Aldsworth**, **Bledington**, **Rendcomb** and **Sevenhampton**. An unusual number of stone pulpits dating largely from this period are also to be found in the Cotswolds.

Throughout the Middle Ages much of the Cotswolds was taken up by the sheep runs of

Stanton Church . . . carefully restored in the early 20th century

William Morris . . . a portrait by George Frederick Watts (The National Portrait Gallery, London)

Another of Morris's favourite Cotswold haunts was **Broadway Tower**, and he stayed here several times with Rossetti and Burne-Jones. It was apparently from here that he wrote the letter protesting against a scheme for the restoration of **Tewkesbury Abbey**. Written in 1876, this was to lead shortly afterwards to the foundation of the Society for the Protection of Ancient Buildings. The effects of this long-needed action have been widespread throughout the country ever since. The direct results of his work may be seen in the Cotswolds in the churches at **Inglesham** and **Buckland**, but the gentle restoration and enrichment of churches like **North Cerney** and **Stanton** also owe much to the influence of his ideas. The vicar of **Burford** may not have approved of his interference, but today we remain very much in Morris's debt. Read more about him in Philip Henderson's *William Morris, his life, work and friends.*

Morris died in the June of 1896. He had loved **Broadway, Burford** and **Bibury**, and his oft-declared enthusiasm for these then unspoilt villages may have played a larger part in their awakening than he might have wished. Few of today's Cotswold visitors call to see his simple grave in the little churchyard at **Kelmscot**, and perhaps even fewer are fully aware of the vast breadth of Morris's work and the extent of his influence both here in the Cotswolds and in the world beyond.

but despite the attractions of Morris's wife, Jane, during Morris's long absences, Rossetti appears to have tired of it rather rapidly. Morris, however, never ceased to love the old house, and when in the closing years of his life he established a private printing press in London, he called it the Kelmscott Press. It was here that he and his old friend Burne-Jones produced the brilliantly typeset and beautifully illustrated *Kelmscott Chaucer* — one of the finest flowers of the whole Pre-Raphaelite movement.

the great monastic houses — institutions which included the abbeys of **Winchcombe, Hailes, Gloucester, Tewkesbury** and **Bruern**. All these monastic institutions were swept away by Henry VIII in the years immediately after 1539, and although some of the abbey churches have survived, the only other abbey buildings to be seen today are the ruins at **Hailes**.

Despite the sweeping changes that followed the English church's break with Rome, our parish churches continued to reflect a strong religious tradition in the centuries that followed. The 18th century saw the partial rebuilding, in handsome classical styles, of several churches in the Cotswolds including **Tetbury, Blockley, Great Witcombe** and **Temple Guiting**. Their contents were often enriched in both the 17th and 18th centuries with splendid monuments. See especially those at **Great Barrington, Chipping Campden, Little Rollright, Swinbrook, Sapperton,** and of course, **Gloucester, Tewkesbury** and **Cirencester**.

In the 19th century, many churches were rebuilt or restored by Victorian architects who were often brilliantly inspired by the past in cold academic terms, but who seldom had any regard for the patina of age and character that they so often swept away. It was not

until the closing years of the 19th and the early 20th centuries that it became clear to William Morris, his friends and some of his contemporaries, that steps should be taken to reverse this trend, and where restoration has been carried out after this time an atmosphere of the past can still often be savoured. It is to Morris in particular that we owe the rare treasure of **Inglesham**, but there are several churches in the Cotswolds whose careful restoration was carried out by architects inspired by Morris and his Arts and Crafts successors, and financed by local benefactors of unusually perceptive taste. See especially **North Cerney** and **Stanton**.

To return now to matters secular, the Normans and their medieval successors built several castles on the fringes of the Cotswolds, of which the most interesting survivors are **Berkeley, Sudeley, Broughton** and **Beverston**. The earthworks of other medieval castles may still be traced at **Ascott-under-Wychwood, Upper Slaughter, Brimpsfield, Chipping Norton,** and **Miserden**, but the surviving medieval manor houses such as **Minster Lovell** and **Horton Court** are of much greater interest.

Following Henry VIII's dissolution of the abbeys in 1539, their great wealth passed into the hands of noble families, merchants and other lay landowners, and it is to them that we are indebted for the series of fine 16th- and 17th-century manor houses and mansions, and the lovely villages often to be found at their gates. There are too many to list all here, but a few which are open to the public include **Snowshill Manor**, **Chavenage House**, **Chastleton House**, **Stanway House**, **Upton House** and **Wroxton Abbey**.

The 18th century produced an even greater number of fine houses in the area, including **Buscot Park**, **Ditchley Park**, **Cornbury Park**, **Rousham Park** and the magnificent **Blenheim Palace**. In many cases fine parks were created, and most of the landscape was now changing fast, with the acceleration of the enclosures. This was a process which had been started in the 16th century and which, apart from a few exceptions like **Westcote**, was largely completed by the beginning of the 19th, as a result of those sweeping changes in agricultural methods now known collectively as the Agricultural Revolution.

On the other hand much of the Cotswolds was hardly touched by the Industrial Revolution, although the 18th and 19th centuries saw the flowering of a great cloth industry in the deep valleys of the south-west around **Stroud** and **Dursley**. This activity, which had previously been of modest proportions and confined to the organisation of outwork in spinners' and weavers' cottages, was now gathered into factories, first water-powered, and later driven by steam. The **Stroudwater Canal** and the **Thames & Severn Canal** were established at this time, but then slowly faded in the bright light of competition from the railways; and then the major part of the cloth industry was overwhelmed by competition from the northern industrial towns.

The early years of the 19th century also witnessed the creation of such eccentricities as **Broadway Tower** and **Sezincote**, and continued with the building of **Woodchester Park**, the **Somerset Monument** and the **Tyndale Monument**. The Arts and Crafts Movement started by William Morris near the end of the century (see previous page) led to the establishment of 'craft colonies' at **Chipping Campden** and **Sapperton**, and although both have now vanished, they have left their mark, on a number of Cotswold churches and on various domestic buildings — **Rodmarton Manor** being an outstanding example.

The coming of the railways in the mid-19th century sent the hitherto robust coaching inns (typified by those at **Burford**) into a state of hibernation from which they only began to awake in the 1930s. And now with the 20th century drawing to a close the railways have retreated, with only a single-track line threading its way up the Evenlode

Valley to Moreton-in-Marsh and beneath the hills beyond Chipping Campden, and the Paddington-South Wales line the only one of real importance still crossing the area. Today the hills are crossed by a number of fast and busy main roads, but happily through traffic now leaves most towns and villages undisturbed. Motorways are visible from afar, but do not intrude upon the hills. Electric power-lines and radio masts are to be seen on many a skyline, but pressure from visitors is perhaps the Cotswolds' greatest future hazard. Retired folk and commuters have increasingly made their mark on small towns and villages, which are now perhaps rather too trim and tidy for those who remember them from earlier years. But the Cotswolds have much to offer the visitor, and it is still possible to move quietly through the area's small towns and villages and its incomparable countryside, and to appreciate the rich diversity of its past.

Cotswold Stone

The great limestone belt of hills stretching from the Humber to the Dorset coast, of which the Cotswolds are a part, contains many differing varieties of stone, all of which have provided the builder with outstanding opportunities. But nowhere have these been grasped so effectively than in the Cotswolds themselves. All Cotswold limestone is known as oolite (egg-stone), being composed of small, rounded, egg-shaped grains, but it is found in several different forms.

Usually close to the surface is the stone suitable for the dry-stone walling that so typifies the Cotswolds. Apart from the boundaries of deer parks and various forests and parks, most of these walls only date from the enclosures of the 18th and 19th centuries. Visitors will continue to marvel at the skill of the dry-stone wall builders, and happily there

Typical Cotswold dry-stone walling

Broadway Tower . . . an outstanding Cotswold viewpoint

are a few who are still able to practise this craft.

Some beds of oolitic limestone are in thin layers, which are suitable for splitting into roofing tiles by exposure to frost, and although they were once quarried in many places, the best-known source was in great caverns beneath Stonesfield, a village between Charlbury and Woodstock. The earliest example of the use of these 'tiles' is to be seen at the 5000-year-old **Belas Knap Long Barrow**, albeit in a much restored condition. They were used here for dry-stone walling, but for many centuries now they have been used for roofing. Observe how they are graded in size on almost all Cotswold roofs, with the massive tiles at the bottom of the roof sometimes weighing over 50lb, and gradually becoming smaller the nearer they are to the ridge. Each size of tile had a different name and these included such delightful ones as 'Short Bachelor', 'Muffity' and 'Short Cock'. The beautifully constructed roofs incorporating these tiles are one of the essential elements of the Cotswold scene, and a series of perfect examples may be seen at close quarters from a small section of flat roof at **Broughton Castle**.

However, an even more potent contributor to the beauty of the Cotswold scene is its beautiful freestone. This is easily worked when newly quarried, but then hardens on exposure to the elements and soon matures to harmonise with its surroundings. It is found in an infinitely varying number of shades — from the golden in the Bath area, through the grey-whites of Painswick, to the honey colour of Broadway and Chipping Campden, and the tawny brown iron-stone of the Oxfordshire hills. Easy working enabled Cotswold masons to produce far more interesting architectural detail than would otherwise have been possible — mullions, transoms, drip mouldings, gargoyles,

churchyard crosses, table tombs and porches, to name but a few.

Because of transport difficulties stone was normally quarried locally to fulfil most needs, but from the later Middle Ages Cotswold stone was also being used for buildings in London, Windsor and Oxford, to which it was carried on barges down the Thames. Most of the stone for this purpose was quarried in the Windrush Valley — at Upton, near Burford, and the nearby villages of Taynton, Great and Little Barrington and Windrush. Much of this was obtained from conventional open quarries, but that from Windrush was 'mined' by driving passages similar to those at Stonesfield into the nearby hill-slopes. There were two important local families of quarrymen, masons and builders — the Strongs and the Kempsters — and by the 17th century their stone and their skills were so well known that they were both employed by Sir Christopher Wren in the building of St Paul's Cathedral and other city churches.

Today only a small amount of Cotswold stone is extracted from the hills, but there are some quarries still working, including two at Coscombe, above Stanway Hill, one at Farmington, one at Westington, above Chipping Campden, and two near Naunton. In addition a quarry supplying stone slates has recently been reopened near Filkins. However, many houses on the Cotswolds are now built of reconstituted stone and roofed with moulded tiles. The degrees of success of these materials vary widely, but in recent years the results have improved and new buildings are mellowing in a reasonably short time. It would perhaps be pleasant if a few more quarries could be worked, but let us at least be thankful that Cotswold stone is too crushable for use beneath modern roads and motorways, and that we are therefore saved from great quarries of the sort that scar the far-off granite hills.

Leisure Activities . . . A Brief Summary

The area covered by this guide provides a wide range of sport and leisure activities and we have listed some of those which we feel will be of particular interest to visitors.

Motoring. You will probably have arrived in your own car, but if you wish to hire a self-drive car or chauffeur-driven car, there is a wide choice available. Self-drive cars are available from the following organisations:
V.J.Collett, Bourton-on-the Water, *Tel: (0451) 20303*
Bristol Street Motors, Cheltenham, *Tel: (0242) 527061*
Europcar, Castle Filling Station, Cheltenham, *Tel: (0242) 221670*
Hertz, Pike House Service Station, *Tel: (0242) 242547*
Central Garage, Chipping Norton, *Tel: (0608) 642014*
New Quarry Motors, Cirencester, *Tel: (0285) 640000*
Europcar, Watts Truck Centre, Gloucester, *Tel: (0452) 28248*
Target Ford, Gloucester, *Tel: (0452) 21581*
P.J.Nichols, Tewkesbury, *Tel: (0684) 292398*
If alternative services are required, or if you require a chauffeur-driven car, use the local Yellow Pages, or Thompson Directory, as there are many other services available.

Bus. Local bus services can be fun if you are prepared to fit in with their schedules, which in most parts of the country are governed by local transport needs. Timetables giving details of times and routes may be obtained from most Tourist Information Centres, or from the City Line, Bristol, *Tel: (0272) 558211*, Midland Red, *Tel: 021-643-0088*, Midland Red (South), *Tel: (0788) 562036*, West Midland Travel, *Tel: 021-622-5151*, Pulham & Sons, Bourton-on-the-Water, *Tel: (0451) 20369*, Castleways, Winchcombe, *Tel: (0242) 602949/603715*.

Train. Details of British Rail's train services in the area may be obtained from most T.I.C.s, or from any British Rail Station, including Birmingham, *Tel: 021-643-2711*, and Gloucester, *Tel: (0452) 29501*. The only non-BR line in the area is that operated by the Gloucestershire Warwickshire Railway, which runs between Toddington and Gretton, and which is hoped eventually to extend between Cheltenham Racecourse and Stratford-upon-Avon.

Caravanning and Camping. There are so many suitable sites in the area covered by this guide that it would be impossible, in a publication of this nature, to provide a truly representative list. There is a useful and inexpensive leaflet entitled 'Caravan and Camping', which is published annually by the Heart of England Tourist Board, PO Box 15, Worcester, WR1 2JT, *Tel: (0905) 763436*, and all the T.I.C.s can also provide further help. If you wish to plan in advance, there are a number of excellent countrywide booklets on sale nationally from early January each year. But if you wish to have the very best camping and/or caravan site information, you would be advised to join one of the national clubs covering these activities. These include: *The Camping and Caravanning Club, 11 Lower Grosvenor Place, London SW1W 0EY*, and *The Caravan Club, East Grinstead House, East Grinstead, West Sussex RH19 1UA*.

Cycling. This is a splendid way of looking around the area, and once you are off the main routes (which is the object of most of our listed tours) the little 'unclassified' roads (yellow on the Landranger maps) are relatively peaceful. If you do not have your own machine, these can be hired from: Crabtrees, Winchcombe St., Cheltenham, *Tel: (0452) 5154291*, Leedon's Park, Childswickham, Nr. Broadway, *Tel: (0386) 852423*, Jeffrey Toyshop, High St., Moreton-in-Marsh, *Tel: (0608) 50756*, Thames and Cotswold Cycles, 21 Church St., Tetbury, *Tel: (0666) 503490*, Anchor Cycles, Winchcombe, *Tel: (0242) 602550*, Cadence Cycle Hire, The Refreshment Room, Foregate Street Station, Worcester, *Tel: (0905) 613501*. If you still have

Typical 'Cotswold Way country' above Winchcombe

difficulty in making arrangements, the very helpful *Cyclists Touring Club, 69 Meadrow, Godalming, Surrey GU7 3HS, Tel: (0483) 417217*, may have other addresses. Why not become a member?

Walking. Walking is the ideal way of exploring the area, and may be combined with any of the above means of transport. In addition to the sixteen **mini-walks** marked on the maps in the **Places of Special Interest** section, there are twelve more detailed walks described on pages 132 — 155, and we hope that these will provide a pleasant introduction to the pleasures of walking with map and guide in this wonderfully unspoilt countryside. Stout shoes and waterproof clothing are desirable, and during the wetter part of the year, walking boots or even wellies to widen the scope of your journeys, to include more of those sodden fields and footpaths than might otherwise have been possible. Small rucksacks are a good idea, and while a compass is useful in this gentle, well charted landscape, it is not essential. Do not always expect to find well defined paths across this countryside's more pastoral corners. Rights of way are clearly shown on both the Landranger map and the Pathfinder extracts, but these may not always show up too clearly on the ground. If in doubt, do try to ask locally regarding rights of way, and at all times do make sure that your dog is on a lead if livestock are anywhere near, and that all gates are left as you found them, which will normally be closed. The Cotswold Way★ and the Oxfordshire Way★ both provide excellent opportunities for the walker, and their courses are marked on the relevant Landranger sheets. The Cotswold Warden Service runs a series of guided walks throughout the holiday season, and a leaflet listing these should be obtainable from any T.I.C.

Horse Riding. Details of the very wide range of available riding facilities may be obtained from any of the T.I.C.s, but here is a list of a few riding centres: Badgeworth Riding Centre, *Up Hatherley, Cheltenham, Tel: (0452) 713818*. Barrington Riding Centre, *Little Barrington, Tel: (04514) 471*. Hare & Hounds Hotel, *Westonbirt, Tetbury, Tel: (0666) 88233*. Talland School of Equitation, *Siddington, Cirencester, Tel: (0285) 652318*.

Water Sports. Despite being so far from the sea, this area has much to offer those who, in some way or other, love to 'mess about in boats'. Small boats may be hired at Lechlade's Riverside Boatyard, *Tel: (0367) 52229*. There are river trips from Tewkesbury on the Severn, *Tel:(0684) 296561*, and on the Avon, *Tel:(0684) 294088*. The last telephone number will also provide details of self-drive

Board sailing at the Cotswold Water Park, one of many leisure activities available here

motor-launches and cabin-cruisers. There is also a canal cruise around Gloucester's revitalised docks, *Tel: (0452) 308018*. There are various water sports facilities at the Cotswold Water Park, details of which are available from the Keynes Country Park Information Centre, *Tel: (0285) 861459*. There is also boating on the 3½-acre lake in Cheltenham's Pittville Park.

Golf. There are at least 13 golf clubs in the area covered by this guide. They include: Broadway, *Tel: (0386) 853683*. Burford, *Tel: (0993) 822583*. Chipping Norton, *Tel: (0608) 642383*. Cirencester, *Tel: (0285) 653939*. Cleeve Hill Municipal, near Cheltenham, *Tel: (0242) 672592*. Cotswold Hills, Ullenwood, Cheltenham, *Tel: (0242) 515264*. Lilley Brook, Cheltenham, *Tel: (0242) 526785*. Minchinhampton, *Tel: (0453) 833866*. Painswick, *Tel: (0452) 812180*. Robins Wood Hill, Gloucester, *Tel: (0452) 411331*. Stinchcombe Hill, Dursley, *Tel: (0453) 542015*. Tadmarton Heath, near Hook Norton, *Tel: (0608) 737278*. Tewkesbury Park, *(0684) 295405*.

Sports Centres and other Sporting Facilities. There are a number of sports and leisure facilities in the Cotswolds, but here is a selection: Bournside Sports Centre, Cheltenham, *Tel: (0242) 239123*. Charlton Kings Sports Centre, Cheltenham, *Tel: (0242) 510182*. Cheltenham Recreation Centre, *Tel: (0242) 528764*. Cotswold Sports Centre, Cirencester, *Tel: (0285) 654057*. Cotswold Water Park, nr. Cirencester, *Tel: (0285) 861459*. Gloucester Hotel and Country Club, *Tel: (0452) 25653*. Gloucester Leisure Centre, *Tel: (0452) 36498*. Gloucester Ski Centre, Robins Wood Hill, *Tel: (0452) 414300*. Stratford Park Leisure Centre, Stroud, *Tel: (0453) 766771*. Tewkesbury Sports Centre, *Tel: (0684) 292953*. Wotton Sports Centre, Wotton-under-Edge, *Tel: (0453) 842626*.

LEISURE ACTIVITIES

Places to Visit, and other items of unusual interest. A summary list showing page number followed by map number/s and map reference. (EH = English Heritage, NT = National Trust)

Flamingos at the Wildfowl and Wetlands Trust, Slimbridge

Bronze Age Sites (not all on public property)
The Hawk Stone (41) (164) (SP 33-23)
The Rollright Stones (EH) (90) (SP 29-30)

Commons and Open Spaces (See also Country Parks, etc., below)
Charlton Kings Common (55) (163) (SO 95-18)
Cleeve Common (48) (163) (SO 98-26)
Minchinhampton Common (80) (162) (SO 85-01)
Rodborough Common (90) (162) (SO 84-04)
Selsley Common (92) (162) (SO 82-02)
Stinchcombe Hill (57) (162) (ST 74-98)

Country Parks, Picnic Areas, etc.
Broadway Tower Country Park (36) (150) (SP 11-36)
Coaley Peak Picnic Area (49) (162) (SO 79-01)
Cooper's Hill (51) (163) (SO 89-14)
Cotswold Water Park (51) (163) (SU 04-95 etc.)
Crickley Hill Country Park (53) (163) (SO 93-16)
Dover's Hill (56) (151) (SP 13-39)
Fish Hill Picnic Area (61) (150) (SP 12-36)
Gretton Meadow (65) (150) (SP 00-30)
Keynes Country Park (51) (163) (SU 02-95)
Kilkenny Picnic Area (73) (163) (SP 00-18)
Robins Wood Hill Country Park (89) (162) (SO 84-15)
Somerford Lakes Reserve (52) (163) (SU 01-94)

Craft Centres, Craft Activities, Mills, etc.
Arlington Mill (28) (163) (SP 11-06)
Combe Mill (50) (164) (SP 40-15)
Cotswold Perfume Exhibition, Bourton-on-the-Water (33) (163) (SP 16-20)
Cotswold Woollen Weavers, Filkins (61) (163) (SP 24-04)
Egypt Mill, Nailsworth (82) (162) (ST 84-99)
Lodgemoor Mill (103) (162) (SO 84-04)
Prinknash Abbey Pottery (88) (162) (SO 87-13)
Selsley Herb Shop, Nailsworth (82) (162) (ST 84-99)
Winchcombe Pottery, Greet (67) (150,163) (SP 03-29)

Follies and Unusual Monuments
Broadway Tower (36) (150) (SP 11-36)
Cromwell Siege Stone (68) (162) (SO 83-09)
Four Shire Stone (62) (151) (SP 23-32)
The Gibbet Tree (96) (163) (SP 27-14)
Kiftsgate Stone (73) (151) (SP 13-38)
St Kenelm's Well (91) (163) (SP 04-27)
Somerset Monument (98) (172) (ST 77-87)
Tyndale Monument (112) (162) (ST 74-95)

Forests and Woodlands
Batsford Park Arboretum (27) (151) (SP 18-33)
Brockworth Wood (52) (163) (SO 89-14)
Buckholt Wood (52) (163) (SO 89-13)
Buckle Wood (52) (163) (SO 91-13)
Chedworth Woods (42) (163) (SP 05-13 etc.)
Cranham Woods (52) (163) (SO 90-12)
Dovedale Woods (32) (151) (SP 16-34)
Frith Wood (146) (162) (SO 87-08)
Guiting Wood (68) (163) (SO 99-16)
Hailey Wood (106) (163) (SO 95-00)
Hilcot Wood (70) (163) (SO 98-16)

Pinchley Wood (70) (163) (SO 99-16)
Redding Wood (146) (162) (SO 88-07)
Siccaridge Wood (151) (163) (SO 93-03)
Silk Wood (114) (162) (ST 84-89)
Standish Wood (89) (162) (SO 83-08)
Stockend Wood (142) (162) (SO 83-08)
Westonbirt Arboretum (114) (162) (ST 85-90 etc.)
Whichford Wood (77) (151) (SP 30-34)
Witcombe Wood (52) (163) (SO 89-13)
Withington Woods (118) (163) (SP 03-14 etc.)
Wychwood Forest (121) (164) (SP 33-17 etc.)

Gardens and Parks
Barnsley House Garden (26) (163) (SP 07-05)
Batsford Park Arboretum (27) (151) (SP 18-33)
Blenheim Palace (30) (164) (SP 44-16)
Cirencester Park (48) (163) (ST 99-02 etc.)
The Coneygree, Chipping Campden (46) (151) (SP 15-39)
Ernest Wilson Memorial Garden (46) (151) (SP 15-39)
Hidcote Manor Garden (NT) (69) (151) (SP 17-42)
Kiftsgate Court Garden (73) (151) (SP 17-43)
Misarden Park (81) (163) (SO 94-08)
Painswick Rococo Garden (87) (162) (SO 86-10)
Pittville Park, Cheltenham (44) (163) (SO 95-23)
Rodmarton Manor (90) (163) (ST 94-97)
Rousham House (90) (164) (SP 47-24)
Sherborne Park (possible) (94) (163) (SP 17-14)
Westonbirt Arboretum (114) (162) (ST 85-90)
Woodchester Park (119) (162) (SO 80-01)
Wroxton Abbey (120) (151) (SP 41-41)

Historic Houses, Castles, etc.
Arlington Row, Bibury (29) (163) (SP 11-06)
Berkeley Castle (27) (162) (ST 68-98)
Blenheim Palace (30) (164) (SP 44-16)
Broughton Castle (36) (151) (SP 42-38)
Buscot Park (NT) (39) (163) (SU 24-96)
Buscot Rectory (NT) (39) (163) (SU 23-97)
Chastleton House (42) (163) (SP 24-29)
Chavenage House (42) (162) (ST 87-95)
Daneway House (53) (163) (SO 94-03)
Ditchley Park (55) (164) (SP 38-21)
Frocester Tithe Barn (62) (162) (SO 78-02)
Hailes Abbey (EH & NT) (68) (150) (SP 04-30)
Honington Hall (70) (151) (SP 26-42)
Horton Court (NT) (71) (172) (ST 76-85)
Kelmscot Manor (72) (163) (SU 25-99)
Lodge Park (NT) (possible) (76) (163) (SP 14-12)
Minster Lovell Hall and Dovecot (EH) (80) (164) (SP 32-11)
Newark Park (NT) (83) (162) (ST 78-93)
Odda's Chapel, Deerhurst (EH) (54) (150) (SO 86-29)

Owlpen Manor (86) (162) (ST 80-98)
Prinknash Abbey (88) (162) (SO 87-13)
Rousham House (90) (164) (SP 47-24)
Sezincote (93) (151) (SP 17-30)
Snowshill Manor (NT) (97) (150) (SP 09-33)
Stanway House (100) (150) (SP 06-32)
Sudeley Castle (104) (163) (SP 03-27)
Upton House (NT) (113) (151) (SP 36-45)
Woodchester Park (119) (162) (SO 80-01)

Iron Age Sites (not all on public property)
Amberley Camp (80) (162) (SO 85-01)
Bagendon Dykes (25) (163) (SP 01-06)
Beckbury Camp (27) (150,163) (SP 06-29)
The Bulwarks, Minchinhampton (80) (162) (SO 86-01)
Camp Gardens, Stow-on-the-Wold (100) (163) (SP 19-25)
Chastleton Barrow (42) (163) (SP 25-28)
Dixton Hill (55) (150) (SO 98-30)
Eubury Camp (59) (163) (SP 15-28)
Grim's Ditch (67) (164) (SP 38-21 etc.)
Grim's Hill (90) (163) (SP 04-24)
Haresfield Beacon (68) (162) (SO 82-09)
Idbury Camp (71) (163) (SP 22-19)
Meon Hill (89) (151) (SP 17-45)
Norbury Camp (nr. Colesbourne) (49) (163) (SO 99-15)
Norbury Camp (nr. Farmington) (60) (163) (SP 12-15)
Nottingham Hill (55) (150,163) (SO 98-28)
Rowbarrow Camp (155) (163) (SP 10-07)
Salmonsbury Camp (33) (163) (SP 17-21)
Shenberrow (100) (150) (SP 07-33)
Uleybury (112) (162) (ST 78-98)
Windrush Camp (117) (163) (SP 18-12)

Medieval Castles & Castle Earthworks (not open)
Ascott-under-Wychwood (24) (164) (SP 30-19)
Beverston (28) (162,173) (ST 86-93)
Brimpsfield (2) (34) (163) (SO 94-12)
Chipping Norton (46) (164) (SP 31-26)
Miserden (81) (163) (SO 94-08)
Newington Bagpath (83) (162) (ST 81-94)

'Lost' Medieval Villages (all on private ground)
Dorn (31) (151) (SP 20-34)
Lark Stoke (74) (151) (SP 19-43)
Lower Ditchford (31) (151) (SP 22-36)
Lower Lemington (77) (151) (SP 21-34)
Northwick (85) (151) (SP 16-36)
Pinnock (106) (150,163) (SP 07-28)
Upper Ditchford (102) (151) (SP 20-37)
Upton (31) (151) (SP 14-34)

Museums, Art Galleries, etc.
Arlington Mill Museum (28) (163) (SP 11-06)
Beatrix Potter Centre (65) (162) (SO 83-18)
Broadway Tower (36) (150) (SP 11-36)
Cheltenham Art Gallery & Museum (44) (163) (SO 94-22)
Chipping Norton Museum (46) (164) (SP 31-26)
Cogges Manor Farm Museum (119) (164) (SP 36-09)
Corinium Museum (48) (163) (SP 02-01)
Cotswold Countryside Collection (84) (163) (SP 02-01)
Cotswold Motor Museum (33) (163) (SP 16-20)
Gloucester Folk Museum (65) (162) (SO 83-18)
Gloucester Museum & Art Gallery (64) (162) (SO 83-18)
Gloucester Transport Museum (64) (162) (SO 83-18)
Gustav Holst Birthplace Museum (44) (163) (SO 94-22)
Jenner Museum (27) (162) (ST 68-98)
John Moore Museum (109) (150) (SO 89-32)
Keith Harding's World of Mechanical Music (83) (163) (SP 11-14)
Little Museum, Tewkesbury (109) (150) (SO 89-32)
Model Railway, Bourton-on-the-Water (33) (163) (SP 16-20)
Model Village, Bourton-on-the-Water (33) (163) (SP 17-20)
National Waterways Museum (64) (162) (SO 82-18)
Oxford City & County Museum, Woodstock (120) (164) (SP 14-16)
Police Bygones Museum, Tetbury (107) (163,173) (ST 89-93)
The Robert Opie Collection, Gloucester (64) (162) (SO 82-18)
Simms Collection of Police Memorabilia, Winchcombe (116) (150,163) (SP 02-28)

At Cogges Manor Farm Museum

LEISURE ACTIVITIES

Stroud Industrial Museum (103) (162) (SO 85-05)
Stroud Museum (103) (162) (SO 85-05)
Tewkesbury Museum (109) (150) (SO 89-32)
Tolsey House Museum (37) (163) (SP 25-12)
Winchcombe Folk Museum (116) (150,163) (SP 02-28)
Winchcombe Railway Museum (117) (150,163) (SP 02-28)
Woolstaplers' Hall Museum (44) (151) (SP 15-39)

Nature Reserves, Trails, etc.
Buckholt Wood (52) (163) (SO 89-13)
Chedworth Woods (42) (163) (SP 04-14)
Cooper's Hill (51) (163) (SO 89-14)
Denfurlong Farm Trail (54) (163) (SP 06-10)
Gretton Meadow (65) (150) (SP 00-30)
Quarry Lakes, Bourton-on-the-Water (34) (163) (SP 17-20)
Siccaridge Wood (151) (163) (SO 93-03)
Stroud Valley Pedestrian and Cycle Trail (103) (162) (SO 84-03)

River Sources
Churn (Seven Springs) (93) (163) (SO 96-17)
Coln (Brockhampton) (36) (163) (SP 03-23)
Evenlode (Sezincote) (94) (151) (SP 17-30)
Frome (Brimpsfield) (34) (163) (SO 94-13)
Isbourne (Charlton Abbots) (41) (163) (SP 03-24)
Leach (Hampnett) (68) (163) (SP 09-15)
Thames (Thames Head) (109) (163) (ST 98-99)
Windrush (Taddington) (106) (150) (SP 09-31)

Roman Sites (not all on public property)
Chedworth Villa (NT) (42) (163) (SP 05-13)
Cirencester Amphitheatre (EH) (47) (163) (SP 02-01)
Cirencester Town Wall (48) (163) (SP 02-01)
Frocester Villa (not open) (63) (162) (SO 78-03)
North Leigh Villa (EH) (84) (164) (SP 39-15)
Spoonley Villa (99) (163) (SP 04-25)
Wadfield Villa (113) (163) (SP 02-26)
Widford Church (115) (163) (SP 27-11)
Witcombe Villa (EH) (117) (163) (SO 90-14)
Woodchester Villa (not open) (119) (162) (SO 83-03)

Witcombe Roman Villa

Stone Age Sites (not all on public property)
Belas Knap Long Barrow (EH) (27) (163) (SP 02-25)
Hetty Pegler's Tump (or Uley Long Barrow) (EH) (69) (162) (SO 79-00)
Hoar Stone Long Barrow (57) (163) (SO 96-06)
The Long Stone (68) (162) (ST 88-99)
Notgrove Long Barrow (EH) (85) (163) (SP 09-21)
Nympsfield Long Barrow (EH) (85) (162) (SO 79-01)
Standish Wood Long Barrow (89) (162) (SO 82-06)
Uley Long Barrow (or Hetty Pegler's Tump) (EH) (69) (162) (SO 79-00)
Whitfield's Tump (80) (162) (SO 85-01)
Windmill Tump Long Barrow (EH) (69) (163) (ST 93-97)

Trackways and Ancient Roads
Akeman Street (22), Buckle Street (37), Campden Lane (40), Ermin Way (59), Foss Way (62), Jurassic Way (72), Ryknild Street (91), Salt Way (92), Welsh Way (114)

Viewpoints
Barrow Wake (26) (163) (SO 92-15)
Beckbury Camp (27) (150,163) (SP 06-29)
Broadway Tower (36) (150) (SP 11-36)
Cleeve Hill (48) (163) (SO 98-26)
Cooper's Hill (51) (163) (SO 89-14)
Crickley Hill (53) (163) (SO 93-16)
Devil's Chimney (54) (163) (SO 94-18)
Dover's Hill (56) (151) (SP 13-39)
Drakestone Point (57) (162) (ST 73-98)
Fish Hill Picnic Area (61) (150) (SP 12-36)
Frocester Hill (63) (162) (SO 79-01)
Haresfield Beacon (68) (162) (SO 82-09)
Ilmington Downs (74) (151) (SP 19-43)
Kilkenny Picnic Area (73) (163) (SP 00-18)
Painswick Beacon (87) (163) (SO 86-12)
Robins Wood Hill (89) (162) (50 84-15)
Shortwood Topograph (143) (162) (SO 82-08)
Somerset Monument (98) (172) (ST 77-87)
Tyndale Monument (112) (162) (ST 74-95)

Wildlife Parks, Farm Parks, etc.
Bibury Trout Farm (28) (163) (SP 11-06)
Birdland, Bourton-on-the-Water (33) (163) (SP 17-20)
Cotswold Farm Park (51) (163) (SP 11-26)
Cotswold Wildlife Park (52) (163) (SP 24-08)
Denfurlong Farm Trail (54) (163) (SP 06-10)
Donnington Fish Farm (55) (163) (SP 16-27)
Folly Farm & Duckpool Valley (61) (163) (SP 12-20)
Prinknash Bird Park (88) (162) (SO 87-13)
Selsley Herb & Goat Farm (92) (162) (SO 83-03)
Trout Farm, Little Faringdon (75) (163) (SP 22-01)
Wildfowl Trust, Slimbridge (97) (162) (SO 73-03)

Special Events
March. *Cheltenham Gold Cup.*
May. *Cheese Rolling Races*, Cooper's Hill. On Spring Bank Holiday Monday.
May. *Randwick Wap*, Randwick. On 1st & 2nd Sundays in May.
May. *Woolsack Races and Fair*, Tetbury. On Spring Bank Holiday Monday.
May/June. *Dover's Games*, Dover's Hill. On the Friday following the Spring Bank Holiday, followed by the *Scuttlebrook Wake*, on the Saturday.
September. *Moreton Agricultural Show. Clipping the Church, Painswick.*
October. *Cheltenham Festival of Literature.*
For a list of other events, dates of which change annually, see the relevant leaflets which are available from the various Tourist Information Centres listed opposite.

Alligators at the Cotswold Wildlife Park

Further Information

Tourist Information Centres

* indicates that the T.I.C. is not open all the year.

Broadway*. *1 Cotswold Court. Tel: (0386) 852937*

Burford. *The Brewery, Sheep Street. Tel: (0993) 823558*

Cheltenham. *Municipal Offices, The Promenade. Tel: (0242) 522878*

Chipping Campden*. *Woolstaplers' Hall, High Street. Tel: (0386) 840289*

Chipping Norton*. *New Street Car Park. Tel: (0608) 644379*

Cirencester. *Corn Hall, Market Place. Tel: (0285) 654180*

Cogges Farm Museum, *nr. Witney. Tel: (0993) 772602*

Gloucester. *St Michael's Tower, The Cross. Tel: (0452) 421188*

Northleach*. *The Cotswold Countryside Collection. Tel: (0451) 60715*

Painswick. *Painswick Library. Tel: (0452) 813552*

Stow-on-the-Wold. *Talbot Court. Tel: (0451) 31082*

Stroud. *Subscription Rooms. Tel: (0453) 765768*

Tetbury*. *The Old Court House, 63 Long Street. Tel: (0666) 503552*

Tewkesbury*. *The Museum, 64 Barton Street. Tel: (0684) 295027*

Winchcombe*. *Town Hall. Tel: (0242) 602925*

Witney. *Town Hall. Tel: (0993) 775802*

Woodstock. *Hensington Road. Tel: (0993) 811038*

Other Useful Addresses and/or Telephone Numbers

Cotswold Tourism, *Corn Hall, Market Place, Cirencester, Glos., GL7 2NW. Tel: (0285) 641182*

National Trust (Severn Region), *Mythe End House, Tewkesbury, Glos, GL20 6EB. Tel: (0684) 850051*

Gloucestershire Trust for Nature Conservation, *Church House, Standish, Stonehouse, Glos, GL10 3EU. Tel: (0453) 822761*

Heart of England Tourist Board, *2 Trinity Street, Worcester, WR1 2PW. Tel: (0905) 763436*

Thames & Chilterns Tourist Board, *The Mount House, Church Green, Witney, Oxon, OX8 6AZ. Tel: (0993) 778800*

A.A. 24 Hour Breakdown Service, Bristol *Tel: (0800) 887766*

R.A.C. 24 Hour Breakdown Service, Bristol *Tel: (0800) 828282*

Police, *Cheltenham. Tel: (0242) 521321*
Police, *Chipping Norton. Tel: (0608) 642021*
Police, *Cirencester. Tel: (0285) 652121*
Police, *Gloucester. Tel: (0452) 21201*
Police, *Moreton-in-Marsh. Tel: (0608) 50324*
Police, *Painswick. Tel: (0452) 812222*
Police, *Stow-on-the-Wold. Tel: (0451) 30618*
Police, *Stroud. Tel: (0453) 766311*
Police, *Tetbury. Tel: (0666) 502334*
Police, *Tewkesbury. Tel: (0684) 293930*
Police, *Winchcombe. Tel: (0242) 602316*
Police, *Witney. Tel: (0993) 703913*
Police, *Woodstock. Tel: (0993) 813499*

Ordnance Survey Agents

F.C.Dodwell & Sons Ltd., 252 High Street, Cheltenham GL50 3HF *Tel: (0242) 522737*

Bellows and Bown, 7 Commercial Road, Gloucester GL1 11W *Tel: (0452) 21206*

Places of Special Interest

Places of outstanding interest are printed in blue. Places referred to in the text which are also covered by a separate entry in this section are identified with the symbol ★.

In addition to the 12 main walks described on pages 132-155, 16 mini-walks starting from the following places are shown on large scale maps in this section:

Ablington (163) (SP 10-07) *1 mi. NW Bibury, 7 mi. NE Cirencester.* Enchanting hamlet on the River Coln with a fine manor house, built in the late 16th century by a wealthy Cirencester wool merchant, John Coxwell. This was once the home of J.Arthur Gibbs, the author of *A Cotswold Village*, that classic evocation of life in the area surrounding Ablington in the closing years of the 19th century. Nearby Ablington House, a beautiful 17th-century building, is complete with gateposts surmounted by lions which once graced the Houses of Parliament, but perhaps the most pleasing buildings in the

Ablington House . . . clipped yews and heraldic lions

hamlet are the two great barns at its centre, one dated 1727. Ablington lies on the course of our **Walk 12**, and it is also possible to walk north-westwards up the valley to Winson ★ and on to Coln Rogers ★.

Adlestrop (163) (SP 24-27) *3 mi. E Stow-on-the-Wold.* This modest village lies between parkland and a belt of trees climbing the hillside to its east. It has several pleasant houses in a cul-de-sac by the church. This stands in a well kept churchyard, but its interior has been over-restored and the only

items of any real interest to visitors are various Leigh family monumental tablets. Their presence reminds us that Jane Austen used to come here often to visit her uncle, Theophilus Leigh, at his rectory, a partly 17th-century building now known as Adlestrop House. Theophilus, who was a member of the family who owned Adlestrop Park, was also Master of Balliol College, Oxford. He died in 1785.

The modest mansion of Adlestrop Park dates back to the 16th century, but its best feature is the south-west front designed in the Gothick style by Sanderson Miller, squire of Radway in neighbouring Warwickshire and a talented gentleman-architect in the best 18th-century tradition. Part of the surrounding parkland was laid out by Humphry Repton, and some of this is crossed by the return path used in our **Walk 5**.

This village's name will always be remembered as the subject of Edward Thomas's highly evocative poem *Adlestrop*, the first two verses of which run:

> Yes, I remember Adlestrop ...
> The name ... because one afternoon
> Of heat the express-train drew up there
> Unwontedly. It was late June.

> The steam hissed. Someone cleared his throat,
> No one left and no one came
> On the bare platform. What I saw
> Was Adlestrop ... only a name.

The station was closed many years ago, but the station sign and a station bench now stand in a small shelter in Adlestrop — a tribute to the young poet by the village he immortalised. Sadly Thomas died on active service at Arras in 1917, aged only 39.

There is a good walk northwards from here over the hill to Chastleton ★, and our **Walk 5** starts from Adlestrop Church.

Akeman Street (163, 164) This important Roman road ran from Cirencester, through Bicester, to St Albans. Unlike several other Roman highways it has not been retained as a part of the Cotswolds' major road network, although several sections in the southern Cotswolds are followed by minor roads, and a few by bridleways and footpaths. Its course passes not far from Widford ★ and North Leigh Villa ★, both of which have Roman connections, but it is perhaps best viewed as it crosses the Leach Valley at (163) (SP 19-06) about 1 ½ miles north of Eastleach Turville ★.

Alderton (150) (SP 00-33) *3 mi. NW Winchcombe.* Lying between the Cotswold edge and outlying Alderton and Dumbleton Hills, this is a transitional village, as much 'Avon Valley' as 'Cotswold' in character. Some half-timbering is to be seen, as well as some stone, and there are several thatched roofs. The largely 14th-century church looks pleasant enough standing in its tidy churchyard, but its interior was ruthlessly restored in the late 19th century, and is not of great interest to visitors apart from its long iron-bound chest, which is a fine specimen of medieval craftsmanship. There is a pleasant bridleway northwards over the wooded hills to Dumbleton.

Aldsworth (163) (SP 15-10) *3 mi. NE Bibury.* Thankfully most of this village is just far enough away to escape the fumes and noise of the busy B4425. Aldsworth's prosperity must have been at its peak when Bibury Racecourse was situated on Upton Down on its immediate south, although no trace of this now remains. The date of Bibury Race Club's foundation is in some doubt, some stating that races were first run here as early as 1621 when Newmarket's regular meeting was prevented by an outbreak of the plague there. Others claim that it was founded here only in 1681, as the result of a visit by Charles II to Burford to see his mistress Nell Gwyn, during the time of his last Parliament's meeting at Oxford. There seems, however, to be little doubt that it was in the latter years of Charles II's reign that, with the promotion of the Duttons of nearby Sherborne ★, it really became a fashionable event. Bibury Race Week was still much in vogue in the days of George IV, when there was an impressive grandstand here complete with a cast-iron balcony. Despite this the course was closed in the mid-19th century, due largely to the ever increasing pressures of agricultural enclosure. The Bibury Race Club is still very much alive, although now located at Salisbury.

The village was also the home of the farmer who ran what was once the last surviving flock of the traditional Cotswold sheep, the animals that brought such prosperity to these hills and which were usually known as 'Cotswold Lions'. Happily this rare breed was just saved from extinction and may now be seen again in small numbers, notably at the Cotswold Farm Park ★, the owner of which has done so much to preserve this and many other rare breeds of farm animal.

Thanks both to its racecourse and no doubt also to its sheep, Aldsworth has a solidly 18th- and early 19th-century flavour, with the church and manor house lying a little to the west, beyond a green crossed by a small stream. The Norman church has a short dumpy spire, and sits most comfortably in a rough, sloping churchyard with a fine collection of tombstones for company. The Perpendicular north aisle is a real beauty, being embellished with a splendid series of grotesque gargoyles outside, and with an elaborately carved niche within. Both porches are full of interest, but the north is particularly attractive, with rib vaulting and a niche thought to be for candles — possibly a 'poor man's chantry' (see Bisley ★).

Alstone (150) (SO 98-32) *3½ mi. NW Winchcombe.* Like neighbouring Alderton ★, this is a 'transitional' village, with a pleasing blend of timber-framing and Cotswold stone. It is quietly situated below Woolstone Hill, an outlier of the true Cotswolds. Its little church was over-restored in 1880, when the walls were scraped and heavily repointed. However, there is a Norman doorway within the 17th-century porch, and the chancel-arch capitals are ornamented with interesting Norman detail.

Alvescot (163) (SP 27-04) *5 mi. SE Burford.* Straddling the B4020, this small village tries hard to ignore the noisy aircraft from the great runways of Brize Norton Airfield just to its north. It has two inns — the Plough, which lies rather inappropriately opposite a quaint little Strict Baptist chapel, and the Red Lion, a little further down the street. There is a small road between the two, leading to the church, which lies in a quiet setting to the north of the

village. This is a pleasant cruciform building with a well proportioned Perpendicular tower and a good 14th-century south doorway. Inside there are lovely old roof timbers resting on carved corbels, some handsome 18th-century monuments, and brasses in the south aisle of Alice Malory (1579) and her husband and children.

It is possible to walk south across fields to Clanfield ★, or west to Kencot ★ and Broadwell ★, but the paths northwards to Carterton ★ are likely to be too disturbed by aircraft noise.

Amberley (162) (SO 85-01) *1 mi. N Nailsworth.* A scattered village on the high, western edge of Minchinhampton Common, with splendid views over the deep valley of the little River Avon. Much of the novel *John Halifax Gentleman* was written here, when Mrs Craik, its authoress, lived for a short time at Amberley's Rose Cottage (see also Tewkesbury ★).

Ampney Crucis (163) (SP 06-01) *2 mi. E Cirencester.* The largest of the three Ampneys, Crucis has a many-gabled inn, the Crown, on the main road, an old mill on the Ampney Brook, and beyond it a beautiful cruciform church tucked away beneath the wall of Ampney Park. In the churchyard is a remarkably well preserved 14th-century cross, whose head was only rediscovered in 1854, having been previously built into the rood loft stair, probably to save it from destruction by the image destroyers who were so active following Henry VIII's break with Rome, and during the Cromwellian period. See also the splendid 16th-century tomb of George and Annie Lloyd, with their five sons and seven daughters kneeling around them, the rare stone Perpendicular pulpit, and behind it a small door leading to the rood loft stair.

Ampney St Mary (163) (SP 08-02) *4 mi. E Cirencester.* This village was originally sited on the Ampney Brook, near the present main road, but it was moved almost a mile to the north-east to the hamlet of Ashbrook, probably owing to a combination of the Black Death and repeated flooding of the brook (SP 07-01) and is well worth visiting. It is a small Norman building with an unusually complete series of Decorated windows, which were restored with a fortunately light hand in 1913. See especially the fascinating Norman lintel over the north doorway, the medieval south door, the stone chancel screen and the extensive series of medieval wall-paintings, including pictures of St Christopher and St George and the Dragon.

Ampney St Peter (163) (SP 08-01) *3½ mi. E Cirencester.* Situated to the immediate north of the A417, Ampney St Peter has several well restored houses and cottages and, like so many Cotswold villages today, is almost too trim. The church, with its small saddleback tower, has a Saxon nave, but the restoration and rebuilding by Sir Giles Gilbert Scott in 1878 have left little feeling of antiquity here. However, do not miss the remains of a 14th-century cross in the churchyard, nor the small, possibly Saxon figure overlooking the font.

There are pleasant walks southwards to Harnhill ★ and Driffield ★ , and on a low hill to the south-east are the extensive but not very exciting earthworks of the Iron Age settlement of Ranbury Rings (no public access).

Andoversford (163) (SP 02-19) *5 mi. E Cheltenham.* Now bypassed by the busy A40, this village has no special features. It is, however, the site of the lively, thrice-yearly 'Stow Horse Fairs', which have been officially moved here from Stow-on-the-Wold ★ . These are held in mid-May, mid-July and mid-October. *(For details ˙from the auctioneers, Messrs Tayler and Fletcher, Tel: (0451) 30383.)*

Arlington (163) (SP 10-06) *6 mi. NE Cirencester.* See Bibury ★ , to which it is attached.

Armscote (151) (SP 24-44) *3 mi. N Shipston-on-Stour.* Attractive mellow stone village situated no more than three miles from the northern bastion of the Cotswolds, Windmill Hill, above Ilmington ★ . It has a fine Jacobean manor house, very Cotswold in flavour, and several no less pleasing houses of the same period. Armscote has no church, but there is an early 18th-century Friends' Meeting House, with a simple, unspoilt interior. Nearby there is a hospitable inn, the Wagon Wheel, and on the road towards Halford, a delightful converted railway-carriage — a remnant from the thirties, when many of these were to be seen in the countryside.

Ascott-under-Wychwood (164) (SP 30-18) *5 mi. NE Burford.* A long, thin village in the lush Evenlode Valley, with a railway still making its mark on the landscape. This is Brunel's old Oxford, Worcester and Wolverhampton Railway, which keeps the Evenlode company all the way from its confluence with the Glyme near Bladon, almost up to its source near Moreton-in-Marsh.

The 16th- and 17th-century manor house stands on the north side of the village, beyond the railway line, within the earthworks of the medieval castle of Ascott Doilly. In the village itself there are two pubs, including the prettily signed Swan Inn, a beautifully converted mill house and a partly Norman church. This sits in a large churchyard with converging avenues of lime trees, and is overlooked by a series of old stone houses on all four sides. The interior has been rather over-tidied (often the fate of those churches restored by the Victorian architect G.E. Street) but there is Norman arcading to the north aisle, and handsome triple sedilia may be seen beneath one of the chancel windows.

Use the Oxfordshire Way ★ to walk up the Evenlode Valley to Shipton-under-Wychwood ★ , or down it to Charlbury ★ . There is also a pleasant walk eastwards over the wolds and beside the edge of Wychwood Forest ★ to Leafield ★ .

Ashley (163, 173) (ST 93-94) *3 mi. NE Tetbury.* Minute village in fields not far from the course of the Foss Way ★ , with a fine 15th- and 17th-century manor house dominating the modest Norman church close by. Do not miss the Norman south doorway with its ornamented tympanum, nor the charming 18th-century monument to Ferdinando Gorges, a descendant of an earlier Ferdinando who had established the North American colony of New Plymouth in 1628.

Ashton Keynes (163, 173) (SU 04-94) *5 mi. S Cirencester.* Described in 1826 by William Cobbett, in his classic description of the English countryside *Rural Rides*, as 'a very curious place', Ashton Keynes still defies description today. The River Thames is here a small stream flowing through country much disturbed by gravel-workings, which are now mostly lakes occupied by various elements of the Cotswold Water Park ★ . The infant Thames, flowing right through the village, divides its houses and cottages from the main street, and it is accordingly crossed by a great number of rather ordinary little bridges. It is only at Church Walk that full justice is done to the stream, and it is well worth idling here before walking across the fields to the church beyond. This has a splendid Norman chancel arch, an ornamented Norman font and a poignant wall monument (1800) by the noted sculptor, John Flaxman, showing Charlotte Nicholas on her death-bed.

Asthall (163) (SP 28-11) *2½ mi. E Burford. (See map on page 105.)* This is one of the classic Windrush villages, complete with water-meadows, willow trees, and gabled Elizabethan manor overlooking a small church and a tidy little inn. It was a great favourite of John Betjeman, who must often have come over here from Oxford when visiting the Mitford family in the thirties. They lived at the manor for six years, after moving from Batsford ★ , and before their father, David, the 2nd Lord Redesdale, built Swinbrook House, north of neighbouring Swinbrook ★ .

Victorian restoration has not been too kind to the interior of the partly Norman church, but the medieval glass in the Cornwall Chapel windows and the effigy of a lady with wimple and flowing robes are well worth looking at. The latter is probably Lady Joan Cornwall, who held the manor in the 14th century. Do not overlook the charming 18th-century tombs in the churchyard.

Asthall lies on the course of the Roman Akeman Street ★ , and a Roman settlement has been traced to the south-east of the village. It is possible to walk beyond the north bank of the Windrush, westwards to Swinbrook ★ and (making part use of our mapped **mini-walk** on page 105) on to Widford ★ , where further evidence of Roman occupation is to be found.

Aston Magna (151) (SP 19-35) *3½ mi. SE Chipping Campden.* Attractive stone village on hill slopes, looking out over flat country that runs towards the valley of the Stour. It has a few pleasant houses and barns, and a little green, on which stand the base and lower part of a medieval cross. Overlooking the green is a church built in 1846 and now converted into a private dwelling. The circular earthworks to the south of the church are the remains of a medieval 'homestead moat', possibly connected with the Jordans, tenants of the bishop of Worcester, and recorded here in 1182. Walk south-eastwards from Aston Magna, across fields and over the Foss Way ★ , to the pleasant little hamlet of Lower Lemington ★ .

Aston Subedge (151) (SP 13-41) *4 mi. NE Broadway.* This quiet village is situated beneath the wooded Cotswold edge, with a small stream beside the road that leads up over the hill towards Chipping

Campden ★. Houses, farms and a little church are situated amongst orchards, reminding us that we are on the very edge of the Vale of Evesham — one of England's outstandingly prosperous fruit and vegetable areas. The little church was built in 1797 and surprisingly there are signs of Greek influence about its bell turret and cornice. There is a delightful old clock, a small gallery and a canopied pulpit, all contemporary with the church itself. Opposite the church is the charming 17th-century manor house, once the home of Endymion Porter (1587-1649), who was an ambassador of Charles I, and well known at the courts of both James I and Charles I. It was here that he entertained Charles's brother, Rupert, when the Prince came to the Cotswold Games organised by Porter's friend, Captain Robert Dover (see Dover's Hill ★).

Avening (162) (ST 88-98) *2 mi. SE Nailsworth.* This substantial village, with its pleasant old houses, shops and inns, was once prosperous from the manufacture of cloth. It is situated near the head of the valley of the little Gloucestershire Avon, the river that once powered its mills and provided vital water for the processing of its cloth. Fine West of England cloth is still made at the large and handsome Longford Mill, north-westwards down the valley towards Nailsworth.

The handsome early Norman church is well sited in a steep, sloping churchyard, and has an interesting interior including a small 'museum' in the south transept, the varied contents of which include models of the church at various stages of its construction, a Saxon skeleton and the tusks of a wild boar. Do not miss the effigy in the north transept of the pirate son of Lord Chandos of Sudeley ★ , Henry Bridges, who in his youth 'indulged in deeds of lawlessness and robbery almost unsurpassed'. Situated on a hillside about ¼ mile to the north of the church are three burial chambers, one with a rare 'porthole' entrance. All three were brought here from a long barrow near Nag's Head ★ , excavated as long ago as 1806.

There is a good walk southwards to Chavenage ★ and Beverston ★ via Longtree Bottom (ST 87-96).

Aylworth (163) (SP 10-22) *5½ mi. SW Stow-on-the-Wold.* The site of a manor recorded in the Domesday Book, this is now only a quiet hamlet in an open valley, with a pleasant 17th- and 18th-century farmhouse. It is possible to walk eastwards down this valley to join the Windrush below Naunton at Harford Bridge ★ .

Badgeworth (163) (SO 90-19) *3 mi. W Cheltenham.* A small and surprisingly quiet village between heavily populated Cheltenham and Gloucester, with its church tucked away at the end of a short cul-de-sac. The large churchyard is approached through an attractively carved lychgate, and beyond lie the base of an old cross and several pleasant 18th- and 19th-century tombs (see especially those to Henry and William Bubb). The church has a well proportioned Perpendicular tower and a beautiful 14th-century north aisle chapel — regarded as the finest specimen of the Decorated period in Gloucestershire — with elaborate ballflower ornamentation to its doors and windows. Do not miss the splendid roof to the chapel, with its lovely angel-figure corbels.

Bagendon (163) (SP 01-06) *3 mi. N Cirencester.* Situated in a quiet wooded valley, this small village has a heavily restored church with Norman saddleback tower and Norman arcading. The chancel is considerably higher than the nave and was made so in medieval times, probably to avoid flooding. Features to note include the attractive triptych, incorporating a list of rectors, and the window in the north wall of the chancel by Christopher Whall.

The earthworks, Bagendon Dykes, situated to the south and west of the village, enclose an area of about 200 acres and are the remains of the Iron Age capital of the Dobunni, the Belgic tribe that flourished here immediately before the coming of the Romans. As part of a consistent policy the conquerors soon 'civilised' the tribes they overcame by moving them into Roman-style provincial capitals — in this case Cirencester ★ , or *Corinium Dobunnorum* as it was then called. Excavations of the Bagendon Dykes took place in the 1950s and were conducted by the formidable local archaeologist, Mrs Elsie Clifford, whose book *A Belgic Oppidum* provides a fascinating insight into the surprisingly high level of civilisation that the Dobunni had achieved well before the coming of the Romans, with a mint for their own coins, and the use of luxury goods imported from the Mediterranean world. Many of the fascinating finds from these excavations may be seen at Cirencester's Corinium Museum.

Bampton (164) (SP 31-03) *4½ mi. SW Witney.* This little market town was once known as Bampton-in-the-Bush, as in winter there were no really usable roads linking it with the outside world. It still has the good fortune to be 'miles from anywhere' (apart from the airfield of Brize Norton). It has many pleasant 17th- and 18th-century houses, a few inns and a minute early 19th-century Italianate Town Hall.

Its church is of considerable interest, with a splendid 170-ft spire, at the base of which are four flying buttresses, each surmounted by a carved apostle. The contents of the interior include canopied sedilia in the chancel, a fine stone reredos, three brasses and an impressive 17th-century monument to George Tompson (1603) in the south transept.

Do not miss the delightful Old Grammar School in Church Street, now used as a library, nor the gatehouse of Ham Court in Mill Street, a building which once formed part of Bampton Castle, which was built by the Earl of Pembroke in the 14th century.

There is a pleasant walk south-west from Bampton, via the hamlet of Weald, to Old Man's Bridge and Radcot Lock, both on the Upper Thames. There is a towpath walk both east and west from here.

Barcheston (151) (SP 26-39) *½ mi. SE Shipston-on-Stour.* Minute hamlet just across the Stour from Shipston, with a manor house, rectory and church. The present manor house is largely 17th-century, but it was here in about 1560 that William Sheldon set up his tapestry-weaving enterprise, having first sent his man, Richard Hicks, to Flanders to learn the craft. The best known productions from the Barcheston looms were the Sheldon tapestry maps, fascinating examples not only of tapestry, but also of the early cartographer's art. Several of these have survived, and good examples are to be seen at the York Museum and in Oxford's Bodleian Library; and Stratford-upon-Avon's New Place Museum has two delightful tapestry panels, with allegorical scenes. Barcheston church has a 14th-century tower, and an interesting medieval interior, the contents of which include the tomb of William Willington and his wife, carved in alabaster, and a brass to Richard Humphray — both from the 16th century. There are pleasant walks beside the Stour, north to Shipston-on-Stour★, and south to Willington and Burmington.

Barnsley (163) (SP 07-05) *4 mi. NE Cirencester.* Traffic on the busy B4425 detracts from an otherwise very pleasing village of neat houses and trim gardens. Although topped by early 17th-century gables and finials, the largely Perpendicular church tower is thought to have been largely rebuilt by Sir Edmund Tame, the prosperous wool merchant who lavished so much of his wealth on the splendid church at Fairford★, and also on the much smaller one at Rendcomb★. Sir Edmund frequently travelled between these two places and, probably for convenience, had a house at Barnsley, the half-way point on his journeys. Apart from its tower, the church is largely Norman in origin, and contains several interesting features. Do not miss the very early Norman window in the organ chamber, hewn out of a single piece of stone, which was moved here from Daglingworth★.

Situated in the village and originally laid out in 1770, the delightful garden of Barnsley House, with its Gothic summerhouse and Classical temple, is regularly open to the public. The elegant Baroque-style early Georgian mansion of Barnsley Park is situated in an extensive park just to the north of the village, but is not open to the public. There is,

Barnsley Church . . . largely Norman in origin

however, a pleasant walk through the park and beyond to Winson★ and Ablington★ in the Coln Valley.

Barrow Wake (163) (SO 92-15) *4 mi. S Cheltenham.* Situated just to the west of the A417, and north of Birdlip★, this is a fine viewpoint on the Cotswold edge, with a wide prospect out over the Severn Valley to the Malverns and the Welsh hills. There are good parking facilities and an unusual stone indicator illustrating the geology of the surrounding area. It was near here, in the excavation of one of a series of Iron Age burial sites, that the famous Birdlip Mirror was unearthed. This

Indicator at Barrow Wake

outstanding example of Celtic (Iron Age) art, together with a variety of other treasures, is to be seen in Gloucester (★) Museum.

Barton (163) (SP 09-25) *5½ mi. W Stow-on-the-Wold.* A modest hamlet, with a delightful 18th-century house overlooking a pool through which the infant River Windrush flows on its way southwards to Naunton★. Records indicate that by 1185 there were two fulling mills here owned by the Knights Templar (see Temple Guiting★), but the little river now drifts by, quite unconcerned with industry of any kind. There is a short but pleasant walk south-westwards, over the even smaller Castlett Stream to unspoilt Guiting Power★, but do not be tempted to try parking a car at Barton.

Barton-on-the-Heath (151) (SP 25-32) *3 mi. E Moreton-in-Marsh.* Quiet village on a small rise, with a tree-shaded green, on which stands a little well-house, with an urn beneath a stone dome supported by three columns. This green is overlooked by handsome 17th-century Barton House, and beyond this lies a modest little Norman church, with small saddleback tower. Two sculptural details, one on the outside and one on the inside of a north chancel window, provide clues to the possible presence of an earlier Anglo-Danish building. These were common in the north and east of England, but it is unusual to find one so far to the south-west. Other features of interest include an amusing fragment of Norman sculpture (a little pig running up the chancel arch), a small brass to Edmund Bury (1559) in the chancel floor, a 15th-century font, and pieces of beautiful medieval stained glass in the chancel's north windows.

Lawyer Robert Dover, the founder of the *Cotswold Olympicks* (see Dover's Hill★), and his wife Sibilla came here in 1650, to live with their son John, who had served as a Captain-of-Horse under Prince Rupert in the Civil War. Robert died in 1652 and was buried here, but his son continued to live at Barton until his own death in 1696.

Walk south from here, either on field-path or road, to Little Compton★, or south and east, up on to high country where the Rollright Stones★ lie.

Batsford (151) (SP 18-33) *1½ mi. NW Moreton-in-Marsh.* A compact little estate-village at the gates of Batsford Park, a large 19th-century neo-Tudor mansion (1888-92), which can best be viewed from its arboretum (see below). Designed by Sir Ernest George, Batsford's building was supervised by the young architect Guy Dawber, who thereafter devoted his life to working in the Cotswolds, and who by so doing evolved his own 'Cotswold style' (see also Eyford Park★). The church is slightly older than the house (1861-62), an ambitious neo-Norman building, with tall spire and apsidal chancel. It is worth visiting for the sake of the handsome wall monument to Thomas Edward Freeman (1808) by the sculptor Joseph Nollekens. Do not overlook the other monuments, to members of the Mitford family, the Lords Redesdale, the forebears of the fabled Mitford sisters, whose early years here, and at Asthall ★ and Swinbrook ★, are so lovingly chronicled in Jessica Mitford's delightful book *Hons and Rebels*. However, for a full account of the Redesdales' life at Batsford and elsewhere, read Jonathan and Catherine Guinness's *The House of Mitford*.

Batsford Park Arboretum (151) (SP 18-33) *Off A44, 1½ mi. W Moreton-in-Marsh.* Here are fifty acres of splendid woodlands, with scenic walks giving fine views eastwards out over the broad Evenlode Valley towards the Oxfordshire Cotswolds. There are over a thousand different species of trees, bamboos and shrubs, many from China, Japan, Nepal and North America, together with bronze statues brought from Japan by the formidable traveller and diplomat, Bertie Mitford, the 1st Lord Redesdale, and creator in the 1880s of this fine arboretum. Read all about Bertie and his descendants in the fascinating biography, *The House of Mitford* (see Batsford ★ above). Plants may be purchased from a nursery by the car park and picnic area, and there is a tea shop open from April to October. *(Tel: (0386) 700409.)*

Baunton (163) (SP 02-04) *2 mi. N Cirencester.* The best part of this small village lies to the east of the busy A435, beyond the little River Churn; the rest is too close to Cirencester and Stratton to preserve its individuality. The small, partly Norman church is quietly situated to the north of the village. It has a heavily restored interior, but should not be missed as it contains an outstanding 14th-century wall-painting of St Christopher wading a stream with the Child Jesus on his shoulder, and also a richly embroidered 15th-century altar frontal.

There is an attractive walk northwards from the church, up beside the Churn to Perrott's Brook, and beyond to North Cerney ★ and Rendcomb ★.

Beckbury Camp (150,163) (SP 06-29) *3 mi. NE Winchcombe.* Large Iron Age promontory fort just to the north of Farmcote ★, with splendid views out over Hailes Abbey ★ towards Bredon Hill and the distant Malverns. The origins of the stone pillar at the north-west corner are obscure, but traditionally it is known as 'Cromwell's Seat' and is supposed to mark the spot where the much reviled Thomas Cromwell, Henry VIII's Commissioner, sat while watching the destruction of Hailes Abbey. There is a good circular walk up to these earthworks, first using part of the Cotswold Way ★ from Hailes, and then northwards down to Wood Stanway ★ before returning westwards to Hailes.

Belas Knap (163) (SP 02-25) *2½ mi. S Winchcombe.* Neolithic (Stone Age) burial mound or long barrow dating from about 2500 BC. One of the finest examples in the country, it has been well restored by English Heritage. The restored false portal at the north end illustrates the great antiquity of the Cotswolds' dry-stone walling tradition. The four burial chambers within the mound are entered from the sides, and the long earth mound is surrounded by a dry-stone revetting wall.

The barrow is situated in high country, and may be reached by walking ¾ mile up from the minor road running south from Winchcombe ★. This path from the road forms part of the Cotswold Way ★ and enthusiastic walkers can follow the Way from Winchcombe to Belas Knap, a distance of just under 3 miles, and then onwards across open country to Cleeve Hill ★.

Berkeley Castle (162) (ST 68-98) *16 mi. SW Gloucester.* Although nearer to the Severn Estuary than the Cotswolds, the presence of this great feudal stronghold must have exerted considerable

Berkeley Castle . . . 'rose red and grey, the colour of old brocade'

influence upon the Cotswolds in medieval times. Its origins date back to 1067 when a castle was built here by Fitz Osborn, Earl of Hereford, but the present building is largely of the 12th century, with substantial alterations and improvements made two centuries later. It was granted by Henry II in 1153 to Robert Fizharding, from whom the Berkeley family are descended, and the Berkeleys still live here today. Described by Vita Sackville-West in her book, *English Country Houses*, as 'rose red and grey, the colour of old brocade', Berkeley Castle continues to impress all who come there with its mellow beauty and great strength. The formidable stone keep contains the Great Hall, the Morning Room (originally the Chapel of St Mary) with its beautifully painted medieval ceiling, and the dungeon where the unfortunate Edward II was so revoltingly murdered in 1327. The castle contains a fine collection of furniture, tapestries, silver, china and carved timberwork and there are attractive ornamental gardens and a Butterfly House. *(Tel: (0453) 810332.)*

While here, do not miss a visit to the Jenner Museum in the Chantry in Berkeley town's Church Lane. This commemorates Edward Jenner, the Berkeley doctor who pioneered vaccination against smallpox. The adjoining coach-house has been converted into a conference centre, thanks to the generosity of Japanese philanthropist, Mr Ryoichi Sasakawa. *(Tel: (0453) 810631.)*

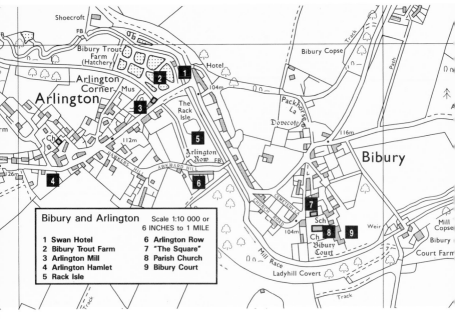

Bibury and Arlington Scale 1:10 000 or
6 INCHES to 1 MILE

1 Swan Hotel
2 Bibury Trout Farm
3 Arlington Mill
4 Arlington Hamlet
5 Rack Isle
6 Arlington Row
7 "The Square"
8 Parish Church
9 Bibury Court

Beverston (162,173) (ST 86-93) *2 mi. W Tetbury.*
Small village on the A4135, with several cottages
designed by Lewis Vulliamy for Robert Holford,
who had purchased the Beverston Estate in 1842,
and for whom Vulliamy also designed London's
Dorchester House in Park Lane, and Beverston's
neighbour, Westonbirt ★.

The church has an interesting Anglo-Saxon
sculpture on the south face of its tower,
representing the Resurrection. The pleasant white-
washed interior reveals several signs of Vulliamy's
restoration of 1844 — the nave roof for instance —
but the original parts of the 15th-century rood
screen and the details in the south arcade capitals
are well worth noting. Also do not miss a glimpse of
the lovely 18th-century rectory on the opposite side
of the roadway to the church.

Here is one of the few surviving Cotswold castles
— a largely 13th-century building with 17th-century
domestic additions and alterations. The original
castle was held in the years before the Norman
Conquest by Earl Godwin, father of King Harold,
and was the family's base during their protracted
grumbles against Edward the Confessor's leaning
towards Norman advisers. After the Conquest, the
castle was granted to Roger de Berkeley, whose
descendants were eventually to base themselves at
Berkeley Castle ★, about twelve miles to the west.
By the time of the Civil War it had been sold to a Sir
Michael Hicks, and although held for a short time by
the Royalists, its surrender was easily obtained.
This was due, so his enemies maintained, to its
garrison commander, the luckless but robust
Colonel Oglethorpe, 'attending upon a young
woman' at a neighbouring farm. The castle is not
open to the public, but glimpses may be obtained
from the A4135, and from the little roadway up to
the church.

Bibury (and **Arlington**) (163) (SP 11-06) *6 mi. NE
Cirencester.* Bibury has perhaps never fully recovered from the day that William Morris described
it, with some justice, as 'the most beautiful village in
the Cotswolds'. But even without Morris's praise it
was inevitable that this enchanting village on the
little River Coln, together with its immediate
neighbour across the water, Arlington, should
become so popular. Do not miss a visit here, but try
to come during a weekday in early spring or late
autumn. Park your car, if possible beyond the
bridge just across from the pleasant creeper-
covered **Swan Hotel (1)**, and explore on foot.

First look at the Swan Hotel and the little
windowless building nearby that once served as the
village lock-up. Then call at the entertaining **Bibury
Trout Farm (2)**, where trout of all sizes may be
observed and fed, and where 'catch-your-own'
fishing is available. Trout may be purchased, and
there is a gift shop and picnic area. *(Tel: (028574)
215.)*

Do not miss a visit to the nearby **Arlington Mill
Museum and Gallery (3)** which is located in an old
corn mill just beyond the Trout Farm. Grindstones
and mill machinery still turn and there is a fascinating
series of displays relating to life and work in the
Cotswolds, including furniture made by Ernest
Gimson and the Barnsley brothers (see Daneway ★
and Sapperton ★) and other members of the Arts and
Crafts Movement, all of whom drew inspiration from
William Morris, to whom a room is specially devoted.
There is also a room illustrating the life and work of
churchman John Keble, who was born at Fairford ★,
and who while at Oxford was for some years curate
of Eastleach ★. At the time of reprinting, the future of
this museum was uncertain. *Please tel: (028574) 368
for the latest information.*

Unless you wish first to walk up into the hamlet of
Arlington (4), with its pleasant cottages around a
small green, cross the B4425 from the mill and walk
along the far side of **Rack Isle (5)**. Now owned by
the National Trust this water-meadow was once
used for drying cloth on racks after it had been
worked by the weavers in the cottages beyond —

the much photographed Arlington Row. Although owned by the National Trust, none of these most attractive early 17th-century cottages between wooded bank and reedy meadow are open to the public, and this adds to, rather than detracts from, their very special appeal. Now walk down *Arlington Row (6)* and cross the River Coln by a little footbridge, inevitably stopping awhile to look into the clear, shallow water to see trout gliding by, apparently quite unconcerned by the noise and movement of ducks and moorhens, another feature of this delightful place.

Turn right onto the path alongside Bibury's greatest enemy, the still-busy B4425, and after a short distance turn right into a mercifully quiet *square (7)*, which is overlooked by a pleasant assortment of 17th- and 18th-century cottages, and beyond which is Bibury's very interesting *church (8)*. Standing in a trim churchyard with cherub table tombs and fragrant rose-trees, this fine building dates back to Anglo-Saxon times, and several features from this period include parts of the chancel arch and the fragments of a cross shaft. From 1130 until the Dissolution in 1539, this church belonged to Osney Abbey near Oxford, and there is no doubt that much monastic wealth was lavished upon it during these four centuries. See especially the Norman north and south doorways, the latter within a Norman porch.

Also beyond the square, on the banks of the winding River Coln, lies *Bibury Court (9)*, a fine, gabled Tudor and Stuart building, which is now a hotel.

Bibury is the start of our **Walk 12** which takes in Ablington ★ and a short stretch of the Coln to the

The Swan Hotel, Bibury

north-west, but it is also possible to walk beyond Ablington ★ up the Coln Valley at least as far as Winson ★ and Coln Rogers ★, or south-eastwards down the valley to lovely Coln St Aldwyns ★ and Quenington ★.

Birdlip (163) (SO 92-14) *5 mi. S Cheltenham.* Small village marking the end of the Roman Ermin Way's ★ steep climb up from the Severn Valley, it is happily now bypassed by the ever-busy A417. Great beech-woods clothe the steep Cotswold edge, and the atmosphere of a welcoming coaching stop still lingers here. There is a small church, built here as recently as 1957 to replace a Victorian one destroyed by fire.

The Cotswold Way ★ passes to the immediate west of Birdlip and this can be used to walk northwards to Barrow Wake ★, or southwards to Cooper's Hill ★ (a route also taken by our **Walk 7**).

Bisley (163) (SO 90-06) *4 mi. E Stroud.* Situated in a fold of the hills at the very head of the Toadsmoor Valley, and well to the north of the Golden Valley ★, this large village is quite delightful. Everywhere the eyes roam they are rewarded with good things. The clothiers of the nearby valleys brought their wealth with them, and spent it wisely — on splendid houses like Over Court with its charming gazebo overlooking the churchyard, on handsome Jaynes Court to the south-west of the church, and on the multitude of more modest but equally pleasant houses and cottages that are to be found throughout the village.

The church has a fine spire and a unique 'Poor Souls' Light'. This 13th-century structure, England's only outdoor example, was used to hold candles for the saying of masses for those who could not afford candles of their own. The interior of the church is rather stark, having been over-zealously restored by the Victorians. However, do not overlook the effigy of a 13th-century knight, nor the font with its Norman bowl upon a 19th-century stem.

Close to the welcoming Bear Inn, with its stone pillars supporting an upper floor, is a pretty, early 19th-century ogee-gabled village lock-up. Some distance away, below the church, are Bisley Wells, which were restored, complete with Gothic detail, by Canon Thomas Keble, John Keble's younger brother, who was vicar here. It was he who revived the ceremony of Well Dressing, which still takes place here on Ascension Day — a custom practised much more widely in Derbyshire's Peak District. It was also largely due to Thomas Keble's enthusiasm that the church of neighbouring Bussage ★ was built.

Local legend tells of how the future Queen Elizabeth I, when about ten years old, was living at Over Court, and that when she died here, her guardians were too frightened to tell Henry VIII. These frightened but resourceful men therefore substituted a local boy, and it was he, the famous 'Bisley Boy', who eventually became 'Queen' —

Bisley's early 19th-century village lock-up

hence 'her' virginity. This whole story appears to have been invented in a light-hearted vein by Canon Keble and his friends, following the discovery of the skeleton of a young girl in the garden of Over Court.

There is a good walk north-eastward from Bisley crossing the heads of two valleys to Miserden ★ .

Black Bourton (163) (SP 28-04) *5 mi. SW Witney.*
On a road cut off at its northern end by Brize Norton Airfield, this small village is subjected to the noise of monstrous jet aircraft taking off and landing nearby. All signs of the great manor house of the Hungerford family, Bourton Place, have vanished, but the church is well worth visiting. There is a pretty little Norman priest's doorway and a large porch leading into a pleasingly plastered interior, which is redolent of the past. The outstanding treasure here is the series of splendid 13th-century wall-paintings — very vigorous and the very essence of medieval faith and art. However, do not overlook the attractive stone corbel figures, nor the handsome monument to Lady Hungerford (1592) — all in pale stone.

Bladon (164) (SP 44-14) *1 mi. SE Woodstock.*
Scattered along the A4095, this village lies just to the south of the great woodlands that make up the far boundary of Blenheim Park. Born at Blenheim Palace ★ in 1874, Sir Winston Churchill chose to be buried at Bladon. His simple grave is situated in the churchyard beside that of his father, Lord Randolph, and will for many years to come be a place of pilgrimage for those who remember him as Britain's greatest statesman.

The church was almost entirely rebuilt in 1891 to the design of that prolific Victorian architect, Sir Arthur Blomfield, but it is not of great interest to visitors.

Bledington (163) (SP 24-22) *4 mi. SE Stow-on-the-Wold.* This large, partly modern village in the broad valley of the River Evenlode is centred upon a rough, wide green complete with the very attractive King's Head Inn and a little stream with noisy ducks. The ducks are apparently all known by their individual names and are greatly cherished, so please drive with special care here! The church is situated on the southern edge of the green with a row of pleasant cottages overlooking the churchyard. Although it has earlier origins most of the good things to be found in the church are from the 15th century, with fine roofs to nave and chancel, a lovely old doorway with its original door, and above all, a splendid series of Perpendicular windows, several of which contain outstandingly beautiful stained glass. These are believed to be the work of John Prudde, the Westminster craftsman who also produced the glass for Warwick's Beauchamp Chapel. The money for all these improvements came from the prosperous Winchcombe Abbey, which held the living, and which probably had a grange here.

Bledington lies on the Oxfordshire Way ★ , and this can be used to walk westwards up on to the wolds at Wyck Beacon and down again to Bourton-on-the-Water ★ , or south-eastwards down the valley, through the woodlands of Bruern Abbey ★ and on to Shipton-under-Wychwood ★ .

Blenheim Palace (164) (SP 44-16) *To immediate SW of Woodstock.* This, the greatest of the English

palaces, was the state's reward to its triumphant general, John Churchill, Duke of Marlborough. Built between 1705 and 1730, it was designed by John Vanbrugh in a heroic, Baroque style. Vanbrugh resigned in 1717 after prolonged disputes with the notoriously difficult Duchess, Sarah, but fortunately the main elements of the palace had by then been almost completed. Vanbrugh's design is magnificent, if perhaps a little overwhelming, but the fantastic 2500-acre park, improved by Capability Brown some fifty years later, has absorbed it effortlessly.

Approached by car- and coach-borne visitors from the A34, at the Oxford end of Woodstock ★ , Blenheim is best seen first by pedestrians, entering through Nicholas Hawksmoor's massive Woodstock Gate, the gateway at the quiet western end of the town (see Woodstock ★). Here is a prospect of palace, bridge and great lake, with sweeping banks clad here and there with noble woodlands — the work of Vanbrugh and Capability Brown brought to glorious perfection. Admission to the park is subject to a modest fee (which also includes access in summer to a butterfly house and a play area), and it is open to pedestrians for 364 days each year. The accompanying map will give some idea of the splendid walking opportunities that the park offers.

Built more as a national monument than a home, the palace offers its visitors a series of magnificent spectacles at every turn. First there is the massive east gate, and then the drama of the Great Court, with its colonnaded wings and its great portico

Blenheim . . . the work of Vanbrugh and Capability Brown brought to glorious perfection

looking northwards, beyond Vanbrugh's bridge and Brown's lakes, to the wide avenue of trees punctuated by the tall 'Column of Victory'.

The Great Hall, with its ceiling painted by Sir James Thornhill, provides an appropriate introduction to the further splendours within. The superb Baroque rooms are richly furnished, their contents including the famous Brussels tapestries, depicting scenes from Marlborough's campaigns, doorways by Nicholas Hawksmoor, paintings by Louis Laguerre, carvings by Grinling Gibbons, and a wealth of paintings added in the centuries that followed. Amongst all this grandeur there is a small room off the west corridor where Winston Churchill was born in 1874, and which now contains an interesting exhibition devoted to his memory. The Long Library contains no fewer than 10,000 volumes in a room 183 feet long.

On the west side of the Great Court is the chapel,

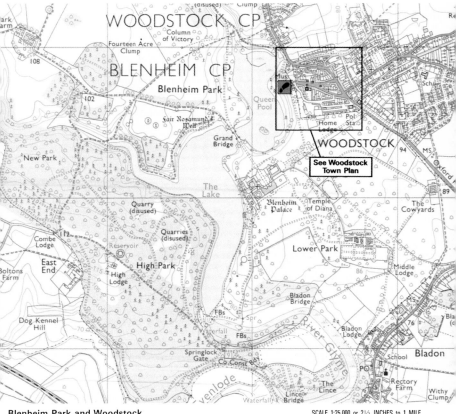

Blenheim Park and Woodstock
(Also see plan of Woodstock on page 120)

SCALE 1:25 000 or 2½ INCHES to 1 MILE

which was completed only in 1731, and which is largely the work of Nicholas Hawksmoor. Here will be found the splendid monument to the 1st Duke and his Duchess, designed by William Kent and executed by Rysbrack — a poignant but fitting climax to any visit to this noble building.

Delightful formal gardens on the south side of the palace complement the great park. There are also restaurants, gift shops, a butterfly house, an adventure playground, a miniature railway, a motor launch and a plant centre. *(Tel: (0993) 811325.)*

Blockley (151) (SP 16-34) *3 mi. NW Moreton-in-Marsh.* A delightful village, owned in medieval times by the bishops of Worcester, and built on the steep slopes of a hollow beneath the high wolds, near the head of a small but prolific stream. It was this stream that provided the power required for no fewer than six silk mills, when Blockley was at the height of its prosperity in the early years of the 19th century. These mills provided much of the silk required by the ribbon manufacturers of Coventry, and at one time well over 500 people were employed here. See the old mill (now a private house) beyond the pool below the church.

Still unspoilt by tourism, Blockley's steep little streets and terraces are full of character, with 17th- and 18th-century houses accompanied by dignified 19th-century buildings. Despite the prosperity of the village, the limitations of geography prevented

the railway coming any closer than Paxford ★, but Blockley was not to be put off entirely, for there remains to this day an inn of character, still proudly entitled 'The Great Western Arms'. The church has a large airy interior, with plenty of plain glass and a flat ceiling. There is a Norman chancel, which was probably once vaulted, and a tower built as late as 1725, by local mason and quarry-owner Thomas Woodward, who appears to have copied certain features from the fine tower of his own parish church at Chipping Campden ★. Do not overlook the series of handsome monuments inside the church to various owners of Northwick Park ★, at least two of which are by the celebrated 18th-century sculptor, J.M.Rysbrack, nor the two monumental brasses, both of priests — one in the chancel floor, and one (unusually) in the centre of the sedilia.

The site of the medieval village of Upton (151) (SP 14-34) is up on the wolds well to the west of the village (see map). Its presence was recorded in the Domesday Book and it has been excavated by archaeologists, but no trace of it now remains above ground. It was almost certainly depopulated in the 14th century on the orders of one of the bishops of Worcester, who would have required it for profitable sheep grazing. The bishops were probably also responsible for the depopulation of three other medieval villages in the area — Dorn (151) (SP 20-34), Upper Ditchford (151) (SP 20-37) and Lower Ditchford (151) (SP 22-36).

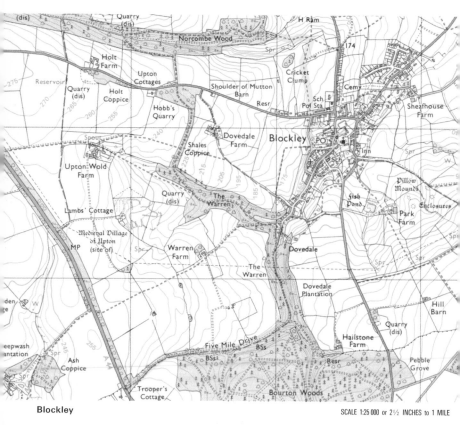

Blockley

SCALE 1:25 000 or 2½ INCHES to 1 MILE

Explore the delights of Blockley on foot, and if possible walk to the south-western end, and up a track into Dovedale Woods following one of our mapped **mini-walks**. The map also shows a circular **mini-walk** starting up a wooded valley known as The Warren and returning to Blockley via Norcombe Wood. There are also attractive walks south-eastwards to Batsford ★ and Bourton-on-the-Hill ★. Blockley's hospitable Crown Inn may ask walkers to remove their muddy boots when entering, but judging by their bar meals, this request should prove to be fully justified.

Rural elegance at Blockley

Bournes Green (163) (SO 90-04) *4 mi. E Stroud.* Pretty hillside hamlet between Bisley ★, Oakridge ★ and France Lynch ★, with steep narrow roads and pleasant views down a small valley where there was once a Roman villa (nothing now visible).

Bourton-on-the-Hill (151) (SP 17-32) *2 mi. W Moreton-in-Marsh.* If only this village could be bypassed, all would be perfection. Even so, traffic rumbling up Bourton's steep and none too wide street does not entirely spoil this charming village. At the top of the hill stands an 18th-century stone built inn, the Horse and Groom; then the road goes down past pretty little terraces of 17th- and 18th-century cottages, past the warm stone church, to the bottom of the village, which is here enriched by the elegant early 18th-century Bourton House, in the grounds of which stands a fine 16th-century barn (dated 1570). In 1598, the previous Bourton House was purchased by the parents of the unfortunate Sir Thomas Overbury, who was poisoned while a prisoner in the Tower of London, at the age of only thirty-two.

Bourton-on-the-Hill was once owned by the abbots of Westminster, who had great sheep runs on nearby Bourton Downs, and no doubt it was wealth from their wool sales that paid for the handsome 15th-century clerestory of the church. This feature together with the church's handsome three-stage tower gives it a totally Perpendicular look. However, within the pleasant cream-washed interior the massive arcade columns reveal its

Norman origins — the pointed arches were probably a 12th- or 13th-century alteration. There are old stone floors and a minute 18th-century gallery near the north door. The beautiful bell-metal Winchester Bushel and Peck, dated 1816, are a rare survival of these English standard measures. A law dated 1587 specified that each parish had to have such measures, and they were used by local magistrates in the settlement of disputes (usually those relating to the payment of the hated tithes). Do not overlook the 15th-century octagonal font, nor the colourful 18th-century wall tablets.

Bourton-on-the-Water (163) (SP 16-20) *3 mi. SW Stow-on-the-Wold*. This large village is probably the most visited tourist attraction of the Cotswolds. It is an unashamedly pretty place, with a series of ornamental bridges (the earliest of which dates back to 1756) spanning the clear waters of the River Windrush, which here runs beside broad, tree-shaded greens. Immediately to the east of the village are the earthworks of Salmonsbury Camp (163) (SP 17-21), an Iron Age settlement, and evidence of Roman occupation has been uncovered near the point where the Foss Way ★ crosses the Windrush.

If arriving by car, park in the **Main Car Park (1)** at the south-eastern end of the village and explore on foot. Immediately to the left, on the road back into the village, is **Birdland (2)**. This delightful bird-sanctuary, which was established by the late, much loved Len Hill, is now situated in stream-side gardens, and also includes a lively display of penguins, a reminder of the fact that Len Hill purchased two small islands in the Falklands some years ago, both of them rich in penguins and other birds. *(Tel: (0451) 20689.)* Not far beyond this, on

Ever-popular Bourton-on-the-Water with its series of bridges across the Windrush

the right of the road, beside the Old New Inn, is the **Model Village (3)**, a beautifully made one-ninth scale replica of the village in Cotswold stone, which inevitably includes a model of the model. *(Tel: (0451) 20467.)*

Walk over the bridge opposite the Old New Inn, to look at the **Pottery (4)** in little Clapton Row, and then turn right into Victoria Road to visit the **Perfume Exhibition (5)**. Not far beyond this will be found the **Cotswold Motor Museum (6)** and the adjacent **Village Life Exhibition (6)**, which are housed in the attractive water-mill. Almost opposite, on the High Street, is the **Model Railway (7)**, while well to the north of this is the **church (8)** which is in an odd mixture of styles. However, its combination of medieval chancel, Georgian tower

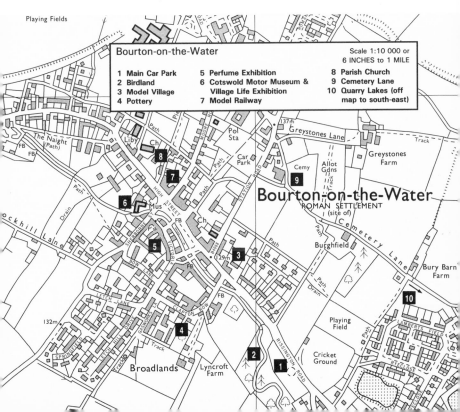

and Victorian nave has resulted in a pleasant and certainly interesting building. Apart from this there is a wealth of lovely buildings in Bourton-on-the-Water, and many stream-side walks.

Before returning to the car park, walk down **Cemetery Lane (9)** which is the best approach to Bourton's expanding **'Pools'** or **'Quarry Lakes' (10)**, flooded gravel workings on which nature reserves are now established. It is possible to spot swans, moorhens, mallard and other wildfowl here. These pools can be included in a pleasant circular walk, first making use of the opening stages of the Oxfordshire Way ★ to Wyck Rissington ★, then turning south to Little Rissington ★, and finally returning to Bourton via the pools.

Other walks from Bourton include one northwards to Lower Slaughter ★, and a long and pleasant one, largely beside the Windrush, north-westwards to Harford Bridge ★ and Naunton ★.

Box (162) (SO 86-00) ½ *mi. NE Nailsworth.* Small village on a steep hillside below Minchinhampton Common, with a little church built as recently as 1953, and some pleasant views down into the Avon Valley.

Boxwell (162) (ST 81-92) *4 mi. E Wotton-under-Edge.* Here in a quiet and beautiful valley well to the west of the A46 is a small 13th-century church which is full of character, and which is complete with a most unusual stone bellcote topped with a miniature spire. This church lies beside Boxwell Court, which looks Victorian at first sight, but which actually dates from the 15th century. It may be possible to drive as far as Boxwell Farm, but from here onwards it is necessary to walk.

Brimpsfield (163) (SO 93-12) *6 mi. S Cheltenham.* Small village in quiet hill country not far from the Cotswold edge at Birdlip. The manor of Brimpsfield

Brimpsfield Church . . . a fascinating architectural puzzle here

was given by William the Conqueror to the Giffard family, who built two castles here, a wooden one on a mound over towards the Ermin Way (close to our **Walk 9**), and later on, a large stone building close to the church. However, in 1322 John Giffard was foolish enough to cross Edward II's path, and he was hanged at Gloucester and his castle demolished. This was never rebuilt, but its substantial earthworks are still visible in trees to the right of the path to the church.

The church is situated on the edge of the village in a large churchyard with many 18th-century tombstones. It has a 15th-century tower which descends into the centre of the building, providing enthusiasts with a fascinating architectural puzzle. Do not overlook the scanty remains, in the walls of a barn over to the left of the churchyard, of a 12th-century priory, which once belonged to the abbey of Fontenay in distant Burgundy.

Our **Walk 9** starts from a point just to the north of Brimpsfield and takes in Syde ★ and Caudle Green ★.

Brimscombe (162) (SO 87-02) *1 mi. N Minchinhampton.* Situated in the deep Golden Valley ★, this is a rather scrappy village with a Victorian church on the hillside above. Brimscombe 'port' was the headquarters of the ill-fated Thames and Severn Canal ★, and it was here that cargoes were transhipped from the broad Severn trows coming up the Stroudwater Canal ★, to the narrow-boats heading eastwards on its narrower counterpart. Several pleasant old buildings beside the canal still bear witness to the architectural harmony of the early Industrial Revolution. Weeping willows and mellow brick enhance this atmosphere despite the presence of a foundry and other industrial works.

Brize Norton (164) (SP 30-07) *3 mi. W Witney.* The great airfield on its doorstep overshadows this once quiet village, but the church still stands in its neat churchyard, and there is a satisfactory Norman south doorway within its medieval porch. Do not overlook the Norman font with its arcade decoration, nor the 14th-century effigy of a knight.

Broad Campden (151) (SP 15-37) *1 mi. S Chipping Campden.* Quieter and much smaller than Chipping Campden, Broad Campden is tucked away in a small valley, with woods never far away — a delicious little village, well removed from the dangers of mass tourism, with a warm little inn, the Baker's Arms, and an outstandingly good guest house, the Malt House. It also has a series of delightful old houses, a small Victorian chapel and an 18th-century Friends' Meeting House with many of its original furnishings intact. Charles Ashbee (see Chipping Campden ★) converted a derelict Norman chapel into a house for himself soon after his arrival in the area in 1905.

Broadway (150) (SP 09-37) *5 mi. SE Evesham.* Situated below the steep scarp face of the Cotswolds, here topped by the stone built folly of Broadway Tower ★, Broadway has a fine wide street bordered by trim greens and a bewilderingly beautiful series of old stone houses dating largely from the 17th and 18th centuries. Although it must have benefited from Cotswold wool in medieval times, its real prosperity dates from the coaching

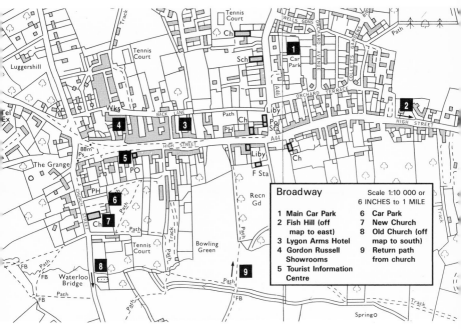

Broadway

Scale 1:10 000 or
6 INCHES to 1 MILE

1 Main Car Park
2 Fish Hill (off
  map to east)
3 Lygon Arms Hotel
4 Gordon Russell
  Showrooms
5 Tourist Information
  Centre

6 Car Park
7 New Church
8 Old Church (off
  map to south)
9 Return path
  from church

era, when, in about 1736, the old turnpike road southwards up to Snowshill was replaced by a new road up Fish Hill ★. From this time onwards the increasingly large volume of coach traffic made use of Broadway as a staging halt on the journey between London, Worcester and beyond, and at one time no fewer than seven coaches were passing through the village each day. The opening of the London and Worcester railway line in 1856 soon brought this era to a close, but Broadway did not have to wait long for its own recovery.

The very railways that had killed the coach trade soon brought enquiring visitors to the area, many bringing their bicycles with them. William Morris, staying with friends at Broadway Tower ★, appears to have been one of the 'discoverers' of Broadway's charms, and he was soon followed by many friends and acquaintances from the artistic world, including Henry James, Sir John Sargent, Mary Anderson, and Frank Millet (who was soon to settle in the village). And so, in a few years, most of Broadway's old houses were restored to new heights of perfection, and its reputation as a show village has continued to grow ever since. A fair proportion of these fine houses are now devoted to the needs of its visitors, with hotels and antique shops much in evidence, but despite this and the intrusion of traffic

Austin House, Broadway . . . on the Cotswold Way

from the busy A44 its character remains largely intact.

If arriving by car, try to park at the **Main Car Park (1)** which is just off the B4632 road to Willersey, and walk through to the High Street. If possible walk up the street first, looking at the fine old houses between here and the end of the village at the bottom of **Fish Hill (2)**. Then turn about and walk right down the wide and always busy High Street, passing a number of shops, hotels and restaurants on the way, including on the right the **Lygon Arms (3)**, one of England's most pleasant country hotels, and not far beyond, the interesting **Gordon Russell Furniture Showrooms (4)**, displaying the fine products of the factory not far to its rear. On the opposite side of the road, there is a bright little shopping precinct, **Cotswold Court (5)**, complete with a **Tourist Information Centre** *(tel: (0386) 852937)*. Behind this precinct is another **Car Park (6)**, which is reached by car from Church Street. The handsomely towered Victorian **'New Church' (7)** is on the left, just beyond the entry to the car park.

If possible walk well beyond this, past the old houses of Bury End and Pye Corner, to the **'Old Church' (8)** of St Eadburgha. This lies on the road up to Snowshill ★, in a quiet valley leading into the hills about a mile to the south of the village, and looking out over a small stream at the bottom of the churchyard. It is a cruciform building with Norman origins and has a delightfully unspoilt interior, which is full of atmosphere. It is possible to walk back from here over the fields to join the main street not far from the turn to the car park. For a more detailed walkabout, read C.C. Houghton's excellent guide, *A Walk About Broadway*.

Broadway lies astride the Cotswold Way ★, and its main car park is also the starting point of our **Walk 1**. There are also several other walks that can be taken from here, all of which are shown on Landranger Sheet 150.

BROADWAY TOWER

Broadway Tower and **Broadway Tower Country Park** (150) (SP 11-36) *1½ mi. SE Broadway*. At 1024 ft above sea level, this is the Cotswolds' second highest point (Cleeve Hill ★ stands at 1083 ft). This 65-ft Gothick folly was completed in the year 1798 to the design of James Wyatt, for the 6th Earl of Coventry, of Croome Court, his country seat about fifteen miles to the north-west. Many divergent theories have been advanced regarding its original purpose, but it now appears likely that it was to celebrate the first centenary of the Coventry earldom — a creation of 1697. This was sufficient justification in an age of follies, and would have provided status for its builder and employment for the needy.

The tower is an outstanding landmark to those who live in the Severn and Avon valleys, and it is one of England's finest viewpoints. On a clear day a dozen counties may be seen from its windy castellated roof, with the massive outline of the Black Mountains in the far west, and the long line of the Berkshire Downs to the south. In the rooms below the roof there are three most interesting exhibitions — one devoted to William Morris, who spent holidays here with his friends Burne-Jones and Rossetti, one to the story of sheep and wool, and one to the history of the tower itself, which was once used by bibliophile Sir Thomas Phillipps to house his private printing press.

The highly eccentric Sir Thomas, who lived at the handsome 18th-century mansion of Middle Hill House, not far to the south of the tower, once wrote (with no small ambition) to a friend, 'I wish to have one copy of every Book in the world.' But this feverish amassing of books was in some ways only secondary to his passion for the collection and preservation of manuscripts, and for this service future scholars were to be much in his debt. For a more detailed account of Sir Thomas's passion for collecting and its effect upon his unfortunate family, read Jocelin Finberg's *The Cotswolds*.

Other facilities provided within the Broadway Tower Country Park include a car park and picnic area, a shop, nature trails, a collection of children's pets including donkeys, an adventure playground, a play area and refreshment facilities. *(Tel: (0386) 852390.)* Broadway Tower, like Broadway itself, is on our **Walk 1**, and it also lies astride the Cotswold Way ★.

Broadwell, near Lechlade (163) (SP 25-03) *3½ mi. NE Lechlade*. Small village not far to the north of the flat Thames gravel country, with two stone gate pillars the only surviving evidence of a long-vanished manor house. There are, however, several pleasant stone houses and an inn of character called the Five Bells. The cruciform, largely Norman church has a fine 13th-century spire which appears to have a slight twist, and by the churchyard gate the extensive remains of a medieval cross. The Norman south doorway has been over-restored, the interior has been ruthlessly scraped, and there are shiny tiles and pitch-pine pews much in evidence. However, do not overlook the dramatic Victorian glass depicting the Three Kings, nor the wall monuments to John Huband (1668) and Sophia Colston (1802).

Broadwell, near Stow-on-the-Wold (163) (SP 20-27) *1½ mi. NE Stow-on-the-Wold*. Pleasant village spread around a wide green and sheltering beneath a hillside which rises up towards Stow-on-the-Wold. The green is overlooked by the hospitable Fox Inn, and there is a small ford at its lower end. Beyond the green is a handsome Georgian manor house, and there are several 17th-century farmhouses not far away. The church stands in a tree-shaded churchyard, with many beautiful 17th-century table tombs. It has an elegant Perpendicular tower, complete with reset Norman tympanum over its outer turret stair entrance. Do not miss the 17th-century monument showing Herbert Weston and his wife both kneeling at a prayer desk.

Brockhampton (163) (SP 03-22) *4 mi. S Winchcombe*. Hamlet with a large, mainly 19th-century mansion now converted into flats, and an inn called the Craven Arms neatly tucked away. This is watershed country, for the lovely River Coln rises near here and flows south to join the Thames, while at nearby Charlton Abbots ★, the little River Isbourne starts its northward journey to the Avon at Evesham. There are good walks west from here up on to Cleeve Common ★, or south down the Coln Valley.

Broughton and Broughton Castle (151) (SP 42-38) *3 mi. SW Banbury*. The small village on the B4035 is itself unexceptional, but the nearby castle and church are of great interest. A fortified manor house was built here in the early 14th century, and in 1377 it came into the ownership of William of Wykeham, Bishop of Winchester and founder of New College, Oxford, and Winchester College. In 1405 Thomas Wykeham turned the manor house into a true castle, and also built the gatehouse. His granddaughter married Sir William Fiennes, Lord Saye and Sele, in 1451, and Broughton has remained in the hands of the Fiennes family until the present day. The castle was modified in the 16th century, being turned into a house by the removal of most of the battlements, the alteration of the roof lines and the heightening of the great hall.

Broughton has remained largely unchanged since that time. It is surrounded by a wide moat, and is one of the most romantically situated castles in the

Broughton Castle . . . surrounded by its wide moat

country. The interior is full of interest and a visitor here will learn much of England's history from the part that various members of the Fiennes family have played, especially in the period leading up to, and during, the Civil War. Celia Fiennes, whose diary gives such a fascinating insight into travel in England in the late 17th century, was a member of the family, and although she was the daughter of a second son, she was a frequent visitor here. Writing in 1687 she refers to Broughton thus: 'its an old house moted round and a parke and gardens, but were much left to decay and ruine, when my brother came to it.' *(Tel: (0295) 262624.)*

The adjoining church has a fine chancel screen and a splendid series of monuments, largely of members of the Fiennes family, but also of earlier owners of Broughton Castle. Despite restoration work carried out by Sir Gilbert Scott and his son G.G.Scott in the 19th century, this church is still full of atmosphere and well worth visiting.

Broughton Poggs (163) (SP 23-03) *(See Filkins & Broughton Poggs ★.)*

Bruern Abbey (163) (SP 26-20) *5 mi. N Burford.* A Cistercian abbey was founded here in the reign of King Stephen, but the dignified 18th-century mansion glimpsed from the road lies a little to the north of the monastic site beside the River Evenlode. The abbey was sold to Sir Thomas Brydges soon after the Dissolution (1539) and the last abbot had to end his days as rector of Wigginton near Banbury. There is very little to see at Bruern, but the roads leading to it from the south and east pass pleasant woodlands, and there is a charming mill house on the Evenlode, close to the mansion. The Oxfordshire Way ★ passes through woodlands close to Bruern Abbey on its way between Bledington ★ and Shipton-under-Wychwood ★, and it is also possible to walk westwards to Idbury ★ or Fifield ★.

Buckland (150) (SP 08-36) *1½ mi. SW Broadway.* This is delightfully situated at the end of a road leading up into a combe in the hills, and overlooked by the not very obvious earthworks of an Iron Age settlement known as Burhill. Buckland is a small village, but it has several pleasant houses and cottages and a fine manor house, which was much restored in the 19th century and which is now a luxurious hotel.

The nearby church has an interesting interior, with some 15th-century glass (restored by William Morris at his own expense), an exquisitely carved and painted panel said to have come from Hailes Abbey ★, splendid Jacobean canopied seating and a pulpit of the same period. The lovely rectory dates from the 15th century and is the oldest medieval parsonage in Gloucestershire still in use, and one of the oldest in the country. It has a fine Great Hall with open timber roof and some interesting medieval stained glass.

There is a pleasant walk over the hill to Broadway ★, or south-westwards over the fields to Laverton ★ and on to Stanton ★. The Cotswold Way ★ runs just to the east, along the hills above the village, and it is easy to link on to it from here.

Buckle Street (150,163) (SP 11-35 etc.) This pre-Roman trackway was called Buggildway in Anglo-Saxon times, but has been known as Buckle Street since the 17th century. It ran southwards from the Jurassic Way ★ on the Cotswold edge, near Broadway Tower ★, in a gently curving line over high wold country to Bourton-on-the-Water ★. Its name was probably derived from an Anglo-Saxon lady called Burghild, and she would possibly gain some satisfaction from knowing that the course of her

road, unlike that of the Romans' Ryknild Street ★ nearby, is still followed by a minor road today. Its name is not shown on the Landranger maps, but it is on the relevant Pathfinder sheets.

Burford (163) (SP 25-12) *9 mi. SE Stow-on-the-Wold.* This lovely old town has an impressive main street lined with a series of fine old houses, and dropping down from the wolds to the valley of the Windrush. The river is crossed by a stout medieval bridge which has resisted the pressures of highway improvers for many years. In coaching days this carried much traffic between the Midlands and the south coast (as it unfortunately still does). However, the main route from London and Oxford to Cheltenham and much of the West Country also originally ran through the town, with a crossing of routes by the old Tolsey House, and it was only in 1812 that the east-west traffic was diverted onto the wolds above.

However, prosperity came to Burford much earlier than this — through trade in wool and cloth, work in the great stone quarries nearby (at the hamlet of Upton (163) (SP 24-12) just to the west of the town, and at the nearby villages of Taynton ★, Little Barrington ★ and Windrush ★), and also the manufacture of fine saddlery, specimens of which were presented to both Charles II and William III. The quarries in the Burford district were worked from early medieval times. In the 17th century their master-mason owners, the Strongs of Great Barrington and Taynton and the Kempsters of Upton and Burford, were noted for their fine craftsmanship, especially in the years following London's Great Fire when members of both families were employed by Sir Christopher Wren in the building of St Paul's Cathedral. Stone from these quarries was also used in the construction of Blenheim Palace ★ and many buildings in Oxford including the Sheldonian Theatre. Saddlery continued to prosper for many years, partly because of the proximity of the Bibury Races which were held regularly for over 200 years on a course near Aldsworth ★, about three miles to the south-west. To add to the jollity Charles II and his mistress Nell Gwyn used to stay in the town during Bibury Race Week, and perhaps for no more than sentimental reasons their son was eventually given the title, Earl of Burford.

As with other towns and cities astride the country's major routes, Burford's great coaching days date from the time when the greatly improved turnpike roads made journeys speedy beyond previous belief. Providing for the feeding and bedding-down of both travellers and their horses, and for the supply of fresh horses, was a considerable trade in itself, and by 1801 Burford's population had reached 1500. 'Burford Bait', the inns' gargantuan meals often incorporating venison 'obtained' (or poached) from Wychwood Forest, was a byword amongst travellers throughout southern England. Coaches coming through here had such splendid names as *Nimrod* and *Tantivy, Defiance, Retaliator* and *Mazeppa*. These were heroic days for Burford and they are brilliantly described in Edith Brill's book, *Old Cotswold*.

It is sad to relate that the coming of the railways brought this colourful era to an abrupt end. Burford's decline had already set in with the diversion of the Oxford to Cheltenham road onto the wolds, and to make matters worse no railway line came its way. The Bibury Races also ceased,

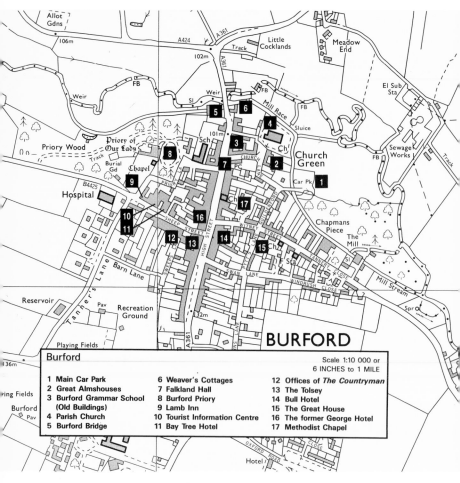

Burford

Scale 1:10 000 or
6 INCHES TO 1 MILE

1 Main Car Park
2 Great Almshouses
3 Burford Grammar School
(Old Buildings)
4 Parish Church
5 Burford Bridge

6 Weaver's Cottages
7 Falkland Hall
8 Burford Priory
9 Lamb Inn
10 Tourist Information Centre
11 Bay Tree Hotel

12 Offices of *The Countryman*
13 The Tolsey
14 Bull Hotel
15 The Great House
16 The former George Hotel
17 Methodist Chapel

owing partly to enclosure of the land on which they had been run. So for a time Burford slumbered, kept alive by the owners of the various fine houses who continued to treasure its qualities, and by agricultural trade from the surrounding countryside. It was also not too long before the first holiday visitors started to arrive, and since the coming of the first motor cars and charabancs to its then dusty streets, their numbers have continued to grow. Today, however, despite its over-busy roads and the demands of its visitors, Burford remains a delight to all who come here.

Explore this charming little town from the **Main Car Park (1)** to the east of the High Street. First walk back over the River Windrush and turn right into Church Lane. Soon pass the attractive **Great Almshouses (2)** which were founded by the Earl of Warwick in 1457, and which were partly rebuilt in 1828. Almost opposite these are some of the old buildings of **Burford Grammar School (3)**, which was founded by prosperous cloth merchant, Simon Wisdom, in 1577.

Just beyond the almshouses, in a churchyard around two sides of which the Windrush flows, is the very interesting **Parish Church (4)**. This has a Norman tower capped by a slender 15th-century spire, and dates largely from the 15th century — a

time when Burford's prosperity from wool was at its peak. See especially the handsome two-storeyed south porch with its fan vaulted ceiling, and the elaborate tomb of Lord Chief Justice Sir Lawrence Tanfield in the North Chapel. Also buried in the church is William Lenthall, noted for his defiance of Charles I when, as Speaker of the Long Parliament, he was recorded as declaring that, 'I have neither eyes to see nor tongue to speak in this place, but as this house is pleased to direct me.' At his own request his last resting place was only marked with an anonymous inscription, but even this was swept away during 19th-century restoration work. Christopher Kempster (or Kit, as he was usually known locally), master-mason of nearby Upton hamlet, has fared better — his monument remains in the south transept complete with weeping cherub carved by his son, William.

On the rim of the church's font will be found the crudely carved inscription 'Anthony Sedley Prisner 1649'. Sedley was one of a party of Roundhead mutineers who were imprisoned in the church, and then forced to watch the execution of three of their comrades before eventually receiving Cromwell's pardon. Lengthy restoration of the church in the 1870s brought much criticism from the ever-watchful William Morris, but the vicar at that time, the Rev. W.A.Cass, was not to be turned from his purpose. He is believed to have responded to Morris's comments thus: 'The church Sir is mine, and if I choose to I shall stand on my head in it.' While there is no record of his ever having performed this gymnastic threat, the final results of his restoration were certainly not to Morris's liking, and do not compare favourably with Morris's own work at Inglesham ★ .

Now walk into the High Street, first turning right to go down to the fine medieval **Burford Bridge (5)** over the Windrush, with the creeper-covered **Weavers' Cottages (6)** on the right, just before it. These were also built by Simon Wisdom as part of his endowment of the Grammar School (see above). Turn round at the bridge and start to walk back up the High Street, first passing on the right the little shopping precinct of Bear Court, once the yard of the Bear Inn. Turn right by the Tudor **Falkland Hall (7)** into Priory Lane, soon passing on the right the fine Elizabethan **Priory (8)** which was once owned by Speaker Lenthall (see above). This is now an Anglican convent.

Continue up Priory Lane and turn left into Sheep Street, first passing the 15th-century **Lamb Inn (9)** on the left, with the Old Brewery next door. This fascinating old building now houses both an off-licence and the town's very helpful **Tourist Information Centre (10)**. (Tel: (0993) 823558.) Immediately beyond this is the 17th-century **Bay Tree Hotel (11)**, which once belonged to Sir Lawrence Tanfield (see above). A short way beyond, on the opposite side of the road, are the offices of that delightful magazine The Countryman **(12)**, the small garden of which is usually open to visitors in summertime.

Now turn right, back into the High Street by the little **Tolsey (13)**, a market house of Tudor origin, where Burford's prosperous wool merchants once held their meetings, and which now houses a small but very interesting local museum. Walk up the High Street far enough to admire the fine view down the hill, here bordered by grassy banks and lined with tall lime-trees. Then cross over to the other side and start to walk downhill. Nearly opposite the Tolsey, pass the handsome 18th-century **Bull Hotel (14)**, the High Street's only brick-faced building. Turn right into Witney Street, to look at the fine 17th-century **Great House (15)**, thought to have been built by Christopher Kempster, and then return to the High Street. Before turning right down High Street, note on the opposite side the archway of the former **George Hotel (16)**, where Charles II once stayed with Nell Gwyn during Bibury Race Week. Being opposite to Witney Street, this archway was well placed to receive the arriving London coaches, which could then depart in the direction of Gloucester from the rear of the hotel yard. Walk down High Street, passing the handsome classical-fronted **Methodist Chapel (17)**, which was converted from a private house in 1849. To complete your walk round Burford, turn right into Church Lane to return to the **Main Car Park (1)**.

away), a pulpit made from a reused Flemish triptych, a fine 17th-century Spanish lectern and delightful monuments to Margaret and Elizabeth Loveden. Beside it is the handsome early 18th-century 'Old Parsonage'. (Visits on Wednesdays in summer only, by written appointment with the National Trust's tenant.)

The village lies a short distance to the east, mostly to the immediate north of the A417. Very much an estate village of Buscot Park, many of its modest buildings were rebuilt or restored in the 1930s. There is an inn on the main road called the Apple Tree, and two National Trust car parks from either of which it is possible (using our mapped **mini-walk**) to walk to Buscot Weir, a lock on the River Thames. Two footbridges cross the river here and beyond them there is a path along its north bank, either westwards to St John's Lock and Lechlade ★ or eastwards to Kelmscot ★. (See below for Buscot Park.)

There is also a small but attractive National Trust car park called the Malthouses, situated on the A417 a short distance to the west of the road down to Buscot Church. Here were once busy warehouses and quays, where goods were transhipped from small craft coming from upstream to larger barges bound mostly for London.

Buscot Park (163) (SU 24-96) 3 mi. SE Lechlade. (See map on page 40.) Owned by the National Trust, this pleasant Adam-style house (1780) is set in a 55-acre park, with beautiful water gardens running down to a tree-bordered lake, and an attractive walled kitchen-garden. The elegant interior of the house is enhanced by a fine collection of furniture and paintings, and the parlour is decorated with the noted series of paintings of the Sleeping Beauty by Sir Edward Burne-Jones. (Tel: (0367) 240786, not weekends.)

Bussage (162) (SO 88-03) 2½ mi. SE Stroud. Small village on steep slopes above the wooded Toadsmoor Valley, with a prettily sited little Victorian church. This was almost entirely paid for by the donations of Oxford undergraduates organised by Thomas Keble, younger brother of John Keble, and vicar of nearby Bisley. The south aisle and the porch were the work of the imaginative architect George Bodley, who also designed the churches at France Lynch ★ and Selsley ★ .

Calcot (163) (SP 08-10) 2½ mi. NW Bibury. A quiet hamlet on the gentle eastern slopes of the Coln Valley with several pleasant cottages lining its sloping single street.

Calmsden (163) (SP 04-08) 5 mi. NE Cirencester. This pleasant little hamlet has a row of attractively glazed early 19th-century estate cottages and a rare 14th-century wayside cross. Come this way in springtime to see water bubbling up amongst daffodils at the nearby spring.

Buscot (163) (SU 23-97) 2 mi. SE Lechlade. Minute village owned by the National Trust, with a small church which can be reached down a separate lane leading from the A417. This has an east window by Edward Burne-Jones (the home of his friend William Morris was at Kelmscot ★, under two miles

Cam (162) (ST 75-99) 1 mi. N Dursley. Large village in the industrialised valley of the little River Cam. One cloth mill remains here, producing high quality West of England cloth, used largely for billiard tables and military uniforms. Upper Cam Church is a large building, believed to have been paid for by

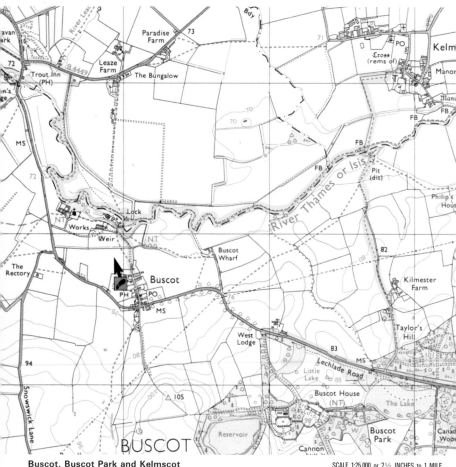

Buscot, Buscot Park and Kelmscot

SCALE 1:25 000 or 2½ INCHES to 1 MILE

Lord Berkeley in the hope of saving his eternal soul following the murder of Edward II at Berkeley Castle ★. The church's interior was partially scraped by the Victorians, but its contents include a Jacobean pulpit on a slender base, a pleasant assortment of 18th-century wall monuments, and an unusual tablet to the Rev. W.C. Holder, featuring a model of his vicarage.

Campden Lane (163) (SP 05-26 etc.) This medieval trackway must have been used by pack-horse trains carrying wool from the warehouses of the Chipping Campden merchants to the port of Bristol, and also probably salt from Droitwich. It follows the approximate course of the Jurassic Way ★ for some of its route, although further south it may have followed the course of the Romans' White Way ★. Part of Campden Lane is followed in our **Walk 3**.

Campden Railway Tunnel (151) (SP 16-40) *1½ mi. NE Chipping Campden.* The best road between Chipping Campden ★ and Hidcote Manor Garden ★ passes a wooded embankment which was created by spoil from a tunnel excavated for the Oxford, Worcester and Wolverhampton Railway, built between 1845 and 1853. This tunnel was the site of

the so-called 'Battle of Mickleton', when the great railway builder and engineer, Isambard Kingdom Brunel, led a gang of no fewer than two thousand navvies armed with picks, shovels and even pistols, in an ultimately successful attempt to oust the navvies of the original contractor, who had refused to leave the site. Read the full story of the battle, and of Brunel's fascinating career, in L.T.C. Rolt's outstanding biography.

Carterton (163) (SP 28-06) *4 mi. SE Burford.* Quite alien in character to the surrounding countryside, this is a garrison town for the great airfield of Brize Norton. However, it does have a heated open-air swimming pool set in a well landscaped recreation ground.

Cassey Compton (163) (SP 04-15) *4 mi. W Northleach.* Here, in the beautifully wooded Coln Valley, is a delightful, partly demolished 17th-century mansion looking south to the point where the Roman White Way ★ crosses the road coming up the valley from Fossebridge ★. 18th-century engravings depict an ambitious house surrounded by formal gardens, but the estate was split up in the 19th century. In the 1920s John Buchan, amongst several others, tried without success to buy the house, and it is easy to see why it would have appealed to a writer with such a strong appreciation of mystery and landscape. Read more about this fascinating house in James Lees-Milne's *Some Cotswold Country Houses.*

Unfenced roads and wooded verges appear to offer picnic opportunities in plenty, but please observe any requests not to park that may be displayed. Walk south-west from here down the White Way, before heading south-east through Chedworth Woods towards Chedworth Roman Villa ★.

Caudle Green (163) (SO 94-10) *7 mi. NW Cirencester.* Quiet hamlet looking north-eastwards across a deep valley to Syde ★, with a small rough green overlooked by a handsome 18th-century farmhouse. This is on the course of our **Walk 9.**

Cerney Wick (163) (SU 07-96) *5 mi. SE Cirencester.* Small village in the flat Thames gravel country, with large flooded pits (part of the Cotswold Water Park ★) to the west and the line of the old Thames and Severn Canal ★ to the east. There is a small Victorian church here and a 'round house' with 18th-century Gothic windows, built for the canal's maintenance men. The little River Churn flows just to the east of the village, on its way to join the Thames at neighbouring Cricklade ★.

Walk from here following the course of the old canal, either south-eastwards to Cricklade ★ or north-westwards to Siddington ★ and Cirencester ★.

Chadlington (164) (SP 33-21) *3 mi. S Chipping Norton.* A long village looking south over the Evenlode Valley towards Wychwood Forest ★. It has at least two inns together with a pleasant 17th- and 18th-century manor house and a substantial church. The church's exterior is enriched with a multitude of fascinating gargoyles, while within will be found a clerestory and a rich series of corbel figures.

There are fine walks northwards over the farmlands of Chadlington Downs, and one of them passes the Hawk Stone (164) (SP 33-23), an isolated eight-foot-high sarsen stone — possibly the sole surviving stone of a long-vanished burial chamber.

Chalford (163) (SO 89-02) *3 mi. SE Stroud.* A large and highly attractive village of the early Industrial Revolution, built on ascending terraces on the south-facing slopes of the Golden Valley ★. Approached by a bemusing series of narrow and often very steep lanes and alleyways is a wealth of late 18th- and early 19th-century houses, most of which once belonged to prosperous clothiers. These are in company with many delightful cottages once inhabited by the more humble weavers. The lanes here are so steep that until recent times panniered donkeys were used to deliver milk, bread and coal. In the valley below there are old mills on the banks of the now derelict Thames and Severn Canal ★, and on the main A419 road there is a rather severe 18th-century church, much altered in Victorian times. This does, however, contain several items of more recent Cotswold craftsmanship including panelling and a font cover by Norman

Jewson, and a lectern by Peter Waals, Gimson's foreman cabinet-maker at Daneway ★, and a close colleague of Jewson's.

Charingworth (151) (SP 20-39) *3 mi. E Chipping Campden.* A modest hamlet on hill slopes looking southwards over orchard country, with a fine early Tudor manor house which is now a luxury hotel. There is a pleasant open road northwards from here, around the Cotswolds' far northern edge below Windmill Hill and then dropping steeply down to Ilmington ★.

Charlbury (164) (SP 36-19) *6 mi. N Witney.* This small town is snugly situated in the Evenlode Valley well away from busy main roads. It looks across the valley to the fine 600-acre Cornbury Park ★, which is itself almost surrounded by the great woodlands of Wychwood Forest ★. For many centuries Charlbury was noted for its gloves, and at the height of its prosperity, in 1852, the town's glovers employed over a thousand people. This trade has now almost ceased, but the coming of the railway, which still survives here, has contributed to Charlbury's special charm. Despite the presence of many retired people and commuting Oxonians, the town has kept much of its rural flavour, and it has a mouth-watering selection of country inns. The largely Perpendicular church was heavily restored by the Victorians, but blends in well with the stone-fronted shops and inns nearby. The small green, known as Playing Close, has a series of attractive cottages looking across to a little neo-Jacobean drinking fountain.

It is possible to walk eastwards from Charlbury, along bridleways running not far from the fine mansion of Ditchley Park ★, and the meandering Oxfordshire Way ★ also passes through the town.

Charlton Abbots (163) (SP 03-24) *2½ mi. S Winchcombe.* A hamlet with fine views out over the 'Sudeley Valley' from its lofty churchyard. The church was virtually rebuilt in the 19th century but in its simple interior will be found a late Norman tub font and an attractive modern oak pulpit. The beautifully gabled manor house close by dates from the Elizabethan and Jacobean periods.

This is all on high watershed country, for in the valley below is the source of the little River Isbourne which flows northwards from here to join the Avon, while less than a mile to the south the River Coln starts its journey southwards to the Thames. Walk westwards from Charlton Abbots over hill country to Cleeve Hill ★, or go northwards beside the Isbourne to link on to **Walk 2** at Waterhatch.

Charterville Allotments (164) (SP 31-10) *3 mi. W Witney, to immediate S of Minster Lovell.* It was here, in 1847, that 300 acres lying each side of the road were purchased by one of the Chartists (forerunners of the Socialists), and in a typically 19th-century exercise in rural paternalism, this land was split up into a number of smallholdings. These were then ploughed up and handed over to poor families from the industrial towns, each having already been endowed with thirty pounds and a pig. But sadly, like so many idealist enterprises, it soon foundered. A handful of the little dwellings remain unaltered, but most have been smartened up beyond easy recognition, and now appear to be the homes of independent folk whose views might not easily be reconciled with the liberal ideals that led to their construction.

Chastleton (163) (SP 24-29) *3 mi. SE Moreton-in-Marsh.* A modest stone village, situated on the lower slopes of the Cotswolds, and whose high point is the splendid Stuart manor of Chastleton House. It was built by Walter Jones, a prosperous Witney wool merchant who had purchased the estate from Robert Catesby in 1602. Probably designed by Robert Smythson, the architect perhaps best known for Hardwick Hall in Derbyshire, it has a fine five-gabled south front and a fascinating and highly atmospheric interior largely undisturbed by 18th- or 19th-century alteration. The most outstanding feature is the Long Gallery at the top of the house which has a beautifully ornamented and tunnel-vaulted ceiling. There is a topiary garden at the side of the house, an attractive 18th-century arched dovecot across the road and medieval barns close by. While visiting here, ask to be told the story of Arthur Jones's plight after the Battle of Worcester, and how he was hidden from Roundhead troops by his enterprising wife Sarah, who spiked their wine flagons with laudanum, thus allowing the now desperate Arthur to escape. *(Tel: (060 874) 355.)*

Chastleton House . . . a Stuart manor house with an atmospheric interior

The nearby church dates from the 12th century, although it was considerably enlarged about 200 years later. See especially the medieval floor tiles, the two interesting brasses and the wall tablets to two members of the Jones family.

Walk southwards to Adlestrop ★ to link onto **Walk 5**, or south-eastwards to Cornwell ★, passing through Chastleton Barrow ★.

Chastleton Barrow (163) (SP 25-28) *1 mi. SE Chastleton.* A well preserved, but thickly wooded, circular Iron Age settlement. Unusually, its builders faced the encircling banks with large blocks of stone and some of these have survived. This may be approached by a bridleway from the road above Chastleton ★.

Chavenage House (162) (ST 87-95) *1½ mi. NW Tetbury.* This delightful Elizabethan manor house is visible from the road and is also sometimes open to

Chavenage . . . Oliver Cromwell slept here

the public. Oliver Cromwell made a special visit here to persuade the owner, Colonel Nathaniel Stephens, to agree to the execution of Charles I. The unfortunate colonel soon deeply regretted giving his agreement and died, full of remorse, less than three months after the king's execution. Cromwell is believed to have slept in the handsome Tapestry Room, which is shown to visitors. *(Tel: (0666) 502329.)*

It is possible to walk behind the manor to the little family chapel nearby, and along a bridleway to Beverston ★. The chapel, virtually rebuilt in the 19th century, is not of great interest apart from some 17th-century tomb figures which have been reset in the porch.

Chedworth (163) (SP 05-11) *4 mi. SW Northleach.* A large village spread out along a quiet valley, through which once ran a railway branch-line complete with a tall and most intrusive viaduct. This structure has now been removed and the best part of the village is centred upon the Seven Tuns Inn, a spring bubbling out of a wall opposite and an interesting church with late Norman origins a short distance beyond. A pleasant cobbled path leads past old tombstones to the south door of this building, which was considerably enriched in the prosperous Perpendicular period. Light floods in through tall windows on the south side, onto a stout Norman tub font and onto the contrastingly elegant 15th-century stone pulpit. Do not overlook the lovely modern sculpture of the Virgin and Child carved by Helen Rock in 1911. If possible climb up the path beyond the church for good views out over the village.

It is possible to walk down the valley to Fossebridge ★ passing through the delectable hamlet of Pancakehill (SP 07-11), but to explore the great Chedworth Woods and the Chedworth Roman Villa ★, use part of **Walk 11** which runs through the village.

Chedworth Roman Villa (163) (SP 05-13) *3½ mi. W Northleach.* Situated in a beautifully wooded stretch of the Coln Valley, this is undoubtedly

Mosaic pavement at Chedworth . . . one of Britain's finest Roman villas

Britain's most attractively sited Roman villa. (The Romans often appear to have been as adept in their choice of villa sites as the Cistercians were in siting their great abbeys.) Discovered in 1864 when Lord Eldon's gamekeeper found a mosaic pavement while digging to retrieve a lost ferret, it proved on excavation to be one of the finest examples of a Roman villa in Britain, whose buildings date from about AD 180 to AD 350. It has been in the care of the National Trust since 1924 and the beautifully preserved remains include bath suites, a hypocaust and mosaic pavements, with one in the west wing depicting the four seasons. There is also a museum complete with a ten-minute video film, and well stocked shop. *(Tel: (024 289) 256.)*

The villa may be approached on foot from Chedworth by using part of our **Walk 11**.

Cheltenham Spa (163) (SO 94-22) *7 mi. E Gloucester.* This large and elegant spa town is situated on the very edge of the Severn Plain, just below the sometimes craggy scarp face of the Cotswolds, and not far from their highest point, Cleeve Hill ★. Once a small market town, its humble beginning as a spa was occasioned by the discovery of salt crystals at a spring in the year 1716. This spring was soon enclosed and incorporated into Cheltenham's first pump-room, but it was some years later that the original owner's son-in-law, one Henry Skillicorne, erected a more permanent building and employed the term spa. The fame of Cheltenham's waters began to spread and the arrival of George III for a five-week 'taking of the waters' in 1788 finally established Cheltenham as a major spa town.

Passing through here in 1826, William Cobbett

Cheltenham

Scale 1:10 000 or
6 INCHES to 1 MILE

1 The Promenade
2 Regent Arcade
3 Tourist Information Centre
4 Montpellier Street
5 Art Gallery & Museum
6 Gustav Holst Birthplace Museum
  (off map to east)
7 Pittville Park (off map to north)
8 Pittville Pump Room Museum
  (off map to north)
9 Cheltenham Racecourse
  (off map to north)
10 Sandford Park
  (off map to east)

Sunlit fountains at Cheltenham Spa

noted 'a new row of the most gaudy and fantastical dwelling places' and described the area in general as 'a nasty, flat, stupid spot, without anything pleasant near it'. However, these were only the views of one rather jaundiced and often prickly traveller, and there were many others who lavished their praises upon a spa town that continued to thrive throughout the 19th century. It was now that a large number of army officers and administrators and their families, many suffering from tropical liver complaints, retired here to benefit from the health-giving waters, thus altering Cheltenham from a town chiefly for spa visitors to a largely residential one.

It continues to thrive today, although now more as a holiday and shopping town, with its considerable light industry being kept well at bay on its fringes. It has been further enhanced by the establishment of three major public schools, two for boys and one for girls. It has some of the finest Regency buildings in the country, these being grouped along terraces, around squares, crescents, parks and gardens, and on either side of Cheltenham's jewel, the handsome tree-lined Promenade, with its fine shops and elegant buildings. There is an annual Festival of Music and also a Festival of Literature, and the famous Cheltenham Gold Cup meeting is held on the fine racecourse just to the north of the town.

Most visitors to Cheltenham will first head for the **Promenade (1)**, which is today complemented by the **Regent Arcade (2)**, a fine two-storey shopping arcade running parallel to it just to the west, and linking in to the busy High Street, where many of the major multiple stores will be found. The **Tourist Information Centre (3)** is also located in the Promenade, in the Municipal Offices on the east side *(tel: (0242) 522878)*. Other elegant shopping areas include **Montpellier Street (4)**, with its attendant Courtyard development, both best approached by a short walk through Imperial Gardens and possibly Montpellier Gardens. The **Cheltenham Art Gallery and Museum (5)**, with various items including its nationally important Arts and Crafts Collection, is in Clarence Street *(tel: (0242) 237431)*, and the **Gustav Holst Birthplace**

Museum (6), where the composer of *The Planets* was born in 1874, is at 4, Clarence Road *(tel: (0242) 524846)*.

On the north side of the town *(all off our map)* will be found the extensive **Pittville Park (7)** with its Nature and Fitness Trails and its swimming pool, and the **Pittville Pump Room Museum (8)** with its emphasis on Cheltenham's history *(tel: (0242) 512740)*. **Cheltenham Racecourse (9)** is situated on the A435, Evesham Road, to the north of the town, well beyond Pittville Park.

On the south-east side of the town *(off our map)* is **Sandford Park (10)**, which has an open-air swimming pool.

Cherington (163) (ST 90-98) *3½ mi. E Nailsworth.* The Cherington Inn and several pleasant 18th- and early 19th-century cottages look across a large green, on which is a Victorian drinking fountain inscribed 'Let Him that is athirst, come'. The largely 13th-century church has a Norman south doorway with tympanum and an Early English chancel which has unfortunately been scraped and heavily repointed. The elegant pulpit incorporates carved medieval panels (possibly Flemish) and there is a handsome Renaissance candle-holder beside it.

It is possible to walk eastwards from here over open farming country to Rodmarton ★.

Chipping Campden (151) (SP 15-39) *5 mi. NW Moreton-in-Marsh.* Chipping was an Old English word meaning 'market', and Campden had a weekly market and no fewer than three annual fairs as early as the mid-13th century. In the 14th and 15th centuries it was without doubt the most important trading centre for wool in the north Cotswolds, and its name must have been familiar to wool merchants on the quays of Bruges and Antwerp, and most other cloth-trading ports of western Europe. William Grevel, described as 'the flower of the wool merchants of all England' on his memorial brass in the parish church, built **Grevel's House (1)** in about 1380. With its splendid Perpendicular style gabled, two-storeyed window, this was to become one of the first of a very beautiful series of buildings in the honey-coloured local stone that were erected in the centuries which followed. Grevel's House is in private hands, but the **Woolstaplers' Hall (2)**, built at about the same time by wool merchant Robert Calf, now houses an interesting small museum, which also incorporates a helpful **Tourist Information Centre (2)** *(tel: (0386) 840289)*.

The lovely **Market Hall (3)** was built in 1627 by Sir Baptist Hicks 'for the sale of cheese, butter and poultry'. He had made his money in the cloth trade, not in Chipping Campden, but in the southern Cotswolds and in London, for by this time Campden's wool trading prosperity had almost ceased, due to the fact that since Edward III's time Flemish weavers had been encouraged to come to England, and wool was handled directly by the clothiers in the Stroud valley and elsewhere, rather than by exporting merchants. Sir Baptist built himself the fine **Campden House (4)** not far to the south of the church, but sadly this was later burnt down by Royalists during the Civil War. It was claimed that this was to prevent it falling into the hands of Cromwell's forces, but it appears more likely to have been set alight in a drunken spree by disgruntled soldiers before they were forced to flee. The only survivals are the lodges and gatehouse,

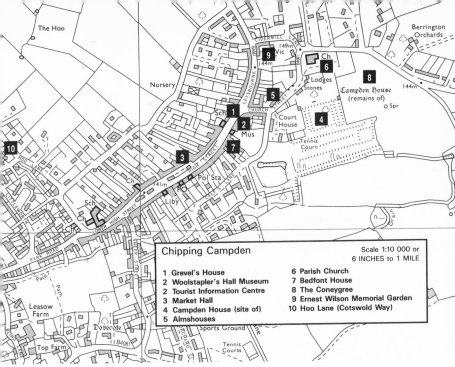

Chipping Campden

| | Scale 1:10 000 or |
| | 6 INCHES to 1 MILE |

1 Grevel's House
2 Woolstapler's Hall Museum
2 Tourist Information Centre
3 Market Hall
4 Campden House (site of)
5 Almshouses

6 Parish Church
7 Bedfont House
8 The Coneygree
9 Ernest Wilson Memorial Garden
10 Hoo Lane (Cotswold Way)

two banqueting houses and an almonry. The East Banqueting House has been beautifully restored by the Landmark Trust. *(Details of short-term holiday letting may be obtained from the Landmark Trust, Shottesbrooke, Maidenhead, Berks. Tel: (062882) 5925.)*

However, just below the church is Sir Baptist's most enduring legacy, a row of delightful **almshouses (5)** built by him in 1612. Sir Baptist became Baron Hicks and Viscount Campden in 1628 (appointments no doubt arising from the substantial loans that he had recently made to his sovereign) but sadly he died only a year later. He and his wife are buried beneath a splendid marble monument in **Campden Church (6)**. This is one of the great Cotswold wool churches, a fine Perpendicular building with a handsome 15th-century pinnacled tower. Its interior is perhaps a little cold in feeling, but it contains a number of interesting monumental brasses, a series of monuments in the Noel Chapel, and an outstanding collection of medieval English embroidery, including copes and altar hangings.

Chipping Campden's prosperity declined greatly in the 18th and 19th centuries, although local mason and quarry-owner, Thomas Woodward, left an enduring mark on the High Street with the building of the elegantly classical **Bedfont House (7)** in about 1745. However, Campden appears to have slept largely undisturbed by intrusions until the early years of the 20th century. Then in 1902 Charles Ashbee, a disciple of William Morris and Ruskin, moved his Guild and School of Handicraft from London's East End to Chipping Campden. This migration of fifty craftsmen and their families was a brave endeavour and full of idealism, but the Guild did not survive the rigours of economic depression, the First World War, and above all, the mutual suspicion that appears to have arisen between the Cockney craftsmen and the natives of Chipping Campden. However, Ashbee's ideals have in part survived, thanks largely to the artist and architect F.L.Griggs, who established the Campden Trust in

1929, and who did so much to preserve the Chipping Campden that we see today; thanks also to George Hart, the craftsman in metal, his son and grandson, who have kept the tradition of the Guild alive; and also, more recently, to Robert Welch, the talented industrial designer, whose work may be seen at his studio shop in the High Street.

Chipping Campden's present-day character still owes much to F.L.Griggs and his friends, and remains largely unspoilt. There are now more tourist shops, restaurants and hotels than there were in Griggs's day, but there are still a few genuine country-town shops and small inns left. It therefore remains a pleasure to walk the length of the High Street, and up past the almshouses, to the splendidly towered church, and on to the open land

Chipping Campden

beyond, **The Coneygree (8)**, which belongs to the National Trust. Before leaving this most attractive of Cotswold towns do not overlook the **Ernest Wilson Memorial Garden (9)**, opened in memory of the great plant collector, who was born at Chipping Campden in 1876, and who made a series of expeditions to the Far East in the first thirty years of this century. This delightful garden is situated in the lower half of the old Vicarage garden, and fronts on to Leysbourne, which runs north beyond the High Street.

Chipping Campden is the northern terminus of the Cotswold Way★, the long-distance footpath which runs from here, following the approximate line of the Cotswold scarp, down to Bath, a distance of about ninety miles. Why not walk the first few miles at least, up over the fields as far as Dover's Hill★? Start by walking west, down the High Street, and turning right into Back Ends and **Hoo Lane (10)**, and then follow the sign to the left marked 'Cotswold Way'.

Chipping Norton (164) (SP 31-26) *14 mi. SW Banbury.* Lively little market town where the everyday lives of those who live and work there have so far not been overshadowed by tourism. It is built on west facing slopes, with the large Victorian Bliss's Valley Tweed Mill in the valley still looking less at home here than it would in some darker, deeper valley in West Yorkshire. It was in fact designed by George Woodhouse, an architect from Yorkshire's neighbour, Lancashire. Built in 1872, it closed only in 1980 and is now converted into flats.

The long **Market Square (1)**, or Chepynge, as it was called in medieval times (hence Chipping), is dominated by a handsome 19th-century **Town Hall (2)** designed by George Repton, son of the better known Humphry Repton, the landscape designer. The Square, which in the 19th century must have resounded to the horns of the twenty-two coaches that were then passing through Chipping Norton daily, is also overlooked by pleasant 17th-, 18th- and 19th-century hotels, inns and shops, and during the summer there is a **Tourist Information Point (3)** at the nearby New Street Car Park. *(Tel: (0608) 644379.)* On the other side of New Street there is a small **museum** in the adjoining **Baptist Chapel (4)** displaying items of local interest.

Almshouses near Chipping Norton Church

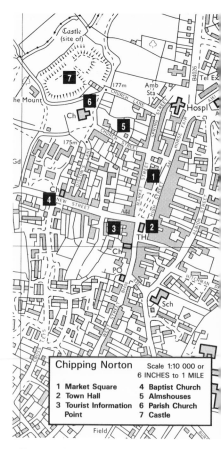

| Chipping Norton | Scale 1:10 000 or |
| | 6 INCHES to 1 MILE |

1 Market Square   4 Baptist Church
2 Town Hall   5 Almshouses
3 Tourist Information   6 Parish Church
Point   7 Castle

The row of quaint, gabled **almshouses (5)** was built in 1640 on Church Street, the cul-de-sac leading down to the **Parish Church (6)**, which lies in the valley bottom. This fine, largely Perpendicular building, which was no doubt mainly funded with money amassed in the wool trade, has an unusual hexagonal porch with a vaulted ceiling. The church tower was rebuilt in 1825, but it is sad to recall that from its tall predecessor was hanged a brave but unfortunate cleric who, in the times following Henry VIII's break with the Church of Rome, obstinately refused to make use of Cranmer's English Prayer Book. The church's handsome interior was over-restored by the Victorians, but the tombs of Richard Croft and Thomas Rickardes, and the interesting series of brasses, make a visit here well worth while. To the immediate north of the church are the extensive motte and bailey earthworks of a 12th-century **castle (7)**.

There is a good walk eastwards from Chipping Norton, down the Glyme Valley, through Old Chalford and Lidstone to Enstone, and returning along the western fringes of Heythrop Park.

Churchill (163) (SP 28-24) *2½ mi. SW Chipping Norton.* Much of this village is strung out along the B4450, but its early 19th-century church is of some interest, being modelled on at least two Oxford buildings. The elegant west tower is a replica of Magdalen College's tower, and the hammerbeam roof within was inspired by the hall of Christ Church. The nearby Memorial Fountain, a rather bizarre exercise in Victorian Gothic, was built in 1870 in memory of James Langston, whose money had paid for the new church. There is also a memorial stone to William Smith, a pioneer of the science of geology, who spent his childhood years at Churchill.

Only the chancel of the old church remains, and this is used as a mortuary chapel. It looks across a broad valley towards Daylesford House ★, reminding us that the great Warren Hastings was born at Churchill in 1732, in an early Georgian cottage which lies on the road between the new and old churches. It was always Hastings's ambition to buy back the family estate at Daylesford, and this aim was eventually achieved on his return from India.

St John's Hospital, Cirencester

Cirencester (163) (SP 02-01) *15 mi. SE Cheltenham.* This busy market town stands on the site of Corinium Dobunnorum, for a time Roman Britain's second largest city, and meeting point of three major Roman roads — the Ermin Way ★, the Foss Way ★ and Akeman Street ★. Evidence of much of the ancient forum and basilica, and also of many houses, has been uncovered over the years, but little now shows above ground apart from a stretch of the Roman town wall on the far side of the Abbey Grounds (see below), and an impressively large, turf-covered **amphitheatre (1)** to the south of the ring road (*off map to the south, but located on* **Tour 5**). This is in the care of English Heritage, and is open at any reasonable time. Although Cirencester was largely neglected by the Anglo-Saxons, it regained its importance in early medieval times. It soon grew rich on the wool trade, owing in the first place to the enterprise of the great Cirencester Abbey, and latterly to the activities of its prosperous wool and cloth merchants. It remains today the undisputed centre of life and work in the southern Cotswolds — a lively market town and attractive tourist centre.

The pressures of modern tourism have been responsible for some change, but many of the cheerfully coloured shops in the **Market Place (2)** have retained their country flavour, and over all preside the magnificent 162-ft Perpendicular tower and three-storeyed south porch of the **Parish Church (3)**. The porch, one of England's finest, was built by the abbey at the end of the 15th century. After the Dissolution it was known as the Town Hall and was only handed back to the vicar in the 18th century. Endowed with the wealth of the town's wool merchants, the splendid interior of this

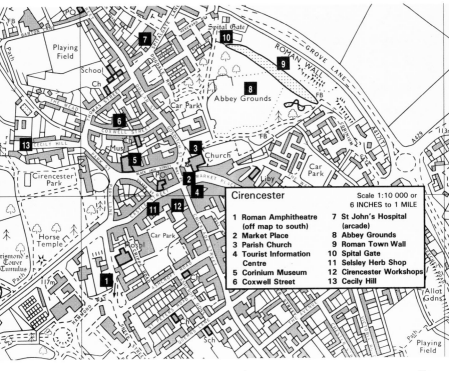

Cirencester Scale 1:10 000 or 6 INCHES to 1 MILE

1 Roman Amphitheatre (off map to south)
2 Market Place
3 Parish Church
4 Tourist Information Centre
5 Corinium Museum
6 Coxwell Street
7 St John's Hospital (arcade)
8 Abbey Grounds
9 Roman Town Wall
10 Spital Gate
11 Selsley Herb Shop
12 Cirencester Workshops
13 Cecily Hill

largely 15th-century church has a fine roof illuminated by clerestory windows, medieval stained glass in the east and west windows, a painted 'wine-glass' pulpit, and also many interesting brasses.

There is a **Tourist Information Centre (4)** in the Corn Hall, which is on the south side of the Market Place, almost opposite the Parish Church. *(Tel: (0285) 654180)*. Not far away, in Park Street, is the most interesting **Corinium Museum (5)**, which has one of Britain's best collections of Romano-British material, together with displays illustrating the medieval Cotswolds and the wool trade. *(Tel: (0285) 655611.)* See also the series of lovely old houses in nearby **Coxwell Street (6)**, the surviving arcade of **St John's Hospital (7)** in Spitalgate Street, the delightful **Abbey Grounds (8)** with swans and wildfowl on a large pool and, to their immediate east, a stretch of the **Roman Town Wall (9)** and the Norman gatehouse known as **The Spital Gate (10)**, the only surviving building of Cirencester Abbey.

Before leaving the town, do not miss a visit to the **Selsley Herb Shop (11)** in Castle Street, which has a herb garden at its rear, nor the **Cirencester Workshops (12)**, a converted brewery in Cricklade Street, housing a number of independent craft businesses, with a craft shop, gallery and coffee shop. See below for **Cirencester Park**, the town entrance to which is at the end of Cecily Hill **(13)**.

Cirencester Park (163) (ST 99-02 etc.) *To the immediate west of Cirencester.* The mansion which lies at the town end of the park was built by the 1st Earl Bathurst in 1714-18 almost certainly to his own design. The house cannot be visited by the public, but most of its great park is open. Notices clearly proclaim that, 'You are welcome on foot and on horseback by permission of the Earl Bathurst. Dogs, cars, cycles or unaccompanied children are not allowed. Take your litter home.'

The writer Alexander Pope gave his advice on the layout of this great park and there is a small rusticated shelter known as Pope's Seat near the polo ground. But the 1st Earl Bathurst lived until the age of ninety-one, dying only in 1775, and for most of the long years following the building of the house, he was constantly adding features to his great park. Apart from Pope's Seat, these include a great Doric column topped by a statue of Queen Anne, the Hexagon, to the north of the Broad Ride, and a large Gothic folly, known as Alfred's Hall. His Broad Ride, or Broad Avenue, stretches westwards

The Broad Ride, Cirencester Park

from the town entrance at Cecily Hill almost to Sapperton ★, and is nearly five miles long.

Wander almost at will in these great woods and open parklands, but always remember that you are a privileged guest, and not there by right. Land-ranger Sheet 163 will be found invaluable. No vehicles are allowed and entrance is normally free, apart from the polo grounds where matches are held on each Sunday from May to September, and where an entry fee is charged (entry for polo spectators is from the A419, Stroud road, some 2½ miles to the west of the town). *(For further information tel: (0285) 653225.)*

Clanfield (163) (SP 28-01) *4 mi. N Faringdon.* This long straggling village is less than two miles north of the Thames, but is still predominantly Cotswold in flavour. It has two attractive inns, the Plough and the Mason's Arms. The interior of the church has been over-restored, but the exterior is well proportioned and is enlivened, high up on the 14th-century tower, by a carving of St Stephen complete with four stones — the symbols of his martyrdom.

Clapton-on-the-Hill (163) (SP 16-17) *2 mi. S Bourton-on-the-Water.* Small village on a hill looking across the Windrush Valley to the ridge where the great hangars of a long-closed airfield remain. The little church has simple Norman features, including a south doorway with a plain tympanum, and a tub font, but the pointed chancel arch is Early English. There is a walk down across the fields to Bourton-on-the-Water ★, and a quiet road leads to Great Rissington ★, crossing the Windrush at New Bridge.

Cleeve Hill and Cleeve Common (163) (SO 98-26) *2½ mi. W Winchcombe.* This broad expanse of

Topograph on Cleeve Hill

open common land slopes gently upwards to West Down, the Cotswolds' highest point (1082 ft). It is grand country to walk or ride over, and there is a wealth of wildlife to be observed in addition to the grazing sheep and cattle, and homo sapiens in the form of the golfers on the northern fringes. There are splendid views out over the Severn Valley to the Malverns, to May Hill, and the distant mountains of Wales in the haze beyond. The best access points are from Cleeve Hill village (SO 98-26), from Postlip ★ (SP 00-27), Corndean Lane (SP 01-26), West Down (SP 00-23), and the vicinity of the radio masts (SO 99-24) three miles north of Whittington ★.

Coaley Peak Picnic Site (162) (SO 79-01) *4 mi. SW Stroud.* A lovely open space above steep scarp slopes near the top of Frocester Hill ★, from whence there are splendid views (with topograph to help with identification) out over the winding Severn Estuary, the Forest of Dean and the distant Welsh hills. There are also a number of display boards depicting the wildlife of the area. This site provides the only public access to the ruined 19th-century mansion of Woodchester Park (see Woodchester ★).

Coates (163) (SO 98-00) *3 mi. W Cirencester. (See map on page 111.)* Small village on the high wolds with a neat Perpendicular-towered church in company with a rectory and farmhouse — two most attractive buildings. Beyond the tidy churchyard and through a Norman doorway, the church itself will be found to have a simple but most pleasing interior. Walk south-westwards from here to the Tunnel House Inn ★ and then south and east along the course of the old Thames and Severn Canal to Thames Head ★, the source of the River Thames. Coates is also on the course of the **mini-walk** shown on the map on page 111.

Coberley (163) (SO 96-16) *4 mi. S Cheltenham Spa. (See map on page 93.)* This small village is delightfully situated near the head of the Churn Valley, less than a mile from the Churn's source at Seven Springs ★. The church lies a little way to the east of the village and is approached by a path beneath an archway in a farm building (visitors may feel that they are intruding, but there is no alternative). The church was largely rebuilt in the 19th century, but the Perpendicular tower and the 14th-century south chapel have survived. This chapel contains the effigies of Sir Thomas Berkeley, who fought at Crécy, and his wife Joan, who remarried after Sir Thomas's death and became the mother of Sir Richard (Dick) Whittington. There is a monument in the sanctuary of a knight holding a heart, commemorating the burial here in 1295 of Sir Giles Berkeley's heart, the rest of his body having been buried at Little Malvern. The high walls by the churchyard and the large flat area beyond are the only surviving evidence of a mansion that stood here until the 18th century.

Follow the **mini-walk** shown on the map on page 93 for a circular walk taking in Upper Coberley ★ and Seven Springs ★. It is also possible to take another pleasant circular walk from here, down the Churn Valley to Cowley ★, Cockleford ★ and Colesbourne ★, returning via Pinswell Plantation and Upper Coberley ★. Landranger Sheet 163 will reveal a wealth of other possibilities.

Cockleford (163) (SO 96-14) *5 mi. S Cheltenham.* Hamlet on the edge of woodland in the Churn Valley with an attractive pool and an excellent inn called the Green Dragon, which would make an ideal halting point on a walk around here (see Coberley, above).

Cold Aston (163) (SP 12-19) *4 mi. N Northleach.* This village used to be widely known as Aston Blank. Documents indicate that it first became known as 'Cold' in 1287, and then as 'Blank' in 1554, and until recent years both names were in common use. Now the arbiters have finally settled

on 'Cold' — and with some justification, for this is a high wold village set in typically rolling Cotswold country, with dry-stone walls providing the only shelter from the strong winds that often blow across here.

The village is centred upon a large sycamore tree on its green, which is itself overlooked on one side by the handsome Georgian Sycamore House, and on the other by the low-built Plough Inn. The largely Norman church has a very plain exterior, but once inside the Norman south door the visitor will find pleasant stone vaulting beneath the tower, a colourful 17th-century monument complete with cherubs, and the remnants of a 14th-century stone reredos in the east wall.

Walk south-westwards from here down a track to Turkdean ★, then possibly on to Hazleton ★, before returning via Notgrove ★ — a fine upland journey of almost ten miles. (Use Landranger Sheet 163.)

Colesbourne (163) (SO 99-13) *6 mi. SE Cheltenham.* Small, scattered village in the wooded Churn Valley. Its church has a Perpendicular tower, and inside will be found a fine 15th-century stone pulpit — vase shaped and on a slender octagonal stem. The large number of exotic trees to be found in the surrounding park is due to the activities of Squire Henry Elwes (1846-1922), soldier, big-game hunter, botanist, and above all forester. Elwes roamed the world in search of exotic tree specimens and brought many of these back to be planted in his park at Colesbourne. Timber for the new bowsprit and masts of the restored SS *Great Britain* at Bristol has all come from the great woodlands of this estate.

Walk north-westwards from here to Upper Coberley ★ passing below the earthworks of the Iron Age Norbury Camp (SO 99-15), and on to Seven Springs ★ to link with the Cotswold Way ★, or return via Coberley ★ and Cowley ★.

Coln Rogers (163) (SP 08-09) *2½ mi. NW Bibury.* The lovely Coln Valley is broad here and there are woods on the far side above the stream, looking back to the Saxon church, which is tucked well away from the road. Much of the original Saxon nave and chancel remains — see especially the chancel arch, and one of the windows in the north side made out of a single piece of stone. Note also the beautifully simple 15th-century stone pulpit.

Walk up the valley to Calcot ★ and Coln St Dennis ★, or down it to Winson ★ and Ablington ★, possibly linking onto **Walk 12** at the latter.

Coln St Aldwyn (163) (SP 14-05) *2½ mi. N Fairford.* This delightful village has a much restored church and an Elizabethan manor house looking out over the clear waters of the Coln and beech-woods beyond. The interior of the church was heavily restored in the mid-19th century and is rather dull, but there are a number of beautifully sculptured tombstones beneath trees in the churchyard. John Keble, father of the famous John Keble, was vicar here from 1782 to 1835, and young John was his curate during the last ten of these years. Memorial windows in the church recall these connections.

The course of the Roman Akeman Street ★ passes just to the north of the village, but there is no right of way for walkers here. However, it is possible to walk beside the little River Coln,

Coln St Aldwyn and Quenington   SCALE 1:25 000 or 2½ INCHES to 1 MILE

upstream to Bibury ★, or downstream to Quenington ★ and part-way to Fairford ★, using the mapped **mini-walk** shown on this page.

Coln St Dennis (163) (SP 08-10) *3 mi. NW Bibury.* Prettily sited village, with a tall-towered Norman church looking out across water-meadows bordering the clear-watered Coln. Apart from its very top even the central tower is Norman, and the west tower arch, although under great stress, still survives intact (the east tower arch had to be rebuilt when the tower's top was added in the 15th century). Do not miss the weird collection of Norman corbel figures supporting the nave roof, nor the attractive 18th-century wall-monuments.

Combe (164) (SP 40-16) *2 mi. W Woodstock.* Attractive village to the west of Blenheim Park ★, with the pretty Cockerel Inn looking across a wide, tree-shaded green towards the church. This is a delightful little building with a vaulted north porch and a Perpendicular doorway opening onto old stone-flagged floors. Inside are a medieval stone pulpit built into a wall, a beautifully carved 15th-century font, triple sedilia and a richly coloured 'Doom' wall-painting.

Enthusiasts have lovingly restored an original mid-19th-century beam engine at Combe Mill on the nearby River Evenlode, and this is put in steam for visitors on many weekends in the summer. *(Tel: (08675) 2652.)*

Compton Abdale (163) (SP 06-16) *3 mi. W Northleach.* Small village in a deep valley, with a church built into a steep bank overlooking its crossroads. This has a finely pinnacled and gargoyled Perpendicular tower, but the rest, including its interior, was over-restored in the late 19th and early 20th centuries. Below the churchyard there is a little stone 'crocodile' from where a spring gushes out, to flow down beside the road on its way to join the Coln at Cassey Compton ★.

There is a good walk south-eastwards from here, over the hills to Yanworth ★, then along the wooded Coln Valley to Cassey Compton ★, before returning to Compton Abdale.

Condicote (163) (SP 15-28) *3 mi. NW Stow-on-the-Wold.* A quiet upland village lying just to the east of the Romans' Ryknild Street ★, the section south of here being known as Condicote Lane. The village is centred upon a large rough green encircled by young trees and which in the spring is bright with daffodils. It is overlooked by a 14th-century wayside cross, four handsome farmhouses and a little Norman church. Unfortunately this was heavily 'restored' in 1888 when the walls were ruthlessly scraped and repointed. However, the Norman south doorway with its patterned tympanum was left largely undisturbed, and there is an interesting little figure beneath the 13th-century piscina. The small earthworks on the east side of the village, marked 'henge' on the Landranger map, are thought to be the remains of a Bronze Age ceremonial site.

It is possible to walk south from here along the course of the Ryknild Street ★, now mostly a grass-grown track, almost to Upper Slaughter ★. There is a pleasant return route from the latter through part of Eyford Park, making use of minor roads in the final stage back to Condicote.

War memorial and church at Condicote . . . a quiet upland village

Cooper's Hill (163) (SO 89-14) *5 mi. SE Gloucester.* This great spur jutting out from the Cotswold edge is now within a 137-acre nature reserve. There is an interesting 1¾-mile nature trail starting from the Fiddler's Elbow Car Park on the A46 (162) (SO 88-13), up through beech-woods and over open grassland, and leading finally to a maypole at the top. There are fine views from here out over the Severn Valley, and the maypole marks the point where the famous cheese-rolling races start. These are held on Spring Bank Holiday Monday and consist of dangerous chases after 7lb wooden discs, representing cheeses, down a 200yd, 1-in-1 slope, each winner being rewarded with a real cheese. There are many other quaint side-events including dancing, wrestling and such bucolic fun as face-pulling through a horse-collar!

The bottom of Cooper's Hill is on our **Walk 7**, and it is possible to use part of this to walk to the interesting remains of Witcombe Roman Villa ★.

Cornbury Park (164) (SP 35-18) *1 mi. SW Charlbury.* Splendid 600-acre deer park with great avenues of trees and a chain of lakes, occupying the north-eastern sector of Wychwood Forest ★. Cornbury House, originally a medieval hunting lodge, is a fine 17th-century mansion, built initially by the great master-mason Nicholas Stone, and completed by Hugh May, Controller of the Royal Works at Windsor Castle. The quarry-owning Timothy Strong of Taynton ★, near Burford, was the contractor. Charles II's Lord Chancellor, the Earl of Clarendon, for whom the house was built, started work on his history of the Great Rebellion here, although he was exiled to France long before its completion. Tantalising glimpses of the 'sweete parke' described by diarist John Evelyn are obtainable from the gates to the immediate south-west of Charlbury ★, but there is no general access for the public, apart from an interesting footpath from Finstock (SP 35-16) running north-westwards to a point (SP 33-18) on the minor road south of Ranger's Lodge.

Cornwell (163) (SP 27-27) *3 mi. W Chipping Norton.* This delightful little village and its fine manor house were 'discovered' by a wealthy American lady in 1938 when they were both in a very run-down state. Realising the possibilities, she bought the whole estate and at once engaged the outstanding Welsh architect Clough Williams-Ellis to restore it for her. Williams-Ellis added several very personal touches which will remind visitors of his better-known work, the colourful, Italianate village of Portmeirion in North Wales. There is a small green with a village hall nearby, and a stream overlooked by cottages on slopes beyond. A short distance along the road to Chipping Norton, there is a glimpse through wrought-iron gates of the enchanting manor house, with its handsome 18th-century front concealing an earlier core. Between house and gates are beautiful terraced gardens which were also laid out by Clough Williams-Ellis when he restored the manor. Sadly the American lady's English husband was killed while serving in the Royal Air Force during the War, and neither of them ever lived in the lovely house that they had so imaginatively brought back to life.

The beautiful gardens at Cornwell Manor

The small church lies in parkland beyond the village and may be approached by a signposted path behind the manor. This low building has a central bell turret, and a pleasant but heavily restored interior. Do not overlook the font with its base made up of four carved lions.

It is possible to walk westwards from here, to link onto **Walk 5** at Daylesford Hill Farm, or north-westwards to Chastleton ★.

Cotswold Farm Park (163) (SP 11-26) *5 mi. W Stow-on-the-Wold.* A unique collection of rare breeds of British farm livestock displayed in a beautiful farm setting in high wold country, with pets and baby animals on show for the benefit of younger children. Breeds exhibited include longhorn cattle, Soay and Orkney sheep, and shire horses. This is the creation of Cotswold farmer, Joe Henson, a pioneer in the preservation of rare breeds, and someone to whom we all owe a great deal. There is an adventure playground, farm trail, restaurant, gift shop and education centre. *(Tel: (0451) 850307.)*

Cotswold Water Park (163) (SU 04-95 etc.) *Approximately 5 mi. S Cirencester.* This developing leisure facility already consists of about a hundred lakes in two distinct areas — the first between Kemble and Cricklade, and the second between Fairford and Lechlade. They are the result of about sixty years of gravel extraction in this part of the Upper Thames Valley, a process which is still continuing. They now provide a significant wetland habitat, and in winter offer splendid opportunities for birdwatchers who come to spot the great quantities of wildfowl which migrate here. There are also three nature reserves within the park.

Details of the varied leisure facilities that the park has to offer, including an invaluable leaflet with map, are available at the Keynes Country Park Information Centre, to the east of Somerford Keynes ★ (163) (SU 02-95). *(Tel: (0285) 861459.)* In addition to bird-watching these facilities include game and coarse fishing, board sailing, lakeside walking, picnics, rowing boat, pedalo and canoe hire, motor boat racing, jet skiing, water skiing, caravanning and camping, and horse riding. It is, of course, the number of lakes and the distance between most of them that allow these very varied activities to take place without seriously impinging upon each other. Parties can also visit the Somerford Lakes Reserve (163) (SU 01-94). *(But first Tel: (0285) 770226.)*

The Cotswold Way (150, 151, 162, 163, 172) This long-distance footpath follows the Cotswold edge country for almost ninety miles between Bath and Chipping Campden. It provides a strenuous walk taking between seven and nine days, although many people will wish to tackle portions of the route on separate days, especially if they have young families. With the prevailing wind blowing from the south-west it is perhaps preferable to start from Bath and finish at Chipping Campden. Most of the route runs through the area covered by this guide, apart from that in the country beyond Wotton-under-Edge. Both Richard Sale's *A Guide to the Cotswold Way* and June Lewis's *Walking the Cotswold Way* are invaluable companions on this challenging and most interesting walk, with its splendid views out over the valleys of the Avon and Severn, and the hill country beyond.

Cotswold Wildlife Park (163) (SP 24-08) *3 mi. S Burford.* This is situated in 200 acres of gardens and parkland surrounding Bradwell Grove, an early 19th-century mansion in the Tudor style. It is attractively laid out, and contains a wide variety of animals, the larger of which are to be found in open areas in the wooded park. Smaller animals are displayed in an imaginatively converted walled

Passenger train at the Cotswold Wildlife Park

garden, and there are picnic areas, a narrow-gauge railway, an adventure playground and a licensed restaurant. *(Tel: (0993) 823006.)*

Cowley (163) (SO 96-14) *4½ mi. S Cheltenham.* Small estate village pleasantly sited in the wooded upper reaches of the Coln Valley. Cowley Manor is a 19th-century Italianate mansion in beautifully maintained grounds, complete with a lake and ornamental ponds. The church, which stands beside the manor, was much restored in the years following the building of its neighbour, and is not of outstanding interest. However, its white-painted interior contains a simple bowl-shaped Norman

font, a primitive Perpendicular stone pulpit and the effigy of a 14th-century priest.

Several quiet roads radiate from Cowley and there are also walks north-west to Crickley Hill ★, and northwards to Seven Springs ★ via Coberley ★.

Cranham (163) (SO 89-12) *6 mi. NE Stroud.* This widespread village lies near the head of the valley running north-eastwards from Painswick ★, and has an extensive common to the south and great beech woodlands to the north and east (see Cranham Woods, below). Here will be found a friendly little inn, the Black Horse, but also rather too many 'between the wars' bungalows. The largely 15th-century church stands high up, well to the south-east of the village, with fine views over the valley. Interesting features include two pairs of sheep shears carved on the second stage of the tower (a reminder once again of the importance of Cotswold wool in times gone by), and within, an early 16th-century rood screen, a lovely triptych reredos and a handsome monument to Obadiah Done (1758) — 'Rector of this parish 57 years'.

In Cranham Woods

Cranham Woods (163) (SO 90-12) *6 mi. NE Stroud.* These splendid woodlands are situated between Birdlip ★ and Prinknash ★, and are largely of beech. They include Cranham Wood itself, and also Buckle Wood, Buckholt Wood (much of which is a National Nature Reserve), Witcombe Wood and Brockworth Wood. All are worth exploring and they are partly covered by our **Walk 7**, which starts from the Fiddler's Elbow Car Park on the A46, Cheltenham to Painswick road (162) (SO 88-13). There are limited car parking possibilities just off some sections of the road through the woods.

Cricklade (163,173) (SU 09-93) *7 mi. SE Cirencester.* Small town on the upper reaches of the Thames (not navigable at this point) and just to the west of the Romans' great road, the Ermin Way ★. Its centre stands within the remains of town walls said to have originated in the time of Alfred the Great, although Romano-British pottery has, not surprisingly, been discovered in their foundations. The town's largely 17th- and 18th-century buildings in the High Street are dominated by the proud tower of St Samson's church, which was built by the Duke of Northumberland in 1553. The large church below has massive arcading, and impressive vaulting beneath the duke's tower, but the smaller and simpler interior of nearby St Mary's Church is possibly of greater interest. This has an excellent Norman chancel arch and an attractive timbered roof with traceried bordering.

It is possible to walk northwards from here, first beside the infant Thames, then following the course of the old Thames and Severn Canal ★ to Cerney Wick ★, and finally westwards to the Cotswold Water Park ★.

Table tombs in the churchyard at Cricklade

Crickley Hill Country Park (163) (SO 93-16) *4 mi. S Cheltenham*. 114 acres of grassland and woodland on the Cotswold edge, owned jointly by the Gloucestershire County Council and the National Trust. There are fine views out over the Severn Valley, the earthworks of a settlement occupied in both Neolithic and Iron Age times, and nearby, the Devil's Table, an attractive rocky outcrop, which should not be confused with the nearby and more dramatic Devil's Chimney ★. This country park is on the course of the Cotswold Way ★ and there are car parks, toilets, picnic areas, walks and information boards.

Cutsdean (150) (SP 08-30) *4½ mi. S Broadway*. Tidy little upland village centred largely on a wide green on slopes above the infant Windrush, less than a mile below its source at Field Barn, Taddington ★. Its church lies beyond a large farmyard, and is a long narrow Victorian building, with a medieval tower providing the only item of any real interest.

Was there an Anglo-Saxon chief called Cod? Did this village take his name, becoming 'Cod's dene'? And did the hill country in which it lies become known as 'Cod's wold' or Cotswold? This is a very likely theory, but it will probably always remain unproved. There is no doubt, however, that Cutsdean's setting amongst the high wolds is the very essence of Cotswold country.

From here it is possible to walk up the valley to the source of the Windrush at Field Barn (150) (SP 09-31), or down to Ford ★ and Temple Guiting ★.

Daglingworth (163) (SO 99-05) *3 mi. NW Cirencester*. Modest village strung out along the valley of the little Duntisbourne stream. The manor house is sited at Lower End to the south, and has in its garden a fine circular medieval dovecot complete with a revolving ladder giving access to all 500 nesting places. The church and rectory stand well above the rest of the village, to the north. The church, largely rebuilt in the 1840s, has a Saxon

doorway, and part of a Roman altar, made into a window by the Saxons. The three carvings set into the walls were rediscovered in 1850 and form a unique and highly satisfying group of primitive Saxon sculpture. See also the interesting Saxon sundial over the doorway, and the fine 15th-century door below.

It is possible to walk southwards from here along a track to the great Cirencester Park ★, or north-westwards up the valley to the lovely little church at Duntisbourne Rouse ★.

Daneway (163) (SO 94-03) *5 mi. W Cirencester*. Here, deep in the Frome Valley, was the western end of the Thames and Severn Canal's ★ two-mile-long tunnel from Coates ★. The Daneway Inn, like the Tunnel House Inn ★ at the Coates end, must have provided countless thousands of pints for the thirsty leggers during the canal's working life between 1789 and 1911. Leggers were the men who had to propel the heavily laden barges through the tunnel by lying along the sides of their decks and pushing with their feet on the tunnel walls. The inn's car park is built on the site of the last of forty-four locks that had to be built between here and Stroud.

Nearby Daneway House, a delightful manor house dating from the 14th century, was used as workshops and showrooms by the Arts and Crafts furniture makers and disciples of William Morris, Ernest and Sidney Barnsley, and Ernest Gimson, in the early years of the 20th century. It was let to them by the Earl Bathurst, together with rent-free cottages in Sapperton, when he required Pinbury Park (see Edgeworth ★) for his own family. They gathered further artists and craftsmen about them, including Norman Jewson, the architect, and Peter Waals, the Dutch foreman cabinet maker. Read more about this richly productive venture in Norman Jewson's autobiography, *By Chance I did Rove*. (*Daneway may be visited by appointment with the owner. Tel: (028576) 232.*)

Our **Walk 10** comes through here after starting from nearby Sapperton, and it is also possible to use part of this to walk down beside the Thames and Severn Canal to Chalford ★. Also walk east-wards along the old canal towpath to the sadly decayed western portal of the canal tunnel, and then steeply upwards to Sapperton ★. Ask the landlord of the Daneway Inn if you wish to use his car park — but only if you are eating or drinking here. The park is sometimes too crowded, but permission may usually be obtained.

The Daneway Inn . . . 'once a leggers' haven'

DARLINGSCOTT

Darlingscott (151) (SP 23-42) *2 mi. NW Shipston-on-Stour.* Minute village, less than two miles to the east of the Cotswold edge, with a pleasant series of Cotswold stone farmhouses and cottages emphasising this proximity. The small church of St George was built as late as 1874, but it has richly carved chancel arch capitals, and other signs of Victorian enthusiasm for carved detail. In 1836, a branch of the Stratford and Moreton Tramway★ was opened, to run between Darlingscott and Shipston-on-Stour. Much of its course may still be traced to the south of the village.

Walk west from Darlingscott, across the fields past Southfield, up near Windmill Hill, and down the drive passing Foxcote House★, towards Ebrington★, to sample the unique flavour of the Cotswolds' northern edge country.

Daylesford (163) (SP 24-25) *4 mi. E Stow-on-the-Wold.* Minute estate village at the gates of Daylesford House, money from which must have paid for the building of the small but splendidly elaborate Victorian church. This was designed by J.L.Pearson, best known as the architect of Truro Cathedral. See especially Pearson's pretty tub-shaped pulpit, the brass to William Gardiner (1632) and the elegant monument outside the east window, simply inscribed 'Warren Hastings 1818'.

Born at nearby Churchill in 1732, Hastings had always hoped to buy back the family estate at Daylesford, and in 1787, four years after retiring from his controversial career as Governor of the East India Company's Bengal, he purchased Daylesford. Not anticipating the crippling expense of defending himself during his seven-year-long trial in the House of Lords, he soon set about building a fine mansion to the design of Samuel Pepys Cockerell, architect to the East India Company, and later the architect of the better-known Sezincote★. Unlike Sezincote, Daylesford is almost entirely classical, and only has a central dome in the Muslim style. It is surrounded by dense woodland, but in winter it is just visible from the public road a few yards south-east of Daylesford village. Our **Walk 5** encircles the estate, but in summer there are no views of the house even from the paths followed.

Walk south from here, down beside the infant Evenlode to Bledington★, or north to Adlestrop★ and Chastleton★.

Deerhurst (150) (SO 87-29) *4½ mi. SW Tewkesbury.* This small village, with its orchards and timber-framed cottages, and its setting in fields just beyond the high banks of the River Severn, is rather far removed from the Cotswolds. However, its church, one of the oldest in England, is one of the few largely Anglo-Saxon buildings to have survived and is well worth visiting. It was part of a monastery founded in the 8th or 9th century, and there are fragmentary clues to the existence of a cloister. There are no fewer than thirty Anglo-Saxon doors and windows to be seen, together with a late 9th-century font, interesting 15th- and 16th-century brasses, and a fine early 17th-century communion rail.

Standing 200 yards to the south-west of the church is a half-timbered farmhouse, at the west end of which is the small Anglo-Saxon Odda's Chapel (in the care of English Heritage). Thanks to the discovery of an inscribed stone, we know that this was built by Earl Odda and was dedicated on 12 April 1065 — an exact dating, which is unique in pre-Conquest building. The nave has survived almost to its full height and is divided from the chancel by an arch.

It is possible to walk from the village over a meadow to the banks of the Severn, and then northwards beside the river to Tewkesbury★, or south to Apperley and Wainlode Hill.

Delly End (164) (SP 35-13) *2mi. N Witney.* Pretty hamlet grouped around a well mown green, complete with a domed war memorial on four slender pillars, and overlooked by a series of delectable stone houses including a handsome early Georgian manor house.

Denfurlong Farm Trail (163) (SP 06-10) *4½ mi. SW Northleach. Turn 2nd right off A429, S of Fossebridge.* This trail makes it possible to visit a working dairy farm on a self-conducted tour, starting the trail from a car park and obtaining a booklet from the entrance room. A taped commentary describes work in the milking parlour (milking daily between 4.30 pm and 6.30 pm). Allow two hours for the longer of two trails. *(Always open, but preferably groups should tel: (024 289) 215 for appointment.)*

Devil's Chimney (163) (SO 94-18) *2 mi. S Cheltenham.* Dramatic limestone pinnacle detached from the Cotswold edge, with splendid views out over it to Cheltenham and beyond to the Malvern Hills. It was formed by quarrymen who left it intact when working the large surrounding quarries, stone from which was used for the building of much of 18th- and 19th-century Cheltenham. It was once a popular challenge for local climbers, who used to leave a coin on the cap for the Devil, and no fewer than thirteen people once stood on its top. This practice is now strictly forbidden, but over the years both this and natural erosion have taken their toll to such an extent that about £25,000 has had to be spent on repairs in recent years.

The Devil's Chimney . . . a limestone pinnacle on the Cotswold edge

To reach the Chimney drive south from Cheltenham on the B4070 for about two miles, and fork left on Leckhampton Hill up a steep road. Park on the left after about half a mile and follow the sign to the Devil's Chimney, using the mapped **mini-walk**

Devil's Chimney   SCALE 1:25 000 or 2½ INCHES to 1 MILE

shown on this page. Because of the extensive quarrying great care should be taken. Some of the path forms part of the Cotswold Way ★ and from here it is possible to walk eastwards along Charlton Kings Common, and then south to Seven Springs ★. There is also a small car park at the foot of the hill, reached by a short road to the east of the B4070. This park is just beyond Tramway Cottage, reminding visitors that it is close to the course of the gravity-worked tramway which once carried stone from the great quarries above. Opened in 1798, this was the very first railway on the Cotswolds.

Didbrook (150) (SP 05-31) *3 mi. NE Winchcombe.* Small village below the Cotswold edge with a pleasant mixture of timber and stone in its buildings — see especially several examples of 'cruck' construction in various cottage ends, these possibly dating back to the 15th century. The church was rebuilt about 1475 by William Whitchurch, the abbot of nearby Hailes ★, and is wholly Perpendicular in style. Note especially the lovely old roof, and the various wood furnishings, including benches, family pew, lectern, pulpit and communion rail. The descent of the tower into the nave, with its three open arches, is most unusual.

It is possible to walk south from here, over the fields to Hailes Abbey ★, then up a track and left to Beckbury Camp ★, and return via Stumps Cross and Wood Stanway ★ — a fine circular walk. Use Landranger Sheet 150.

Ditchley Park (164) (SP 38-21) *4½ mi. NW Woodstock.* A splendid mansion in a 300-acre park, complete with pleasant gardens, a lake, temples and woodlands. The house, which happens to lie on the exact course of the Iron Age Grim's Ditch ★, was designed in the 1770s by James Gibbs, the architect of St Martin-in-the-Fields, with interior decorations by William Kent. Ditchley was the weekend headquarters of Winston Churchill during the War, and it is now an international conference centre. *(Usually open for about 12 days per year. Tel: (0608) 677346.)*

There is an attractive approach road running from the A34 at Over Kiddington (164) (SP 41-22), but the most used entry is from the north-east side of Charlbury ★.

Dixton (150) (SO 98-30) *2½ mi. NW Winchcombe.* Hamlet below the Cotswold edge with a fine 16th-century gabled manor house, and above it the earthworks of a probable Iron Age settlement on Dixton Hill. Walk south from here, up over Nottingham Hill (the site of another Iron Age settlement) to Cleeve Hill ★.

Donnington (163) (SP 19-28) *1½ mi. N Stow-on-the-Wold.* There are fine views out over the Evenlode Valley from this modest hamlet in the hills. It was here that Lord Astley, with 3000 Royalist troops, surrendered to the Parliamentarians on 21 March 1646, in the final defeat of the long and bitter Civil War. Sitting dejected amongst his captors at the end of the battle the weary Lord Astley was heard to say, 'Gentlemen, yee may now sit downe and play, for you have done all your worke, if you not fall out among yourselves.'

Over a mile to the west, beyond the A424, lies **Donnington Brewery** (163) (SP 17-27). Although not open to visitors this must surely be Britain's most delectable brewery. The accompanying lake, or mill pond, is the source of the little River Dikler, and its waters still turn a great mill-wheel. Donnington Brewery owns a fair number of inns, all in and around the Cotswolds, and was brewing real ale long after the large breweries ceased to do so, and long before the Campaign for Real Ale forced many of them to resume. It is a truly Cotswold undertaking, with these inns always appearing to add to, rather than detract from, the charm of the towns and villages in which they are situated. If you appreciate real ale, keep an eye open for Donnington's well painted inn signs.

Donnington . . . surely Britain's most delectable brewery

Not far to the west of the brewery, on the road towards Condicote, the **Donnington Fish Farm** (163) (SP 16-27) is largely concerned with the rearing of rainbow trout. Visitors may see trout at various stages of development, feed the larger fish, purchase fresh or smoked trout, and fly-fish in a small lake. *(Tel: (0451) 30873.)*

Doughton (162) (ST 87-91) *2 mi. SW Tetbury.* A hamlet astride the busy A433 with a number of 17th- and 18th-century stone houses having a feel of Wiltshire about them; Doughton is in Gloucestershire, but the Wiltshire border is only about two miles to the south. Handsome 18th-century Highgrove House, standing in a modest park to the immediate west of the hamlet and not visible from the road, was built for the Paul family, wealthy clothiers of Huguenot descent, one of whom, Sir George Onesiphorus Paul, became a noted prison reformer (see also Northleach ★, Rodborough ★ and Woodchester ★). Highgrove House is now the country home of the Prince and Princess of Wales.

Dover's Hill (151) (SP 13-39) *1 mi. NW Chipping Campden.* This is a delightful crescent-shaped field-walk poised on the very edge of the Cotswold scarp, and was acquired by the National Trust in 1928, thanks to the efforts of Chipping Campden's F.L.Griggs, and to the generosity of that great historian, G.M.Trevelyan. There is a small car park here, and one can walk along the hillside, down to the edge of dense woodland below, or even back down to Chipping Campden ★ on the footpath shown on the map, which is part of the Cotswold Way ★. On a clear day views out over the Avon Valley and the Midland Plain extend to Bredon, the Malverns, and the distant outlines of the Black Mountains and the Long Mynd. Identification of these distant hills is made easier and more interesting by a well engraved viewing topograph not far beyond the car park.

Dover's Hill was the site of the famous 'Cotswold Olympicks', founded in 1612 by local lawyer Robert Dover with the approval of James I, the monarch having been approached through Dover's friend at Court, Endymion Porter, who lived at nearby Aston Subedge ★. These games, then held on the Thursday and Friday after Whit Sunday, included the usual horse racing, hare coursing, dancing and wrestling, but there were also two essentially local contests of a more violent nature: single-stick fighting, in which the contestants fought with one arm tied behind their backs, sometimes for hours at a time, with the sole intention of 'breaking the other's head'; and shin-kicking, the purpose of which was to reduce one's opponent to such agonies that he was forced to withdraw defeated. The more enthusiastic shin-kickers used to 'harden up' by beating their own shins with planks, or even in extreme cases with hammers, in the weeks prior to the games.

Although temporarily suppressed during the Cromwellian period, the games were otherwise held regularly each year until the mid-19th century. By this time they had become the scene of considerable violence and drunkenness, a situation greatly worsened by the presence of Irish navvies, who were then building the nearby Campden Railway Tunnel ★, and they were discontinued in 1853, following an Act of Parliament enclosing the land. In 1951 the games were again revived, and since then they have been held each year on the Friday following the Spring Bank Holiday, followed on the Saturday by the Scuttlebrook Wake, a colourful fair which culminates in a torch-light procession from Dover's Hill back down into Chipping Campden.

Dowdeswell (163) (SP 00-19) *3 mi. E Cheltenham.* This minute village is pleasantly situated on a hillside and happily just far enough away from the busy A40 to avoid its noise. The cruciform church, with its small stone spire, is situated below the road, beside a Tudor farmhouse. It has two mid-19th-century galleries within, one for the use of the manor and one for the rectory. Do not miss the 16th-century brass of a priest, nor the handsome monument on the chancel wall, to William Rogers (1734).

The A40 road beside Dowdeswell Reservoir is one of the few places in Britain where the writer has seen a notice declaring 'Drivers beware — toads crossing road'. The road forms part of a regular migratory route and an effort is being made to save as many as possible of this threatened species. The Cotswold Way ★ crosses the A40 just below the reservoir dam on its way between Cleeve Hill ★ and the Devil's Chimney ★.

Down Ampney (163) (SU 10-97) *5 mi. SE Cirencester.* A long straggling village in flat countryside about two miles north of the Thames, with only two buildings of any real interest, both of which lie quietly amongst trees at its southern end — the cruciform church and nearby Down Ampney House.

The church has a fine 14th-century spire and a large porch about a hundred years younger. The interior was richly restored, perhaps over-restored, at the turn of the century, but it contains a number of items which should not be missed. Amongst these are the effigies of a knight (in black marble) and a lady (in stone) in the south transept, a 17th-century monument to two knights of the Hungerford family, Sir John and Sir Anthony, acting as a reredos in the north transept, and the excellent copy of Giorgione's *Madonna of Castel Franco.* There is a stained-glass window in memory of the airmen who flew from the nearby airfield, and who did not return. Standing beside the church is Down Ampney House, the fine 15th-century manor house of the Hungerford family, which was embellished by Sir John Soane in 1799.

The composer Ralph Vaughan Williams was born in the village in 1872, the son of its vicar, and he spent the first three years of his life at what is now the Old Vicarage. He named his best-known hymn 'Down Ampney', in memory of his childhood years here.

Draycott (151) (SP 18-35) *3 mi. SE Chipping Campden.* An expanding hamlet lying in a broad valley overlooked by low wooded hills, with an attractive row of cottages leading to a small 18th-century farmhouse. Walk southwards from here, up the fields to the road above Batsford Park ★, and then down again to Blockley ★.

Driffield (163) (SU 07-99) *3 mi. E Cirencester.* Small village with pleasantly noisy duckpond, and a church which was rebuilt in 1734 and heavily restored in 1836, almost certainly by the redoubtable Victorian architect, William Butterfield, perhaps best known for his design for Keble College, Oxford. Do not miss the inscription to George Hanger, Lord Coleraine, whose gambling debts almost certainly explain the odd high-walled garden nearby: this was part of a mansion sold to pay his debts and subsequently demolished. The inscription reads: *'He lived and died a firm believer in one God and in one God only. He was also a practical Christian as far as his frail nature did allow him to be so.'* But this statement appears to have been over-charitable to a rake whose 'eccentric manner', according to another source, 'became too free and coarse even for the Prince Regent'. In fear of the Devil, he asked to be 'buried' above ground, but he was eventually interred beneath the organ.

Duntisbourne Abbots (163) (SO 97-07) *5 mi. NW Cirencester.* Situated in the valley of the little Dunt stream, this small but very trim village once belonged to the abbots of Gloucester — hence its name. Dating back to Norman times, the church has a low saddleback-roofed tower. The chancel has been restored since the War — white painted and very pleasant — but the rest is still scraped and rather severe, a legacy of its 'restoration' in 1872. There is a Youth Hostel nearby.

The Hoar Stone Long Barrow, with the Hoar Stone itself at its eastern end, is situated close to a road about a mile to the south of the village (163) (SO 96-06).

Duntisbourne Leer (163) (SO 97-07) *4½ mi. NW Cirencester.* The unusual name of this hamlet in the Dunt Valley is derived from the abbey of Lire in far off Normandy, to which it belonged until 1416, when it was given to Cirencester Abbey. Here are

Ford at Duntisbourne Leer

two farmhouses and attendant buildings, all attractively grouped around a ford.

Duntisbourne Rouse (163) (SO 98-06) *4 mi. NW Cirencester.* Here is a largely Norman church, still displaying evidence of its Saxon origins, and standing in a sloping churchyard overlooking the Dunt stream, with a fine 14th-century cross for company. Like Duntisbourne Abbots it has a saddleback roof to its tower, and it has a delightful interior complete with box pews, octagonal Norman font, stalls in the chancel with misericords (which probably came from Cirencester Abbey), and medieval paintings upon its north chancel wall. It is built upon such a steep slope that there is a crypt at its eastern end — a most unusual feature in so small a church.

There is a pleasant walk above woodlands on the east side of the valley down to Daglingworth ★.

Duntisbourne Rouse Church

Dursley (162) (ST 75-97) *8 mi. SW Stroud.* Busy market town beneath the Cotswold edge, with extensive industry which has replaced its long-vanished cloth trade. It is centred upon a delightful 18th-century market house, which also acts as the Town Hall, and which displays an elegant statue of Queen Anne in a niche well above its arcading. The nearby church has a beautifully vaulted Perpendicular porch, but its interior was over-restored in the 19th century. However, it has a most impressive tower, which was rebuilt in the Gothic style in the early years of the 18th century after most of the earlier tower and spire had collapsed in 1698.

Part of Stinchcombe Hill, about a mile to the west of the town, is used as a golf course, but there is parking space for cars, good walking opportunities and fine views out over the Berkeley Vale, especially from Drakestone Point (162) (ST 73-98). This is on the course of the Cotswold Way ★, which may be followed south from here to North Nibley ★ and Wotton-under-Edge ★.

Eastington (163) (SP 12-13) *1 mi. SE Northleach.* Hamlet in a bowl-like setting in the wolds, with the little River Leach flowing beside the road. There are fine barns and a small mid-Victorian chapel on a slope overlooking the valley. At Upper End, half a mile to the north-east, are a lovely 15th-century manor house and a circular dovecot, both of which belonged to Gloucester Abbey before the Dissolution. There is a pleasant road running south-eastwards from Eastington, beside the beech-woods of Lodge Park ★ and on over open country to Aldsworth ★.

It is possible to walk up the valley of the little River Leach to Northleach ★ and onwards to this river's source at Hampnett ★, using the mapped **mini-walk** on page 84 for the latter part.

Eastleach Martin and **Eastleach Turville** (163) (SP 20-05) *4 mi. N Lechlade.* Here are two parish churches looking at each other across the clear waters of the little River Leach. Today Turville is by far the larger of the two settlements, but Martin has the larger church. This was founded by Richard Fitzpons, one of William the Conqueror's knights, and a few of its original Norman features remain, including the south doorway and the supporting piers of the chancel arch. However, one of its best features is the 14th-century north transept with its three beautiful Decorated-style windows. Turville's church, although smaller than Martin's, is even more interesting, with an early 14th-century saddleback tower and a Norman tympanum over the south doorway. Inside the largely 13th-century interior will be found a fine canopied tomb and a pleasing pulpit, reading desk and lectern.

Be sure to spend time wandering up the slopes of Turville, past the war memorial, as far as the friendly little Victoria Inn, and back down again to cross the stone footbridge to return to Martin. This is known as Keble Bridge, probably because the lordship of the manor of Turville was held by the Kebles in the 16th and 17th centuries, and not because the better-known John Keble held the curacy of the two parishes as a mere non-resident in the 19th.

Come here in early spring to find the banks of the Leach scattered with daffodils, but avoid Sundays if possible, when this spot tends to be much visited by local motorists. The road southwards from

Keble Bridge, Eastleach

Martin to Southrop ★ is open to the Leach in places, but to enjoy this delightful valley to the full take the footpath southwards from Turville, also to Southrop ★. However, the finest walk from Turville is that up the valley of the Leach to the point where it crosses the Akeman Street ★, and over Macaroni Downs to Ladbarrow Farm and beyond to Windrush ★. See Landranger Sheet 163 for details.

Ebrington (151) (SP 18-40) *2 mi. E Chipping Campden.* A beautiful village overlooking a valley, through which the little Knee Brook flows on its way to join the Stour above Shipston-on-Stour ★. 'Yubberton', as many of the locals still call it, has many attractively thatched stone cottages lining its little sunken roads leading to the centre, which is overlooked by a war memorial and the handsomely signed Ebrington Arms.

The church stands on a small ridge close to the largely 17th-century manor house, and above the rest of the village. It has a good solid tower and a Norman south doorway with a geometric design upon its tympanum, rather similar in style to the one at Great Rollright ★. Inside the church there are a few medieval bench-ends, a large, heavily restored pulpit dated 1679, and a charming little medieval glass roundel illustrating the month of October — probably one of a series of twelve — with a jaunty peasant sowing grain. This feature is illustrated in the delightful little book by Edith Brill and Peter Turner entitled *The Minor Pleasures of Cotswold*.

The whole interior has been over-restored, but there are several fine monuments to members of the Keyte and Fortescue families. See especially the monument to Sir John Fortescue, who was Lord Chief Justice of England during some of the most troubled years of the Wars of the Roses. Despite a reversal of his fortunes after the defeat of the Lancastrians at Tewkesbury in 1471, he was allowed a gentle retirement at Ebrington until his death some years later, at the age of ninety. This was most unusual in an age when defeated enemies were generally despatched without hesitation, in a variety of barbarous ways.

The two 17th-century Keyte monuments are equally interesting and we particularly like the notice reading, 'William Keyte Esq., A.D. 1632, left by will the milk of ten good and sufficient kine to the poor of Ebrington from May 10th — November 1st for ever'. It is sad to read a note below which indicates that 'This charge was redeemed 1952'; no doubt a practical step, but how dull! William Keyte's son, Sir John Keyte, must also have been a man of substance, as it is known that he raised a troop of horse 'at his own expense' in the loyal support of his sovereign, during the Civil War.

The best walk from Ebrington leads north-eastwards, past Foxcote House ★ to Ilmington ★, returning via Nebsworth and Ebrington Hill. Links

may also be made to the road northwards over Lark Stoke ★, or across to Hidcote ★. All these walks are over windy, often open wold country, with fine views out over the Midland plain, the Northamptonshire uplands and the line of hills on the borders of Oxfordshire.

Edge (162) (SO 84-09) *3 mi. N Stroud.* Small village with views westwards over the Severn Valley, and eastwards to Painswick ★. Its modest Victorian church has a neat little stone spire, but is otherwise unexceptional. There was at least one cloth mill here until the early 19th century. Beatrix Potter used to stay at Harescombe Grange, just to the north of the village, and it was while here that she was inspired to write her delightful story, *The Tailor of Gloucester* (see Gloucester ★ for the 'House of the Tailor of Gloucester').

Walk south-west from Edge and then west, along the Cotswold edge to Haresfield Beacon ★, making use of our **Walk 6**, and also following part of the Cotswold Way ★.

Edgeworth (163) (SO 94-06) *5 mi. NW Cirencester.* Here are a church and a manor house looking down over wooded slopes into the deep valley of the little River Frome. The church has retained certain evidence of its Saxon origins, and its Norman features include a south doorway and much of the chancel. The interior has been over-restored, but there are a few 15th-century bench-ends with poppy heads, and the medieval stained glass featuring a bishop should not be missed. There is a medieval cross in the churchyard, which overlooks the valley.

The nearby Jacobean manor house was much restored and enlarged in the 19th century, but remains an enviably beautiful building. The stables are topped by a pretty little bellcote which overlooks the adjoining churchyard.

Pinbury Park (SO 95-04), an idyllic manor house on the eastern slopes of the valley between here and Daneway ★, was once the home of the noted Gloucestershire county historian, Sir Robert Atkyns, who is buried at Sapperton. In the early years of the 20th century it was let by the Earl Bathurst to the Arts and Crafts Movement's Ernest

Edgeworth . . . a Jacobean manor much restored in the 19th century

Gimson and the Barnsley brothers, who had workshops in the adjoining buildings. On Pinbury being required by Lord Bathurst for his family, he let Daneway★ to them for their workshops and showrooms, and allowed them to build cottages for themselves at Sapperton★.

Our **Walk 6** passes Edgeworth and Pinbury Park, but Landranger Sheet 163 will reveal a wealth of alternative walks in this outstandingly beautiful area with its deep valleys and great beech-woods.

Elkstone (163) (SO 96-12) *6 mi. S Cheltenham.* This small, rather undistinguished village is relieved by both its handsome 18th-century rectory and its exceptionally interesting church. Standing in a churchyard with pleasant table tombs, this has a fine Perpendicular west tower, but it is the fascinating corbel figures around the outside of the nave, and the splendid tympanum over the south doorway, that provide an introduction to what must be the best-preserved Norman church in the Cotswolds. Inside will be found a beautiful little vaulted Norman chancel with a wealth of fine architectural detail. There are also box pews and good 17th-century furnishings including pulpit, reading desk and communion rails. Do not miss this remarkable little church.

Ermin Way (163 etc) A Roman road which extended from Silchester, near Reading, through Cricklade★ and Cirencester★, to the legionary fortress at Gloucester★. Modern roads still follow its course across the Cotswolds — the A419 as far as Cirencester, and the A417 north-westwards to Gloucester. Superb Roman engineering has left us with a long straight road, and this provides a number of opportunities for over-fast driving — so beware when turning onto or off, or crossing, this often very busy road.

Eubury Camp (163) (SP 15-28) *To NE of Condicote.* Crescent-shaped earthworks in pleasant wold country just beyond Condicote★. The Camp is possibly the remains of an Iron Age settlement, although its origins are far from clear.

Evenlode (163) (SP 22-29) *2 mi. SE Moreton-in-Marsh.* Lying in the broad valley of the River Evenlode, this scattered village has a Georgian rectory and several pleasant farmhouses, one with pretty Gothick windows. The attractive church lies on the western edge of the village in a churchyard containing several interesting 18th- and 19th-century tombs. It has a fine late Norman chancel arch with a mason's mark on its south side, a pleasing rood loft stair and a carved 15th-century pulpit.

Ewen (163) (SU 00-97) *3 mi. S Cirencester.* This attractive residential hamlet lies in flat countryside with the infant Thames flowing only a few yards to its south. The attractive Wild Duck Inn provides excellent restaurant and bar meals. Walk southwards from here, partly beside the Thames, to Somerford Keynes★ and the western fringes of the Cotswold Water Park★.

Eyford Park (163) (SP 14-24) *2½ mi. W Stow-on-the-Wold.* An elegant 'Queen Anne' mansion built by Sir Guy Dawber in 1910 in a fine park with a lake, near the source of the River Eye — the small stream later to enrich Upper and Lower Slaughter★. This house stands on the site of a mansion built in 1870, which was contemporary with the surviving lodge on the B4068. This Victorian mansion stood near the site of an earlier house, where the Duke of Shrewsbury, Charles Talbot, once entertained William III.

Apparently there is a tablet on a well in the park claiming that Milton wrote part of *Paradise Lost* while seated beside it. Neither this nor the house is visible from the B4068, but there is a pleasant walk northwards from this road, passing close behind the house before heading across country to a minor road near Chalk Hill (163) (SP 13-26). There is an attractive row of late 18th-century cottages close to the point where the walk leaves the B4068.

Fairford (163) (SP 15-00) *4 mi. W Lechlade.* In the 19th century an Anglo-Saxon cemetery was excavated just to the west of Fairford, so the history of this warm little town on the River Coln stretches far back into the past. However, the great antiquary John Leland, Henry VIII's librarian, claimed that 'Faireforde never flourished afore ye Tames came to it', and there is no doubt that its prosperity in late medieval times was almost entirely due to the wealth of one of the Cotswolds' greatest wool merchant families, the Tames. It was the most illustrious member of this family, John Tame, and his son Edmund who built the magnificent late Perpendicular **Fairford Church (1)**.

This wonderfully proportioned building stands at the north end of the High Street, beyond the Market Place. It has a massive central tower, the rich sculptural details of which include the arms of John Tame. The interior has a fine oak-beamed roof supported on interesting stone corbels, great piers supporting the central tower, and a fascinating series of carved misericords beneath the choir stalls. But the greatest glory of Fairford is its remarkably complete series of stained-glass windows. Most of

In Fairford churchyard . . . an old friend remembered

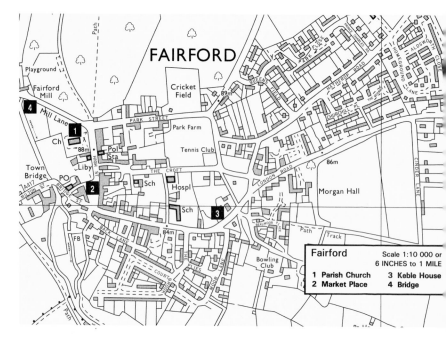

FAIRFORD

Playground

Fairford Mill

4

Mill Lane

Ch

88m

Pol Sta

Town Bridge

Liby

PO

2

Sch

Hospl

Sch

3

FB

Cricket Field

89m

Park Farm

Tennis Club

THE CROFT

84m

Courts

Bowling Club

86m

Morgan Hall

Fairford   Scale 1:10 000 or 6 INCHES to 1 MILE

1 **Parish Church**   3 **Keble House**
2 **Market Place**   4 **Bridge**

these are almost certainly the work of the Fleming, Barnard Flower, who was employed by Henry VIII to glaze the windows of both his new Lady Chapel at Westminster Abbey and King's College Chapel, Cambridge (which was not completed until after Flower's death). It is thought that, although all the glass came from the same workshops, a number of English and possibly French craftsmen must also have contributed their skills. Before leaving this most beautiful church, pause for a while at John Tame's fine altar tomb between the choir and the Lady Chapel, to remember the debt that we owe both to him and to the craftsmen he employed. Another well-known Cotswold craftsman is buried in the churchyard beneath a fine table tomb — master-mason Valentine Strong, one of the quarry-owning Strongs of Taynton ★, who died while he was building the mansion of Park House (see below). Read all about the Strong family in Edith Brill's interesting book, *Life and Tradition in the Cotswolds*.

The buildings in the **High Street** and the **Market Place (2)**, although not as impressive as the church, are a pleasant mixture, largely of the 17th and 18th centuries, the number of hotels and inns reminding us that Fairford was once an important posting stage on the London to Gloucester coaching run. See especially the charming old Bull Hotel. John Keble was born in 1792 at **Keble House (3)** on the north side of London Road, for although his father was the vicar of nearby Coln St Aldwyns he preferred to live in Fairford.

The church overlooks the water-meadows of the River Coln, which flows to the west of the town, and there is a pleasant mill house and an old **bridge (4)** from where one can look upstream across the parkland of Park House — itself demolished in 1955. Milton End lies on the west side of the river, and is separated by it from the rest of the town. For further details of Fairford's story read June Lewis's brief but excellent *History of Fairford*.

Farmcote (150,163) (SP 06-28) *2 mi. E Winchcombe.* This hamlet is perched on the very edge of the Cotswold scarp and has wonderful views out over valley country to Bredon Hill and the Malverns. It has a delightful little church, or to be ecclesiastically correct a chapel of ease. Its exterior appears to have been heavily restored, but once inside the visitor will be pleasantly surprised to find it a simple and unspoilt Norman building. See especially the Jacobean two-decker pulpit and altar rail, the 16th-century benches and the handsomely canopied tomb of Henry and Mary Stratford, in pale, unpainted stone.

It is possible to link onto our **Walk 3** by walking down the road less than a mile southwards, or to join the Cotswold Way ★ by going northwards down a bridleway to Hailes Abbey ★. The Iron Age promontory fort of Beckbury Camp ★ is about half a mile to the north of the hamlet, and this may also be reached by using part of the Cotswold Way ★.

Farmington (163) (SP 13-15) *1½ mi. NE Northleach.* Small village on high ground between the valleys of the Leach and the Sherborne Brook and centred upon an extensive green on which stands a little octagonal pumphouse. Farmington Lodge is partly 18th- and partly 19th-century, and has four massive Doric columns gracing its front — all rather swish for little Farmington. The church which lies across the road from the Lodge is a largely Norman building, complete with Norman south doorway, chancel arch and north aisle arcade. The well proportioned tower was added in the 15th century and is a good example of late Perpendicular work. Lying just to the west of the village is Norbury Camp, an Iron Age settlement with the remains of a Stone Age long barrow within the north-west corner of its earthworks.

It is possible to make a circular walk from here, taking in Eastington ★, the head of the Leach

Valley, and Northleach ★. (Use Landranger Sheet 163.) There is also a pleasant minor road eastwards down the Sherborne and Windrush Valleys to Sherborne ★, Windrush ★, Little Barrington ★ and Burford ★.

___

Fifield (163) (SP 24-18) *4 mi. N Burford.* Modest village looking out over the Evenlode Valley to the woodlands around Bruern Abbey ★, which were the major source of timber for the hurdle makers of Fifield, who until the 1950s had worked here for centuries. The church stands in a wide, open churchyard and has a small octagonal 14th-century tower topped by a minute spire. Although much restored, it is worth visiting, if only to look at the charming 17th-century brass of Mary Palmer, complete with her eight children and a baby in christening robes. While here, do not overlook the interesting fragments of medieval glass.

Take a circular walk by first dropping north-eastwards into the valley, and returning through woods to Bould (SP 24-21) and neighbouring Idbury ★. (Use Landranger Sheet 163.)

___

Filkins and Broughton Poggs (163) (SP 24-05 & 04) *3½ mi. NE Lechlade.* Situated in low country only about four miles north of the Thames, these two are now virtually one village and all is happily bypassed by the busy A361. Broughton Poggs Church is a small Norman building with a squat saddleback tower, and is tucked away behind farm buildings. It has several Norman features including two small doorways, a narrow chancel arch and a tub-shaped font.

Not far to the north is the cheerful Five Alls Inn, and then beyond it is Filkins Church. This was designed in the French Gothic style by G.E. Street, a Victorian architect best known for his work on London's Law Courts. Not far away are another inn, the Lamb, and a cheerful little Post Office stores. There are also several pleasant houses in the village, and many of the cottage gardens are edged by large stone slabs or slates. This unusual method was used by Sir Stafford Cripps's estate foreman, and ex-quarryman, George Swinford. It was thanks to George and to Sir Stafford and Lady Cripps that the little Swinford Museum was established. *(Tel: (036786) 209.)* It is good to hear that a quarry supplying stone slates has recently been reopened near Filkins.

Also continuing in the spirit of George Swinford's work, craft workshops have now been established in the village, and here will be found the Cotswold Woollen Weavers. Visitors may watch traditional weaving machinery at work, but they should read the rather sad notice displayed in the mill, which reads: 'No one in the world makes replacements for our looms and when this machinery finally grinds to a halt full scale cloth production will disappear.' It is to be hoped that this situation does not arise for a very long time. There is also a permanent and most interesting exhibition, tracing the history of sheep and wool-weaving in the Cotswolds, a woollen shop, an art gallery and a coffee shop. *(Tel: (036786) 491.)* Other craft shops and workshops in the adjoining buildings include a stone mason's and an art gallery, a rush-weaving and wood-turning workshop, and a furniture restorer's workshop.

___

Fish Hill and the Fish Inn (150) (SP 11-37) *½ mi. E Broadway.* Long winding hill out of Broadway up onto the Cotswold edge. There is some doubt as to the date when this replaced the old road to London up Conigree Lane, now the private drive to Middle Hill, but Fish Hill is certainly shown on Ogilvy's *Britannia*, first published in 1675. In 1736 Fish Hill was engineered into 'a well-formed serpentine road', and this construction probably coincided with the building near its top of what is now the Fish Inn, an interesting little 18th-century stone building, originally intended as a gazebo by its builder, Sir John Coterill. Almost opposite the Fish Inn will be found the Fish Hill Car Park and Picnic Area, which is complete with toilets, useful information boards showing woodland walks starting from here and a viewing topograph. The Cotswold Way ★ passes through this area on its route between Chipping Campden ★ and Broadway ★. The Broadway Tower Country Park ★ is about half a mile to the south-west.

___

Folly Farm and Duckpool Valley Farm Trail (163) (SP 12-20) *2½ mi. W Bourton-on-the-Water.* Here, near the source of a small stream below open wold country, is a collection of rare breeds of poultry, waterfowl and wildfowl, including several endangered species. These are displayed on lakes and in open pens in a typical Cotswold farm setting. There is also a garden centre. *(Tel: (0451) 20285.)*

At the Cotswold Woollen Weavers, Filkins

Duckpool Valley, Folly Farm

FORD

Ford (150,163) (SP 08-29) *4 mi. E Winchcombe.*
Pleasant hamlet on the slopes of the upper Windrush, less than two miles below its source above
Taddington★. There is a hospitable inn, the
Plough, which has an oft-quoted verse on a board
above its door exhorting 'ye weary travellers that
pass by ... to step in and quaff my nut brown ale ...
twill make your lagging trotters dance.' Please read
it all if you pass this way.

It is possible to walk up the Windrush Valley to
Cutsdean★ and Taddington★, or down it to
Temple Guiting★. There is also a good walk
eastwards along tracks, and then along a wooded
valley to Hinchwick★.

Fossebridge (163) (SP 08-11) *3 mi. SW Northleach.* This small hamlet marks the point where the
Foss Way★ drops into a steep-sided valley to cross
the River Coln. There is a pleasant hotel here beside
the bridge, and it is possible to walk from here up
the valley to Yanworth★ and Chedworth Roman
Villa★, or up the valley of a small tributary stream
to the village of Chedworth★, using part of our
Walk 11.

Foss Way This Roman road runs diagonally across
the Cotswolds through the towns of Moreton-in-
Marsh, Stow-on-the-Wold and Cirencester, on its
way between Lincoln and Exeter, a total distance of
182 miles. Its course between the Stour Valley near
Shipston-on-Stour and Cirencester is followed by
the A429, and for a few miles beyond Cirencester by
the A433. Beyond this it is, apart from an early
interruption at Kemble Airfield, classified as 'a
byway open to all traffic', and later as 'a road used
as a public path'. In practice however it is not
always easy to follow, even on foot.

The permanent Roman occupation of Britain
commenced in 43 AD, almost a hundred years after
Julius Caesar's brief invasions in 55 and 54 BC, and
within only four years the new Governor, Ostorius,
had concluded its first stage by establishing his civil
boundary along a line that was soon to become the
fine road now known as the Foss Way. This then
became a temporary frontier between the subjugated Iron Age tribes of the south and east, and
their wilder, still unconquered counterparts in the
more mountainous and less easily controlled north
and west.

In the years that followed its construction, its
purpose must have been largely military, with forts
and marching camps established upon it at regular
intervals (of which there is little visible evidence in
the area covered by this guide), and with roads
leading off it to north and west carrying the legions
towards the more troubled areas that lay beyond. It
is one of the most direct of all Roman roads, and it
is claimed that its course never diverges more than
six miles from a theoretical straight line between
Lincoln and Axminster in Devon. The best accounts
of the Foss Way, and the other Roman roads in the
area, the Ermin Way★, Ryknild Street★ and the
White Way★, are to be found in I.D.Margary's
classic work, *Roman Roads in Britain*.

The Four Shire Stone (151) (SP 23-32) *1½ mi. E
Moreton-in-Marsh.* A handsome 18th-century
monument topped by a sundial and ball, marking
the original meeting point of four counties: Oxfordshire, Gloucestershire, Warwickshire and Worces-

The Four Shire Stone

tershire. This still applies to the first three, but the
isolated 'island' of Worcestershire, which owed its
presence here to the once wide-ranging domains of
the bishops of Worcester, has been swallowed up in
Gloucestershire for many years.

Foxcote, near Andoversford (163) (SP 01-18)
4 mi. SE Cheltenham. Small hamlet about a mile to
the south-west of Andoversford★, with a handsome 17th-century manor house just to its south.
There is a pleasant path southwards from here to
Withington★.

Foxcote, near Ilmington (151) (SP 19-41) *1 mi.
SW Ilmington.* This fine early 18th-century mansion, possibly built by Edward Woodward of
Chipping Campden, is only open to visitors by prior
written appointment with the owner, but there is a
public right of way for walkers down its long
curving drive, and beyond it on a rougher track, to
the village of Ebrington★. Starting from the road
between Ilmington★ and the hamlet of Char-
ingworth★, this is an attractive walk, and a return
journey may be made via Ebrington Hill and
Nebsworth (SP 19-42).

Frampton Mansell (163) (SO 92-02) *6½ mi. W
Cirencester.* This small village stands on the steep
southern slopes of the Golden Valley, with a
handsome neo-Norman church and a delightful little
inn called the Crown. The sound of steam trains
coming up the old GWR line in the valley below is
no longer to be heard, but diesel-hauled trains may
still be seen crossing the tall viaduct below the
village, and there are pretty stretches of the old
Thames and Severn Canal★ in the depths of the
valley, beside the little River Frome.

France Lynch (163) (SO 90-03) *3½ mi. E Stroud.*
This steep hillside village is today almost part of
Chalford★, and has the same delightful flavour. It
has a small inn and an unusually effective Victorian
church, which was the work of the architect George
Bodley, perhaps best known as the designer of far-
off Washington Cathedral. Designed in the French
Gothic style, it includes a splendidly ornate chancel,
with coloured marble inlays and the carvings of
three angels playing different musical instruments.

The more recent altar-rail kneeling-mat was worked by the ladies of the parish 'and includes a picture of one of the donkeys which were once used to deliver bread and milk up the steep village streets, both here and at neighbouring Chalford ★ .

Frocester (162) (SO 78-03) *4 mi. SW Stroud.* Small village lying beneath the Cotswold edge and centred upon a crossroads overlooked by the colourfully painted Royal Gloucestershire Hussar Inn. The 'new church' was largely rebuilt in the 19th century and is not of great interest to visitors. The remains of the 'old church' are about a mile to the west of the village, and consist of only a Victorian Gothic tower and spire. Medieval Frocester Court was owned by the abbey of Gloucester and its tithe barn is one of England's finest specimens, being over 180 feet in length. The barn is open during all reasonable daylight hours. *(Tel: (045382) 3250.)* A large Roman villa has been excavated here, but its remains are not on view.

Frocester Hill (162) (SO 79-01) *4 mi. SW Stroud.* A lovely open space on the Cotswold edge, with splendid views out over the winding Severn Estuary. Gliders from the nearby club add further colour and interest. The best approach is from the adjoining Coaley Peak Picnic Site ★ .

Fulbrook (163) (SP 26-13) *¾ mi. NE Burford.* Large village astride the A361 and only separated from Burford by the River Windrush and the water-meadows through which it flows. Its interesting Norman church stands in a quiet setting just to the north of the A361. It has a beautiful Norman south doorway, a fine 16th-century roof supported on well carved corbel figures, a series of solid 12th-century arcade capitals and an opulently colourful 17th-century monument in the chancel.

Gatcombe Park (162) (ST 88-99) *5 mi. SE Stroud.* This handsome late 18th-century mansion, once owned by the political economist, David Ricardo, is now the home of the Princess Royal. The house is not open to the public, but the delightful park is used at least once a year for horse trials.

Gloucester (162) (SO 83-18) *7 mi. W Cheltenham.* Situated, like neighbouring Cheltenham, just below, and to the west of, the Cotswold scarp, this city, the capital of Gloucestershire, has a long and interesting history. In the years after their invasion of 43 AD, the Romans soon established a fort at the very end of the Ermin Way, at what is now Kingsholm (SO 83-19) on the north side of the city. This was used to house the famous 2nd Legion, but by the late sixties a new and larger fort had been built on the site of the present city centre, and was by then already known as Glevum. By the end of the century the 2nd Legion had moved westwards to its new fortress at Caerleon to subjugate and control the Welsh tribes, and Glevum became a non-military colony. By the end of the 2nd century the city had grown to considerable importance and had become one of the four great *coloniae* of Britain, along with Lincoln, York and Colchester.

As in the rest of Britain the departure of the legions saw the eventual decline of Roman civilisa-

tion, and it was not until the Anglo-Saxons had firmly established themselves that Gloucester was reborn. The monastery of St Peter was established here as early as 681, a royal palace was built at Kingsholm probably in the late 9th century and St Oswald's Priory was founded in 909, by Ethelfleda, the Lady of the Mercians. She was probably also responsible for the building of the walls and streets. Although loosely based on Glevum's pattern of building, the present street plan owes less to the Romans than to the Saxons, with the streets of Northgate, Eastgate, Southgate and Westgate meeting at the Cross. At this time the whole of Anglo-Saxon England was divided up into shires and it was then that Gloucester became the capital of its own shire.

It was Edward the Confessor who established the tradition of holding a court here at Christmas, and William the Conqueror continued to do the same. It was here, in 1085, that William had 'deep speech with his Witan' (his council of wise men), and it was at this meeting that the decision was made to start the great Domesday survey. It was only three years later that work was started on the great new abbey church of St Peter, the fine building that was later to become the basis for Gloucester Cathedral. The Norman and Angevin kings continued to regard Gloucester as a place of great importance, and Henry II granted a Charter to the city giving it a status equal to that of Winchester and Whitehall. In 1216 the young Henry III was crowned here, and just over a hundred years later, in 1327, Edward II was buried here following his dreadful murder at Berkeley Castle ★ .

Although overtaken by Bristol as a commercial centre because of the distance of its port from the sea, Gloucester continued to flourish in medieval times, from its trade, its agricultural markets and from the number of pilgrims visiting the tomb of Edward II in the great abbey. Many churches were built and there were no fewer than three friaries in the city. Great changes took place during the Dissolution between 1536 and 1539: the friaries and the monastery were closed, and the great abbey church soon became a cathedral with its own diocese. With Henry VIII's daughter Mary on the throne the fortunes of the Protestant church went into reverse, and in 1555 Gloucester's bishop, John Hooper, was burnt at the stake in his own cathedral city.

It was in the reign of Mary's sister, Elizabeth, that Letters Patent were granted establishing the City Docks, the basis of those that have survived to this day. In the century that followed the city had mixed fortunes. During the Civil War it successfully endured a long siege by the Royalists and this fact was not forgotten by Charles II who, after his Restoration, had the city walls and the castle demolished, and more importantly reduced the city's land holdings from 29,000 acres to only 400, thus cancelling a privilege hard won from his ancestor Richard III.

The docks were relatively busy in the 18th century, but it was the opening of the Gloucester and Sharpness Canal in 1827 that brought renewed prosperity. By the mid-1860s, however, the size of ocean-going ships had increased so much that the docks again went into a decline, and it is only now that plans to revive them for leisure purposes are reaching fruition.

To explore some of the best of Gloucester it is suggested that you first call at the *Tourist Infor-*

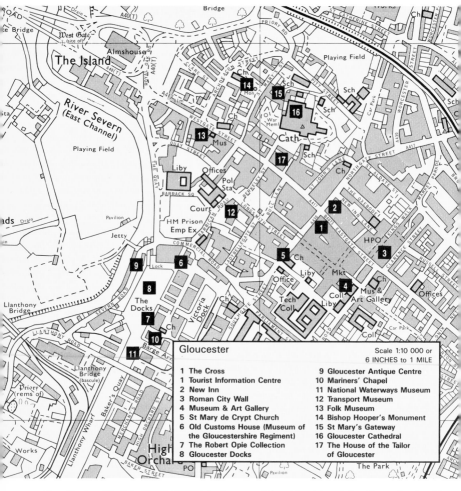

Gloucester

Scale 1:10 000 or
6 INCHES to 1 MILE

1 The Cross
1 Tourist Information Centre
2 New Inn
3 Roman City Wall
4 Museum & Art Gallery
5 St Mary de Crypt Church
6 Old Customs House (Museum of the Gloucestershire Regiment)
7 The Robert Opie Collection
8 Gloucester Docks
9 Gloucester Antique Centre
10 Mariners' Chapel
11 National Waterways Museum
12 Transport Museum
13 Folk Museum
14 Bishop Hooper's Monument
15 St Mary's Gateway
16 Gloucester Cathedral
17 The House of the Tailor of Gloucester

mation Centre (1) (tel: (0452) 421188) in St Michael's Tower by **The Cross (1)**. Now go into Northgate Street to look at the **New Inn (2)** with its beautiful galleried courtyard, and then turn right into New Inn Lane and right again into King's Walk, passing the remains of the **Roman City Wall (3)** on the left. Cross Eastgate Street to Queen's Walk and head slightly to the left of Jubilee Gardens to visit the outstandingly interesting **Gloucester Museum and Art Gallery (4)** (tel: (0452) 24131), with its Roman mosaics and sculptures, and freshwater aquarium. Now turn right up Greyfriars passing the ruins of the 16th-century Greyfriars church on the right.

Turn left into Southgate Street by the largely Perpendicular **St Mary de Crypt Church (5)**, and soon fork right into Commercial Road, passing the **Old Customs House (6)** which houses the **Museum of the Gloucestershire Regiment** (tel: (0452) 22682). Now turn left and follow signs to **The Robert Opie Collection at the Museum of Advertising and Packaging (7)** (tel: (0452) 307009), with its fascinating displays concerning packaging and advertising, housed in a large 19th-century warehouse in **Gloucester Docks (8)** (see below). Now walk back to Commercial Road and

turn left and then left again into Severn Road to visit the **Gloucester Antique Centre (9)** (tel: (0452) 29716), which has over sixty individual shops and a restaurant, all housed in yet another 19th-century warehouse.

Gloucester Docks (8) are fascinating in themselves and it is well worth walking around them, visiting the **Mariners' Chapel (10)** and the Mariner's Walk Shopping Centre. On some days it is also possible to cruise around the docks in the passenger ferry Heather Spray. (Tel: (0452) 308018.)

The National Waterways Museum (11) which is housed in the nearby Llanthony Warehouse provides a fascinating variety of displays on the colourful history of canals and other inland waterways, with novel live exhibition areas outside and canal boats in the barge arm alongside. (Tel: (0452) 307009.)

Now walk back into Commercial Road, turn left into Barbican Road, and then into Bearland, where some of the city's finest 18th-century houses will be found, including Bearland House and Lady Bellgate House. Pass the small **Transport Museum (12)**, with its horse-drawn vehicles always visible from the road. Now walk down Quay Street, turn right

Horse-drawn bus at the National Waterways Museum, Gloucester (British Waterways Board Photo Library)

down Lower Quay Street, and then right again into Westgate Street. Soon pass the **Folk Museum (13)** *(tel: (0452) 26467)*, which is housed in Bishop Hooper's Lodging, a group of half-timbered buildings where the bishop is reputed to have spent his last night before being burnt at the stake.

Now turn left not far beyond St Nicholas's Church, down the narrow Three Cocks Lane which runs into St Mary's Street. **Bishop Hooper's Monument (14)**, on the left, marks the spot where this brave but unfortunate prelate met his end. Now turn right through **St Mary's Gateway (15)** and into the Cathedral Close with its fine 16th-, 17th- and 18th-century houses, then visit the splendid **Gloucester Cathedral (16)**. This is a triumphant blend of the Norman and high Perpendicular styles. A visit here should take at least two hours, but see especially the early Norman crypt, the great Norman pillars of the nave, the Norman chapter house,

Gloucester Cathedral and the Bishop Hooper Memorial

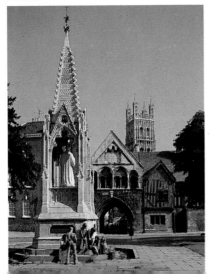

the splendid Perpendicular choir and cloisters, the beautifully vaulted Lady Chapel, the magnificent east window, and the massive 225-ft pinnacled tower. See also the outstandingly beautiful tomb of the murdered Edward II and the fascinating collection of carved misericords beneath the choir stalls. Coffees, teas and light lunches are available in the refectory.

After walking right round the Cathedral Close, leave College Green by College Court, calling in at **The House of the Tailor of Gloucester (17)**. This minute shop is the home that Beatrix Potter chose for her delightful 'Tailor of Gloucester'. It is now a Beatrix Potter Centre with a museum depicting her life, her art and her writing. There are gifts on the Beatrix Potter theme available and there is a reconstruction of the 'Tailor's Kitchen' complete with mice stitching the famous waistcoat. *(Tel: (0452) 422856.)* Now turn left into Westgate Street and return to **The Cross (1)**, thus completing your walk around this most interesting city.

Gloucestershire Warwickshire Railway ('The G.W.R.') (150) (SP 05-32) *At Toddington, 3½ mi. NE Winchcombe.* The long-term aim of this preservation project is to reopen most of the former Great Western main line between Stratford-upon-Avon and Cheltenham. The line already connects Toddington, Winchcombe Station (nearer Greet than Winchcombe) and Gretton Meadow, where there is a 7-acre Nature Reserve complete with Picnic Area. Plans are in hand to reach Cheltenham Racecourse and then to concentrate on reopening the line northwards, through Broadway and on to Honeybourne Junction, where a link with British Rail may be possible once again. Steam and diesel-hauled trains both operate over the existing length of track. The restored Toddington Station has a book and souvenir shop and a cafeteria, and vintage locomotives and rolling stock are on display. *(Tel: (0242) 621405.)*

As it grows longer, this line will become increasingly useful for walkers wishing to sample the delights of the Cotswold edge, either by using sections of the Cotswold Way ★ or by planning their own routes.

The Golden Valley (162,163) (SO 88-02 etc.) *1 mi. SE Stroud, etc.* This description is normally applied to the length of the Frome Valley that runs between Chalford and Brimscombe, but it appears to have derived its name from the prosperity brought here by the cloth weavers who were established all along the valley by the end of the Middle Ages. This prosperity increased with the building of mills in the years of the early Industrial Revolution, and was at its height in the early years of the 19th century. It was then that cloth manufacture began to move northwards to Lancashire and Yorkshire, and although light industry has now replaced some of the closed mills, much of this delightful valley now slumbers once again, and is 'golden' for very different reasons.

Great Barrington (163) (SP 20-13) *3 mi. W Burford.* This small village in the Windrush Valley has several pleasant 17th- and 18th-century houses, many of which had been allowed to deteriorate in the middle years of the 20th century. Fortunately many have now been restored, and others are soon

The Barringtons SCALE 1:25 000 or 2½ INCHES to 1 MILE

the porch, nor the rather sad verse on the tablet to Thomas Cambray, which reads:

Whilst in this sad world I did remain
My latter days were grief and pain
Full fifteen years and something more
But now the Lord hath set me free
From grief and pain and misery

There is a pleasant walk southwards, over the fields, and then beside the River Windrush, to the village of Windrush ★. It is also possible to walk north to Little Rissington ★ and onwards to Wyck Rissington ★ to link on to the Oxfordshire Way ★. The massive airfield on the hill above the village is, at the time of writing, disused.

Great Rollright (151) (SP 32-31) *2½ mi. N Chipping Norton*. Windy upland village just over the county boundary from Warwickshire into Oxfordshire, with fine views south out over a broad valley towards rolling hill country around Chipping Norton ★. There are no real features of interest here, apart from the Norman church. This has some grotesque gargoyles on its well proportioned Perpendicular tower and a Norman doorway whose tympanum has a fish inserted amongst various geometric carvings. The porch in which it shelters is two-storeyed and its cornice is richly carved with an assortment of animals, flowers and the heads of men and women. Inside there is much evidence of over-zealous Victorian restoration, but do not overlook the brass to John Battersby, rector here until his death in 1522, nor the pleasant roof, with the names of the churchwardens in the year 1814 on one of its beams.

Walk north from here, down the scarp slope, across a valley, and beside a great wood, to the village of Whichford ★ in Warwickshire, or eastwards to delightful Hook Norton ★. If driving westwards from Great Rollright, possibly to the Rollright Stones ★, do not miss the splendid panoramic views, to both north and south of the road.

Great Tew (164) (SP 39-29) *5½ mi. E Chipping Norton*. This is largely a 'model village' constructed at least in part by the early 19th-century landscape gardener, John Loudon (who managed the estate from 1809 to 1811), as part of an extensive park overlooking the Worton Valley. It is for this reason that there are so many evergreen trees to be found in 'Tewland'. There are 'picturesque' stone cottages, a small inn, the Falkland Arms, and stocks on the village green, but it was all conceived so long ago that it no longer appears contrived.

Nothing remains of the fine manor house where, before his untimely death at the Battle of Newbury in 1643, the brilliant Lucius Cary, Viscount Falkland, once entertained poets and philosophers from, Oxford. It has been replaced by an odd 19th-century mansion, built by the descendants of Matthew Boulton, partner of James Watt in Birmingham's famous Soho Foundry. Idyllic Great Tew therefore owes its very existence to wealth created by Black Country sweat in the early years of the 19th century.

One of the Boultons, Mary, is remembered in the church above the manor, where there is a brilliant monument to her by the great 19th-century sculptor, Sir Francis Chantrey. The approach to the church is through a fine 17th-century gateway,

due for restoration. The village is dominated by Barrington Park, a fine Palladian mansion built for Earl Talbot, Lord Chancellor in the reign of George II, possibly by William Kent. The house, which overlooks a beautifully landscaped park through which the Windrush flows, is not visible from the road, but the wrought-iron gates on the road north towards Great Rissington and the exquisite temple visible through them provide tempting glimpses of otherwise hidden splendours.

The largely Norman church lies on the edge of the park, and has an unusually high Norman chancel arch and several interesting monuments. These include a delightful memorial to Mary, Countess Talbot, by the fashionable 18th-century sculptor, Joseph Nollekens, and another one, to two children of the Bray family, previous owners of the manor of Barrington, with the little boy and girl being led heavenwards by an angel.

The bridge over the Windrush between the church and the Fox Inn was built by local mastermason, Thomas Strong (see also Burford ★). Traces of the great quarries in the area worked by the Strongs and the other family of master-masons, the Kempsters, are not easily found, for most of them were underground. They are all on private land, largely between the Windrush Valley and the A40 and well to the south of Great Barrington. See also Taynton ★ and Windrush ★.

Use our mapped **mini-walk** to go south, across the River Windrush to Little Barrington ★, and return via the friendly Fox Inn. (The latter might make a good alternative starting point, but only if the landlord is willing to allow cars to be parked here, by those also using the inn.)

Great Rissington (163) (SP 19-17) *3 mi. SE Bourton-on-the-Water*. Situated on a gently sloping hillside, this widespread village looks westwards out over the broad Windrush Valley. Its main street runs down from a small triangular green towards a fine 17th-century manor house. This and the nearby church are attractive buildings, both showing clear evidence of sympathetic restoration and care.

The cruciform church has a 15th-century tower with pinnacles and battlements, and in the south transept there are three memorial tablets, that to John Barnard and his wife being especially pleasing. Do not miss the interesting little 15th-century carving of the Crucifixion which has been reset in

Thatched cottages at Great Tew . . . a 19th-century estate village now delightfully matured

thought possibly to be the work of Nicholas Stone, and up a delightful tree-lined path.

There is a pleasant walk south-westwards from here, through Little Tew to the edge of Heythrop Park and then south to Enstone.

Great Witcombe (162) (SO 91-14) *5 mi. SW Cheltenham.* Quiet village tucked away beneath the wooded Cotswold edge at Birdlip, with hills on three sides and reservoirs just below. Here are a few half-timbered cottages, a dignified little 19th-century school and school house, and an interesting church. This has a massive yew tree close to its attractive 18th-century porch, the latter being contemporary with the handsome tower. The interior is even more pleasing, with a Norman chancel arch, a barrel-vaulted ceiling to the nave, a medieval rood beam, and fragments of medieval glass in the north aisle windows.

There is fly-fishing available on the nearby reservoirs. *(Tel: (0452) 864413.)* Witcombe Roman Villa ★ is less than a mile to the south-west and may be approached from our **Tour 5**. The villa is also visited on our **Walk 7**, as are the reservoirs and the village.

Great Wolford (150) (SP 24-34) *3 mi. NE Moreton-in-Marsh.* This modest village looks out towards neighbouring Little Wolford ★, across a valley through which the Nethercote Brook flows north to join the Stour, and so on to the Avon and Severn; but less than two miles away, streams flow south to join the Evenlode, which flows into the Thames. So, although the village stands less than 400 feet above sea level, this is watershed country, and it was perhaps for reasons of strategy that a small Iron Age settlement was built here, the earthworks of which may be seen to the immediate south-east of the village. Wolford's medieval church was destroyed by fire in the early 19th century, and was replaced by a broad building, with a short chancel containing some monuments to the Ingram family. Its best feature is the tall spire, which is an outstanding landmark in this gentle south Warwickshire landscape.

Greet (150) (SP 02-30) *1 mi. N Winchcombe.* This large hamlet has a pleasant manor farmhouse complete with a 17th-century dovecot, and a half-timbered house opposite, but both buildings have been overshadowed by considerable modern development. A short distance to the east, near the B4632, is the Winchcombe Pottery, which has been creating excellent craft work for many years. There is a modest shop and enthusiasts will probably be able to watch the potters at work. *(Tel: (0242) 602462.)* Less than half a mile to the west of the pottery there is a station on the Gloucestershire Warwickshire Railway ★.

Gretton (150) (SP 00-30) *1½ mi. NW Winchcombe.* Situated beneath 900ft-high Langley Hill, this small village has several attractive half-timbered cottages prettily situated around the 15th-century tower of its otherwise demolished medieval church. Great care and attention was lavished upon its Victorian successor by the architect, John Drayton Wyatt, Sir Gilbert Scott's principal draughtsman. The end result, however, is not over-inspiring, and the interior lacks atmosphere. The nearby inn has for some years been known as the Bugatti, in recognition of the nearby Prescott ★ Hill Climb, and the figure on the inn sign is that of Rivers Fletcher, the well-known Bugatti owner and driver.

It is possible to walk southwards from Gretton, up over Langley Hill, to Winchcombe ★, or south-westwards to Cleeve Hill ★.

Grim's Ditch (164) (SP 38-21 etc.) A now disconnected series of banks and ditches, which once formed part of a defensive system built by an Iron Age (Belgic) tribe in the first part of the 1st century AD. The best sections are visible in Blenheim ★ and Ditchley ★ Parks.

Guiting Power (163) (SP 09-24) *5 mi. SE Winchcombe.* This delightful village is built around a small sloping green, and is a fascinating example of the

The Post Office at unspoilt Guiting Power

unconscious harmony created by Cotswold masons over the centuries. The cottages, shop and inns are all beautifully cared for. Both the Farmers' Arms in the village and Ye Olde Inn on the road leading to Winchcombe are worth visiting, and form welcome breaks on a number of walks that can be taken in this area — north-westwards to Guiting Wood ★, linking with our **Walk 3**, south-eastwards down the Windrush Valley to Naunton ★, or south-westwards to Hawling ★.

The church of St Michael has substantial Norman north and south doorways, but restoration by the Victorians has resulted in a certain lack of atmosphere within. However, there are pleasant views from its tidy churchyard towards Naunton.

Guiting Wood (163) (SP 07-26) *3 mi. SE Winchcombe.* Extensive woodland bordering the valley of the little Castlett Stream. It may be approached from Guiting Power★, Kineton★, Temple Guiting★ or Farmcote★, and is also partly covered by our **Walk 3**. The minute car park used for the start of **Walk 3** makes a very useful base from which to explore the area, and is overlooked by a handsome 17th- and 18th-century stone manor house standing above its own miniature park. A very minor road, signed as 'Unsuitable', runs northwards and then westwards from here partly beside the Castlett Stream, and this provides a fine, almost mud-free walk, even in the depths of winter.

Hailes Abbey and Hailes (150) (SP 04-30) *2 mi. NE Winchcombe.* Here beneath the Cotswold edge are the remains of a great abbey founded in 1246 by Richard, Earl of Cornwall, who had earlier vowed to do so, following his escape from a shipwreck off the Isles of Scilly. It was colonised by monks from Beaulieu in Hampshire, a Cistercian house founded by Richard's father, King John. Hailes's popularity as a place of pilgrimage was then assured by Richard's son Edmund, who gave the monks a relic of the 'Holy Blood of Christ', which had been authenticated by the Pope himself. From this time forth pilgrims poured into Hailes and it was only at the Dissolution of the Monasteries by Henry VIII that its fame came to an end.

Christmas Eve 1539 witnessed the final surrender of the abbey to the agents of the king, and according to legend its destruction was witnessed by the king's hated Commissioner, Thomas Cromwell, from Beckbury Camp★, on the hillside above. The only remains now are parts of the cloisters and various low walls, but the plan of the magnificent abbey church has been perpetuated by the planting of trees and the attractive site is well worth visiting. There is a small but interesting museum close by containing many medieval tiles, a beautiful series of roof bosses, many other finds from the excavation of the abbey and life-size figures of Cistercian monks.

The nearby parish church of Hailes, a small building nearly a hundred years older than the abbey, has ancient stone floors, medieval wall-paintings and stained glass, a 15th-century rood screen and attractive 17th-century woodwork. This delightful little building was sympathetically restored in 1961 and is still full of an atmosphere of the past.

Hailes is on the course of the Cotswold Way★.

Summertime at Hailes Abbey

and this can be used to climb up onto the hill on a pleasant bridleway almost to Farmcote★. It is also possible to follow the Way over the fields to Winchcombe★, along a path still known as the Pilgrims' Way. Motorists will find a pleasant, partly open road leading southwards up over Salter's Hill, following the course of the ancient Salt Way★, and still known here as Salter's Lane.

Hampen (163) (SP 05-19) *6½ mi. E Cheltenham.* Minute hamlet in unspoilt upland country to the south of the A436, on a bridle road running between Salperton★ and Shipton Oliffe★. The long-vanished 'Banbury and Cheltenham Direct Railway' ran just to the north of the hamlet, and its embankments and cuttings are still much in evidence hereabouts.

Hampnett (163) (SP 09-15) *1 mi. NW Northleach. (See map on page 84.)* This attractive village is thinly spread around a field-like village green, which gives birth to one of the Cotswolds' loveliest streams — the Leach. The church is largely Norman, but its interior was subjected to some very unusual stencil decoration in the 1880s. This work, largely carried out by Hampnett's vicar, detracts from the clean Norman lines, although it should be remembered that in medieval times most churches were decorated with a variety of patterns similar to this. Do not miss the finely carved birds on the capitals supporting the chancel arch — they are a fine example of late Norman work.

Walk south-east from here down the valley of the infant Leach to Northleach★ using part of the **mini-walk** on the map on page 84. It is also possible to walk south-westwards over the hills to Yanworth★.

Hampton Fields (162) (ST 88-99) *1 mi. SE Minchinhampton.* There is a pleasant row of 18th- and early 19th-century cottages in this small hamlet in partly wooded hill country. The Long Stone, the only surviving stone from an otherwise defunct long barrow, stands in a field to the east of the road from here to Minchinhampton.

Haresfield Beacon (162) (SO 82-08) *3 mi. NW Stroud.* There is a topograph, or viewing table, near a car park in the Shortwood area, and beyond this a further car parking space for those who wish to walk along to the Beacon itself, a hill-top surrounded by the earthworks of an Iron Age promontory fort. There are splendid views out over the Severn Estuary from this dramatic edge country, most of which is owned by the National Trust.

The Cotswold Way★ passes through this area and a short distance along it to the north-east will be found the 'Cromwell Siege Stone', a simple monument commemorating 5 September 1643, the day when the Royalist siege of Gloucester was lifted, due to the imminent arrival of a strong Parliamentary force commanded by the Earl of Essex. See also our **Walk 6**, which starts from the Shortwood Car Park and passes this way.

Harford Bridge (163) (SP 12-22) *4 mi. SW Stow-on-the-Wold.* Here is a pleasant little ford across the Windrush, overlooked by a modest farmhouse. The Domesday Book records a village of Harford, but no

Ford at Lower Harford

trace of this remains. It was probably depopulated by sheep graziers in the 15th or early 16th century. There is a public road through here, but the ford is often deep and it is anyway far more pleasant to walk here from Naunton ★, and on down the Windrush Valley to Bourton-on-the-Water ★.

Harnhill (163) (SP 07-00) *2½ mi. E Cirencester.* Compact village in flat country to the east of Cirencester, with a small conically towered Norman church standing almost in the garden of a largely Georgian rectory. The church's chief treasure is its Norman south doorway's tympanum which depicts St Michael locked in combat with a dragon, but there are also lovely fragments of medieval glass in the east window. This church was lucky enough to escape the attention of the Victorians and was most sympathetically restored in 1909.

Close by the church is a fine 16th-century manor house with an attractive square dovecot in its grounds.

Hatherop (163) (SP 15-05) *2½ mi. N Fairford.* This is a largely 19th-century estate village, the creation of the Lord de Mauley, the owner of Hatherop Castle. The castle itself is a 17th-century manor house ambitiously enlarged and partly rebuilt in the 1850s, complete with battlements and other trimmings. This was the work of Henry Clutton, an architect much influenced by the eccentric William Burges, and also to some extent by the great French Gothicist, Viollet le Duc. The nearby French Gothic church was also the work of Henry Clutton and contains the dramatic monument in white marble to Lady de Mauley, who died in 1844, twelve years before her husband.

Hawling (163) (SP 06-23) *4 mi. SE Winchcombe.* Situated in high sheep country just to the east of the ancient Salt Way ★, this is a small, quiet village with a fine Elizabethan manor house next door to its church. The latter was largely rebuilt in 1764 and was probably still in such good order in the 19th century that it escaped the more ruthless 'restoration' experienced by so many other churches. It has a handsome Georgian pulpit, an unusual set of 17th-century brass plaques to various members of the Stratford family and a colourful little ceiling beneath its tower, this being the only medieval part of the church to survive.

There is a pleasant, partly unfenced road running eastwards from here to Guiting Power ★, and for walkers there is a bridleway leading northwards over open wold country to Deadmanbury Gate (163) (SP 05-26) on the edge of Guiting Wood ★, linking with our **Walk 3**.

Hazelton (163) (ST 92-98) *4½ mi. E Nailsworth.* This fine 16th- and 17th-century manor house and farmstead stands on the site of a 12th-century priory and is just visible to the north of the road between Rodmarton ★ and Cherington ★. Windmill Tump Long Barrow (163) (ST 93-97), to the south of the road, is a classic chambered long barrow complete with a false entrance between two projecting horns, similar to that at Belas Knap ★. It is in the care of English Heritage and may be visited at any reasonable time.

Hazleton (163) (SP 07-18) *2½ mi. NW Northleach.* An unspoilt village situated high up on the wolds, on the line of the ancient Salt Way ★. The church has Norman origins, although its tower and most of its windows are 15th-century Perpendicular. There is a fine Norman south doorway and chancel arch, and a massive 13th-century font.

Walkers will enjoy the attractive bridleways eastwards to Turkdean ★, north-eastwards to Notgrove ★ and northwards to Salperton ★.

Hetty Pegler's Tump (or Uley Long Barrow) (162) (SO 79-00) *On B4066, ½ mi. S Frocester Hill.* A Neolithic chambered long barrow about 180ft long, surrounded by a dry-stone revetting wall and containing a central passage of stone with three burial chambers. In the care of English Heritage, it may be visited at 'any reasonable time'. The very low entrance is usually kept locked, but the key may be collected from a cottage half a mile to the south on the B4066. Visitors are advised to wear old clothes and to take a torch.

Hidcote Boyce (151) (SP 17-41) *2 mi. NE Chipping Campden. (See map on page 79.)* Here is a pleasant hamlet below the western slopes of high Ilmington Downs. It has a single, gently sloping street bordered by flower-filled cottage gardens. Some distance to its north, the road is overlooked by Hidcote House, a delightful manor house which was built in 1663, probably by Francis Keyte of neighbouring Ebrington ★. This has attractively curved gable-ends and mullioned windows, and pretty fan-tailed doves are usually to be seen flying to and from their nesting boxes overlooking the gateway.

The mapped **mini-walk** on page 79 goes through Mickleton, Hidcote Boyce and neighbouring Hidcote Bartrim ★. It is also possible, by using its eastern portion only, to walk up onto Ilmington Downs and back down through Hidcote Bartrim.

Hidcote Manor Garden, Hidcote Bartrim (151) (SP 17-42) *3 mi. NE Chipping Campden. (See map on page 79.)* This was given to the National Trust in 1948 by the great horticulturist, Major Lawrence Johnson, who had by that time devoted forty years of his life to its creation. When he came to Hidcote in 1905 there was only the minute hamlet of Hidcote Bartrim, and its 17th-century manor house in company with only a cedar tree, a clump of large beeches and a few walls.

The garden that we see today was therefore created from eleven acres of open Cotswold hill country. In fact Major Johnson made not one garden but a series of small gardens, separated by now mellowed walls and by hedges of hornbeam, yew, green and copper beech, box and holly.

Brilliant flower-beds at Hidcote Manor Garden

Amongst these magnificent hedges are to be found the Fuchsia Garden, the White Garden, the Bathing Pool Garden, and, in contrast to these formal creations, a wild garden beside a stream. These are enriched by grass walks and lawns, mellow brick gazebos and wrought-iron gates through which one can glimpse distant views of Bredon Hill and the Malverns, across the blue haze of the valleys through which the Avon and Severn flow. See also the Theatre Lawn, which is usually the scene of an open-air Shakespeare Play at some time each summer, the Long Walk in the Kitchen Garden, which contains a fine collection of old French roses, the alley of lime trees, and the fine avenue of beech trees. The National Trust describe Hidcote as 'one of the most delightful gardens in England', and it would indeed be hard to dispute this claim. The Trust have one of their excellent gift shops here, and refreshments available include coffees, light lunches and cream teas. *(Tel: (0386) 438333.)*

Use our mapped **mini-walk** on page 79 to walk down to Mickleton★, via neighbouring Hidcote Boyce★, and back up the hill via Kiftsgate★. This can also be extended by taking a track up the hill from Hidcote Bartrim which leads over the top of Ilmington Downs, from where it is possible to walk down into nearby Hidcote Boyce, and return across fields to the start. But do not use the National Trust's car park, which is for the use of those visiting the garden.

Hilcot and Pinchley Woods (163) (SO 99-16 etc.) *5 mi. SE Cheltenham.* This is a delightful and little-known area of woodland in a valley which gives birth to the Hilcot Brook, a tributary of the River Churn. Public footpaths are few, but the roads approaching from Withington★, Andoversford★, Seven Springs★ and Colesbourne★ are normally quiet enough to be used for walking. Upper Hilcot farmhouse is half-timbered — an unusual feature in this countryside of Cotswold stone, and perhaps a reflection of this hidden valley's rich timber resources in days gone by.

Farmhouse at Hilcot

Hinchwick (151) (SP 14-30) *4 mi. NW Stow-on-the-Wold.* An early 19th-century manor house and a few cottages, on the line of the Romans' Ryknild Street★, at the southern end of a tranquil, wooded valley, with a series of small lakes amongst the trees (please do not trespass). This valley should contain the upper reaches of the little River Dikler, but although it must have its origins on Bourton Downs, it remains underground and it is not until Donnington Brewery★ that it finally emerges for good at the head of a beautiful lake, by now in sufficient volume to justify a large mill-wheel. Our **Walk 4** uses a path north from Hinchwick, leading up the dry valley, and over the wold country of Bourton Downs.

Holwell (163) (SP 23-09) *2½ mi. SW Burford.* Quiet hamlet in open wold country with pleasant farm buildings not far from a small church, which was entirely rebuilt in 1895. The interior is not of great interest, apart from the pulpit which has delightful 17th-century Flemish panels built into it depicting various scenes from the Nativity.

Honington (151) (SP 26-42) *1½ mi. N Shipston-on-Stour.* A most attractive village centred around a wide, tree-shaded green, with a beautiful assortment of houses and cottages in timber, mellow brick and stone, blending together to produce a highly satisfying scene. Honington is approached from the A34, Stratford to Shipston road, by a small road leading over a pretty five-arched bridge with balls upon its parapet. This is probably contemporary with the late 17th-century Honington Hall, an exceptionally handsome mellow brick mansion visible well over to the left in parkland beside the River Stour. This was built in 1685 by a London merchant, Sir Henry Parker, and is enriched by a series of oval recesses between the upper and lower windows, in which busts of the twelve Caesars sit most comfortably. The house was lovingly restored in the mid-1970s, and incorporates a wealth of richly contrived 18th-century plasterwork, especially in its entrance hall and octagonal Saloon. *(Tel: (0608) 61434.)*

Apart from its 13th-century tower, the adjoining church is contemporary with the house, and its elegantly decorated interior reminds one of a Wren City church. It was also restored in the 1970s and contains several handsome monuments to members of the Parker and Townsend families. See especially the self-important but sumptuous monument to Sir Henry Parker and his son Hugh, a piece of work that typifies the spirit of the age in which they lived. In contrast, there are two monuments by the 19th-century sculptor Sir Richard Westmacott, less exciting, but also less worldly — the one to Lady Elizabeth Townsend, depicting a mourning male figure by an urn, exhibiting a typically poignant Westmacott treatment.

There is a pleasant little road north from Honington, to Halford, with views out over the River Stour from its northern end.

Hook Norton (151) (SP 35-33) *5 mi. NE Chipping Norton.* A large village situated in remote hilly country that once yielded great quantities of ironstone. The old ironworks have long since vanished, but other evidence of Hook Norton's past importance as an ironstone centre may still be seen

'Sagittarius the Archer' . . . on the font at Hook Norton

— a series of dramatic piers, the only remains of a massive railway viaduct that once spanned the broad valley to its east, carrying the long-vanished 'Banbury and Cheltenham Direct Railway'. There is also a Victorian brewery here (its red-brick fabric an unusual intrusion into the Cotswold scene) which still brews the most delectable Hook Norton Ale. This beer, like the village in which it is brewed, is known far and wide as 'Hooky', to all those who know a thing or two about real ale.

This village, with its orange-brown stone and thatched roofs, is well worth exploring. 'The Green' and 'East End' are both very pleasant, but we particularly favour the terrace in the centre of the village, with the Bell Inn at one end and the church at the other. The latter is a large building of Norman origin with a finely pinnacled Perpendicular tower and a spacious, pleasantly bare interior, in which is a fascinating Norman font complete with sculptured figures of Adam and Eve, Sagittarius the Archer, and other signs of the Zodiac.

Walk south-east from here, across the broad valley over which the viaduct once ran, and up over the hill to the delightful little village of Swerford in the next valley.

Horton and Horton Court (172) (ST 76-85) *5 mi. S Wotton-under-Edge*. Situated beneath the wooded Cotswold edge, Horton Court is a lovely manor house in the care of the National Trust. Its fine Norman hall and its detached 16th-century ambulatory are both open to the public. The latter was built by William Knight, who was Henry VIII's envoy to the Pope when the king was attempting to obtain a divorce, and its elegant Renaissance style, complete with the medallion heads of four emperors, must have been inspired by his visit to Rome. *(Tel. NT Regional Office for opening times: (0747) 840224.)*

The nearby church has a well proportioned Perpendicular tower and a vaulted porch of the same period. In the pleasantly white-painted interior are a Jacobean pulpit and two handsome 18th-century wall monuments, the one to Anne Paston being most tenderly worded.

Hyde (162) (SO 88-01) *1½ mi. NE Minchinhampton*. Upper Hyde hamlet overlooks the Golden Valley ★, and Lower Hyde, itself in the valley, has a delightful little 'round house' built beside the Thames and Severn Canal ★, a restored stretch of which runs here. These round houses were built for the canal's maintenance men, known as length men, as each was responsible for the upkeep of a certain length of the waterway.

Icomb (163) (SP 21-22) *2½ mi. SE Stow-on-the-Wold*. Situated beneath 800ft-high Icomb Hill, this pleasant village has a variety of houses and cottages, almost all of which are a delight to the eye. The small church has a blocked-up Norman north doorway and an Early English chancel, but all has been rather heavily restored. However, visitors should not overlook the effigy of Sir John Blaket, a 15th-century knight in armour upon a fine tomb chest, and almost certainly the builder of Icomb Place, the medieval manor house hidden away from view at the southern end of the village.

A path leads south from the vicinity of the church to join the Oxfordshire Way ★ in less than a mile. Use this to walk eastwards to Bledington ★, and then down the Evenlode Valley to Bruern ★ and Shipton-under-Wychwood ★.

Idbury (163) (SP 23-19) *4½ mi. SE Stow-on-the-Wold*. Situated on the western slopes of the broad Evenlode Valley, and not far to the east of the earthworks of a large Iron Age settlement, Idbury is a minute village with far-ranging views across to the Oxfordshire Cotswolds. The lovely Tudor manor house was once the editorial headquarters of that delightful little magazine, *The Countryman*, as it was then the home of the publication's founder, Robertson Scott. There is a tablet over the door inscribed, 'Oh more than happy countryman, if he but knew his good fortune'. There is also a more poignant reminder of the Scott connection on a wall by the roadside nearby inscribed, 'This tree is planted in proud memory of Peter Scott, A.F.C., of Idbury, who died in 1943, in Canada'. It is at least good to know that *The Countryman* continues to flourish, with its editorial office having been in Sheep Street, Burford ★ for many years now.

The interior of Idbury's largely Perpendicular church has an unspoilt medieval flavour, with a blocked-up Norman doorway, beautiful 15th-century nave roof supported on corbel figures, and a pulpit made up from three medieval bench-ends. See also the medieval bench-ends still serving their original purpose, the 19th-century box pews, the unusual 'walk-through' squint and the particularly lovely octagonal font. In the churchyard will be found the tomb of Sir Benjamin Baker, the civil engineer who designed the original Aswan Dam and the still-famous Forth Railway Bridge.

There is a bridleway heading eastwards from here into the Evenlode Valley, joining up with the Oxfordshire Way ★ at Bruern Abbey ★.

Ilmington (151) (SP 21-43) *5 mi. NE Chipping Campden*. A most attractive stone village lying beneath Windmill Hill, the most northerly bastion of the Cotswolds, and still very 'Cotswold' in flavour. It spreads itself comfortably below the hill slopes, and to be properly savoured should be explored on foot. Here will be found a wealth of old houses and

INGLESHAM CHURCH

Ilmington SCALE 1:25 000 or 2½ INCHES to 1 MILE

cottages, many beside small paths which stray away from the road that encircles the village. There is a lovingly restored manor house, the beautiful gardens of which are normally open to the public at least twice a year. There are also two very pleasant inns, the Howard Arms and the Red Lion.

The **mini-walk** on our map follows a pleasant circuit taking in many of the village's best features, and using it you will soon encounter the church beyond a quiet little pathway, overlooking two pools in a field in the very heart of the village. This is a largely Norman building, with Norman north and south doorways and chancel arch, and Norman windows in the aisle. Once beyond the 16th-century porch, one comes upon splendid oak pews and other furnishings. These were all installed in the 1930s, and are the work of master-craftsman, Robert Thompson, whose descendants still produce their stout oak furniture in his original workshops in the little village of Kilburn, beneath the steep slopes of the far-off North York Moors. All of Robert Thompson's work, and that of his descendants too, includes a unique signature, an individually carved mouse. Can you find the eleven mice that he carved upon the Ilmington oak? However, during your search for the mice, do not overlook the severely classical monument to Francis Canning and his wife, by the early 19th-century sculptor, Sir Richard Westmacott, other examples of whose work will be found at Honington ★ and nearby Preston-on-Stour. Westmacott, much in the spirit of his times, was very fond of weeping figures and classical urns, and these features will be found in all three of the village churches concerned. The unusual lantern-like structure by the south porch is an early 19th-century monument to members of the Sansom family.

There is a pleasantly quiet road running south from Ilmington, along the eastern slopes of Windmill Hill to Charingworth ★, with fine views over the Vale of Red Horse to the distant line of Edge Hill.

Inglesham Church (163) (SU 20-98) *1 mi. S Lechlade.* Situated by a farm beside the Thames, this charming little building was sensitively preserved by the man to whom we owe so much — William Morris. His work has left the medieval flavour of Inglesham undisturbed, and it is well

worth visiting. Be sure not to miss the hauntingly beautiful 13th-century Madonna and Child.

The River Coln flows into the Thames not far away, and it was there also that the Thames and Severn Canal ★ ended its long run over the Cotswolds to join the Thames.

The Jurassic Way (150,151,162,163,172) This is the name that some archaeologists have given to the prehistoric 'ridgeway' running south-westwards from the mouth of the Humber to Salisbury Plain and the coast beyond. Although its course through the Cotswold area is not at all clear it appears to have followed the high ground some distance behind the long west-facing scarp — from the Rollright Stones in the east, to the hills above Bath in the far south-west. Some of its course is still followed by modern roads, and much of it was also used by medieval traders, especially those transporting wool to the port of Bristol by pack animals. See **Walk 3**, which uses part of the Campden Lane ★, a medieval trading route partly following the approximate course of the Jurassic Way. For more information on this and other ancient trackways, read G.R. Crosher's excellent book, *Along The Cotswold Ways.*

Kelmscot (163) (SU 25-99) *2½ mi. E Lechlade. (See map on page 40.)* Lying just to the north of the Thames, this small village will for ever be associated with the man who lived at the lovely manor house here from 1871 until his death in 1896 — William Morris, craftsman, poet, social reformer and visionary. In a letter to a friend in 1871, Morris wrote:

'I have been looking about for a house for the wife and kids, and whither do you guess my eye is turned now? Kelmscot, a little village about two miles above Radcot Bridge — a heaven on earth; an old stone Elizabethan house — and such a garden! close down on the river, a boat house, and all things handy ...'

The manor, an Elizabethan building with 17th-century additions, still bears the stamp of Morris's powerful personality, besides containing furnishings, wallpapers, and fabrics designed by him, and pictures by his friends Rossetti and Burne-Jones. *Owned by the Society of Antiquaries and let to a tenant, it is only open on written application.*

A stone carving on the village's Memorial Cottages depicts Morris sitting beneath trees, and the nearby Morris Memorial Hall, designed by Ernest Gimson (see Daneway ★), was opened by none other than George Bernard Shaw. The small cruciform church contains much evidence of its Norman origins, and in the churchyard will be found Morris's tomb which, like the Memorial Cottages, was designed by Philip Webb.

Walk from Kelmscot using our mapped **mini-walks** on page 40, starting near the Plough Inn and crossing the Thames to Buscot Park ★, or going across Buscot Weir to Buscot ★. It is also possible to walk on along the north bank of the Thames to St John's Bridge and Lechlade ★.

Kemble (163) (ST 98-97) *4 mi. SW Cirencester.* This village astride the A429 grew in importance in the years when it was a junction on Brunel's busy railway line to the west: hence the number of 19th-century buildings to be found here. The branch lines from it to Tetbury and Cirencester are long gone, but the little station here is still a favourite with those travelling to London from the southern Cotswolds. The line of the old Thames and Severn Canal ★ passes about a mile to its north, and not much further away is the source of the Thames at Thames Head ★, Trewsbury Mead. The church was largely rebuilt in the 19th century, but retains some interesting older features. The whole of the south transept was brought from nearby Ewen ★, where it had served as a chapel. There is also a beautiful Norman inner doorway, and hidden behind the organ is an effigy of a 13th-century knight in chain mail.

It is possible to walk south-eastwards from here to Poole Keynes ★ and the western fringes of the Cotswold Water Park ★, or northwards to Thames Head.

Kencot (163) (SP 25-04) *4 mi. NE Lechlade.* This pleasant village to the immediate north of Broadwell ★ has the misfortune to lie close to the airfield at Brize Norton and noise here is a problem. However, flying does not go on all the time, and Kencot is an otherwise quiet village with an interesting little church beyond a small triangular green. This building has an unusual turret stair and a Norman south doorway with a tympanum depicting 'Sagittarius the Archer' (quite a favourite in this area — see also Hook Norton ★ and Salford ★). The interior has been restored as recently as 1962, and, as a modest notice proclaims, 'this was made possible by the generosity of Edith Bundy of San Francisco'. There is an attractive little early 19th-century gallery, a Jacobean pulpit and a 17th-century monument, to Mary Oldisworthy and Elizabeth Mountsteven.

Kiftsgate Court Garden (151) (SP 17-43) *3 mi. NE Chipping Campden. (See map on page 79.)* This is perhaps not as well known as neighbouring Hidcote Manor Garden ★, but it should on no account be missed. Kiftsgate Court, situated on the very edge of the Cotswold scarp above Mickleton, is a largely Victorian house, with an 18th-century portico which was moved piece by piece up from Mickleton Manor on a specially constructed light railway. Most of the garden was created in the years following the First World War, by Mrs Heather Muir, and she was no doubt helped and inspired by her neighbour and friend, Major Johnson, the creator of nearby Hidcote Manor Garden ★. Kiftsgate Garden's steep hillside setting is more dramatic than Hidcote's, and Mrs Muir took full advantage of this in her splendid design.

Mrs Muir's daughter and granddaughter, Mrs Binny and Mrs Chambers, have carried on the Kiftsgate tradition, and today the garden continues to evolve. There are paths, flower-beds, shrubs and trees on the terraced areas above the scarp, and a steep cliff with pine-trees, and winding paths leading to a swimming pool on a grassy terrace at its foot, with views down a wooded combe to the Vale of Evesham. Come here in summertime, when the air is heavy with the scent of roses, and the blue swimming pool, viewed through the pine-trees from the steep hillside above, brings a hint of the Mediterranean to this lovely garden enfolded in the Cotswold hills. Teas are available here. *(Tel: (0386) 438777.)*

The mapped **mini-walk** shown on page 79 passes Kiftsgate Court Garden on its way between Mickleton ★ and Hidcote Manor Garden ★.

The Kiftsgate Stone (151) (SP 13-38) *1 mi. W Chipping Campden.* This rather unexciting monolith lies half hidden in woodland just to the north-west of the road towards Broadway, on the hill to the west of Chipping Campden. It marks an ancient 'moot' or meeting place, where people used to gather to organise their affairs and dispense justice (often of a very rough nature), and this was in fact the original administrative centre of the Kiftsgate Hundred. 'Hundreds' were sub-divisions of shires, part of a system of local government which grew up in Saxon times, and one which was so firmly established by the time of the Norman Conquest that it was absorbed into the Norman framework of administration. Traditions attached to the Kiftsgate Stone itself were indeed so strong that its use ceased only in the years following the proclamation of George III in 1760, the last occasion which was celebrated here.

Kilkenny and Cold Common (163) (SP 00-18) *1½ mi. SW Andoversford.* Here at Cold Common on the A436, just to the west of the Kilkenny road junction, is a large car parking area, with information points. There are wide panoramic views out over the Severn Valley, and an attractive minor road running southwards into the Hilcot and Pinchley Woods area ★.

Kineton (163) (SP 09-26) *5 mi. E Winchcombe.* The attractions of this hamlet lie mainly in the two fords spanning the little tree-lined Windrush, which flows southwards from its source above Cutsdean ★. The southerly of the two fords is easily negotiated, but do not try the northerly one. There is a pleasant Donnington Brewery pub here — the Half Way House.

Head westwards from here to cross another ford, before arriving at the crossroads in miniature parkland which mark the start of our **Walk 3**. (See also Guiting Wood ★.)

Kingham (163) (SP 25-23) *4 mi. SW Chipping Norton.* Lively village in the broad Evenlode Valley, with wide greens at the northern end, and at the southern a very handsome 17th-century rectory. Beyond the rectory, the small tower of Kingham church looks out across the Evenlode meadows. The unusual stone pew-ends and backs were installed in the church as part of a restoration in 1853 and are elegant but rather stark. Do not miss the monument to the Rev. William Dowdeswell, who built the splendid rectory, nor the monument to Lieutenant-Colonel Davis, showing a soldier

Handsome 17th-century rectory at Kingham

leaning on his tomb with a reversed rifle. See also the brass to Katherine James (1588), depicting her kneeling figure surrounded by children.

Use the Oxfordshire Way ★ to walk westwards across the Evenlode Valley to Gawcombe and over to Wyck Rissington ★, or to walk southwards down the valley to Bruern Abbey ★ and Shipton-under-Wychwood ★.

King's Stanley (162) (SO 81-03) *2½ mi. W Stroud.* This village lies beneath the Cotswold edge and is rather overpowered by modern development. However, Messrs Marling and Evans's fine old Stanley Mill, which was built in the early years of the 19th century, continued to produce West of England Cloth here until the late 1980s. Happily the building still stands, but it is now used for the production of industrial felt. At the north end of the village there is a partly Norman church, in a churchyard with clipped yews.

Langford (163) (SP 24-02) *3 mi. NE Lechlade.* This quiet village looks southwards over flat Thames Valley farmland to the distant line of the Berkshire Downs beyond. Langford's church is a treasure house of early medieval art and architecture and should not be missed. Built into the south porch are a rare and beautiful Saxon carving of the Crucifixion, and a 14th-century carving with the figures of Mary and John. There are also other fascinating figures carved on the central tower, which itself was probably built by Saxon craftsmen working soon after the Norman Conquest. The Norman and Early English arches beneath the tower of this cruciform church are unusually lofty, and it is thought that its ambitious conception was possibly due to the parish having been in royal hands (as it certainly was by the time of the Domesday Survey of 1086). Do not miss a visit to this exceptionally interesting church.

Lark Stoke and Ilmington Downs (151) (SP 19-43) *1½ mi. W Ilmington.* At 850 feet above sea level, this is the highest point in Warwickshire, and one of the northern bastions of the Cotswolds. Despite the presence of a small TV transmitting station, this is still reasonably good walking country, and there are fine open views northwards out over the Avon valley, and eastwards to the wooded silhouette of Edge Hill and the rolling Northamptonshire uplands that lie beyond. Lark Stoke received a separate entry in the Domesday Book (1086), but there is now no trace of any ancient village on these windy hillsides, nor in the woodlands below.

Walk south from here to Ebrington ★, and then south-west to Chipping Campden ★; or make a small circular walk by taking in Hidcote Boyce ★ and Hidcote Bartrim, calling in of course at the splendid Hidcote Manor Garden ★. Motorists can use a narrow, partly unfenced road, leading up from the minor road between Ilmington ★ and Mickleton ★.

Lasborough (162) (ST 82-94) *4 mi. SW Nailsworth.* A fine 17th-century manor house and a small Victorian church overlook a quiet valley in which lies Lasborough Park, an 18th-century mansion built by James Wyatt. A drive or a walk as far as the church makes a pleasant diversion from the busy A46.

Latton (163) (SU 09-95) *1½ mi. NW Cricklade.* This small village lies on the Ermin Way ★ in water-meadow country near the union of the old Thames and Severn Canal with the Thames, with one of the canal's little 'round houses' nearby (see Hyde ★). The stout Norman church was restored by the renowned Victorian architect, William Butterfield, and as a result lacks any feeling of the medieval past. However, there are pleasant stone floors and an amusing series of corbel figures supporting the nave roof.

Laverton (150) (SP 07-35) *2 mi. SW Broadway.* Large hamlet beneath the Cotswold edge, with an attractive Post Office stores and several pleasant farmhouses. There are paths from here to Buckland ★ and Stanton ★, and a pleasant bridleway up the hill linking onto the Cotswold Way ★, and beyond to Snowshill ★.

Lechlade (163) (SU 21-99) *9 mi. S Burford.* Here on the southern borders of the Cotswolds, the Rivers Coln and Leach join the Thames, and Inglesham ★, just above Lechlade, marks the head of its navigation. After 1789 it was possible to tranship to narrow boats (see also Buscot ★), for it was in that year that the Thames and Severn Canal ★ was opened. It was also from Lechlade and nearby Radcot (163) (SU 28-99) that much of the stone quarried in the Burford area was shipped downriver for the building of St Paul's Cathedral and a multitude of other buildings in London and Oxford. Lechlade church was itself built almost entirely of

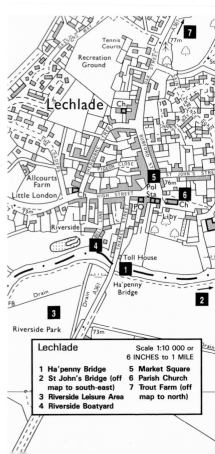

Lechlade	Scale 1:10 000 or 6 INCHES TO 1 MILE
1 Ha'penny Bridge	5 Market Square
2 St John's Bridge (off map to south-east)	6 Parish Church
3 Riverside Leisure Area	7 Trout Farm (off map to north)
4 Riverside Boatyard	

St John's Lock, Lechlade

wealth of pleasant 17th-, 18th- and early 19th-century buildings and are well worth visiting.

There is a *Trout Farm (7)* on the A361 just to the north of the town *(off map)*, beyond the River Leach and the flooded gravel pits beside it, one of the latter providing opportunities for sailing. These 'lakes' are at the far, eastern end of the Cotswold Water Park ★. Just beyond is the hamlet of Little Faringdon (163) (SP 22-01), which has a small Norman church with several interesting features, notably the sculptural details to its north arcade capitals — very probably by the same craftsman who worked at Langford ★, Fulbrook ★ and North Cerney ★.

In addition to the walk upstream from Ha'penny Bridge, referred to above, it is possible to walk south-eastwards across the meadows to St John's Bridge, where there is a cheerful inn, The Trout, and the highest lock on the Thames, St John's. (It is possible to link here onto the mapped **mini-walk** shown on page 40, to go down beside the river to Buscot ★ and Kelmscot ★.) St John's Lock is busy with colourful boats and boating people all summer long, and there is a fine view from here across the meadows to Lechlade Church.

Leckhampton (163) (SO 94-19) *1 mi. S Cheltenham.* This large suburb of Cheltenham is situated on its southern fringes beneath the steep quarries of Leckhampton Hill (see the Devil's Chimney ★). Despite Cheltenham's proximity it has retained a flavour of its own. The church of St Peter is pleasantly sited, with its slender 14th-century tower and spire viewed against a backdrop of the hills. Almost all the rest of the church was rebuilt in the 19th century, but there are interesting monuments to be seen, including the fine effigies of Sir John Giffard and his lady (1327), and the attractive brass of Elizabeth Norwood (1598), complete with husband, nine sons and two daughters. In the churchyard will be found a monument to Edward Wilson, one of Captain Scott's ill-fated companions on their journey to the South Pole in 1912.

Little Barrington (163) (SP 20-12) *3 mi. W Burford. (See map on page 66.)* A very pleasing village with most of its houses grouped around a sloping, bowl-shaped green, which was originally a quarry. At least two cottages have reset medieval stone doorways. The church, away from the centre on the east side of the village, has a Norman doorway and nave, and a Norman tympanum, depicting Christ in Majesty, over the outside of a blocked-up doorway in the north aisle. Do not miss the charming early 18th-century memorial tablet built into the outer east wall of the porch.

To the north-east of the village there is an inn of character called the Fox, which overlooks an old bridge across the Windrush built by local master-mason, Thomas Strong (see Burford ★). The Inn for All Seasons, an attractive hotel and restaurant, is situated about half a mile to the south, on the busy A40.

Use the **mini-walk** shown on the map on page 66 to walk via the Fox Inn to Great Barrington ★, returning via Barrington Mill to Little Barrington. The Fox Inn might make an alternative starting point, but only if the landlord would permit the parking of cars by those also intending to use the inn's services.

It is also possible to walk westwards from here

stone from Burford's neighbour, Taynton ★.

This small market town is still busy with the comings and goings of boats, but now they ply for pleasure only. There are two fine bridges here — 18th-century *Ha'penny Bridge (1)* with its little square tollhouse overlooking the boatyard at the southern end of the town, and *St John's Bridge (2)*, dating from as early as 1228, in meadows well to the south-east *(and therefore off map)*. In summertime, many boats moor on the river banks between the two bridges, and there is a busy *Riverside Parking and Leisure Area (3)* just upstream from Ha'penny Bridge, and reached from the A361 to its south. For those wishing for more tranquillity, small boats may be hired from the *Riverside Boatyard (4)* to explore the narrow, shallow river meandering past Inglesham ★ up towards Hannington Bridge (163) (SU 17-96). *(Tel: (0367) 52229.)* There is also a path leading south-westwards beside the south side of the river almost as far as the point where the Thames and Severn Canal joined the river. This is marked by a little 'round house' (see Hyde ★).

The town itself, which appears to make few other concessions to tourism, is centred upon its small triangular *Market Square (5)*. This is overlooked by dignified 18th- and early 19th-century buildings, including the handsome mellow brick New Inn, with its archway reminding the visitor that Lechlade was once a busy coaching stop. The Square is dominated from its far corner by Lechlade's fine Perpendicular *Parish Church (6)*, with its tower topped by a slender spire — described by the 16th-century antiquary John Leland in his famous *Itinerary* as a 'pratie pyramis of stone'. The interior is handsomely proportioned, with a high clerestory and a magnificent chancel roof with carved bosses. See also the beautifully carved door leading to the vestry, the 15th-century brass of wool merchant John Townsend and his wife, and the finely executed monument to Mrs Anne Simons (1769). It was the churchyard at Lechlade that inspired the poet Shelley to compose his *Summer Evening Meditation*, and there are few better places to stop awhile than this quiet corner.

Do not let the charms of the Square and the churchyard deter you from exploring the three streets that stem from here — Burford Street, running northwards, High Street to the west and St John Street to the east. All three are blessed with a across the fields to the village of Windrush ★, and from there northwards up the Windrush Valley to Great Rissington ★. For those not wishing to walk, there is a quiet little road down the Windrush Valley from Little Barrington to Burford ★, with beautiful views of the meandering river in the meadows beyond.

Little Compton (151) (SP 26-30) *4 mi. SE Moreton-in-Marsh.* Situated in a sheltered hollow between Barton Hill and the main Cotswold edge, this pleasant village, Warwickshire's southernmost, is over the watershed into the 'land of the Thames'. This great river may seem very far away, but the stream on which Little Compton lies flows west to join the Evenlode below Moreton-in-Marsh, where this river is itself near the start of its quiet journey to join the 'sweet Thames' just above Oxford. The little church retains its 14th-century tower with saddleback roof, but the rest of the building dates from the 1860s, and is not of great interest to visitors. In the churchyard there is a gravestone carved by one of the 20th century's outstanding sculptors, Eric Gill; a simple but fine example of his craft. The lovely 17th-century manor house next to the church was the home of Bishop Juxon, who had the unenviable task of attending Charles I at his trial and subsequent execution on the scaffold outside the Banqueting Hall, Whitehall. During their walk to this place of execution, Juxon was observed by the king to be weeping, and the king is supposed to have exclaimed, 'Leave all this my Lord; we have no time for it.' This terse comment appears at least to have stopped Juxon's tears, and after some years he received substantial consolation, for when his monarch's son Charles II was finally crowned in 1660, he was appointed Archbishop of Canterbury — a post he held until his death, sadly only three years later.

If you pass through Little Compton during 'opening hours', call at the Red Lion. This cheerful inn serves Donnington Ale — real ale which is brewed at the delectable little Donnington Brewery ★, a short distance to the north of Stow-on-the-Wold.

Walk northwards from Little Compton, on the quiet road over Barton Hill to Barton-on-the-Heath ★, or over the fields on a path parallel to the road, past Salter's Well Farm.

Little Rissington (163) (SP 19-19) *1½ mi. E Bourton-on-the-Water.* Situated on the eastern slopes of the Windrush valley, this small village has pleasant views out over several flooded gravel pits, some of which now provide nature reserves (see Bourton-on-the-Water ★). The church, which is approached by a pathway over fields, was restored twice in the 19th century and is not of great interest apart from its Norman south doorway. In the neat churchyard will be found the graves of several young men who were killed while flying from the great airfield on the hill above. This was once the RAF's Central Flying School, and the original home of the Red Arrows Display Team, but at the time of writing it is not in use.

There is a good bridle road southwards to Great Rissington ★, and it is also possible to walk northwards to Wyck Rissington ★, to link onto the Oxfordshire Way ★, or westwards, down to Bourton-on-the-Water ★, passing one of its gravel-pit lakes.

Little Rollright (151) (SP 29-30) *2 mi. NW Chipping Norton.* Here, in a quiet setting beneath the hills, are a fine 17th-century manor house, a modest rectory of the same period, a few cottages, and a delightful little church. This is a largely Perpendicular building, but its squat tower and south window date from the 17th century. It has a simple interior, with pleasant Perpendicular windows and two gorgeous 17th-century monuments — canopied tomb chests to members of the Dixon family which make it clear that the Dixons were persons of considerable substance, probably sheep graziers. Do not miss a visit to this very satisfying little building.

Although most visitors will arrive at the fascinating Rollright Stones ★ by car, it is also possible to reach them by walking north-eastwards over the fields from Little Rollright.

Little Washbourne (150) (SO 99-33) *4 mi. NW Winchcombe.* This small hamlet has a minute Norman church prettily sited in an orchard, with a bellcote and a completely unspoilt Georgian interior. There is a Norman chancel arch, and a Norman lancet window in the chancel, but the principal attractions of Little Washbourne church are its two-decker pulpit and its lovely 18th-century box pews, each with its own candle-holder. Visitors wishing to sample the simplicity of 18th-century England can do no better than to sit for a few moments in this charming little building.

Little Wolford (151) (SP 26-35) *4 mi. NE Moreton-in-Marsh.* A hamlet of Victorian estate cottages and unexciting council houses, situated in gently undulating countryside, with views towards the spires of Todenham ★ and Great Wolford ★, out over the valley through which the little Nethercote Brook flows, on its way to join the Stour a mile or so to the north. Any dullness is relieved by tantalising glimpses of Little Wolford's fine Tudor manor house. This is in a pleasing blend of stone and timber-framing — appropriate in an area which lies between the ancient forest country of Warwickshire and the bare stone uplands of the Oxfordshire Cotswolds. Walk south and east, up the valley, past Pepperwell and Kings Brake Farms, to Long Compton ★, and return via the open road across Weston Park ★.

Lodge Park (163) (SP 14-12) *2½ mi. SE Northleach.* This charming little mid-17th-century build-

Lodge Park, a 17th-century building with an unusual origin

ing standing in open wold country was commissioned by the hunchback John 'Crump' Dutton of nearby Sherborne Park ★. It was designed in the French style, probably by Valentine Strong, the Little Barrington quarry-owner, as a grandstand from which Dutton's guests could watch the coursing of deer by greyhounds. It was converted into a dwelling only in 1898, and has recently been bequeathed to the National Trust, along with most of the Sherborne Estate. It is hoped that this will be open to the public in 1994, but a glimpse through the handsome wrought-iron gates will give a foretaste of pleasures yet to come. Read more about Lodge Park in James Lees-Milne's delightful book, *Some Cotswold Country Houses*.

Longborough (163) (SP 17-29) *2½ mi. N Stow-on-the-Wold*. Attractively sited village on a hill slope looking out eastwards over the broad Evenlode Valley, with a pleasant inn called the Coach and Horses, many neat houses and cottages and a church with Norman origins which once belonged to Hailes Abbey ★. This has a 13th-century tower with an added upper stage in the best Perpendicular tradition, complete with pinnacles and gargoyles. The sunken path to the south porch is overlooked by the beautiful Decorated-style windows of the 14th-century south transept. This houses the very grand 17th-century monument to Sir William Leigh, complete with his wife and children, and a monument to a 14th-century knight and his lady, for whom this transept was probably built. The north transept, added after the demolition of nearby Sezincote church, is sealed off and houses the tomb of Sir Charles Cockerell, the builder of Sezincote ★. This church contains several other items of interest, but make a point of looking at the beautiful 14th-century font — a tall richly sculptured piece.

Walk north from here to Sezincote ★, and on to Bourton-on-the Hill ★ and Batsford ★, with fine views out over the Evenlode Valley from many points along the way.

Long Compton (151) (SP 28-32) *4 mi. NW Chipping Norton*. This attractive stone village stretches out along the A3400 for over half a mile, to the very foot of the long hill that climbs up over the Cotswold edge, across the county boundary

from Warwickshire into Oxfordshire. There is considerable modern building at its northern end, and the main road is always busy with traffic; but despite this Long Compton has much to offer. It has a cheerful inn, many trim houses and cottages, and a church whose handsome Perpendicular tower looks westwards out over a large bumpy field which must have been the site of the original village. The church's lovely south porch is approached by a yew-lined path leading from a delightful little two-storeyed lychgate, which is believed to be a small timber-framed cottage with its lower storey removed. The core of the church is 13th-century, but externally it appears to be almost entirely Perpendicular. See the nave roof, the charming little Perpendicular south aisle chapel, and in the porch the pathetically worn effigy of a lady. For a full account of life at Long Compton and in the countryside that surrounds it, read Edward Rainsberry's delightful book, *Through the Lych Gate*, published by the Roundwood Press, but unfortunately now out of print.

The best walk from Long Compton leads across fields north-eastwards to Whichford ★, skirting the southern edge of the great Whichford Wood. There is also a good walk leading south-westwards over a spur of the hills, and down into Little Compton ★.

Lower Lemington (151) (SP 21-34) *1½ mi. NE Moreton-in-Marsh*. This is now no more than a quiet little hamlet with a farm, a few houses and a small church — all spread around an open field-cum-farmyard. However, the undulating fields surrounding it conceal the remains of a larger medieval village, and on the road to its south there is a substantial 16th- and 17th-century manor house. The little church in its stone-walled churchyard has a small bellcote where the nave roof meets that of the chancel, and a narrow Norman doorway within its porch. The chancel was damaged during the Civil War, but the exceptionally narrow Norman chancel arch, with minute squints on either side, has survived. There are pleasant old Commandment Boards, an early Norman tub font, an 18th-century two-decker pulpit and a small 17th-century brass to two brothers, Charles and Peter Greville.

Lower Slaughter (163) (SP 16-22) *1½ mi. N Bourton-on-the-Water*. Most of this delightful and

The Slaughters

SCALE 1:25 000 or 2½ INCHES to 1 MILE

Waterside cottages at Lower Slaughter

much visited village seems to have been planted upon the banks of its stream, the little River Eye, the two sides of which are linked by a series of small, simply built bridges. The water-mill with its pond and its mellow brick chimney provides a fitting entrance for the stream, whose departure is marked by graceful willows, as it hurries away to join the River Dikler just to the east of Bourton-on-the-Water. The manor house, now much altered, was built in about 1650 by Valentine Strong, the quarry-owner of Little Barrington, and in its grounds is one of Gloucestershire's largest dovecots. The nearby church was rebuilt in 1867 and is not of great interest to visitors.

With mixed success this village, with its attractive village shop tucked away at the rear of the mill, has tried hard to resist repeated attempts to commercialise its undeniable charms. Use our mapped **mini-walk** to explore both Lower and Upper Slaughter, which are linked by a delightful footpath beside the little River Eye. There is another pleasant walk from here, southwards across the fields to Bourton-on-the-Water ★.

Lower Swell (163) (SP 17-25) *1 mi. W Stow-on-the-Wold.* Much of this tidy, well built village is astride the still-busy B4068 road, once the main Stow to Cheltenham road. It has a pleasant 17th-century inn, the Golden Ball, and a small hotel close by. In the valley at its eastern end there is a bridge over the little River Dikler, which has here just completed its short journey through the park of Abbotswood, a fine early 20th-century house designed by Sir Edwin Lutyens. Abbotswood Gardens are particularly lovely and may possibly be open to the public on one or two Sunday afternoons. To the left of the road up to Stow, a short distance beyond the bridge, will be found Spa Cottages, built in a slightly oriental style and thought to have been inspired by S.P. Cockerell's work at Sezincote ★. There is an inscription on one of them stating that a chalybeate spring was discovered here in 1807, and it was intended that this feature should be the basis for a spa — a plan that never fully materialised.

Lower Swell's church lies to the north of the village, on the road to Upper Swell. The original Norman building now forms the south aisle and this still retains the former Norman chancel arch, which

is enriched with a splendid series of animal carvings. The Norman south doorway is equally interesting, and has a tympanum above it depicting a dove eating fruit from a 'tree of life'.

Marston Meysey (163) (SU 12-97) *3 mi. SW Fairford.* A long, thin village in flat country not far from the monstrous runway of Fairford airfield, once used by Concorde in the years of its flight testing. The church is Victorian and not of great interest to visitors, but there are many lovely old tombs in its churchyard. Well to the south of the village there is one of the 'round houses' built for the

Cherubs in the churchyard at Marston Meysey

maintenance men of the long-vanished Thames and Severn Canal ★. This is reached on foot from Marston Meysey, and there is a path beyond, across water-meadows to Castle Eaton on the Thames.

Maugersbury (163) (SP 20-25) *½ mi. SE Stow-on-the-Wold.* Quiet hamlet on the south-eastern slopes of Stow-on-the-Wold's hill, with pleasant views across to Icomb Hill. There are several pleasant farmhouses, but no features of special interest apart from St Edward's Well (SP 19-24). This is situated in an overgrown late 18th-century garden (on private ground) on either side of the road between the village and the Foss Way, and connected by a tunnel under the road. It is not certain with which St Edward the well is supposed to be connected — Edward, King and Martyr, Edward the Confessor, or Edward the Hermit — the latter being a shadowy local figure from early Christian times. The same mystery surrounds this 'St Edward connection' at Stow-on-the-Wold ★.

There is a good bridle road southwards from Maugersbury to Icomb ★.

Meysey Hampton (163) (SU 11-99) *2 mi. W Fairford.* This very trim village has a semi-circular green overlooked by a small inn, the Mason's Arms, and a fine Georgian manor house. The 13th-century cruciform church was probably built by the Knights Templar and is a neat-looking building. Within its rather cold interior will be found four well sculptured tower arches, handsome triple sedilia with a piscina in a fourth niche, and a very engaging 17th-century monument incorporating the effigy of physician James Vaulx, plus those of his two wives and their many offspring. Vaulx, a doctor with a considerable reputation, was once asked by James

I, who was considering a change of physician, how he had come by his great skill. But when he was told by Vaulx that he had acquired it by practice, that somewhat dour monarch is supposed to have replied, 'Then, by my soul, thou hast killed many a man and shalt na' practise on me.' Alas, poor Vaulx!

Mickleton (151) (SP 16-43) *3 mi. N Chipping Campden.* This busy, almost town-like, village has considerable modern development on its fringes, and is rather disturbed by traffic on the still-busy B4632. However, it lies in an attractive setting immediately beneath the Cotswold edge, and has several attractive stone houses and cottages in addition to those of thatch and half-timber. The little Victorian Memorial Fountain close by the Three Ways Hotel is an attractive feature — an unusually restrained piece of work by William Burges, the architect of Cardiff Castle and Castle Coch, two supreme examples of the High Victorian Gothic.

Turn up beside handsome 'Cotswold-Queen-Anne' style Medford House, to visit the church, which lies on the southern edge of the village, with pleasant views up towards the wooded Cotswold edge. This has a fine 14th-century tower and spire, and a most unusual 17th-century two-storeyed porch. Inside will be found a 12th-century crucifix or rood (over the north aisle chapel altar), some stout, late Norman arcading, and a monument to the 18th-century architect, builder and quarry-owner, Thomas Woodward of Chipping Campden, erected by his grandson, Edward. There is considerable evidence of Victorian restoration in the shape of the east window and most of the woodwork, but Mickleton church has retained an atmosphere that makes a visit here well worth while.

The attractive though challenging mapped **mini-walk** leads up the hill from the church to Kiftsgate ★, Hidcote Manor Garden ★ at Hidcote Bartrim, and then up onto Ilmington Downs, before going down again through Hidcote Boyce ★ to return to Mickleton. This walk may be shortened by cutting across to Hidcote Boyce from Hidcote Bartrim. There is also a walk leading southwards, over the hill to Chipping Campden ★, passing close to the southern entrance to Campden Railway Tunnel ★.

Middle Duntisbourne (163) (SO 98-06) *4 mi. NW Cirencester.* A disappointing hamlet in the lovely Duntisbourne Valley, with a rather deep ford overlooked by scrappy farm buildings.

Milton-under-Wychwood (163) (SP 26-18) *4 mi. N Burford.* This widespread village in the broad valley of the Evenlode has much modern development on its fringes, and a church designed by G.E.Street, the Victorian architect perhaps best known for his work on the Law Courts in the Strand. Church, lychgate, school and school-house all bear witness to his very considerable skill. The long village street beyond the Quart Pot Inn has a series of shops and houses, but apart from the little stone bull's head above the butcher's shop, there is nothing of exceptional interest here.

Minchinhampton (162) (SO 86-00) *1½ mi. NE Nailsworth.* Situated on the eastern fringes of Minchinhampton Common ★, high above valleys once prosperous with the production of cloth, this is an especially attractive little Cotswold town. It is centred upon its High Street and old Market Square, the chief features of which are the late 17th-century Market House supported on stone columns, the handsome Crown Hotel, and the Post Office, a genuine Queen Anne building.

The interesting church, with its truncated spire, looks out over the Market Square, but at the same time stands slightly aloof from it. It was given to Caen's Abbaye aux Dames by William the Conqueror, and then in 1415 passed to Syon Abbey, in whose hands it remained until the Dissolution. The present building dates from the 12th century and is full of interest. See especially the fine 14th-century south transept with its Decorated-style tomb recesses and effigies, and the vaulting beneath the tower. There is also an outstanding series of

Mickleton and Hidcote

SCALE 1:25 000 or 2½ INCHES to 1 MILE

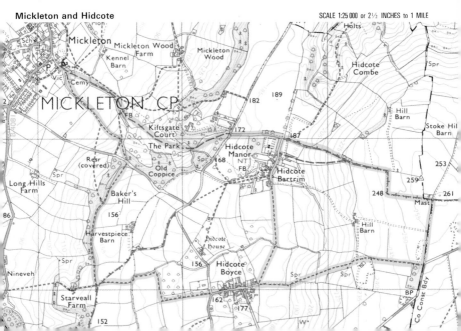

The Market Square, Minchinhampton

monumental brasses.

There are old cloth mills in the valleys to the south, notably at Ball's Green (162) (SO 86-99) where the great Longfords Lake once provided water for power and washing at Longfords Mill. See also Hampton Fields ★ and Gatcombe Park ★

Minchinhampton Common (162) (SO 85-01) *1 mi. NW Minchinhampton.* Owned by the National Trust, this 590-acre sweep of turf country is situated high up between the deep Frome and Nailsworth Valleys. It is a favourite with walkers and horse riders alike, and there are fine views on every side and interesting archaeological remains, including The Bulwarks, parts of an Iron Age defensive system, and Amberley Camp, an Iron Age settlement. Whitfield's Tump is a long barrow, so named because it was from here that one of the founders of Methodism, the famous preacher George Whitfield, addressed a large crowd in 1743, despite having been assaulted in Minchinhampton a few hours earlier.

Minster Lovell (164) (SP 31-10) *2½ mi. W Witney.* A trim stone and thatch village set in the lovely Windrush Valley, with a small hotel called the Old Swan not far from its bridge across the stream. The church, standing at the eastern end of the village, was once in company with a small priory (hence the village's name), but this was dissolved in 1414, as it had by then become an alien house in the ownership of Ivry Abbey in distant Normandy. The fine cruciform, 15th-century church has beautiful vaulting beneath its central tower, and some benches and stained glass both of which may be contemporary with the church. See also the tomb of a knight — probably William Lovell, the builder not only of the church, but also of the adjoining manor house.

The splendid 15th-century manor house of the Lovells, Minster Lovell Hall, has been a ruin since it was dismantled in 1747, but its setting on the willow-bordered banks of the Windrush is incomparable and it is well maintained in its present form by English Heritage. It was built as a fortified manor house, much like a small castle, and its quarters, ranged around a quadrangle, include a great hall with solar and kitchens. Its circular dovecot is situated in an adjoining farmyard and is also open to the public.

Francis, the 13th Lord Lovell, was associated with the ill-fated Lambert Simnell Rising in 1487, and following its failure it is thought that he sought refuge in a secret room at Minster Lovell. The location of this room was apparently known only to one trusted servant, and when he suddenly died, his master was trapped, and in due course starved to death. During repairs to the house in 1708 the skeletons of a man and a dog were found in a secret room, and this discovery appears to bear out the story of Lord Lovell's disappearance — unless it was thought up by the 1708 repairers to explain their macabre find, in a similar manner to the story of the Bisley Boy (see Bisley ★).

Another of the village's Lords of the Manor also met an unpleasant (but in this case well-deserved) end — on the gallows. This was a certain Mr Freeman, who lived here in some style in the early

Minster Lovell

SCALE 1:25 000 or 2½ INCHES to 1 MILE

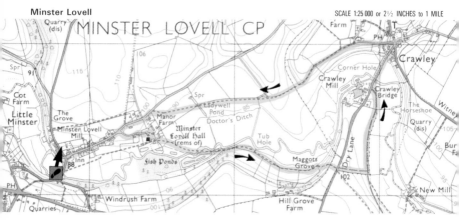

Miserden and Winstone

SCALE 1:25 000 or 2½ INCHES to 1 MILE

1800s, until it was discovered that he was the highwayman responsible for a large number of hold-ups on the toll roads of Oxfordshire and the Cotswolds.

By using our mapped **mini-walk** it is possible to walk from the car park well to the south-west of the Old Swan Hotel, up the village street, through the churchyard beyond the far side of the manor house ruins, and soon over a footbridge crossing the Windrush. From here the walk goes down the valley to the delightful little village of Crawley and then returns over slightly higher ground to Minster Lovell. This walk is nearly three miles long, but well worth while.

Minster Lovell Hall . . . romantic ruins beside the Windrush

Miserden (163) (SO 93-08) *7 mi. NW Cirencester.* A very trim, largely 19th- and 20th-century village, with a small octagonal shelter built around a massive sycamore tree and overlooked by the hospitable Carpenter's Arms (noted for its cold buffet). The church, standing in a churchyard enriched with yew and beech, has late Saxon origins but was heavily restored in the 1880s. See especially the elaborately carved and gilded reredos and the splendid series of 17th-century monuments. The war memorial was designed by Sir Edwin Lutyens, who also carried out extensive work at Misarden Park, an Elizabethan mansion overlooking the wooded Frome Valley to the immediate east of the village. The lovely gardens surrounding the house are normally open on Wednesdays and Thursdays throughout the summer. At nearby Anvil

Barn the local blacksmith works not only in iron and steel, but also in copper and bronze. It is possible to visit his forge and showrooms. *(Tel: (028582) 244.)*

There are the earthworks of a motte and bailey castle in the valley to the immediate west of the

Springtime at Misarden Park

River Frome. These probably mark the site of a castle built soon after the Norman Conquest, and already ruined by the end of the 13th century. Our mapped **mini-walk** uses a path from Miserden, eastwards across the valley to Winstone ★, passing close to these earthworks, but they are on private land. This walk returns to Miserden through parts of Misarden Park — please keep to right-of-way. There is also a longer walk southwards to Edgeworth ★, linking there with our **Walk 10**.

Moreton-in-Marsh (151) (SP 20-32) *4 mi. N Stow-on-the-Wold.* The intrepid late 17th-century traveller and diarist, Celia Fiennes (see also Broughton and Broughton Castle ★) visited Moreton several times, as she had a widowed aunt living there. Her succinct description of 'Morton Hindmost' as 'a little neate stone built town, good Innes for traveller' could hardly be bettered today. As Mistress Celia pointed out, it lay on the main route from London and Oxford to the cities of Worcester and Hereford, and the centre of Wales; and this probably accounted even more strongly for Moreton's prosperity than did its position astride the Foss Way.

It appears that this 'little neate stone built town' was also once called Moreton Henmarsh, the

81

Moreton-in-Marsh

Henmarsh being low-lying country much frequented by coots and moorhens; but we still find Celia's 'Morton Hindmost' an even more endearing name. The origins of the town are somewhat obscure, but the oldest part grew up around the church, a former chapel of ease for nearby Bourton-on-the-Hill ★. The present *Parish Church (1)*, lying to the east of the High Street, and south of Oxford Street, is almost entirely Victorian, and is not of great interest to visitors. However, the elegant 18th-century house to its immediate east should not be overlooked.

Almost all of interest in Moreton-in-Marsh is situated on its High Street, with a series of stone built shops, houses and coaching inns facing each other across the broad Foss Way, but divided by incessant traffic passing along it between the Midlands and the South-West. The Manor House Hotel and the Redesdale Arms are both pleasing buildings, and the White Hart Royal Hotel claims the distinction of having provided shelter for Charles I — on 2 July 1644. The little 16th-century *Curfew Tower (2)* on the corner of Oxford Street

has a bell dated 1633, and this was rung each evening until as recently as 1860. On the other side of the High Street is the dominant feature of Moreton-in-Marsh, the confidently neo-Tudor *Redesdale Market Hall (3)*, built in 1887 to the designs of Sir Ernest George, who was soon to carry out a similar commission for Lord Redesdale — the design of a 'Cotswold-Elizabethan' mansion, at nearby Batsford Park ★.

The coming to Moreton in 1843 of Brunel's Oxford, Worcester and Wolverhampton Railway brought a connection with the outside world that some of Moreton's neighbours must have envied at the time, and a certain robust quality appears to have survived here to this day (see also the Stratford and Moreton Tramway ★). So despite the traffic, do take time off to walk down both sides of Moreton's long High Street — there are several interesting and attractive shops, and the tree-lined greens at the northern end are especially pleasing.

The best walk from Moreton-in-Marsh is north-westwards, up over the hills to Blockley ★, skirting the southern edge of Batsford Park ★, and possibly calling in to look round the Batsford Park Arboretum ★. To make a long circular walk, move south-west from Blockley, via Dovedale and Bourton Downs, to Hinchwick ★, and then head east, making some use of public roads to return to Moreton, skirting to the south of Sezincote ★.

Nag's Head (163) (ST 89-98) *3 mi. E Nailsworth.* This delightful little hamlet takes its name from an inn that used to be here. It has a row of small houses looking southwards over a quiet valley, some with interesting architectural detail. Walk eastwards from here, over the fields to Cherington ★, and beyond to Hazelton ★ and Rodmarton ★.

Nailsworth (162) (ST 84-99) *4 mi. S Stroud.* The centre of this modest cloth town stands at the union of two valleys, and is much dominated by the busy A46. There is a mid-20th-century clock tower in its centre and its old cloth mills have been put to new uses. Egypt Mill, on the A46, has been restored, with two of its great water-wheels and attendant gearing, and is now a restaurant. On the slopes above the valley bottoms there are a multitude of attractive streets and alleyways, which will amply repay those who explore on foot. See especially the steep little Chestnut Hill, with Stokes Croft at its foot, and the Quaker Meeting House a short distance beyond — both attractive 17th-century buildings. Also do not miss a visit to the Selsley Herb Shop at 4, George Street, by the side of the river and overlooking the clock tower. The late Victorian church is not of great interest to visitors.

It is possible to walk southwards from here, over open hill country to Chavenage ★ and Beverston ★.

Naunton (163) (SP 11-23) *5 mi. W Stow-on-the-Wold.* This is a delightful, elongated village, spread out along the floor of the deep Windrush Valley, and looking like a model from the B4068 above. The church has a handsome Perpendicular tower with pinnacles and gargoyles, and although time has not dealt as kindly with the interior as it might have, this has a beautifully carved early 15th-century stone pulpit and an interesting font of the same period. There are two small 17th-century brasses in the chancel

Map

Moreton-in-Marsh
Scale 1:10 000 or
6 INCHES to 1 MILE
1 Parish Church   3 Market Hall
2 Curfew Tower

Naunton . . . a village sheltering in the lovely Windrush Valley

and a wall tablet to Ambrose Oldys who died in 1710, with 'better fortune' than his father Dr William, who, the tablet relates, was 'barbarously murdered by ye rebells' in 1645.

Rest awhile at the little bridge over the Windrush near the lovely Old Rectory, before walking down the village to the hospitable Black Horse Inn, passing on the way a charming 17th-century dovecot overlooking the stream to the right.

Walk north-west from here, up the Windrush Valley to Guiting Power ★, or south-east to Harford Bridge ★ and then down the Windrush Valley to Bourton-on-the-Water ★.

Nether Lypiatt Manor (162) (ST 87-03) *2 mi. SE Stroud.* An especially lovely 17th-century manor house standing close to a minor road junction, and looking westwards over Stroud from a hilly edge. It is owned by Prince and Princess Michael of Kent. Read more about this house and its various fascinating owners in James Lees-Milne's delightful book, *Some Cotswold Country Houses.*

Newark Park (162) (ST 78-93) *2 mi. E Wotton-under-Edge.* This was originally a hunting lodge, built in Elizabethan times by the Poyntz family, on the edge of a cliff looking eastwards over the valley of Ozleworth Bottom. It was converted in 1790 into a four-square castellated country house by the redoubtable architect, James Wyatt, who provided a new south front incorporating a Gothick porch. Owned by the National Trust, it is being rehabilitated by the Trust's tenant. *(Tel: (0453) 842644.)*

Gothick porch at Newark Park

Newington Bagpath (162) (ST 81-94) *4 mi. E Wotton-under-Edge.* Minute hamlet in a quiet valley overlooked by the circular earthworks of a medieval castle and a small church beside them. Visitors may find this isolated church locked and the churchyard will probably be overgrown. However, there are pleasant views over the valley and a feeling of utter tranquillity not often encountered today. The church's squat tower has an attractively hipped roof, and there is a Jacobean pulpit together with medieval choir stalls and reredos. Little else appears to have survived the restoration of 1858.

There is a fine circular walk from here taking in Lasborough ★ and Ozleworth ★.

North Cerney (163) (SP 02-07) *4 mi. N Cirencester.* Pleasant village in the Churn Valley, with the hospitable Bathurst Arms set in a streamside garden and looking across the busy A435 to the little saddleback tower of a largely Norman church. This was exquisitely restored and refurnished in the early years of the 20th century, thanks to the generosity of Mr W.I. Croome. Much of this work was carried out under the direction of F.C. Eden, the fruits of whose peculiar genius the writer first encountered at the village of Blisland on the remote western fringes of Bodmin Moor. Eden's work includes the porch gates, three stained-glass windows, a vestment press, the rood loft and screen, and the reredos. See also the Norman south doorway, the roof with its fascinating corbel figures of monks, kings and queens, the handsome gallery, the fine 15th-century stone pulpit, the beautiful medieval glass, and the lovely 18th-century monument to William Tyndale in the Lady Chapel. This list tells but half the story, so be prepared to spend time here — it will be well rewarded.

There is a fine late 17th-century rectory opposite the church, and handsome Cerney House is just beyond. It is possible to walk northwards from this village, beside the River Churn to Rendcomb ★, or southwards to Baunton ★.

Northleach (163) (SP 11-14) *10 mi. NE Cirencester.* In the Middle Ages this was one of the Cotswolds' most important wool trading centres and acknowledged only Cirencester and Chipping Campden as its superiors. Situated in the valley of the infant River Leach just to the east of the Foss Way, and now happily bypassed by the busy A40, this attractive little town has regained the tranquillity it enjoyed before the coming of the motor car. It is now probably less busy than it was in the days following Thomas Telford's diversion of the main road to bring coaches through the town — a move that placed it on the great coaching route between London, Oxford, Gloucester and South Wales. The town's small square stands just above the road, to the east of the church, and is a focal point of the modest High Street, itself lined with pleasant houses, shops and inns dating from the 16th to the early 19th century, a few of them half-timbered. The Dutton Almshouses 'for women' were built by Thomas Dutton of neighbouring Sherborne ★ in 1616, and of special interest to visitors is **Keith Harding's World of Mechanical Music** at Oak House in the High Street, where there are regular demonstrations of mechanical musical instruments, musical boxes and automata. *(Tel: (0451) 60181.)*

But this little town is dominated by its magnificent 'wool church' which was entirely rebuilt in the

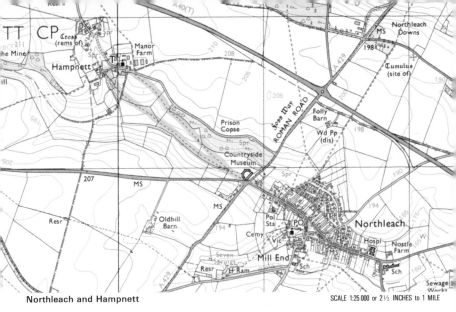

Northleach and Hampnett

SCALE 1:25 000 or 2½ INCHES to 1 MILE

15th century — a splendid example of the Perpendicular style. It has a fine tower and the elegantly pinnacled south porch is one of the finest in England. The interior is beautifully proportioned and well lit by clerestory windows. Its contents include a lovely 15th-century goblet-shaped pulpit, and new seating designed by Sir Basil Spence, and made in the furniture workshops of Gordon Russell in Broadway ★. The outstanding monumental brasses commemorate the great wool merchants of Northleach, men whose wealth rebuilt the church and enriched its fabric — Thomas Busshe, Merchant of the Staple of Calais, John Taylour, Thomas Parker, William Midwinter, John Fortey and Thomas Fortey. These families grew rich on trading in Cotswold wool, and many of them enjoyed a significant position not only in the commerce of England, but in that of Europe generally.

Northleach

At the Cotswold Countryside Collection, Northleach

At the crossing on the Foss Way, just to the west of the town, there is a late 18th-century 'house of correction' or prison. This was built by the philanthropist and prison reformer, Sir George Onesiphorus Paul, a member of the prosperous family of Huguenot clothiers from Woodchester, who built Highgrove House at Doughton ★, the present home of the Prince of Wales. Sir George was also the builder of three other similar prisons, but despite his reforming zeal a treadmill was still installed at Northleach and this must have provided a punishing means of exercise for the still unfortunate prisoners. The prison building now houses a most interesting museum of rural life, including a restored 18th-century cell block, and this museum is known as the **Cotswold Countryside Collection**. *(Tel: (0451) 60715.)* There is also a small Tourist Information Centre here.

Use our mapped **mini-walk** to go north-west from here up beside the little River Leach to its source on Hampnett ★ village green, and return over slightly higher ground. It is also possible to walk south-eastwards down the valley to Eastington ★.

North Leigh Roman Villa (164) (SP 39-15) *3½ mi. W Woodstock.* Situated in gentle wooded countryside, not far from the banks of the River Evenlode, are the remains of a large 4th-century Roman villa

Mosaic pavement at North Leigh Roman Villa

on a site first occupied in the 1st century. First excavated as long ago as 1813, these remains (in the care of English Heritage) surround a courtyard and include living quarters with mosaics and a bath. It is possible to walk northwards from here, over the Evenlode to Stonesfield, a village once noted for its Cotswold stone tiles.

North Nibley (162) (ST 74-95) *2 mi. SW Dursley.* This small village is situated just below the Tyndale Monument ★, and claims, like Slimbridge ★, to be the birthplace of William Tyndale, the priest who first translated the New Testament into English. It has a largely Perpendicular church on its western edge, with fine views over to Stinchcombe Hill. This building has an unusually attractive 19th-century French-Gothic chancel, which was designed by J.L. Pearson, the architect best known for his creation of Truro Cathedral. Do not miss the 17th-century wall monument to Grace Smyth complete with coloured heraldry.

There is a path south-eastwards, up the hill by the Tyndale Monument ★, and southwards past the woodlands which contain the extensive earthworks of an Iron Age settlement known as Brackenbury Ditches.

Northwick Park (151) (SP 16-36) *1 mi. N Blockley.* A large 16th- and 17th-century mansion built on the site of a vanished medieval village, in a great park on the slopes of the hills to the north of Blockley. It has an east front built in 1732 to the designs of the great advocate of Palladianism, Lord Burlington, and both house and outbuildings have now been extensively restored and converted into houses and flats. The nearby encampment, built during the last war, is now used as a 'business centre', and although not of great beauty, provides valuable local employment.

Notgrove (163) (SP 10-20) *3 mi. N Northleach.* Situated in high wold country, but just sheltered from the worst excesses of the north winds, this modest village spreads thinly around a rough green, with church and rebuilt manor house at its southern edge. These two buildings are at the end of a tree-lined driveway and both look out over a valley containing the headwaters of the little Sherborne Brook, which rises in the village. The small, stone spired, largely Norman church has a primitive Saxon crucifix on its exterior south wall, while the heavily restored interior is enlivened by a colourful 20th-century tapestry representing the outline of the reredos that it covers. There is Norman arcading, a Norman tub font, two effigies of medieval priests, and a large monument to various members of the Whittington family, the descendants of Sir Richard (Dick) Whittington.

The best walk from here runs south-westwards to Hazleton ★.

Notgrove Long Barrow (163) (SP 09-21) *4 mi. N Northleach, 1½ mi. NW Notgrove.* In the care of English Heritage, this long barrow is situated in high country to the immediate south of the A436. Most of the earth covering the burial chambers has long been removed, and the massive stones that remain provide an interesting impression of what the gallery and chambers must once have looked like. However, for 'prehistoric flavour' most visitors will still prefer Belas Knap ★ and Hetty Pegler's Tump ★.

Nympsfield (162) (SO 80-00) *4 mi. NE Dursley.* Small village sheltering near the head of a valley just to the east of the Cotswold edge. It used to lie on the Gloucester-Bath coach route and in the mid-18th century there were no fewer than five inns here. The pleasant Rose and Crown Inn has survived to this day, and this is not far from the 19th-century church, which has a Perpendicular tower complete with gargoyles, a turret stair and a handsome clock-face. The nearby Nympsfield Long Barrow (SO 79-01) (in the care of English Heritage) is open to the sky, and provides a good opportunity to see the layout of a typical Cotswold long barrow. This can best be visited from the nearby Coaley Peak Picnic Site ★.

Oakridge (163) (SO 91-03) *4 mi. E Stroud.* Small village above the steep slopes of the Golden Valley ★, with its views southwards marred by massive aircraft hangars on the skyline. At the south-western end of the village, below a pleasant triangular green, is the church, which was built in 1837 when Thomas Keble held the living here. It has a lofty, well restored interior, but no features of outstanding interest to the visitor.

Oddington (163) (SP 22-25) *2½ mi. E Stow-on-the-Wold.* An attractive village spread thinly on the lower slopes of the hill between Stow and the River Evenlode, and made up of Upper and Lower Oddington. It has several very pleasant houses including early 17th-century Oddington House, which was extensively remodelled in the early 19th century, and the nearby Old Rectory, which has had very much the same history. There are two inns, the Fox in 'Lower', and the Horse and Groom in 'Upper'. There is also an unassuming mid-19th-

Oddington Old Church . . . a remarkably unspoilt interior

century 'new' church, but the village's best feature is some way off.

This is the old church of St Nicholas, which lies by itself at the end of a quiet road south of the village, although there is a long bridleway onwards from here to Bledington ★. It is also on the course of our **Walk 5**. This remote church has had a number of illustrious owners, ranging from the Abbot of Gloucester to the Archbishop of York, and various kings of England, and it is known that Henry II stayed at Oddington several times. This distinguished ownership resulted in relatively ambitious building in the 13th and 14th centuries, and thanks to its being largely unused in the 19th century, it has remained wonderfully unspoilt. See especially the Jacobean pulpit on its turned newel post, the lovely old chancel roof, the 15th-century font and Oddington's greatest treasure — its extensive and horrific late 14th-century 'Doom' wall painting. A few minutes' study of this fascinating relic of medieval times will show how easy it must have been for the clergy of the day to keep their primitive flock in a truly 'God-fearing' frame of mind.

Owlpen (162) (ST 80-98) *3 mi. E Dursley*. A delightful group of buildings in a deep hollow beneath woodlands. Here is a fine 15th-century manor house with 16th-, 17th- and 18th-century alterations, a small Victorian church above it, and a little 18th-century mill not far away. All this is framed by clipped yews and backed by steep woods above — a perfect example of a small Cotswold estate.

The present condition of the manor house owes much to the work of the architect Norman Jewson, a disciple of Ernest Gimson and the Barnsley brothers (see Daneway ★), who bought and res-

Church and Manor House at Owlpen

tored it in the 1920s, but who then sadly could not afford to live in it. *It is not open to the public.* The interior of the nearby church is enriched by much painting and mosaic work, and there are no fewer than eight monumental brasses to members of the Daunt family, dating from 1542 to as late as 1803. Read more about Owlpen in James Lees-Milne's most interesting book, *Some Cotswold Country Houses*.

There is a pleasant walk from here, northwards to the village of Nympsfield ★.

Oxfordshire Circular Walks Reference to these walks will be found on Landranger Sheets 163 and 164, amongst others. One of these is a walk with many varying circuits around the Windrush Valley to the west of Witney — from 2½ to 13 miles in length. *(Details of this and other Oxfordshire Circular Walks may be obtained from the Oxfordshire County Council, Department of Leisure and Arts, The Countryside Service, The Library Service H. Q., Holton, Oxford OX9 1QQ.)*

The Oxfordshire Way This 65-mile field path links the Cotswolds and the Chilterns. It starts from Bourton-on-the-Water, and then heads through or past Wyck Rissington, Bledington, and Shipton-under-Wychwood. From here it runs down the Evenlode Valley, passing Charlbury, North Leigh Roman Villa, and the northern edge of Blenheim Park, before leaving the area covered by this guide, on its way to the Chilterns. *(Guides to this walk are published by the CPRE, and by the Oxfordshire County Council — see Oxfordshire Walks, above.)*

Ozleworth (162) (ST 79-93) *2½ mi. E Wotton-under-Edge*. This small group of buildings is situated in a delightfully quiet, well wooded valley overlooked by both the National Trust's Newark Park ★ and a tall but less beautiful concrete communications tower. It is possible to walk up the short drive towards handsome 18th-century Ozleworth Park and round behind it to visit the little Norman church. Standing in a circular churchyard, this has a very rare central hexagonal tower. Ozleworth Bottom, the valley running south-westwards from here, once sheltered several watermills. These were first used for the grinding of corn or fulling, but in the 16th and 17th centuries they were converted into cloth mills. Little trace of these now remains.

Walk eastwards from Ozleworth, up another beautifully wooded valley to Lasborough ★ and Newington Bagpath ★.

Painswick (162) (SO 86-09) *3 mi. N Stroud*. Painswick is situated on a high spur between two valleys, with a series of old mills on the stream in the valley to its south-west. These mills were once used for the production of cloth, and it was both the wool trade and the dyed-cloth industry that brought prosperity to this delightful little town in the 17th and 18th centuries, the latter witnessing its peak. The dyeing of cloth had become a speciality here owing to the purity of its streams and especially its spring water.

Before starting to explore the town try to pay a visit to the Tourist Information Centre at the Library to the south-west of the church, on Stroud Road. *(Tel: (0452) 813552.)* The church's 15th-century tower is topped by a fine 17th-century spire, and also houses a peal of twelve bells. The interior, with its vaulted nave ceiling and painted chancel ceiling, is remarkably uncluttered. It does, however, contain a number of interesting monuments including a 15th-century tomb-chest in Purbeck marble in St Peter's Chapel. This was used for a second time for the body of Sir William Kingston, Constable of the Tower of London at the time when the unfortunate Anne Boleyn was beheaded. The third and final users of the tomb lie upon it in effigy — 17th-century Doctor John Seaman and his wife, with a pile of law books between them.

However, it is Painswick's churchyard that is bound to attract the majority of visitors. Here is a splendid colonnade of architecturally clipped yew trees, most of which were planted in 1792. Legend has it that only ninety-nine will grow at any one time, as the Devil always kills off the hundredth. Some have become so intertwined over the years that it is now impossible to confirm or deny the truth of this charming story. The annual clipping service is held on the Sunday following the patronal festival. During this open-air service children join hands (clipping means 'embracing') and encircle the church while singing a traditional hymn. Tradition also ensures that the children wear flowers in their hair, and that for their part in the ceremony they each receive a 'Painswick Bun' and a coin.

Painswick churchyard is also noted for its splendid series of 17th- and 18th-century Renaissance-style table tombs, many of which were carved by

Painswick from Bull's Cross

Joseph Bryan and his two sons, John and Joseph. John Bryan was also responsible for the handsome pair of gate-piers at the north-east entrance to the churchyard. See also the headstone to freemason, Thomas Hamlett, complete with a display of mason's tools. The stocks in nearby St Mary's Street were installed here in the mid-19th century 'for the punishment of those who carry on carousels to the annoyance of neighbours'.

In the streets around the church will be found a rich array of houses, shops and inns, almost all of which are built of Painswick's creamy grey-white stone, and many of which are also embellished with pleasing architectural details. Take time to stroll round Painswick, a large village (or small town) which was fortunate to grow up at a time when prosperity brought such perfection. This feeling of pleasant affluence is also reflected in the most attractive hilly countryside around it, which is rich in elegant houses and enviably lovely cottages. Half a mile to the north, to the left of the B4073,

Gloucester road, will be found the delightful **Painswick Rococo Garden**, the 18th-century Painswick House's six-acre garden, which has been restored to the original form as depicted in an 18th-century painting by Thomas Robins. Do not miss this. *(Tel: (0452) 813204.)*

It is possible to walk north-eastwards from Painswick, up the valley and into lovely Cranham Woods ★, or south-westwards, down the valley to busy Stroud ★. Painswick is also situated astride the Cotswold Way ★, and this can be followed north to Prinknash ★, or south to Stonehouse and on to Dursley ★.

Painswick Beacon (162) (SO 86-12) *1½ mi. N Painswick.* About 250 acres of common land — pleasant, open country with pine-trees, old quarries and a golf course nearby. The Cotswold Way ★ passes just below it, to the east. This area can become very crowded on Sunday afternoons.

Pitchcombe (162) (SO 85-08) *2 mi. N Stroud.* Appropriately named village on a steep hillside, with lovely Pitchcombe House standing close to a terrace of older houses looking southwards. The church was entirely rebuilt in the 19th century and is a dignified if rather dull building relieved only by the handsome table tombs and clipped yews in the churchyard — both of these in the best Painswick tradition.

Postlip (163) (SP 00-27) *1 mi. W Winchcombe.* Here is a fine Jacobean manor house, Postlip Hall, charmingly situated at the head of the Isbourne Valley below the bare heights of Cleeve Common ★. In its grounds is a small Norman chapel, now used as a Roman Catholic church. This has a Norman south doorway and chancel arch, and a 16th-century roof. The nearby 15th-century tithe barn has a little stone figure on its western gable-end which is said to represent Sir William de Postlip, who lived in the reign of King Stephen. Legend has it that whenever Sir William hears the midnight chime, he comes down off his gable to drink at the nearby well. A little further down the valley, nearer to Winchcombe, is a papermill, which has been making fine quality papers since the mid-18th century, taking advantage of the pure, iron-free waters of the little River Isbourne.

There are good walks up over Cleeve Common from Postlip, going for a short time through open country rather like parts of the Peak District.

Poulton (163) (SP 10-01) *3 mi. W Fairford.* A small village in flat country with no outstanding features. It has a modest little inn overlooked by an equally modest late 17th-century manor house. The nearby church and school were both built by the redoubtable Victorian architect William Butterfield. Within the church's large, rather bare interior will be found a water-colour painting of the charming little church that was swept away with such Victorian zeal. Two crossroads on the road north are marked on the Landranger map as 'Betty's Grave' and 'Ready Token' ★, but the reasons for these descriptions are unfortunately far from clear.

Prescott (150, 163) (SO 98-29) *2½ mi. W Winchcombe.* Small hamlet beneath steep Nottingham

PRESTBURY

Hill, which is itself topped by the ramparts of an Iron Age settlement. Prescott is renowned throughout the world of motor sport as the site of the Prescott Speed Hill Climb. This is operated by the Bugatti Owners' Club and meetings are held here about six times a year. *(Tel: (0242) 673136.)*

Walk south from here, up over Nottingham Hill, and on to Cleeve Hill ★.

Prestbury (163) (SO 97-23) *1½ mi. NE Cheltenham.* Sheltering beneath the steep western scarp face of Cleeve Hill, this large, busy village is now almost part of Cheltenham. Its old houses are built either of stone or of timber, and the little half-timbered King's Arms is a particularly attractive inn. Nearby Prestbury Park has been the site of Cheltenham's world-famous racecourse since 1823, and the great jockey Fred Archer trained here while living at the King's Arms — an inscription here informs the passer-by that Archer, 'who trained on toast, Cheltenham water and coffee, lived at this Prestbury inn'.

The church was over-restored by G.E.Street in 1864, but several medieval features have survived, including a Perpendicular tower, 15th-century arcading and chancel arch, and a double piscina in the Lady Chapel. 'The Priory', a nearby house of 14th-century origin, reminds the visitor that the long-vanished Priory of Llanthony, at Gloucester, once owned both this and the church.

There are two steep lanes heading eastwards up on to Cleeve Hill ★, to link with the Cotswold Way ★. Once up on Cleeve Common ★, walking possibilities are limitless.

Preston (163) (SP 04-00) *1 mi. SE Cirencester.* A minute village in flat country to the immediate east of the Ermin Way (A419). It has a small church approached by a narrow pathway bordered with pollarded limes. The 14th-century triple bellcote is worth noting, and the contents of the church's over-restored interior include a stout, cylindrical Norman font. The beautiful farmhouse next door will be the envy of all who come this way.

Prinknash Abbey (162) (SO 87-13) *2½ mi. NE Painswick.* This establishment dates from 1928, when a Benedictine community moved here from Caldey Island, off the Pembroke Coast, having handed over Caldey to the Cistercians. The 'old abbey' was built in the 14th century as a grange and hunting lodge for the abbots of Gloucester, but inevitably passed out of monastic hands at the Dissolution. Writing to a friend in 1774, Horace Walpole tells that, 'Yesterday I made a jaunt to Prinknash. I wished you there. It stands on a glorious but impracticable hill, in the midst of a little forest of beech and commanding Elysium.' Coming here today, he would perhaps be surprised by the lines of the new abbey, but he would not be disappointed with its setting or the magnificent views out over the Vale of Gloucester to the distant Malverns.

The new abbey was completed in 1972 using stone from the quarries of Guiting, and is an unashamedly modern structure owing little to the traditions of the medieval building that it replaced. Clay was discovered here when the foundations of the new abbey were being dug, and this material soon became the basis for Prinknash's main com-

Prinknash Abbey . . . an unashamedly modern structure

mercial activity — its well-known pottery. However, vestments, incense, stained glass and iron-work are also created here. It is possible to visit the abbey church, the pottery, the walled garden, and nearby tearoom. *(Tel: (0452) 812239 for abbey; (0452) 812455 for pottery and tearoom.)* The adjoining Prinknash Bird Park is also well worth visiting, and consists of nine acres of parkland, with numerous species of waterfowl, West African Pygmy Goats, and a herd of Fallow Deer. *(Tel: (0452) 812727.)*

Quenington (163) (SP 14-04) *2 mi. N Fairford. (See map on page 50.)* A highly attractive village, with many pleasant houses and cottages on slopes above the little River Coln. Notable amongst these is Quenington Court, a largely 19th-century house on the site of a preceptory of the Knights Templar, which later passed into the hands of the Knights Hospitaller. This has an interesting 13th-century gatehouse, and a circular dovecot which is probably about the same age. The little church nearby was over-restored in the late 19th century, but its Norman north and south doorways, each with a richly carved tympanum, should on no account be missed. The tympanum over the south doorway depicts the Coronation of the Virgin, and that over the north doorway the Harrowing of Hell. Both are outstanding examples of Romanesque art.

Use the mapped **mini-walk** on page 50 to explore part of the Coln Valley, taking in some of neighbouring Coln St Aldwyns ★. It is also possible to walk on north-westwards from the latter, beside the Coln to Bibury ★.

Quinton, Upper and Lower (151) (SP 18-47) *2 mi. NE Mickleton.* There is a large military housing estate here, but most of Lower Quinton remains unspoilt, with a village green overlooked by several thatched, timber-framed cottages, a handsome mellow brick 17th-century house with Cotswold stone tiles, and a well restored inn, the College Arms. This displays the arms of Magdalen College, Oxford, which still owns much land in the area. All this is overlooked by the splendid 130ft-high spire of Quinton church. This has Norman south arcading and a Norman font, and many interesting features from the centuries that followed, including a Perpendicular clerestory, and an effigy of a knight who fought at Agincourt, Sir William Clopton, and a fine brass of his widow, Lady Clopton. On Sir William's death, this lady took a vow of widowhood, and is believed to have lived as an anchorite, or hermit, in a cell nearby. It is probably to her that we are indebted for the clerestory and the splendid spire.

It is possible to walk across the fields to **Upper Quinton**, where there is an early timber-framed manor house with very close vertical timbers. To the south of Upper Quinton is Meon Hill, one of the northern outliers of the Cotswolds. There are memories here of suspected witchcraft in comparatively recent times, and the hill's summit is crowned by the ramparts of an Iron Age settlement.

Randwick (162) (SO 82-06) *1½ mi. NW Stroud.* The lower parts of this village are now more a suburb of Stroud, but the rest is full of character. It is attractively sited on steep hillsides beneath Standish Wood. There is an inn called the Vine Tree and, sitting below the road in a tree-shaded churchyard, a largely Victorian church, which has retained its Perpendicular tower.

This church is the focus of the Randwick Wap, an ancient ceremony, the first part of which is held on the first Sunday in May. Three cheeses are carried here on litters decorated with flowers, and after being blessed during a short service they are rolled three times round the church before being cut up and distributed by officers in ceremonial dress. On the following Sunday, the second part of the ceremony takes the form of a mock mayor-making.

There are the earthworks of two round barrows and a long barrow in Standish Wood (most of which belongs to the National Trust), just above the village. There is a path near the church heading up into this wood, thus providing a link with the Cotswold Way ★, which passes through it.

Ready Token (163) (SP 10-04) *5 mi. E Cirencester.* There was once an inn at this point, where the Romans' Akeman Street ★ is crossed by the Welsh Way ★. No doubt it was a popular stopping point for the ever-thirsty Welsh drovers, especially in summertime when the dust from the great herds of cattle must have parched many a Welsh throat. Why the name 'Ready Token'? There appears to be no clear answer to this question.

Rendcomb (163) (SP 02-09) *5 mi. N Cirencester.* Situated on the slopes of the beautifully wooded Churn Valley, this is a small estate village at the gates of Rendcomb Court, a 19th-century Italianate mansion, which has been a boys' boarding school since 1920. The Court was built most meticulously by the famous contractor Thomas Cubitt to the designs of Philip Hardwick, an architect much influenced by the ideas of Sir Charles Barry.

Close to the school is Rendcomb's largely Perpendicular church, which was built by the prosperous Sir Edmund Tame, wool merchant of Fairford ★. Sir Edmund was the son of John Tame, the builder of the magnificent church at Fairford, and there are definite similarities between the two buildings in certain aspects, especially in the carving of their screens. The stained glass, although only fragmentary, is clearly the work of craftsmen influenced by the Renaissance to a far greater extent than those at slightly earlier Fairford. See also the little sculpture of the Crucifixion over the east gable, the fine 15th-century south door, which is contemporary with the church itself, and the outstandingly beautiful Norman font, with figures

Rendcomb's splendid Norman font

of eleven apostles beneath arcading in high relief, and the figure of Judas left uncarved. This font is thought to have come from Elmore (162) (SO 78-15), a village on the banks of the Severn below Gloucester. Before leaving do not overlook the cross in the churchyard — a 19th-century head on a stout medieval base.

Walk south from here, down beside the Churn to North Cerney ★ and Baunton ★.

Robins Wood Hill Country Park (162) (SO 84-15) *2 mi. S Gloucester.* Robins Wood, an outlier of the Cotswolds, lies entirely within the boundary of the city of Gloucester, and the 250-acre country park is owned by the City Council. There is a small Information Centre (*tel: (0452) 413029*), and guided tours on summer Sundays, horse trails, nature trails, footpaths and even a BMX track. At the very top of the hill there is a viewing topograph which helps to identify the features that can be seen on distant horizons. The best approach to the park is by turning off the St Barnabas Roundabout on the ring road, onto Reservoir Road.

The rest of the hill is owned by the Gloucester Country Club, which provides a wide range of sporting facilities, including a golf course and one of England's highest dry-ski slopes.

Matson House, below the north-eastern slopes of the hill, was the headquarters of the Royalists during their siege of Gloucester, and the top of the hill above must have provided the besiegers with a superb vantage point.

Rodborough (162) (SO 84-04) *1 mi. SW Stroud.* This scattered village is now a hilly suburb of Stroud, and much walking up and down its sloping streets is required to appreciate its remaining character. Its manor, burnt down in about 1900, was once the home of Sir George Onesiphorus Paul, the local prison reformer of Huguenot descent (see also Doughton ★, Northleach ★ and Woodchester ★). Up on windy Rodborough Common, well above the village, Rodborough Fort is a prominent landmark. This was built in 1761 as a 'pleasure-house' by local dyer, George Hawker, but having been entirely rebuilt in 1870 it now looks typically Victorian. There is a good caravan site here, pleasant walks over to the south side of the common and wide views out over the still-busy valleys below. Well beyond the village, on the southern edge of the common, there is a comfortable hotel called 'The Bear at Rodborough'.

Rodmarton (163) (ST 94-97) *4½ mi. NE Tetbury.* This has a small green overlooked by quiet cottages and an attractively spired church. Pollarded trees create a 'lychgate' effect over the churchyard gate, and there are several pleasant tombs in the churchyard. Unfortunately the interior was ruthlessly scraped by Victorian 'restorers', but there are old stone floors, several handsome 18th- and 19th-century monuments, and the brass of a 15th-century lawyer dressed in his cap and gown.

The nearby manor house was built for Claud Biddulph, between 1909 and 1926, to the designs of Ernest Barnsley, one of a group of artists and craftsmen much influenced by William Morris's 'Arts and Crafts' philosophy (see also Daneway ★). As part of Biddulph's and Barnsley's plan, the house was built entirely by estate workers and local specialist craftsmen, using local materials but no machinery and nothing modern. Its furniture includes items by Ernest Barnsley himself, his brother Sidney, and their friend Ernest Gimson. The interior of the manor cannot be visited, but the chapel and the delightful garden surrounding the house are open to the public. (*Tel: (028584) 219.*)

Walk westwards from here to Cherington ★ via Hazelton Manor ★ .

Roel Gate (163) (SP 05-24) *3½ mi. SE Winchcombe.* Lonely crossroads about 900 feet above sea level, with fine views down the 'Sudeley Valley' to Winchcombe. Roel Gate lies on the Salt Way ★ , at one of the highest points on its course between Droitwich and the Thames. There is a seat here, in memory of 'Arthur Edwin Boycott — Pathologist, Naturalist and Friend — 1877-1938', and it would be hard to find a finer place at which to be remembered.

There is an Iron Age settlement at Grim's Hill, half a mile to the west, and a mile and a half in the opposite direction lies Roel Farm, an old manor house which provided shelter for Lord Chandos, his family and retainers from Sudeley Castle, during the troubled times of the Civil War. A village of Roel is recorded in the Domesday Book, but this was probably depopulated in the 14th century when great sheep runs were established here and elsewhere in the Cotswolds by the Abbot of Winchcombe, and no trace of it remains apart from slight undulations in a field next to the farm.

The Rollright Stones (151) (SP 29-30) *2½ mi. NW Chipping Norton.* These consist of three separate features. The King's Men make up a Bronze Age stone circle about a hundred feet in diameter, and date from between 2000 and 1800 BC. This group is situated to the immediate south of a road between the A34 and the A44. The Whispering Knights, the remains of a Bronze Age burial chamber, stand 400 yards to the east of the circle, and finally the King Stone, an isolated 'standing stone', is nearly opposite the King's Men, and almost certainly associated with them, although its exact

The Rollright Stones . . . a Bronze Age stone circle

purpose is not known. These features all lie in fine upland country, and there are splendid views, especially northwards from the King Stone. The ridge on which these stones are situated is believed to have carried one of Britain's earliest and most important tracks — the so-called Jurassic Way ★ , leading south and west along the limestone belt from the shores of the Humber, to Salisbury Plain and the coast beyond. For further reading on the subject of trackways in this area, see G.R.Crosher's *Along the Cotswold Ways*.

The 18th-century antiquary, William Stukeley, referred to the Rollright Stones as being 'corroded like wormeaten wood by the harsh jaws of time', but despite their exposed upland setting they still survive. In earlier times they were the subject of a legend relating to a king intent on the conquest of England, who was confronted here by a witch who spoke thus:

If Long Compton thou canst see,
King of England thou shalt be.

Unfortunately for the king and his followers this proved to be impossible at the time, and the witch continued:

As Long Compton thou canst not see
King of England thou shalt not be.
Rise up stick, and stand still, stone,
For King of England thou shalt be none.
Thou and thy men hoar stones shalt be,
And I shall be an eldern tree.

And so, it is sad to relate, the king, his men and his knights were all turned into stone, and the witch into an elder tree.

Rousham House and Gardens (164) (SP 47-24) *6 mi. NNE Woodstock.* A Jacobean mansion enlarged and enriched by William Kent in 1783, and still in the hands of the family who built it — the Dormers, latterly the Cottrell-Dormers. While the house with its fine collection of portraits and furniture is of considerable interest, a visit to its landscaped gardens is a quite unique experience.

These were laid out by William Kent, and are the only surviving example of his landscape design, still including many of the features which proved so enticing to 18th-century visitors. Horace Walpole was one of these visitors and described the garden as 'the most engaging of all Kent's works'. Sited amongst woods along the rushy tree-shaded banks of the River Cherwell, the garden's various features include ponds, cascades in 'Venus' Vale', the 'Cold Bath', and the seven-arched 'Praeneste'. This is a

At Rousham Park . . . the only surviving example of William Kent's landscape designs

lovely classical summer-house with views across the valley to a sham ruin on the skyline — known, like several other examples in various parts of the country, as an 'eyecatcher'.

See also the lovely flower borders in the old walled garden, the 16th-century dovecot with revolving ladder, and the nearby church with its fine Cottrell-Dormer monuments. To quote from the descriptive leaflet, 'Rousham is uncommercial and unspoilt with no tea room and no shop. Bring a picnic, wear comfortable shoes and it is yours for the day.' Need we say more, apart from asking readers to leave their dogs at home and to bring no children under fifteen. There is no better place to visit on a hot summer's day. *(Tel: (0869) 47110.)*

Ryknild Street (150,151,163) This Roman road was an important route running northwards from the Foss Way near Bourton-on-the-Water, and down the Cotswold edge between Saintbury and Weston-sub-Edge. From here it ran across the Midland plain, past Birmingham and Derby, and ended up at Templeborough near Sheffield. Its line across Bourton Downs is not easy to spot on the ground, although slight humps where it crosses two roads at (151) (SP 13-33) provide a fascinating clue which has been substantiated by excavation at Bourton Far Hill Farm, a short distance to the south. Further evidence will be apparent to those who make use of **Walk 4**, north from Hinchwick ★. Apart from this, the best section of road for walkers is the track known as Condicote Lane which runs southwards from Condicote ★ almost to Upper Slaughter ★.

Ryknild Street, south of Condicote . . . known here as Condicote Lane

Saintbury (150) (SP 11-39) *2 mi. NE Broadway.* Small village poised on the slopes of the Cotswold edge, with a single street leading up from a medieval wayside cross on the B4632, past a series of enviably lovely stone houses and cottages, to the slender-spired church at its top. There are fine views from the church's north porch, which itself shelters a pleasant early Norman doorway complete with patterned tympanum. The interior is delightfully unspoilt, with light flooding in onto old benches through the clear glass of the Perpendicular west window. There is a lovely old roof to the nave, a fine 15th-century font complete with an ogee-shaped 18th-century wooden cover, and several other attractive items including fragments of 17th-century wall-painting.

St Kenelm's Well (163) (SP 04-27) *1 mi. E Winchcombe.* This is a 19th-century reconstruction of a Holy Well connected with St Kenelm, the martyred boy prince, who was murdered in AD 819 in the far-off Clent Hills, and whose shrine at Winchcombe Abbey brought it such prosperity. The well lies about a quarter of a mile north of the road up from Winchcombe which passes the rear of Sudeley Castle. The footpath is muddy and unsigned, and the going is steep, but the views are worth while and the spring feeding the well still flows. It is possible to walk on from here to the top of Salter's Hill, and then down Salter's Lane, following the line of the Salt Way ★, to Hailes Abbey ★.

Salford (163) (SP 28-28) *2 mi. W Chipping Norton.* This modest village just off the busy A34 has no special features apart from its church. This was largely rebuilt by the very competent Victorian architect, G.E. Street, although it is not one of his better works. However, there is the base of an old cross in the churchyard, an interesting Norman font with interlaced arcading, and a crudely carved tympanum over the north doorway which may represent 'Sagittarius the Archer'. This subject was quite a favourite in the Cotswolds — see also Kencot ★ and Hook Norton ★. It is possible to walk eastwards from Salford across the fields to Chipping Norton ★.

There is trout fishing at lakes to the east of the village. *(For details, tel: (0608) 643209.)*

Salperton (163) (SP 07-20) *4 mi. NW Northleach.* Here is a minute village in a quiet fold of the hills between the A40 and the A436, and on the probable line of both the Salt Way ★ and Campden Lane ★, a wool trading trackway between Chipping Campden and the southern Cotswolds (see also **Walk 3**); the two medieval trading routes appear to have converged here. The name Salperton is almost certainly derived from the early English *salt-paeth*, the salt path.

Nearby Salperton Park is a 17th-century manor house much altered in the 19th century. The adjoining church has a small tower complete with painted clock-face. The church is Norman in origin and has many Norman features, including its chancel arch. To the north of the tower arch is a late medieval wall-painting of a skeleton with a scythe and arrow — Death, the Grim Reaper, perhaps? There is a coat of arms of George III, and a handsome 18th-century wall monument to John

THE SALT WAY

Browne with a draped coffin, urns and cherubs. Salperton Park is private property, but there appears to be a public path to the church in front of the house (please check locally if in doubt). Do not miss the attractive 17th-century table-tombs in the churchyard.

Walk southwards from here to Hazleton ★ following the probable course of the Salt Way, and then eastwards along a good bridle road to Turkdean ★

The Salt Way (150,163) Several trackways across the Cotswolds were used by medieval traders in salt, and some Cotswold manors even had their own salt-workings in the Droitwich area. However, the best-known of these tracks, known as the Salt Way, linked the main workings at Droitwich with the head of the navigable Thames in the vicinity of Lechlade ★, from whence the salt could easily be moved downriver to London. Study of Landranger sheets 150 and 163 will soon reveal its approximate course, as it is still referred to as the Salt Way in several places, as it follows sometimes modern roads, sometimes bridleways and at others just ill-defined pathways. Our **Walk 12** follows its course near Bibury ★ for a short time. For more details on this fascinating subject read G.R. Crosher's book, *Along the Cotswold Ways*, and J. Finberg's *The Cotswolds*.

View of the 'Sudeley Valley' from the Salt Way

Sapperton (163) (SO 94-03) *5 mi. W Cirencester.* Situated just beyond the western extremities of the great Cirencester Park ★ and poised above the deep Frome Valley, this is a trim little village, with an inn of great character called the Bell, and an attractive terraced road beyond its church. This lies at the lower end of a long path sloping beneath yew trees. It is a largely 18th-century building, having round-headed windows with their original glass, and a very stylish interior which has utilised much Jacobean woodwork removed from Sapperton House, itself demolished in about 1730 to make way for the western end of Cirencester Park's Long Ride. There are two very fine monuments here, both with life-size figures — one to Sir Henry Poole and his family and the other to Sir Robert Atkyns, the noted county historian and author of *The Ancient and Present State of Gloucestershire*. In the churchyard outside will be found the base and shaft of an 11th-century cross, and, beneath trees on either side of a sloping path, the tombs of the three artist-craftsmen who carried on the traditions of William Morris in the surrounding area — Ernest Gimson, and the

Monument in Sapperton Church

brothers Ernest and Sidney Barnsley (see also Daneway ★). For further memories of the life and work of these three and their fellow craftsmen, read the account by their best-known disciple, the architect Norman Jewson, entitled *By Chance I Did Rove*. This was originally published in 1920, but was reprinted in 1973.

The Thames and Severn Canal ★ runs in a tunnel beneath the village, to emerge at its north-western end at Daneway ★ in the valley below.

The best walk from here runs north-eastwards along the valley slope to lovely 17th-century Pinbury Park (see Edgeworth ★), once the home of Sir Robert Atkyns, and for a few years at the beginning of the 20th century, that of Ernest Gimson and the Barnsleys. The walk then returns through woods down beside the infant Frome. See also our **Walk 10**, which starts from Sapperton and runs in the opposite direction.

Sarsden (163) (SP 28-23) *3 mi. SW Chipping Norton.* A quiet hamlet in rolling, wooded parkland, with a few thatched cottages, two round barrows, a medieval wayside cross, and a beautiful late 17th-century mansion in a park landscaped by Humphry Repton. Beside the mansion is a church rebuilt in 1760 — an austere building with little of interest for the visitor.

Selsley and Selsley Common (162) (SO 83-04) *2 mi. SW Stroud.* Small hillside village which is almost a suburb of Stroud. It has an interesting church, which was paid for by the prosperous mill-owner Samuel Marling. Despite his wish that this should resemble the church of Marling in the Tyrol, which he had recently visited, it was designed more in the French-Gothic style much favoured by his talented architect, G.F. Bodley (see also Bussage ★ and France Lynch ★). This church contains stained glass by almost all the leading figures of the Pre-Raphaelite circle, including William Morris himself, Philip Webb, Ford Madox Brown, Edward Burne-Jones and Dante Gabriel Rossetti, and for this reason also is well worth visiting.

In Water Lane, to the south-east of the village, will be found the attractive Selsley Herb and Goat Farm. As their leaflet states, 'goats and herbs don't mix,' but visitors may look round the orchard where the goats are kept, and of course visit the delightful herb garden. There is a barn shop and light refreshments are available (but tel: (0453) 766682 for details).

Selsley Common extends along a ridge south-westwards from the village and is a fine open stretch of country, with many picnic possibilities and a series of extensive views.

Sevenhampton (163) (SP 03-21) *4 mi. S Winch-combe.* This modest village has a small ford across the infant Coln, a river which rises about a mile to its north. The ford is overlooked by a few cottages and not far away there is a Norman church. This was much altered and improved by the benefaction of a rich wool merchant, John Camber, who died in 1497, and whose likeness is well portrayed on a memorial brass to be found within. Flowering rock plants line the path to the south door, which is sheltered by a handsome little porch, and the base of John Camber's Perpendicular tower provides a fascinating architectural story, with flying but-tresses within the body of the church, and vaulting high up above the tower crossing. The interior has been over-restored, but there are several interesting monuments to be seen.

It is possible to walk northwards from here, up the head of the Coln Valley, over the watershed to Charlton Abbots ★ , and down to Winchcombe ★ .

Seven Springs (163) (SO 96-17) *3 mi. S Chelten-ham.* Although this has sometimes been claimed to be the 'highest source of the Thames', it is in fact only the source of its attractive tributary, the Churn. It consists of a rather muddy little pool, no doubt fed by seven springs, and is situated beside the A436 and a much-used lay-by.

Walk south from here using our mapped **mini-walk** — down the Churn Valley to Coberley ★ , then eastwards to Upper Coberley ★ before returning to Seven Springs. The course of the Cotswold Way ★

At Seven Springs . . . source of the River Churn

passes within a few yards of Seven Springs, and this can be used to walk north and north-west to Charlton Kings Common and the Devil's Chimney ★ .

Sezincote (151) (SP 17-30) *2½ mi. SW Moreton-in-Marsh.* In medieval times there was a small village here, but its church was destroyed by Cromwell's forces, apparently because the estate was in the hands of an ardent Royalist family. In 1795 Sezincote was purchased by Colonel John Cockerell, a 'nabob' recently returned from Bengal. He died only three years later, leaving the estate to his younger brother Charles, who had served with him in the East India Company. Charles, who became a Baronet in 1809, and a Member of Parliament for Evesham, built a new house, employ-ing another brother, Samuel Pepys Cockerell (the family were distantly related to the diarist), as his architect.

S.P.Cockerell, who had already designed nearby Daylesford ★ for Warren Hastings, was also Sur-veyor to the East India Company. He worked closely with Thomas Daniel, an artist who had also recently

Seven Springs and Coberley
SCALE 1:25 000 or 2½ INCHES to 1 MILE

Sezincote . . . Oriental magnificence on a Cotswold hillside

returned from India, and together they created a magnificent house in the Indian manner. This was inspired at least in part by the extensive works of the 16th-century Mogul Emperor, Akbar, who had deliberately mixed Islamic and Hindu styles in an attempt to integrate the diverse cultures of the two races. The result achieved at Sezincote is unique — a grand house in the authentic Mogul style in a rural English setting, the beauty of which was further enhanced by the outstanding landscape artist, Humphry Repton, who helped to create the lovely water gardens and lakes on the gently sloping hillside that gives birth to the River Evenlode. In addition Sezincote offers a most elegant classical interior, which has been beautifully restored in the mid-20th century, and a visit here should certainly not be missed. *(Tel: (0386) 700444.)*

Sezincote was visited in 1806 by the Prince Regent who was staying at the time with the Marquess of Hertford at Ragley, near Alcester, and it is thought that he was so impressed by Sezincote's style that he advanced his plans for the 'Indianisation' of his Pavilion at Brighton. Sadly, however, the commission was given to the Prince's favourite architect, John Nash, rather than to Cockerell.

For a delightfully nostalgic account of Colonel and Mrs Dugdale's frequent house-party weekends at Sezincote in the early 1930s, read John Betjeman's long poem, *Summoned by Bells.* This is extensively quoted in James Lees-Milne's highly informative book, *Some Cotswold Country Houses.*

Sheepscombe (163) (SO 89-10) *1½ mi. E Painswick.* A long village beautifully situated on both sides of a quiet valley beneath luxuriantly wooded hillsides. In the 18th century this was a cloth-weaving village and a few of the cottages still have the large three-light windows which were built to provide the maximum possible light for the weavers. In the early years of the 19th century there was no church here, but there were no fewer than eight unlicensed alehouses. Its inhabitants had by then mostly become factory workers at the Brookland Mill, and they had acquired a reputation throughout the district for drunkenness and riotous behaviour. However, by 1825 a church had been built and a Sunday School opened, and Sheepscombe soon became known as the 'Peaceful Valley'. This almost miraculous transformation appears to have been a permanent one. Today there is one inn — the little Butcher's Arms — complete with a colourful carved sign, and across the valley, immediately above a sloping green, the quaint little church still stands proudly, with its minute tower 'stuck on' to an ornate west end.

Walk northwards from Sheepscombe, up through woods and over to Cranham ★.

Sherborne (163) (SP 17-14) *4 mi. S Bourton-on-the-Water.* The village has been part of the Sherborne House Estate for centuries. The site was once owned by the abbots of Winchcombe ★, who had a substantial farm here. Apparently the abbot would spend most of the month of May here to supervise the shearing of the vast flocks gathered in from his abbey's great sheep runs, which stretched over the Cotswolds from Snowshill ★ and Roel ★, through Charlton Abbots ★ and Hawling ★, to Sherborne. At least one wool-buyer from Italy is known to have visited Sherborne in 1436, and until the English clothiers took up most of its output, the majority of the abbey's fleeces would have been exported to Italy and Flanders.

Following the Dissolution of 1539, the Sherborne estate was purchased in 1551 by Thomas Dutton, who at once built himself a fine house here. His grandson John 'Crump' Dutton, the hunchback Royalist colonel, who at the end of the Civil War was clever enough to convince Cromwell that he had only served the king under duress, employed Valentine Strong, quarry-owner and builder of nearby Taynton ★, to enhance the original building (see also Lodge Park ★, another house built for him, also probably by Valentine Strong). Using stone from underground quarries (or mines) in the park, Sherborne House was regrettably rebuilt in the 19th century, largely by Lewis Wyatt, but also by Anthony Salvin, the architect who is best remembered for his extensive rebuilding work at Windsor Castle. The house was a boarding school for some years, but has now been converted to luxury flats. The estate remained in the hands of the Dutton family, latterly the Lords Sherborne, until recently, but it has now been generously bequeathed to the National Trust. There is a small car park (SP 159-44) at Ewepen Barn, on a track to the east of a minor road north from the A40. Display boards in the barn relate to the history of the estate and to the waymarked walks through woods and parkland which can be started from here.

The church lies close to the park, but although its tower and spire are medieval, the rest was rebuilt during the first half of the 19th century. However, its well-proportioned interior was refurnished in the 1930s, and also contains a splendid series of monuments to various members of the Dutton family. See especially the fine monument to Sir John Dutton by the celebrated sculptor, John Rysbrack, and the one to John Lennox Dutton, by Richard Westmacott the elder.

The village itself is delightfully situated in the valley of the little Sherborne Brook, not far from its confluence with the more important River Windrush. It is divided into two parts, to the east and the west of the park, and both have a number of attractive houses and cottages not far from the brook. At the eastern end of the village there is a cottage with a small reset Norman arch.

Walk eastwards from here, down the valley to Windrush ★ and Little Barrington ★

Shilton (163) (SP 26-08) *2½ mi. SE Burford*. This charming village is tucked away in the quiet valley of the Shill Brook, just below the busy B4020 and only a mile away from the garrison town of Carterton and the adjoining airfield of Brize Norton. Apart from the noise of aircraft overhead, Shilton is near perfection, with a stream, a pond edged with chestnut trees and a forded road leading up beside a farm and a dovecot. It also has rose-decked cottages, flower-filled gardens and a small but very friendly inn — the Rose and Crown.

Church and rectory lie to the south of the village, and in the church, which has many Norman features, will be found an exceptionally beautiful font enriched with 14th-century carvings on all four sides depicting scenes from the Passion, with the Evangelists at each corner.

Ford at Shilton . . . near perfection when the skies are empty

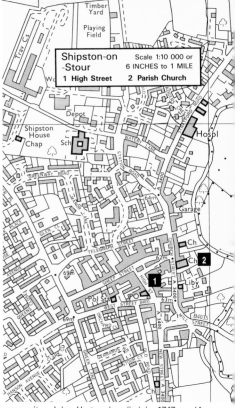

Shipston-on -Stour Scale 1:10 000 or 6 INCHES to 1 MILE

1 High Street 2 Parish Church

Shipston-on-Stour (151) (SP 25-40) *7 mi. NE Moreton-in-Marsh*. 'Sheepstown', as its name implies, was once an extremely important market for sheep, and its many delightful houses from the 17th, 18th and 19th centuries bear witness to a prosperity lasting for at least three hundred years. That it continued to thrive in the 19th century must have been due in part to the enterprise of the local canal and railway promoter William James of Henley-in-Arden, who in 1826 completed a tramway linking the canal wharfs of Stratford-upon-Avon with Moreton-in-Marsh, with a branch line to Shipston opening ten years later (see Stratford and Moreton Tramway ★). Eventually, in 1889, many years after Brunel's main Oxford, Worcester and Wolverhampton line came through Moreton-in-Marsh, part of the tramway was converted into a railway branch line between there and Shipston. Another factor contributing to Shipston's continuing prosperity was its position astride a busy north-south coaching route, and a number of its old coaching inns survive to this day, amongst them those in the very pleasant *High Street (1)*, Shipston's little market square. This is just far enough away to escape the busy traffic of the A3400, Stratford to Oxford road. Shipston today is a thriving little shopping town, with many shops attractive enough to tempt customers from far and wide.

St Edmund's Church (2) has retained its 15th-century west tower, but is otherwise the creation of Victorian architect, G.E.Street. The interior is not of outstanding interest, but do not miss the very unusual conversion of a sounding-board from an earlier pulpit into an octagonal table. There is also a handsome little monument to another person to whom Shipston must have owed some of its prosperity, John Hart, who died in 1747 — 'A considerable Improver and Promoter of Manufacture in this his native Town'.

There is an attractive walk, partly beside the River Stour, to Barcheston ★ , and on to Willington, and also one south-westwards across the fields to Todenham ★ .

Shipton Oliffe (163) (SP 03-18) *6 mi. E Cheltenham*. Long straggling village on a tributary of the Coln with a small ford, a Methodist chapel in bright red brick looking startlingly like a Victorian railway station, and a pretty church overlooking ornamental gardens by the stream. The little church with its 13th-century bellcote has been rather tidied up inside, but has a colourful Royal Coat of Arms in plaster relief, blocked-up Norman doorways, remnants of medieval wall-paintings and old oak pews which were originally in the church at neighbouring Shipton Solers.

It is possible to walk north-eastwards from here to Hampen ★ and on to Salperton ★ .

Shipton Solers (163) (SP 03-18) *5½ mi. E Cheltenham*. This is smaller than its neighbour Shipton Oliffe, but there are delightful glimpses of the manor house's stream-side gardens, and the little 13th-century church, which is situated just above the road, was very sympathetically restored in 1929. Its contents include a 17th-century pulpit complete with sounding board and a plain 15th-century font. The Frogmill Inn, well to the west of the village, was once a well used coaching halt on the Gloucester to London road and is now a hotel and restaurant.

Walk south from Shipton Solers to Cleevely Wood (SP 03-17), and then walk beside the stream to Withington ★ .

SHIPTON-UNDER-WYCHWOOD

Shipton-under-Wychwood (163) (SP 27-17) *4 mi. NE Burford*. This large village was once the centre of the great Wychwood Forest ★ and a large fair was held here each year. Shipton is situated in the broad valley of the River Evenlode and has several very pleasant old houses, including the handsome 17th-century Shipton Court behind its high wall. The largely 15th-century Shaven Crown Hotel was once a guest house run by the monks of Bruern Abbey ★, and is claimed to have held a licence since the year 1384. This fine old building has a central hall and a carriage entrance opening onto a partly cobbled yard. It was at the Shaven Crown that the fascist leader Sir Oswald Mosley and his wife Diana (one of the 'Mitford Girls' of nearby Swinbrook ★) were detained by the authorities for a short time during the War.

The Shaven Crown looks out across a fine, wide village green to Shipton's tall-spired church. This has a Norman tower and a 15th-century vaulted porch opening into a large, rather bleak interior, this condition being partly due to the heavy-handed work of Victorian architect, G.E. Street. It does, however, contain a handsome 15th-century stone pulpit, a large font of the same period, and a charming Tudor wall monument with husband and wife at a prayer desk and their children in attendance. At the southern end of the village will be found the hospitable Lamb Inn, a small hotel and restaurant, with a reputation for excellent buffet lunches.

About two miles to the south-east is the farmhouse of Langley (164) (SP 30-15), a largely mid-19th-century building on the site of a royal hunting lodge. Most of the Tudor monarchs stayed here when hunting in Wychwood Forest ★, and it was certainly used by the Royal Court for this purpose as late as 1614. Langley is unfortunately now dominated by a large number of radio transmitting masts.

The Gibbet Tree (163) (SP 27-14), shown on the map to the east of the A361, about two miles south

The Shaven Crown at Shipton-under-Wychwood . . . unusual guests during World War II

of Shipton, was the single oak tree where two of the notorious Dunsdon brothers were hung in chains in 1785, following their earlier hanging at Gloucester. These three brothers, named Tom, Dick and Harry, were highwaymen who had acquired a notoriety not far short of Dick Turpin's, and the writer suspects that it is to them that we may owe the oft-used phrase, 'Tom, Dick and Harry'. They were born at nearby Swinbrook ★, but appear to have worked from Icomb ★, using an old underground quarry beneath their cottage both to stable their horses and to store their loot.

Shipton-under-Wychwood is on the line of the Oxfordshire Way ★, and this can be used to walk north-westwards up the Evenlode Valley to Bruern Abbey ★ and Bledington ★, or eastwards down the valley to Charlbury ★.

Shurdington (163) (SO 92-18) *3 mi. SW Cheltenham*. This large village below the Cotswold scarp is now almost a suburb shared between Cheltenham and Gloucester, and its peace is shattered by traffic on the A46 road. However, the church lies away from this busy road, with yew trees lining the long path to its south porch. This is overlooked by a slender 14th-century spire, which is even more graceful than its contemporary at nearby Leckhampton ★. Inside its much restored interior there is fine rib vaulting below the tower, and beneath it a pleasant 14th-century font, but otherwise there is little of interest to the visitor here.

It is possible to walk south-eastwards, up Shurdington Hill, to link onto the Cotswold Way ★.

Siddington (163) (SU 03-99) *1 mi. SE Cirencester*. Now almost a suburb of Cirencester, Siddington has somehow managed to preserve its individuality in the area immediately surrounding its tall-spired church. Much of this was rebuilt by the Victorians, but there is a splendid Norman south doorway with beak-head decoration and an outstanding tympanum depicting Christ in Majesty. There is also a beautiful Perpendicular north aisle chapel with a fine roof supported on angel corbels. Unfortunately for Siddington, the fine 15th-century glass from here was transferred to Cirencester church, where it now forms the central feature of the massive east window there. The cylindrical Norman font is so tall that it is thought to have been used at one time for adult baptisms. While visiting the church do not miss the pleasant 16th-century barn overlooking the churchyard.

Siddington is on the course of the long-closed Thames and Severn Canal ★. Traces of this may be seen to the south of the village and it is in fact still possible to use part of its old towpath to walk southwards to South Cerney ★.

Slad (162) (SO 87-07) *2 mi. NE Stroud*. Strung out along the B4070 on the side of a valley dropping down into Stroud, this small village is now inevitably linked with the poet and author, Laurie Lee. His childhood years in the village are brilliantly recalled in his book, *Cider with Rosie*. Despite its fame Slad has remained remarkably unspoilt, so let us help to keep it this way by trying not to linger too long here. The small Victorian church is certainly for architectural enthusiasts only.

There is a pleasant, winding road westwards from here to Bisley ★, and our **Walk 8** starts from nearby

Bulls Cross, coming down through woodlands to Slad.

Slimbridge and the Wildfowl and Wetlands Trust (162) (SO 73-03) *12 mi. SW Gloucester.* This

modest sized village lies in flat, non-Cotswold country between the M5 and the shores of the Severn Estuary, and like Berkeley Castle should really be outside the scope of this guide. There are, however, two reasons why it has been included. Firstly it has a fine 13th-century church — one of the area's best examples of the Early English style. The three-stage tower is topped by a tall, beautifully proportioned spire, and the 13th-century architectural detail within is full of interest. William Tyndale, the first translator of the New Testament into English, was probably born at Slimbridge, in the year 1484, but the Tyndale Monument★, erected to his memory in the 19th century, stands on the Cotswold edge some miles to the south, above North Nibley★, a village which also claims to have been his birthplace.

Having looked round the church, drive beyond the village, cross the broad waters of the Gloucester and Sharpness Canal, and head for the place that has brought world-wide fame to the name of Slimbridge — the Wildfowl and Wetlands Trust's splendid reserve (162) (SO 72-04).

Established by Sir Peter Scott as a registered charity in 1946, this organisation was originally called the Severn Wildfowl Trust. It has four aims — education, research, conservation and recreation — and thanks to the dedication of Sir Peter and his colleagues, these aims have been achieved with outstanding success. The Wildfowl and Wetlands Trust, as it is now called, has established similar reserves at Peakirk, Cambridgeshire; Martin Mere, Lancashire; Washington, Tyne and Wear; Arundel, Sussex; and Llanelli in South Wales. At Slimbridge and all the above reserves there is a combination of tame waterfowl from all over the world, and wild native species in their natural habitat. At two other reserves — Caerlaverock, Dumfries and Welney, Norfolk — there are no tame birds, but there is an abundance of wild ones.

A visit here at any time of the year will prove to be a delight, for here is the world's largest and most varied collection of wildfowl, including colourful flocks of all six of the world's species of flamingos. There is also a tropical house with humming birds flitting amongst jungle foliage. In winter the skies are alive with swans, geese and ducks, and they can be observed from comfortable hides. The visitor centre has exhibitions, displays and a 100-seat cinema. There is also a gift shop and excellent restaurant. A visit here will help to support the fine aims of the Wildfowl and Wetlands Trust. *(Tel: (0453) 890333.)*

The Wildfowl and Wetlands Trust, Slimbridge . . . the magical creation of Sir Peter Scott

Snowshill Manor

Snowshill (150) (SP 09-33) *2½ mi. S Broadway.* This charming hillside village is situated at the head of a quiet valley, on slopes just below Oat Hill, one of the high points along the Cotswold edge. Hardly any two of Snowshill's roof lines are on the same level, and there are beautifully framed views over the Avon Valley and to the Midland Plain beyond. Viewed from the little road above it, the church sits comfortably into the hillside and appears to be almost part of the earth itself. It was rebuilt in the mid-19th century and is not of great interest, although its contents do include a good Perpendicular-period octagonal font, and a pulpit constructed of 17th-century carved panels.

A series of attractive houses and cottages are grouped around the small sloping churchyard and village green, while below the church will be found a busy and welcoming inn, the Snowshill Arms. Not far beyond the inn is the National Trust's **Snowshill Manor** — a beautiful Tudor building with a William and Mary south front. It is set in lovely terraced gardens which overlook orchards below and farmland which rises beyond. Once owned by the abbey of Winchcombe, and then by Catherine Parr, the last of Henry VIII's six wives, it was purchased just after the First World War by Charles Paget Wade, whose family had amassed great wealth from sugar plantations in the West Indies. An architect, artist, craftsman, eccentric and scholar, he first restored the manor, and then proceeded to fill it with a most extraordinary collection. As a result the house is packed from ground floor to attic with a series of fascinating bygones — toys, telescopes, sedan chairs, ship models, clocks, musical instruments, weavers' and spinners' tools, Japanese armour and even bicycles. Each of the many rooms in which the collection is housed bears a name beautifully painted above its door — names like *Nadir, Meridian, Seraphim, Dragon, Admiral, Top Gallant* and *Seventh Heaven*. Mr Wade, who gave Snowshill Manor and its contents to the National Trust in 1951, lived in extreme simplicity, never having electric light in the house, and sleeping in an adjoining cottage in a Tudor cupboard-bed. However, very late in life he married, and eventually retired to the West Indies, where he died in 1956. The house and its contents, and the delightful gardens which surround it, make a visit here very rewarding, but try to avoid peak times. There is a

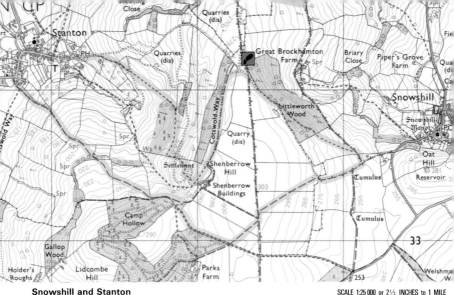

Snowshill and Stanton

special car park close by, at the northern end of the village. *(Tel: (0386) 852410.)*

One item of local interest not to be seen in the manor's collection is a device claimed to be the world's earliest sewing machine. This is to be found in the Science Museum in South Kensington, but it was made at Snowshill in the year 1842 by a certain Charles Keyte, known to his friends rather appropriately as 'Schemer Keyte'.

There are a number of walks from Snowshill — to Buckland ★, Laverton ★, Stanton ★, and Stanway ★. The best starting point for walks in this area is a small car-parking space (150) (SP 083-341) on the course of the Cotswold Way ★, which can be reached by a narrow public road running from the village, first westwards and then north-westwards. This parking space is the start of the mapped **mini-walk** on this page which links the villages of Snowshill and Stanton ★. Snowshill is also on the course of our **Walk 1** from Broadway.

Somerford Keynes (163) (SU 01-95) *4 mi. S Cirencester.* A pleasant stone village with a hospitable inn and, in a park-like setting between the manor and the rectory, a most interesting church with Saxon origins. The tall narrow doorway in the north wall has been reopened, and with its single stone arch may be over a thousand years old. Inside will be found a fragmentary carving which may be Danish in origin, showing the confrontation of two strange beasts, but many visitors will find the elegant 17th-century monument to Robert Strange, complete with bewigged effigy, more to their liking.

Somerford Keynes lies just to the east of the infant River Thames, and it is possible to walk northwards close beside it to the pleasant hamlet of Ewen ★.

The Keynes Country Park (163) (SU 02-95), well to the east of the village, is one of the main features of the very extensive Cotswold Water Park ★, and details of its facilities will be found under this heading.

The Somerset Monument (172) (ST 77-87) *3½ mi. S Wotton-under-Edge.* This high stone tower, with its slightly oriental flavour, was designed by the architect Lewis Vulliamy in 1846 for the Duke of Beaufort, and commemorates General Lord Robert Somerset, a member of the Beaufort family who served under Wellington at Waterloo. It is sometimes possible to climb the 144 steps to a platform, from where views ranging from Flat Holm in the Bristol Channel to the Forest of Dean and the distant mountains of Wales may be obtained. *(Enquire locally.)* The monument lies on the course of the Cotswold Way ★, and this provides a good walk north-eastwards to Lower Kilcott.

Southam (163) (SO 97-25) *3 mi. NE Cheltenham.* Situated beneath Cleeve Hill's steep scarp slopes, Southam has grown considerably in the last few years, with many new houses being built for those working in nearby Cheltenham, of which it is almost a suburb. Worth visiting is the small Norman church, which had fallen into disuse by the mid-19th century when it was partially rebuilt, much restored and also richly furnished, by Lord Ellenborough, who had retired to Southam after a term as Governor-General of India. Lord Ellenborough lived at Southam Delabere, an Elizabethan mansion nearby which he enlarged, adding a neo-Norman keep and a Gothic tower. It is now a thriving luxury hotel.

There is a steep walk from Southam up onto Cleeve Hill ★, linking with the Cotswold Way ★.

South Cerney (163) (SU 04-97) *3 mi. SE Cirencester.* A large village on the banks of the River Churn, only about four miles above its confluence with the Thames at Cricklade ★. It is also on the edge of the large gravel pits which, now flooded, are providing the basis for the extensive Cotswold Water Park ★. Two lakes near the village are devoted to fishing and a third to sailing.

The village itself is of considerable interest, with an 18th-century octagonal gazebo by the River Churn, a number of pleasant old houses in Church Lane and Silver Street, and a walk near the George Inn with the delightful name 'Bow-Wow'. The large church dates back to the Norman period and above the Norman south doorway are sculptured details of Christ in Glory and the Harrowing of Hell. The large central tower was once topped by a spire, but this was dismantled in 1862, during restoration work carried out by the architect J.P. St Aubyn. Do not miss the fragments of a 12th-century rood, with the head and foot of a crucifix, one of the earliest and most outstanding pieces of wood-carving in the country.

The course of the Thames and Severn Canal ★ passes to the north of the village, and it is possible to use the old towpath, to walk north to Siddington ★ or south-eastwards to Cerney Wick ★, where there is a canal 'round house' (see Hyde ★), and on to Cricklade ★.

Southrop (163) (SP 20-03) *2½ mi. N Lechlade.*
Small village beside the willows and water-meadows of the lovely River Leach, with a fine manor house and a pleasant mill house nearby. There is a creeper-covered inn called the Swan, a pretty row of cottages, a gabled dovecot, and tucked away behind the manor an interesting little Norman church. This has a small bellcote, a Norman north doorway with geometric patterns in its tympanum, and a simple Norman chancel arch. John Keble was curate at Southrop between 1823 and 1825 (he was born in nearby Fairford) and it was he who was apparently responsible for rediscovering the Norman font, which for many years had been built into the south doorway. This font is a superb example of mid-12th-century craftsmanship, and in the view of most experts the finest specimen in the Cotswold area. Its subjects range from 'Moses with the Tables of the Law' to 'The Virtues trampling on The Vices'. Do not overlook the 16th-century effigies of Sir John Conway and his lady.

The nearby Old Vicarage was the home of John Keble during his short curacy (see above) and it was here that the first stirrings of the Oxford Movement must have taken place, for Keble used to invite friends from Oxford to come here for reading parties during vacations.

The manor house dates largely from the 16th and 17th centuries, but the discovery of a Norman archway appears to confirm the belief that it stands on the site of a very early building. The manor was purchased in 1612 by Dorothy Wadham, the founder of Wadham College, Oxford, and it formed part of her endowment, remaining in Wadham College's hands until as recently as 1926.

Walk north from here beside the River Leach to Eastleach ★, or south-eastwards, also beside the river, to Little Faringdon, with its flooded gravel pits.

Spelsbury (164) (SP 35-21) *1½ mi. N Charlbury.*
There is a pleasant blend of stone and thatch in this quiet village looking out over the Evenlode Valley towards Wychwood Forest ★. It has an attractive row of gabled 17th-century almshouses and a Victorian drinking fountain. Its fine, largely 18th-century church has a handsome tower and a series of splendid monuments to the Lee family, latterly the Earls of Litchfield, of nearby Ditchley Park ★.

Spoonley Roman Villa (163) (SP 04-25) *2 mi. SE Winchcombe.* Situated in Spoonley Wood, near the head of the 'Sudeley Valley' and about three quarters of a mile north-west of Roel Gate, are the remains of a Roman villa excavated in the late 19th century. This lies on private property, although there is a pleasant public footpath through the wood, passing close by (see our **Walk 2**, which

uses this path). It is regrettable that the remains of this delightfully situated villa have been allowed to deteriorate, especially as its courtyard layout plan was used to illustrate that classic textbook, *Everyday Life in Roman Britain*. Did the Romans' White Way ★ extend as far north as this from Cirencester? The answer is far from certain, but it seems likely that the owners of the villa would have wished to make frequent visits to this centre of local civilisation. Use Landranger Sheet 163 to arrive at your own conclusions.

Stanley Pontlarge (150) (SO 99-30) *2 mi. NW Winchcombe.* A hamlet beneath high Langley Hill, over which it is possible to walk to Winchcombe ★. The small Norman church has an original north doorway and chancel arch, but most of the remaining 'Norman' features are Victorian copies. As a result of this over-zealous restoration there is less atmosphere here than might have been hoped for.

Stanton (150) (SP 06-34) *3 mi. SW Broadway. (See map on page 98.)* An outstandingly beautiful village situated below the wooded Cotswold edge, and tempting enough to have brought the course of the Cotswold Way ★ down the steep slopes of Shenberrow Hill, through the village, and on to Stanway ★. The village was lovingly restored by its owner, the architect Sir Philip Stott, in the first quarter of the present century. The house he once owned, Stanton Court, is a fine Jacobean example and rather outshines the 16th-century manor house, but almost every building in Stanton is a delight to the eye.

The church has a well proportioned Perpendicular tower and spire and a very attractive two-storeyed porch complete with pinnacles and battlements. Inside, its Norman origins are revealed by the stout north arcading, and there are the remains of early 14th-century wall-paintings in the north transept. There are two pulpits here — a Jacobean one, and a late medieval one, no longer in use. The church was splendidly refurnished by one of the 20th century's finest restorers, Sir Ninian Comper, and his work

Springtime at Stanton . . . on the way towards the Mount Inn

has enhanced an already beautiful medieval interior. See especially the altar and communion rails, the gallery, the rood screen and the reredos, and above all the 15th-century stained glass, which originally came from Hailes Abbey, and which was reset by Comper.

The young John Wesley often stayed at his 'dear delightful Stanton' with the Reverend Lionel Kirkham and his sons and daughters, who were all great friends of his. In these years before his departure to America in 1735, Wesley preached several times from the pulpit at Stanton, and also at nearby Buckland and Broadway. For more details read V.H. Green's *The Young Mr Wesley*.

Walk beyond the old wayside cross, up the quiet village street to the hospitable little Mount Inn, which awaits you on its small knoll below the wooded scarp. From here it is possible to walk up over the hills to Snowshill ★, passing the small car-parking area (150) (SP 083-341) which straddles the Cotswold Way ★. This parking area is also the start of the mapped **mini-walk** shown on page 98, a suggested circular affair taking in both Stanton and Snowshill. Other walks from Stanton include a path over the fields to Laverton ★, and, using the Cotswold Way, either up to Shenberrow Hill (where there are the earthworks of a large Iron Age settlement) and eventually heading for Broadway ★, or through semi-parkland to neighbouring Stanway ★.

Stanway (150) (SP 06-32) *4 mi. SW Broadway.* This small village lies at the foot of long, winding, beautifully wooded Stanway Hill. Thatched stone cottages and the attractive Bakehouse Restaurant are situated between the bottom of the hill and the wooded crossroads where a handsome war memorial stands. This is a bronze by Alexander Fisher of *St George and the Dragon*, mounted on a plinth designed by Sir Philip Stott of neighbouring Stanton, with lettering by Eric Gill.

A short distance to the north of this crossroads stand the church, Stanway House and its splendid 17th-century gatehouse. Stanway church was over-restored in the late 19th century, but it has a Jacobean pulpit, a beautiful little bronze by Alexander Fisher and an altar made by Sir Ninian Comper, who worked so extensively at neighbouring Stanton ★.

Stanway House is a handsome Jacobean manor house containing fine period furniture, including a working shuffleboard table and 'Chinese Chippendale' day-beds. The house stands in lovely gardens beneath steep, wooded parklands enhanced by an 18th-century stone belvedere called the Pyramid, from the base of which once descended a cascade similar to that at Chatsworth in Derbyshire. There was once an ornamental canal between the base of the cascade and the house, but this was filled in many years ago and is now covered by a lawn.

Stanway's gatehouse is an enchanting piece of architecture, so beautiful that it was once attributed to Inigo Jones. However, it is now thought to have been the work of Timothy Strong of Taynton, one of the Cotswolds' outstanding masons and quarry-owners, and kinsman of Thomas Strong, who built the bridge over the Windrush at Little Barrington ★. Timothy also worked as a contractor at Cornbury Park ★ under the direction of the great Nicholas Stone, and it seems likely that some of Stone's influence was at work in the design of Stanway. In

St George and the Dragon at Stanway's wooded crossroads

the grounds is a fine 14th-century tithe barn, used by the abbots of Tewkesbury when they held the manorial rights here, and close by is a thatched wooden cricket pavilion set on staddle stones. This was presented to the village by Sir James Barrie, the writer perhaps best known for his haunting children's story, *Peter Pan*. *The house and grounds are open to the public at certain times. (Tel: (038 673) 469.)*

Stanway lies astride the Cotswold Way ★, and this can be used for walks to Stanton ★, or to Wood Stanway ★, both relatively level stretches of the Way. However, the best walk from Stanway is up through the great woodlands below Lidcombe Hill and over to Snowshill ★. A glance at Landranger Sheet 150 will also indicate a fine circular walk, up through the same woods, down to Stanton by way of Shenberrow Hill, and back along the Cotswold Way to Stanway.

Stowell (163) (SP 08-13) *2 mi. SW Northleach.* Here is a fine Elizabethan mansion in a large park looking westwards over the Coln Valley to the Chedworth Woods. This is not open to the public. However, behind the mansion there is a small Norman church. This has been over-restored externally, but the interior is full of character and its contents include some fascinating and very early 'Doom' paintings, which must have been executed between 1150 and 1200, soon after the church was built. See also the two Norman piscinas, and the two 18th-century wall monuments in the chancel. This church lies within the bounds of the estate and it is suggested that visitors walk up the drive from the Northleach to Yanworth road. Parking on the roadside can be a problem, but the possibly long walk is well justified.

Stow-on-the-Wold (163) (SP 19-25) *4 mi. S Moreton-in-Marsh.* This attractive little market town is the focal point of the northern Cotswolds, with no fewer than eight roads converging upon its windy site 700 feet above sea level. There was an Iron Age settlement here — an area of about thirty acres enclosed by earthworks, the partial remains of which are visible (but not worth searching for) in

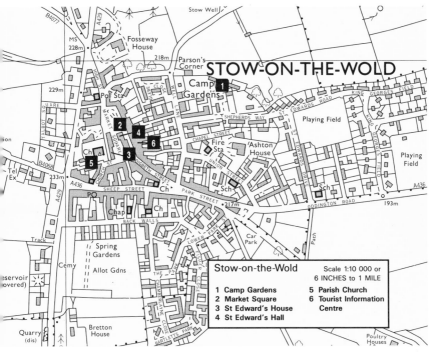

Camp Gardens (1). Later there was also a Roman villa, sited not far to the west of the Foss Way ★, which itself now runs along the western edge of the town.

The best of Stow is centred upon its large **Market Square (2)**, and a weekly market and two annual fairs, known as the Charter Fairs, have been held here since 1107, when Henry I granted Borough status to 'Edwardstow', as it was then called. The connection of Stow-on-the-Wold with 'St Edward' remains a mystery as there are three possible candidates to be considered — Edward the Hermit, a shadowy figure from early Christian times, Edward, King and Martyr, the young king stabbed to death at Corfe Castle, and the better-known King Edward the Confessor. The writer prefers the earliest candidate, Edward the Hermit, and likes to feel that this old bewhiskered saint spent his days in zealous prayer near the well below nearby Maugersbury ★ that still bears his name.

Stow's fairs were renowned for the sale of wool and sheep, and Daniel Defoe, who once visited one of them, noted that over 20,000 sheep were sold. However, since Defoe's time they have become better known for the sale of horses, and until only a few years ago the Stow Horse Fairs were held in fields just to the west of the town. Officially they have been moved to Andoversford ★, but many horses still change hands at the time of the two Charter Fairs which are still held in Stow, one in May and one in October, and which are now largely funfairs.

Although undisturbed by none of the main roads entering the town, the Market Square is still usually busy with visitors and local country shoppers. The town's excellent **Tourist Information Centre (6)** can be found here (tel: (0451) 31082), together with several antique shops, picture galleries, hotels, restaurants and inns — all facing into the Square —

and most are traditional 17th- or 18th-century Cotswold buildings, apart from **St Edward's House (3)**, a handsome building with Corinthian pilasters. There is a medieval cross here, although this has a headstone made in 1878, the year that **St Edward's Hall (4)** was built a little to its north. This substantial Perpendicular-style building tends to divide the Market Square into two separate areas. It now houses the town's library. Beyond St Edward's Hall, the northern and more open half of the Square, known as the Green, has wide grass verges and the old town stocks which were once used for the punishment of evil-doers.

Quiet corner at Stow-on-the-Wold

STRATFORD AND MORETON TRAMWAY

St Edward's Church (5) lies well back from the Square, between this and the Foss Way. It is a large building with medieval origins, but much restored in the 17th century, following extensive damage caused whilst it was used to house prisoners during the Civil War. The last battle in this bitter struggle between king and Parliament was fought at nearby Donnington ★, although it is usually referred to as the Battle of Stow. The church's interior was again restored in the 19th century, when the roof was rebuilt. The work was carried out by J.L.Pearson, the architect best known for the building of Truro Cathedral, but Stow's restoration does not appear to have been one of his better efforts. However, do not miss the impressive painting of the Crucifixion in the south aisle, thought to be by the 17th-century Flemish artist, Gaspar de Craeyer, nor the floor slab in memory of Francis Keyte, one of the Keytes of Ebrington ★, who was killed at the Battle of Stow.

Before leaving Stow, explore the small streets leading from the southern end of the Square where there are further shops and hotels, all contributing something to Stow-on-the-Wold's qualities as an excellent touring centre for the northern Cotswolds.

The Stratford and Moreton Tramway (151) (SP 20-54) — (SP 20-32) This was the brainchild of William James of Henley-in-Arden, near Stratford-upon-Avon, and was part of an ambitious scheme to link his other transport and mining interests to London, by a projected line entitled the Central Junction Railway. However, James was only able to gain local support for a line as far as Moreton-in-Marsh ★ with a branch to Shipston-on-Stour ★. An Act of Incorporation for this scheme was passed on 18 May 1821, only six weeks earlier than the Act of Incorporation for that world pioneer line, the famous Stockton and Darlington Railway. It is interesting to speculate on what would have happened to Shipston-on-Stour and Moreton-in-Marsh if James's scheme for the Central Junction had been accepted in full. As it was, the local scheme soon ran into difficulties, both with problems of civil engineering, and with the prevention by the authorities of the use of steam trains on at least the first six miles south of Stratford-upon-Avon. The line to Moreton was finally opened in 1826, but by then James had been declared bankrupt, and all passenger and goods traffic was restricted to horse-drawn wagons provided not by the company but by toll-paying local traders.

In 1836 a branch line was opened to Shipston-on-Stour ★, and when Brunel's main Oxford, Worcester and Wolverhampton Railway line was built in 1853, the tramway provided a useful link to it at Moreton-in-Marsh ★.

The Moreton-Shipston section was eventually converted to take steam trains, as a branch of the Great Western Railway, an arrangement that lasted until its final closure in 1960. The most enduring monument to the tramway is its mellow brick bridge over the Avon at Stratford-upon-Avon, and on the town side of the bridge there is an old tramway wagon on display, between the gardens and the timber-yard. The line of the tramway may be followed in several places, especially beside the Shipston Road out of Stratford, but its total disappearance in others is a reflection of the problems often facing archaeologists looking for signs of civilisation many hundreds or even thousands of years older. Read the most interesting

story of this tramway in John Norris's book, *The Stratford and Moreton Tramway*.

Stratton (163) (SP 01-03) *1 mi. NW Cirencester.* Now almost a suburb of Cirencester, most of old Stratton is situated astride the still-busy Ermin Way ★. The church, situated at its north-western end, was largely rebuilt in 1850, although the south wall of the original Norman building has survived, complete with one Norman window and, above a late Perpendicular doorway, a Norman tympanum with a Tree of Life. Apart from the white-painted chancel, the interior has been scraped and pointed, and this is relieved only by a few 18th- and 19th-century wall monuments.

It is possible to walk north-westwards from here, up the Duntisbourne Valley to Daglingworth ★, and on to the Duntisbournes ★.

Stretton-on-Fosse (151) (SP 22-38) *4 mi. NE Moreton-in-Marsh.* An unspoilt village on a little hill just to the west of the busy Foss Way. The 'e' added to the word 'Foss' in the village's name is evidence of continuing confusion over the correct spelling of one of Britain's best-known Roman roads. The church here was entirely rebuilt in 1841, and is not of great interest to visitors, but the William and Mary Old Rectory and the Georgian Court House add interest to the village. From a distance, the unusually restrained 19th-century Manor House could easily be mistaken for a building some 300 years older. It overlooks the Foss Way, which crosses the line of the old Stratford and Moreton Tramway ★ in the valley below. This was once the site of a small railway station, and the mellow brick building that still stands here was once the Golden Cross Inn. This has been a private house for many years, but there is a welcoming inn in the village — the Plough.

It is possible to walk south-westwards from here, over the fields passing the site of the medieval village of Upper Ditchford, and on to Aston Magna ★. A return could be made eastwards to Todenham ★, and then north-westwards back to Stretton-on-Fosse.

Stroud (162) (SO 84-05) *8 mi. S Gloucester.* Built on steep slopes at the junction of no fewer than five valleys, this busy town has retained considerable character despite its industrialisation in the late 18th and early 19th centuries. It had established itself as the pre-eminent centre of the Cotswold cloth industry as early as the 15th century, and the availability of the splendid Cotswold wool, of water for washing, and of minerals for dyeing and cleaning ensured that it remained so for several hundred years. At the height of its prosperity there were at least 150 cloth mills in the valleys centred upon Stroud; 'Uley Blue', 'Stroudwater Scarlet' and other West of England cloths were renowned throughout the world as the basis for a wide range of military and naval uniforms and high-class civilian wear — a reputation that has lasted to this day. As the 19th century progressed, more and more cloth manufacture moved to the mills of Yorkshire's West Riding, and competition from here and more recently from abroad has by now resulted in the closure of all but two companies. However, these two are still very active, many light industries have come here to replace the others, and Stroud and its

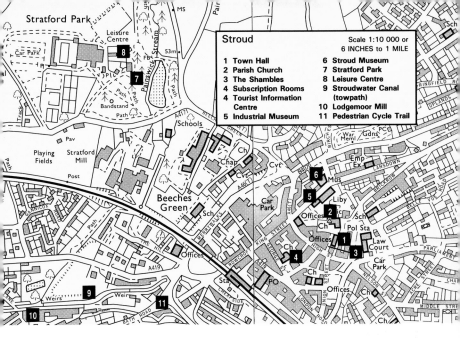

surrounding valley country continue to thrive.

Most of Stroud's prosperous clothiers chose to build their houses in the countryside beyond, but many of its steep and often narrow streets retain a character formed by the town's early industrial success. Beside the Tudor *Town Hall (1)* and to the south side of *St Lawrence's Church (2)* is *The Shambles (3)*, once a meat market, and now the site of a busy market on Wednesdays and Fridays. The nearby *Subscription Rooms (4)*, in George Street, are housed in an elegant early 19th-century neo-classical building. Numerous local functions are held here and they also house the *Tourist Information Centre (4). (Tel: (0453) 765768.)*

Apart from its fine 14th-century tower, St Lawrence's Church was rebuilt in the 1860s, and although its interior contains some earlier monuments it is not of great interest to visitors. In the street called Lansdown there is a small *Industrial Museum (5)* representing a wide range of local crafts and industries. Just beyond it on the other side, the interesting *Stroud Museum (6)* is located in the Lansdown Hall. It is largely devoted to items of local interest, including a 20ft model of a dinosaur, a collection of early lawnmowers, and displays illustrating the story of Stroud's cloth industry. *(Tel: (0453) 763394.)* For further details refer to the booklet *A Walk round Stroud*, published by the Stroud Civic Society, and copies of which are obtainable from the Tourist Information Centre.

The delightful *Stratford Park (7)*, just to the north-west of the town, has a large lake and a fine *Leisure Centre (8). (Tel: (0453) 766771.)* Another of Stroud's features is the *Stroudwater Canal (9) ★*, which runs up the Frome Valley, and which once formed a link here between the Severn at Framilode and the Thames and Severn Canal ★. It is possible to walk along its towpath, and that of the Thames and Severn Canal ★, eastwards up the valley, most of the way from Eastington ★ to Daneway ★. This walk is well described in the locally produced *Canals Towpath Guide*, which should be available from the Tourist Information Centre.

Also of interest are the Stroud Civic Society's

two *Wool Walk* booklets, also available from the Tourist Information Centre. *Wool Walk One* passes, amongst other features of the cloth industry, *Lodgemoor Mill (10)*, which still produces fine West of England cloth. *Wool Walk Two* explores more cloth industry features, in the Nailsworth Valley, which runs south from Rooksmoor (162) (SO 84-03) to Woodchester ★. Both of these walks make part use of another excellent facility, the *Stroud Valleys Pedestrian and Cycle Trail (11)*. This uses the abandoned railway track-bed between Nailsworth ★ and Stonehouse, with a branch to Stroud. A leaflet describing this trail should also be available from the Tourist Information Centre.

Stratford Park, Stroud

Stroudwater Canal (162) (SO 75-10) — (SO 85-04) This canal, linking the River Severn at Framilode with the busy industrial town of Stroud ★, was opened in 1779. Within ten years it had become part of a link between the Severn and the Thames, with the opening of the Thames and Severn Canal ★, between Stroud and Inglesham near Lechlade. The

SUDELEY CASTLE

Thames and Severn was never a commercial success and the last recorded journey through it was made in 1911. However, the Stroudwater Canal was more successful and was not finally abandoned until 1954. Brave attempts are being made to restore sections of both canals, and parts of their towpaths make delightful walks, especially near Stonehouse (162) (ST 81-04) and along the Thames and Severn Canal between Stroud and the western portal of the Sapperton Tunnel at Daneway ★ (see also **Walk 10**). For further details read Ronald Russell's *Lost Canals and Waterways of Britain*, and Michael Handford's *The Stroudwater Canal*.

Sudeley Castle (163) (SP 03-27) *½ mi. SE Winchcombe.* This is beautifully situated just outside the little town of Winchcombe ★, and looks out towards the wooded slopes of Cleeve Hill ★.

Sudeley Castle

Sudeley was in royal hands from the time of King Ethelred the Unready, and it included a fine deer park which took up most of the valley running into the hills to its south, and of which many of the boundaries can still be traced today. Ethelred granted the estate to his daughter Goda, who was the sister of Edward the Confessor. Thanks to her distant relationship with the Duke of Normandy it was not confiscated by the Normans, and she was able to pass it on to her son, Ralph de Sudeley. His descendants held it until a new castle was begun in 1441 by the victorious Admiral of the Fleet, Sir Thomas Boteler, who was created Baron Sudeley by Henry VI.

No trace of the earlier castle or castles remains, but much of Boteler's magnificent building has survived, including St Mary's Chapel, the ruined Banqueting Hall, the Tithe Barn and the Portmare Tower. This tower is said to have been named after a captured French admiral, whose ransom money very largely financed the castle's rebuilding. In 1455 the Wars of the Roses broke out, and within six years Boteler's master, the Lancastrian Henry VI, had been succeeded by the Yorkist Edward IV. Boteler was soon forced to forfeit his beloved Sudeley, and it once more became royal property. Queen Catherine Parr, the only one of Henry VIII's six wives to outlive him, came with her court to Sudeley on his death. Within a short time the scheming Sir Thomas Seymour had secretly married Catherine and persuaded the young Edward VI to create him Baron Sudeley. In August 1548, with Sir Thomas already making free with other ladies at court in London, Catherine gave birth to a

daughter. A few days later she died of puerperal fever, and was buried in the beautiful little St Mary's Chapel, with the ill-fated Lady Jane Grey as one of the chief mourners.

Queen Mary granted Sudeley to Thomas Brydges and created him Lord Chandos of Sudeley. Her sister Queen Elizabeth visited the castle on three occasions and, as was the custom, she was of course lavishly entertained. During the Civil War the castle was held by the Royalists, but in 1644 it was forced to surrender to the Parliamentarians after a siege. At the end of the war it was, like most castles which had been held by Royalists, 'slighted', or effectively ruined, by the victorious Parliamentarians, and a process of decay set in, which was only to be reversed after nearly 200 years had passed.

It was in 1837 that the estate was purchased by two highly successful glove makers from Worcester, the brothers John and William Dent. They immediately set about the massive task of restoring the castle, employing the distinguished architect Sir Gilbert Scott to restore the chapel. By the early 1840s Sudeley was again habitable, but sadly the two brothers had both died by 1855, and the estate passed to their nephew John Dent. He, however, had the good sense to marry Emma Brocklehurst, the daughter of a Cheshire Member of Parliament.

Emma Dent, even when widowed, carried on the work of restoration and improvement, contributing much to this and to the community in general. She must have been a formidable figure — tireless, demanding, generous — in many ways resembling Queen Victoria in her later years, especially in her looks. She died in 1900, but the castle has remained in the same family ever since.

Today Sudeley is full of interest, its restored rooms containing many art treasures, including works by Constable, Turner, Rubens and Van Dyck, along with tapestries, needlework and armour. Moreover the powerful personality of Emma Dent still seems to linger here. Thanks to Gilbert Scott, the chapel's interior, including the tomb of Catherine Parr, is rather heavily Victorianised, but its lovely Perpendicular exterior has survived intact. See also the craft exhibitions, the regular falconry displays and the Elizabethan Garden. There is also a restaurant. *(Tel: (0242) 602308.)*

Swinbrook (163) (SP 28-12) *2 mi. E Burford.* Delightful village with a rough, sloping green. It is enlivened by a small stream which flows into the River Windrush close to the Swan Inn, once Swinbrook's mill. The church with its small tower should on no account be missed. A fine Perpendicular window fills the whole of the east end and light floods in upon two splendid three-decker wall monuments, in which there are the effigies of no fewer than six male members of the Fettiplace family, all lying on their right sides, looking not upwards but outwards. The Fettiplaces once owned a great mansion, which stood between the church and the Windrush, but of this there is now no trace apart from vague terraces and a fishpond. See the 15th-century choir stalls with their misericords (the carved undersides of their seats), the brasses of John Croston and his three wives, and of Anthony Fettiplace, and several other wall monuments including one by the celebrated sculptor, Richard Westmacott.

In the churchyard, in addition to the considerable number of handsome table tombs in the best

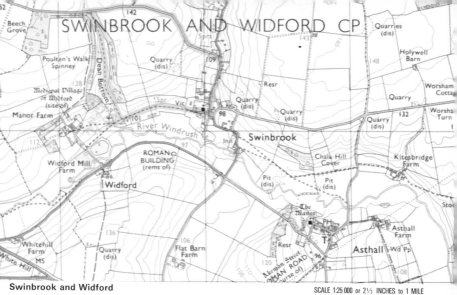

Swinbrook and Widford

SCALE 1:25 000 or 2½ INCHES to 1 MILE

Cotswold tradition, will be found the gravestone of Unity Mitford and her sister Nancy, whose childhood years at Swinbrook are so wonderfully described by their sister Jessica in her book *Hons and Rebels*. They lived at nearby Asthall ★ for a time, and then at Swinbrook House, which was built by their father, Lord Redesdale, some way to the north of Swinbrook village. Read more about this fascinating family in Jonathan and Catherine Guinness's book, *The House of Mitford*.

Use our mapped **mini-walk** to go westwards along the Windrush Valley to visit the fascinating little church at Widford ★, then go up Dean Bottom and down a quiet road back to Swinbrook. It is also possible to walk eastwards down the valley to Asthall ★.

Fettiplace Monument in Swinbrook Church

Syde (163) (SO 94-10) *7 mi. NW Cirencester*. A quiet hamlet looking across the deep, wooded valley of the upper Frome to Caudle Green ★. Its early Norman church has a small saddleback tower and a pleasing 15th-century, almost barn-like roof. Beyond the plain Norman chancel arch the chancel is Victorian, but unusually even this is pleasant. See also the 17th-century box pews, the octagonal 15th-century font, and the little 15th-century glass roundel of St James of Compostela, in lovely muted colours.

There is a tithe barn on the south side of the churchyard, and the cottage on the right-hand side of the road down towards Caudle Green ★ has 14th-century windows, and is believed to be based on a chantry chapel founded here in 1344 by Sir Thomas Berkeley.

Walk down into the valley and then northwards, up beside the infant Frome to Brimpsfield ★, or down the valley to Caudle Green ★ and Miserden ★. Syde is also on our **Walk 9**.

Syde Church, with its little saddleback tower

Syreford (163) (SP 02-20) *5 mi. S Winchcombe.*
This hamlet north of Andoversford has a pleasant
mill house, but few other special features. A Roman
settlement was excavated here many years ago and
amongst the articles recovered was a delightful
four-inch-high statuette of the god Mars. Walk
north from here beside the infant River Coln to
Sevenhampton ★ and Brockhampton ★ .

Taddington (150) (SP 08-31) *2 mi. S Snowshill.*
Small, windy upland hamlet with a few houses and
a fine 17th-century barn with the date 1632 upon its
porch. There are low earthworks to the north of the
hamlet, the remains of a larger medieval settlement
probably depopulated by sheep graziers. This is in
high watershed country and under half a mile to its
east is the substantial farmhouse Field Barn, with a
reed-bordered pool beside it giving birth to what is
arguably the loveliest of Cotswold rivers — the
Windrush.

Walk south from here, down the head of the
Windrush Valley to Cutsdean ★ , Ford ★ and Temple Guiting ★ , or westwards to the great woodlands
above Stanway ★ .

Tarlton (163) (ST 95-99) *4 mi. W Cirencester.* This
scattered little village has a small, largely neo-
Norman church, the result of a complete rebuild in
1875. There is a simple Norman chancel arch
retained from the original building, and the Norman
tub font appears to have been recut in low relief in
the 14th century. There is a pleasant walk northwards through the great Hailey Wood and on to
Sapperton ★ , or north-eastwards to the Tunnel
House Inn ★ , which is close to the south-eastern
portal of the Thames and Severn Canal ★ tunnel
beneath the Cotswolds.

Taynton (163) (SP 23-13) *1½ mi. NW Burford.*
Trim stone village in the Windrush Valley with views
out towards the willow-bordered river. Yew trees
line the wide path to the north door of the church,
which has a slender Perpendicular tower. The 14th-
century north aisle is a fine example of the
Decorated style, with much ballflower ornamentation and rich stone tracery. Other notable features
include an elaborate early 15th-century font, interesting corbel figures, carved roof bosses and an old
alms chest. There is a pleasant assortment of
17th- and 18th-century tombstones in the churchyard.

Stone has been extracted from the great Taynton
quarries since medieval times, and it has been used
in the construction or repair of Windsor Castle, St
Paul's Cathedral, Blenheim Palace ★ and most of
the Oxford colleges. The Clerk of Works at Windsor
during the reign of Edward III was named Richard
Taynton, and he no doubt acquired his skills in his
home village before moving on to greater things. In
his fascinating *Natural History of Oxfordshire*, the
eccentric Dr Plot relates that he once saw a wagon-
load of Taynton stone being hauled by no fewer
than twenty-one horses. It was probably being
driven southwards to the Thames at Radcot Bridge
or Lechlade, where it would have been loaded onto
barges for carrying down to Oxford or London.

Unlike the quarries at Windrush ★ and Barrington,
which were driven underground into the ridge
which now carries the A40, the Taynton quarries
have always been open to the sky. Now much

overgrown, they lie in a valley about a mile and a
half to the north of the village, on land owned by
the Lee family, farmers of Taynton.

Teddington (150) (SO 96-33) *5 mi. E Tewkesbury.*
Pleasant village beneath the steep, orchard-clad
slopes of Oxenton Hill, an outlier of the true
Cotswolds. Although Norman in origin, with a tall
early Norman chancel arch, the church has much
from the 13th, 14th and 15th centuries. The tower
was built in 1567 and the fine Early English tower
arch and west window were imported from Hailes
Abbey ★ , which was by then a total ruin. The
plastered nave walls are decorated with various
paintings, including a handsome Royal Arms of
William and Mary. See also the 17th-century pulpit
and reading desk.

At Teddington Hands, on the main A435 road,
half a mile to the north, there is an attractive stone
guide-post, put up here in 1676 by a certain Edmund
Attwood.

The best walk from Teddington is southwards
along the flanks of Oxenton Hill, to Oxenton and on
to Gotherington, neither of which is covered by this
guide.

Temple Guiting (150,163) (SP 09-28) *4 mi. E
Winchcombe.* This minute village shelters in the
pleasantly wooded valley of the Windrush, with
pools both above and below a small bridge over this
delectable river. There is a small bow-fronted shop,
and several attractive houses. These include the
early 16th-century Manor Farm, which may have
been one of the summer residences of the Bishop of
Oxford, and the elegant 18th-century Temple Guiting House, which looks across the Windrush Valley
to the church. This was once given to the preceptory of Quenington ★ , itself owned by the Knights
Templar, but only fragments of their Norman
church remain. The architectural history of the
remainder is most involved, and restoration and
rebuilding have occurred many times. The fine
tower was built as late as the 18th century, while its
pinnacles are an even later (19th-century) addition.
We are also indebted to the 18th-century builders
for the Georgian classical windows, the pulpit, the
tower arch, the reredos and the handsome Royal
Arms of George II, in white plaster. See also the
Decorated piscina and font, the early 16th-century
stained glass and the 18th-century wall tablets.

The best walk from here is northwards up the
Windrush Valley to Ford ★ , from whence it is
possible to walk westward to Slade Barn Farm. By
using Landranger Sheet 163, it is possible to plot a
return to Temple Guiting via Pinnock Farm.

Tetbury (163,173) (ST 89-93) *10 mi. SW Cirencester.* Situated on the busy A433, this largely unspoilt
little market town is centred upon its delightful mid-
17th-century **Town Hall, or Market House (1)**.
This is supported by three rows of dumpy Tuscan
pillars, and has a stone roof and a handsome cupola
topped by a weathervane with gilded dolphins. To
the north of the Market House is the mid-19th-
century **Snooty Fox Hotel (2)**. Formerly the White
Hart, this was rebuilt by Lewis Vulliamy, the
architect of Westonbirt ★ , with the large ballroom
on its first floor specially designed to accommodate
the junketings of the celebrated Beaufort Hunt, but
now subdivided into bedrooms.

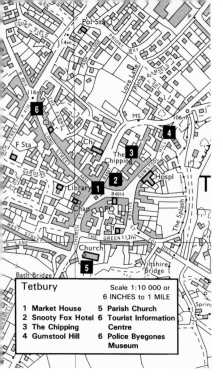

Tetbury

Scale 1:10 000 or
6 INCHES to 1 MILE

1 Market House
2 Snooty Fox Hotel
3 The Chipping
4 Gumstool Hill
5 Parish Church
6 Tourist Information
Centre
6 Police Byegones
Museum

is part of the lively Tetbury Festival (or Woolsack Day), which takes place on Spring Bank Holiday Monday, with stall-holders in medieval dress, a town jester, morris dancers and other revivals of ancient revelry.

The Church of St Mary (5) was built in the Gothic style in 1781, by the architect and builder Francis Hiorn of Warwick. He retained the fine medieval tower and spire, but these had to be rebuilt about a hundred years later. The tall, beautifully proportioned interior, with its panelled galleries, box pews and several pleasing monuments, is splendidly lit by tall Perpendicular-style windows. The two handsome 18th-century chandeliers add further elegance to a church which should on no account be missed.

Tetbury's Tourist Information Centre (6), which is open from Easter to the end of October, is situated together with an interesting little Police Bygones Museum (6) in the Old Court House, at the far end of Long Street near the north end of the town. (Tel: (0666) 503552.) There is a pleasant variety of shops in the town, including several fine antique shops and another devoted entirely to the sale of cheese, of which there is an outstanding selection. For a more detailed description of Tetbury's architectural gems refer to the Tetbury Society's interesting Walkabout Guide and Map, which is available at the Tourist Information Centre.

Beyond the Snooty Fox is The Chipping (3), a former lesser market. The Chipping is overlooked by a number of attractive 17th- and 18th-century houses. These, and many other buildings of the same period in other parts of the town, bear witness to the continuing prosperity of Tetbury, due largely to its importance as a wool collecting centre for the cloth towns and villages to its north and west. The Chipping Steps lead down from the Chipping's north-east corner to the foot of the steep Gumstool Hill (4), up which it is possible to return to the Market House. Gumstool Hill is the scene of Tetbury's famous Woolsack Races, when the young men and girls of two local teams have to race down to the cattle market and back up this 1-in-4 hill, from the Crown Inn to the Royal Oak, each carrying a 65lb sack of wool. This feat of endurance

Tuscan pillars supporting Tetbury's Market House

Tewkesbury (150) (SO 89-32) 10 mi. NE Gloucester. Not truly Cotswold in character or location, the delightful old town of Tewkesbury is just too good to omit from this guide. There is some evidence that there were monks here as early as AD 715, but the great Benedictine abbey from which the town drew its medieval prosperity was founded by the Norman, Robert Fitzhamon, who imported stone from Caen for its construction. Fitzhamon died in 1107, fourteen years before it was consecrated, but on his death his patronage was continued by his son-in-law, the bastard son of Henry I, Robert Fitzroy, Earl of Gloucester. The 'Honour of Tewkesbury', as this patronage was known, then descended to the powerful de Clare family, and thanks to their endowments and support, the abbey grew into one of the country's most powerful religious houses, owning great tracts of land on the Cotswolds, and several great tithe barns including the one that still stands at Stanway ★. The abbey remained the focal point of the town for over 400 years, but at the Dissolution of the Monasteries in 1539, its great abbey church was sold to the town for what must even then have been the very modest price of £453.

It was in the meadow off Lincoln Green Lane (known from that day forward as 'Bloody Meadow'), to the south of the abbey, that one of the bloodiest and most decisive battles of the Wars of the Roses took place, when on 4 May 1417 the Lancastrian army of Margaret of Anjou, wife of the imprisoned Henry VI, was massacred by the Yorkist army of Edward IV. Some of the defeated troops sought sanctuary in the abbey itself, but despite the protests of the abbot, they were still put to the sword in the aisles. The queen's illegitimate son Edward was slain during the battle, but Margaret escaped, only to be imprisoned later in the Tower, until ransomed by her father, the king of France. Ask for a copy of the Tewkesbury Battle Trail at the Tourist Information Centre (see below).

The town that grew up in the shelter of the great

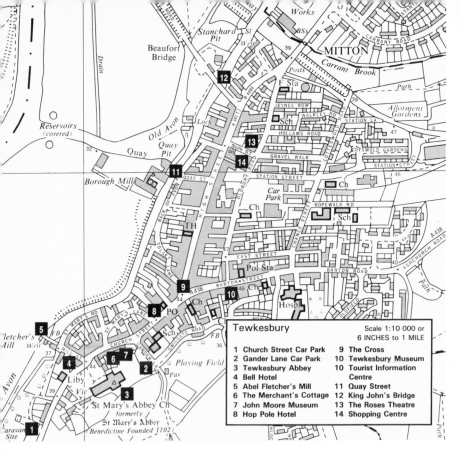

abbey was confined by the Rivers Severn and Avon, which join just to its west (and which were, and still are, very liable to flood), and by the abbey's lands to its east and south. But within these confines it continued to grow — not in size, but in density. In the 17th and 18th centuries especially, the areas behind the three main streets, Church Street, High Street and Barton Street, were threaded with a fascinating but no doubt insanitary series of alleys and courts. Several of these have survived to this day and bring a special quality to this town of timber-framed and mellow-brick houses, which also has a pleasing number of genuine country-town shops amongst the inevitable chain stores.

Exploration of the town is best started from one of the two car parks close to the abbey, one at the end of Church Street *(1)* on the road out to Gloucester, and one in Gander Lane *(2)* just to the east of the abbey itself. First visit this great **Abbey Church of St Mary (3)**, with its massive 132ft-high and 46ft-square Norman tower. From the top of the tower there are fine views out over the town and the two rivers beyond, to Bredon Hill and the Malverns, and in the other direction, towards the long scarp face of the Cotswolds. The west front has a 65ft-high Norman recessed arch, one of the largest ever built, and light floods in through the window it surrounds, which is a 17th-century replacement. This illuminates the fourteen massive Norman columns which support the splendidly vaulted 14th-century roof of the nave, with its fifteen bosses illustrating the life of Christ. From the ambulatory behind the apsidal choir, also 14th-century, six

chapels radiate outwards, and in this area there are a number of beautiful monuments, including several to the de Clares and to members of the family with whom they became linked by marriage, the Des-

Half-timbered cottages and the Norman abbey church at Tewkesbury

pencers; here also is the lovely Warwick Chantry Chapel, endowed by the Beauchamp family, many of whose members are buried in the abbey. Perhaps of even greater beauty are the choir's seven 14th-century stained-glass windows. However, this is a brief summary of some of this great abbey church's outstanding features. To enjoy it to the full, purchase one of the detailed guides available at the abbey's well stocked bookstall, and take time to explore it in detail.

Now go down Mill Street, passing the richly timbered *Bell Hotel (4)*, to *'Abel Fletcher's Mill' (5)*, a restored water-mill thought to have provided inspiration for Mrs Craik, the Victorian writer who used Tewkesbury as the model for 'Nortonbury' in her novel *John Halifax, Gentleman*. From here it is possible to walk out over the wide water-meadows of Severn Ham to look at the weir and lock on the Severn at Upper Lode (150) (SO 88-33). It is also possible to walk beside the Avon, passing an attractive row of timbered cottages, and into St Mary's Lane. However, it is probably better to return to the Bell Hotel and turn left into Church Street, where there is soon an alley or court down to the left leading to a delightfully unspoilt Baptist Chapel. With origins in the 15th century, this was skilfully converted into a chapel in the 17th, and it still retains the flavour of this era. Almost opposite the turn to the chapel there is a restored row of medieval merchants' cottages, one of which houses *'The Merchant's Cottage' (6)*, which is furnished to illustrate the life of the original occupants. Another is the *John Moore Museum (7)*, a countryside museum which commemorates the local author John Moore, who died in 1967, and whose books were very largely based on Tewkesbury and the surrounding countryside. Read his *Portrait of Elmbury* for a flavour of Tewkesbury in the first half of the 20th century.

Now continue along Church Street, passing an excellent bookshop, to the Georgian-fronted *Hop Pole Hotel (8)*, where Charles Dickens's Mr Pickwick and his friends did so well on 'ale, Madeira and five bottles of port'. From here it is a short distance to *The Cross (9)*. This is now the war memorial, but it stands on the point where the medieval High Cross stood before its demolition by the Puritans in 1650. Here is the true centre of the town, where its three streets meet — Church Street, High Street and Barton Street. First go down Barton Street for a short way to visit (on the right-hand side) the interesting *Tewkesbury Museum (10)*, an 'architectural heritage centre', with its local history items including a model of the Battle of Tewkesbury. This is also the town's *Tourist Information Centre (10)*. *(Tel: (0684) 295027.)* Various leaflets are available here including one describing the *Tewkesbury Battle Trail*, which follows a footpath through the Bloody Meadow.

Walk back to *The Cross (9)* and turn right into the High Street. Soon turn left into *Quay Street (11)*, near which it is possible to hire a boat on the River Avon. For other boating opportunities from Tewkesbury, please enquire locally. It is also possible to walk over the bridge leading to the large flour mills (do not trespass into the mill area), and to follow the right of way immediately to the right, on a riverside path leading past the last lock on the Avon before it joins the River Severn. From here it is a short way to the main road which crosses the Avon over the rebuilt *King John's Bridge (12)*. Turn right, cross the bridge, turn right into High

Street and head back for the Cross, passing on the right *The Roses Theatre (13)* and the *Shopping Centre (14)* on the way. From here it is not far to walk back to either of the starting car parks.

Walks out from Tewkesbury include one northwards beside the Avon to Twyning Fleet (150) (SO 90-36). This can be extended into a nine-mile walk returning beside the Severn, but for details see the *Circular Walk Leaflet No 1*, available at the Tourist Information Office. There is also a walk southwards beside the Severn, from Lower Lode to Deerhurst★, and beyond to Apperley (150) (SO 86-28) and even as far as Gloucester★.

Thames Head (163) (ST 98-99) *3 mi. SW Cirencester*. This is at Trewsbury Mead, the true source of the River Thames. There are pleasant paths across the fields, either southwards from Coates★, or northwards from the Thames Head Inn, on the Foss Way (163) (ST 98-98). In his *Itinerary*, Henry VIII's antiquary John Leland states, 'Wher as the very head of Isis ys, in a great sommer drought apperith very little or no water.' Things appear to have changed but little, and visitors will probably still find no more than a muddy depression beneath a tree, relieved only by a granite slab declaring this to be the true source of the Thames. This modest stone replaces a handsome statue of Neptune, which was removed in 1974 to St John's Lock below Lechlade★, as it sadly became the subject of vandalism soon after its installation here by the Thames Conservancy in 1958.

The Thames Head Bridge, some distance to the south-east, once carried the Foss Way★ over the Thames and Severn Canal★. The canal has long been abandoned, and the bridge is now on a lay-by just to the west of the road, with a plaque fixed to its parapet. The group of buildings (now converted into a private house) just to the south-east of the Foss Way is all that remains of the old Thames Head Pumping Station, where a pumping engine drew water from a deep well to top up the summit level of the canal. Use Landranger Sheet 163 to follow a path from the Foss Way south-eastwards and then south towards Kemble★, to come to the first appreciable flow of Thames water — probably at Lyd Well. Leland appears to have missed this.

Thames and Severn Canal (162) (SO 85-04) — (163) (SU 20-98) Designed by Robert Whitworth, this was opened in 1789 to link the Stroudwater Canal★ at Stroud with the head of the navigable Thames at Inglesham★, near Lechlade★. Unlike the Stroudwater it was never a great success. There were no fewer than forty-four locks between Stroud and the western end of the tunnel. The 2¼-mile tunnel at Sapperton★ was a constant problem, and there were often water shortages on the summit level, despite the pumping station at Thames Head★. The Upper Thames navigation was also never good, and the Oxford Canal, which opened only one year after the Thames and Severn, provided a better link between London and the Midlands. Both were soon to be overshadowed by the Grand Junction Canal, which opened in 1800.

The last recorded journey on the Thames and Severn was made in 1911 and it was finally abandoned in 1927. Its closure was one of the great tragedies of English canal history, and although brave efforts are being made to restore certain sections of both this and the Stroudwater Canal★,

The south-eastern portal of the Thames and Severn Canal's long tunnel beneath the Cotswolds. Note the Tunnel House Inn in the background

it is hard to believe that this outstandingly beautiful link between our two great river systems will ever be reopened in its entirety. See also Daneway ★ and the Tunnel House Inn ★ .

Several sections of the old canal course may still be walked, including a length on our **Walk 10** from the western end of the Sapperton Tunnel to the Daneway Inn and beyond, down beside a long flight of sadly empty locks. Much of the canal's course can be traced on Landranger Sheets 162 and 163, and it is interesting to note the clumps of trees at intervals between Sapperton and Hailey Wood, to the north of the Tunnel House Inn, which neatly conceal the mounds of spoil around the top of each ventilation shaft. See also Ronald Russell's excellent *Lost Canals and Waterways of Britain*, and for a more detailed study of the canal's history read Humphrey Household's *The Thames and Severn Canal*.

Tidmington (151) (SP 25-38) *1½ mi. S Shipston-on-Stour*. Here is a 17th-century bridge over the River Stour, crossed here by the still-busy A3400, and overlooked by an old water-mill. Well to the north, beside the garden of Tidmington House, a largely 17th-century building with a handsome 18th-century front, is one of Warwickshire's smallest churches. This has a late 12th-century tower with pyramid roof, and a 16th-century chancel; the rest was rebuilt about 1875. However, the early Norman font has an interesting carving of Christ

upon it, and makes a visit here well worth while. It is possible to walk beside the Stour northwards to Shipston.

Toadsmoor Valley (162) (SO 88-04) *3 mi. E Stroud*. A deep wooded valley running up from the larger Golden Valley ★ at Brimscombe ★ , almost as far as Bisley ★ . There are old cloth mills here, but these are now long closed. There is an interesting account of the once thriving cloth industry in this valley in Jennifer Tann's *Gloucestershire Woollen Mills*.

Toddington (150) (SP 03-32) *3½ mi. NE Winchcombe*. This village is broken up into two halves.

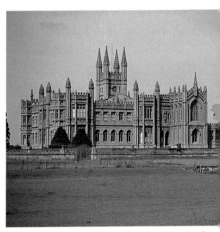

Toddington Manor . . . an outstanding example of Victorian Gothic

The old village extends northwards from the B4077, with a farmhouse and several pleasant houses before the church is reached in a well wooded area on the edge of parkland. This is an impressive 19th-century building, the creation of G.E. Street, one of the most talented of Victorian architects and perhaps best known for his work on London's Law Courts in the Strand. It has a handsome tower topped by an elegant spire, and its interior, in neo-Decorated style, is a formidable combination of starkness and extravagance — qualities that are typified by the splendid white marble tomb of Charles Hanbury-Tracy, 1st Lord Sudeley of Toddington, and his wife.

To the immediate west of the church are the ruins of the gatehouse of the Tracys' largely Jacobean manor house, which was inhabited until the early years of the 19th century. Toddington Manor, the massive Victorian Gothic mansion just visible in the park beyond, was designed by the owner, Charles Hanbury-Tracy. He was an amateur architect who was considered capable enough to be appointed chairman of the commission which adjudicated on the designs for the new Houses of Parliament. The massive mansion was built between 1820 and 1835 and many of its features were inspired by various Oxford colleges, Hanbury-Tracy having been an undergraduate there in the closing years of the 18th century. It is not open to the public.

The new part of the village, New Town, extends in three directions from the roundabout on the

B4632, and lies about a mile to the east of the old village. There is a large garden centre here, and next to it are the headquarters of the fascinating Gloucestershire Warwickshire Railway ★.

It is possible to walk south from the old village, to Greet ★ and on to Winchcombe ★.

Todenham (151) (SP 24-36) *3 mi. NE Moreton-in-Marsh.* An attractive and unspoilt village, with views out across quiet countryside to the low wooded hills around Cherington and Stourton. It has a handsome late Georgian manor house, and next to the church a little mellow-brick 18th-century inn, the Farrier's Arms.

The church of St Thomas of Canterbury is largely 14th-century in origin and has a fine tower and octagonal, broached spire. There are many pleasing items in the Decorated style here, including the east window, the sedilia, and the little priest's door on the south side. On the north side of the chancel will be found Perpendicular windows, which were added by the Greville family when they built a north chapel and north aisle in the early 16th century. Victorian restoration was carried out here with a very much lighter hand than at neighbouring Lower Lemington ★, and the interior of Todenham church is well worth a visit. See especially the 13th-century font with the names of the churchwardens of 1773 inscribed upon it, the brass to William Molton and his wife (1614), and outside, the memorial tablet on the south wall complete with skull and crossed bones.

Walk north-west, over the fields, to Stretton-on-Fosse ★, or eastwards to Little Wolford ★, in both cases back from Gloucestershire into Warwickshire.

Tredington (151) (SP 25-43) *2 mi. N Shipston-on-Stour.* An elegantly beautiful village in the valley of the Stour, with wide, well-mown grass verges and several interesting old houses. However, everything has been so polished and tidied up that Tredington's real character has been somewhat eroded, and to the west of the busy A3400 there is also considerable modern housing development. But do not let this description deter you from exploring Tredington, for it is still very pleasant to walk along the small roads leading to the church of St Gregory, which is itself well worth visiting. It has a tall tower topped by a noble 15th-century spire — a landmark visible from many points of the delightful south Warwickshire countryside. It also has a Norman south doorway and a Perpendicular two-storey north porch, beyond which will be found old stone floors, beautiful old benches, a handsome Jacobean pulpit, a Perpendicular rood screen, lovely roofs of the same period in nave and transepts, and several interesting brasses. Architectural enthusiasts will also note evidence of St Gregory's Anglo-Saxon origins, but everyone who comes here will sense the atmosphere of the past that lingers in this fine building.

Tunley (163) (SO 93-04) *5 mi. E Stroud.* Minute hamlet in a deeply wooded combe thrusting northwards from the Frome Valley. The attractive thatched cottage, Sherwood Hill, was once the home of the potter Alfred Powell, a friend of Ernest Gimson (see Daneway ★). Our **Walk 10** passes close by this quiet hamlet, and there is also a delightful walk continuing up the combe to Sudgrove (163) (SO 93-07) and over to Miserden ★.

The Tunnel House Inn (163) (SO 96-00) *4½ mi. W Cirencester.* A pleasant 18th-century building close to the south-eastern end of the Thames and Severn Canal's ★ 2¼-mile tunnel under the Cotswolds.

Tunnel House Inn and Coates

SCALE 1:25 000 or 2½ INCHES to 1 MILE

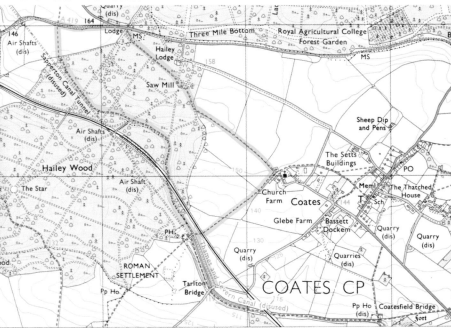

During the canal's heyday this inn, like the Daneway Inn ★ at the other end of the tunnel, must have been a popular port of call for the thirsty leggers at the end of each journey. For many years the tunnel's portal, with its handsome Doric columns, stood neglected at the end of a long canal 'ditch' shaded by massive beech trees, but happily it has now been restored. Near the southern end of this section of canal will be found one of the delightful little Gothick 'round houses' which were built to accommodate the canal's lengthmen (maintenance men).

Use our mapped **mini-walk** to walk from here through part of Hailey Wood to the A419, and return through Coates. Please ask the landlord if you wish to use the inn's car park. Permission will almost certainly be given to those making use of the inn's facilities. It is also possible to walk south-east from here, following the course of the canal, to the source of the River Thames at Trewsbury Mead (see Thames Head ★).

Turkdean (163) (SP 10-17) *2 mi. N Northleach.* This small village is pleasantly sited on a hillside, with the hamlet of Lower Dean in the valley below, the two being joined by a road leading down through a magnificent avenue of beech trees. The Norman church, situated in a large churchyard bordered by chestnut trees, has some interesting items of early sculpture built into the lower stages of its tower. There is also a blocked-up Norman doorway in the south wall of the chancel. The Perpendicular north doorway is sheltered by a porch of the same period, and opens into an interior which contains a Norman chancel arch and a stout Perpendicular stone pulpit. Do not overlook the interesting photograph of the vaulted undercroft, or crypt, of nearby Rectory Farm.

Turkdean lies midway between Hazleton ★ and Cold Aston ★, both of which may be reached by pleasant bridle roads. A glance at Landranger Sheet 163 will indicate a good circular walk from Turkdean, making use of both these sections of bridle road and taking in the village of Notgrove ★ .

Tyndale Monument (162) (ST 74-95) *2 mi. SW Dursley.* This 111ft-high tower above the little village of North Nibley ★ was built to the designs of S.S. Teulon in 1866, in memory of William Tyndale, the first translator of the New Testament into English. There are fine views to the Severn Estuary from the gallery near its top, and there is an inscription here, part of which reads: 'born near this spot' (a fact disputed by the inhabitants of Slimbridge ★) 'he suffered martyrdom at Vilvorde in Flanders on 6th October, 1536.' Ask for the key to the tower in the village below.

Uley (162) (ST 79-98) *2 mi. E Dursley.* Situated in a deep valley this large village has many delightful 18th-century houses — evidence of Uley's prosperity as a cloth centre in the years immediately prior to the Industrial Revolution. Beautifully sited above the valley, Uley's handsome Victorian church was designed by the talented architect, S.S. Teulon, who also designed the Tyndale Monument ★ . Beside the churchyard there is a path leading steeply up the hill to the Iron Age settlement of Uleybury, from which there are spectacular views in almost every direction.

Uley Long Barrow *(See Hetty Pegler's Tump ★)*

Upper Coberley (163) (SO 97-15) *4 mi. SE Cheltenham. (See map on page 93.)* Attractive hamlet overlooking the upper Churn Valley, not far from the source of the Churn at Seven Springs ★ .

Use the **mini-walk** shown on the map on page 93 for a pleasant circular ramble taking in Seven Springs ★ and Coberley ★ . There is also a good walk north-eastwards, passing Needlehole, and turning right onto an unfenced road running southwards through Pinchley Wood. To return to Upper Coberley, either turn right at Hilcot ★ , or walk further southwards on a minor road, before turning sharp right to return via Pinswell Plantation. Brief study of Landranger Sheet 163 will clarify these rather complex directions, and also reveal a host of alternative walks in this delightful area.

Upper Slaughter (163) (SP 15-23) *3 mi. SW Stow-on-the-Wold. (See map on page 77.)* This

Early spring at Upper Slaughter

village is situated on the banks of the little River Eye, less than two miles from its source below Eyford Hill. It is fortunately less visited than its neighbour Lower Slaughter ★ , but is equally delightful. Its gabled manor house is perhaps one of the finest examples of Elizabethan domestic architecture in the Cotswolds, and has a beautiful two-storeyed porch with Doric and Ionic pilasters. Although it is not open to the public, there is a tantalising glimpse down its front drive. Further into the village will be found the pleasant Lords of the Manor Hotel. Beyond this is a small square overlooked by a group of eight trim cottages much restored by the distinguished early 20th-century architect, Sir Edwin Lutyens. The passing of time and the genius of Lutyens have together ensured that this group blends in perfectly with its tranquil surroundings.

Just to the north of the square is Upper Slaughter's late Norman church, with its attractively pinnacled tower. This church was largely rebuilt in 1877, when the results of earlier tinkering with its Norman features were to a large extent rectified. Despite the care taken, the interior is inevitably Victorian in feeling, and this effect is increased by the presence, in a specially built mortuary chapel to the north of the chancel, of a very grand monument to F.E.Witts, the local rector and lord of the manor, who died in 1854. The diary of this most energetic of country parsons was published in 1979, and anyone wishing to gain insight into life in the Cotswolds and the towns of Cheltenham and Gloucester between 1820 and 1852 should read this, *The Diary of a Cotswold Parson*.

Beyond the church there is a small road leading down to a minute bridge over the River Eye, here no more than a modest stream. This is itself sheltered by a massive tree and overlooked by a mound just to its east, on which are the none-too-obvious earthworks of a long-vanished motte and bailey castle (see map on page 77). There is a farmyard not far beyond and on summer afternoons cattle may sometimes be seen being driven down the bank and across the stream towards their milking shed.

Use the **mini-walk** shown on the map on page 77 to explore both Upper and Lower Slaughter, which are linked by a pleasant footpath beside the little River Eye. There is also a fine walk northwards up the Eye Valley to the B4068, and by using a short length of this (with great care) it is possible to move north again skirting part of Eyford Park ★.

Upper Swell (163) (SP 17-26) *1 mi. NW Stow-on-the-Wold.* This small village overlooks the valley through which the little River Dikler runs. This is crossed by a small 18th-century bridge, above which is the moss-covered weir retaining an extensive mill pool. The water-mill still has its wheel, and waterfowl are usually to be seen on the pool. Do not try to park here, but use the small lay-by beyond on the Stow-on-the-Wold road.

Above the mill there is a fine manor house with a two-storeyed porch, an outstanding example of late 16th- or early 17th-century Cotswold domestic architecture. This was built by the Stratford family of Farmcote ★ and Hawling ★, after they had acquired the land which had previously belonged to Evesham Abbey.

Bridge and Mill at Upper Swell

The little church nearby is largely Norman in origin and has a good Norman south doorway within its 15th-century porch. Inside will be found a 14th-century piscina and sedilia and a handsomely carved Perpendicular font.

Upton House (151) (SP 36-45) *7 mi. NW Banbury.* Given to the National Trust by the 2nd Viscount Bearsted, this fine William and Mary mansion is built of local Hornton stone and stands at the end of a straight driveway, off the main A422, Stratford-upon-Avon to Banbury road. It is situated less than half a mile behind the Edge Hill scarp, and from its south front there are pleasant views out over wide grassy terraces and beautiful, steep sloping gardens (which should not be missed), to its Temple Pool. This is enhanced by a little temple at the far end in the Tuscan style, said to have been designed by Sanderson Miller, squire of nearby Radway, and architect extraordinary (see also Adlestrop ★). Miller may also have carried out improvements to the house in the 1730s, but about this there appears to be some doubt.

The interior of the present house is largely the work of the 20th-century architect, Morley Horder, who created a series of fine neo-Georgian rooms in about 1927. These provide a perfect setting for the remarkable collection of works of art presented by Lord Bearsted to the National Trust in 1948. This includes 18th-century furniture, Brussels tapestries, and 18th-century porcelain, both English and European. But of outstanding interest is the superb collection of pictures, with works by Bosch, the Brueghels, Holbein, Rembrandt, Van Dyck, Cana-letto, Goya, El Greco, Tiepolo, Tintoretto, Constable, Hogarth, Reynolds, Romney and Stubbs. On no account should a visit here be missed, for it provides, in the heart of the English countryside, a sparkling insight into the rich diversity of European culture — an experience that many believe can only be achieved by visiting one of the great art capitals of the world.

However, visitors should not allow the wealth of art treasures to prevent them from seeing Upton House's extensive gardens. Time should be allowed for both. *(Tel: (029587) 266.)*

Upton St Leonards (162) (SO 86-14) *3 mi. SE Gloucester.* Situated below the scarp on which Prinknash Abbey ★ stands, this is a rather scattered village, with its timber-framed farms and cottages now greatly outnumbered by modern houses. Gloucester is not far away and the noisy M5 motorway is depressingly close to Upton's church. This has a handsome Perpendicular tower, but is now largely the result of Victorian rebuilding. However, there is a fine monument to Sir Thomas Snell in the north chapel, and some pleasant table tombs in the churchyard.

Wadfield Roman Villa (163) (SP 02-26) *1½ mi. S Winchcombe.* This Roman villa was excavated in the 19th century, thanks no doubt to the enthusiasm of Mrs Emma Dent, the formidable chatelaine of Sudeley Castle ★. Our **Walk 2** (and the Cotswold Way ★) passes close to a small shed which still houses a small mosaic pavement, but it should be stressed that this is private property. Strangely, the best pavement taken up during the excavation, well documented and removed to Sudeley Castle, has since vanished without trace. It is thought that it lies hidden under the turf in a quiet part of Sudeley's garden, but this theory has yet to be proved.

The Welsh Way (163) (SP 05-05 etc.) *3 mi. NE Cirencester.* There are several rough tracks across the Cotswolds which were used by Welsh cattle drovers to bring their beasts to the London markets before the coming of the railways. The section of the Welsh Way running westwards from Barnsley ★ probably had its origins in prehistoric times, but it is still used as a minor road and provides a pleasant contrast to the busy A417, as it winds across country towards the Foss Way. Much of its course must have been used by the prosperous wool merchant Sir Edmund Tame, on his frequent journeys between his estates at Fairford ★ and Rendcomb ★ .

For more details of this and other Cotswold roads and trackways read G.R. Crosher's *Along the Cotswold Ways.*

Westcote (163) (SP 22-20) *3½ mi. SE Stow-on-the-Wold.* Made up of Church Westcote and Nether Westcote, this small village has fine views eastwards over the broad Evenlode Valley to the distant wooded slopes of Wychwood Forest ★. It has a handsome 16th-century manor house and several pleasant old houses nearby, but its church is the result of several 19th- and 20th-century reconstructions, and is not of great interest to visitors. However, in the churchyard, which is colourful with primroses and daffodils in early spring, can be seen the sculptured base of a 13th-century cross.

Here, at least until the 1960s, on land to the west of the A424 just north of the Hunter's Lodge Inn (163) (SP 23-18), were to be found the last vestiges on the Cotswolds of the medieval farming practice of the open field — the division into strips of land, the produce of which was shared between the peasant renting the strip and the lord of the manor. Open fields still survived in many Cotswold parishes in the early 19th century, although the process of enclosure was by then gathering momentum.

Walk north-westwards from Westcote to link onto the Oxfordshire Way ★ at nearby Gawcombe (163) (SP 21-21), or north-eastwards across the valley to Bledington ★ .

Westington (151) (SP 14-38) *To immediate south of Chipping Campden.* This is the quiet and somewhat over-trim south-western part of Chipping Campden, with some bewilderingly beautiful houses and cottages, many of which are thatched. On Westington Hill, on the B4081 south of the village, there is a little stone conduit by the roadside, built by Sir Baptist Hicks in 1612 to supply water to his almshouses below Chipping Campden church ★ .

Westonbirt Arboretum (162) (ST 85-90 etc) *3 mi. SW Tetbury.* The magnificent neo-Elizabethan Westonbirt House was designed by the architect Lewis Vulliamy for Robert Holford, for whom he had also designed Dorchester House in London's Park Lane (now the Dorchester Hotel). The mansion is now a girls' boarding school, and for most visitors to the Cotswolds, Westonbirt is perhaps better known for its splendid arboretum — the creation of Robert Holford, his son Sir George

Holford, and Sir George's nephew, the fourth Earl Morley. Since 1956 it has been owned by the Forestry Commission, who have continued to develop the woodlands and to provide visitor facilities.

This world-famous collection of over 13,000 trees and shrubs covers 116 acres, and includes an unrivalled variety of different species in carefully contrived harmony, with maples, rhododendrons, azaleas and camellias in great profusion, all linked by woodland paths and grassy glades. The Silk Wood, a very extensive area of semi-ornamental woodland to the immediate south-west of the car-parking area, should also not be missed. *(Car parking and picnic area, visitor centre and cafeteria open daily from spring to autumn. Tel: (0666 88) 220.)*

Sunlit pathway at Westonbirt Arboretum

Weston-sub-Edge (150) (SP 12-41) *3 mi. NE Broadway.* There are several attractive stone houses in this village and at least one with a timber frame upon a stone base, emphasising Weston's position on the borders between the Cotswolds and the Vale of Evesham. The church is at the upper end of the village looking across the earthworks of a medieval moat towards the steep, wooded slopes of the hills above. Its attractively pinnacled tower is Perpendicular, and although the rest of the building has been heavily 'Victorianised' its interior does contain several items of interest, including a handsome late Jacobean pulpit, a brass to a very smart Elizabethan gentleman named William Hodges, and several other monuments.

The Roman Ryknild Street ★ runs just to the west of the village, and its course up part of the Cotswold scarp is followed by a well defined bridle road ending up just above neighbouring Saintbury ★ .

Westwell (163) (SP 22-10) *2 mi. SW Burford.* A delightful and still totally unspoilt village in open wold country with church, rectory and manor house looking out across a rough green complete with duck-pond. The impressively simple war memorial consists of a great block of stone into which has been set a figure 'I' rescued from the shattered Cloth Hall at Ypres — a poignant reminder of the 'war to end all wars'. The nearby Norman church stands amongst a fascinating array of beautifully lettered 17th- and 18th-century table tombs and is overlooked by an exquisite late 17th-century rectory. Amongst several interesting features within the church will be found a charming 17th-century monument to Charles Trinder, his wife and their fourteen children.

Whichford (151) (SP 31-34) *5 mi. N Chipping Norton.* Here is a wide green surrounded by houses and cottages of almost every age — not outstandingly beautiful, but one of the most comfortable villages in southern Warwickshire. It is enfolded in beautifully wooded hill country, not far from the Oxfordshire border, but well sheltered from the winds that blow around Great Rollright, on the hills to its south. The 18th-century rectory in mellow stone is one of the most elegant country buildings one could wish to encounter, and the church close by is equally attractive. This has a Norman south doorway, a rugged early 14th-century tower, and in contrast a finely built Perpendicular clerestory. The white-painted interior was restored in 1845, when neo-Gothic pews were installed, and these now blend in well with their surroundings. Do not miss the medieval stained glass in some of the window heads, nor the coffin lid, thought to be that of Sir John de Mohun, who fought at the Battle of Boroughbridge in 1322, and who died shortly afterwards. See also the alabaster relief of John Merton, and the tomb chest with brass of Nicholas Asheton, both men rectors of Whichford in the 16th century.

The best walk from Whichford is along the southern edge of Whichford Wood, and southwest, down over the fields to Long Compton ★. It is also possible to walk eastwards round the flank of Whichford Hill, to Hook Norton ★, or northwards to Brailes (151) (SP 30-39), past Whichford Mill and New Barn Farm.

Whiteway (163) (SO 91-10) *6 mi. SE Gloucester.* A community was founded here in 1898 by a group of idealists from The Brotherhood Church of Croydon, who wished to follow the principles of the writer Tolstoy. Their original ideas based on shared land and resources had to be drastically modified, and the bleak hill farm they had bought had to be split up into self-contained smallholdings, each with its own small house or bungalow. The architectural results are hardly inspiring, but the courage that it must have required to espouse a philosophy of life and follow it through in practical terms, even modified ones, is still unquestionable. For a fuller account of Whiteway read Josceline Finberg's most revealing book, *The Cotswolds.*

The White Way (163) (SP 03-11 etc.) *North from Cirencester.* This was a minor Roman road, the purpose of which appears to have been the serving of the numerous villas that lay between Cirencester and the Cotswold edge in the vicinity of Winchcombe. See Chedworth ★, Spoonley ★, Wadfield ★ and Withington ★.

Whittington (163) (SP 01-21) *4 mi. E Cheltenham.* Small village not far to the south of Cleeve Common and Cleeve Hill ★. It has a pleasant row of cottages, a Victorian wayside well succinctly inscribed 'Waste not, want not' and, away from the village, a small church sheltering beneath the high walls of the romantic 16th-century Whittington Court.

The church, which has some Norman details, has a small bellcote and a pretty little north porch. However, the most interesting treasures here are the three 14th-century effigies — two of knights and one of a lady. There is also a brass (dated 1556) of the builders of Whittington Court, Richard Cotton and his wife, with the unusual wording 'in the reign of King Philip and Queen Mary' included in its inscription. Do not miss the two little figures used as headstops to the arcading — a gentleman and a lady, who both look quite Chaucerian.

There are small but convenient access roads to Cleeve Common ★ northwards from here. If possible use Landranger Sheet 163. It is also possible to walk northwards from here to Cleeve Common ★, West Down, Belas Knap ★ and Winchcombe ★.

Widford (163) (SP 27-11) *1 mi. E Burford. (See map on page 105.)* Situated just above the watermeadows of the Windrush Valley, this hamlet consists of a pleasant 16th- and 17th-century manor house and a minute 13th-century church. This was built on the site of a Roman villa and a small portion of mosaic floor lies exposed amongst the old stone flags of the chancel floor. But quite apart from this most interesting feature, the interior is delightfully unspoilt, with Jacobean pulpit, early 19th-century box pews and 14th-century wall-paintings.

Use our mapped **mini-walk** on page 105 to walk up Dean Bottom, down a quiet road to Swinbrook ★, and back along the Windrush Valley to Widford. This walk can be extended from Swinbrook to Asthall ★.

Wildfowl Trust *(See Slimbridge ★)*

Willersey (150) (SP 10-39) *1½ mi. NE Broadway.* Situated just below the steep Cotswold scarp, this modest village sits astride the still-busy B4632. The little Bell Inn looks across to handsome 17th-century Pool House, with its stone gate-pillars standing between the house and a lively village duck-pond. Opposite this pond there is a quiet cul-de-sac leading to the church, which lies on the eastern fringes of the village looking up and across to Saintbury church, itself poised half-way up the Cotswold edge. Willersey church has an imposing Perpendicular tower, almost certainly built by Evesham Abbey, which then owned this parish. It is complete with pinnacles and gargoyles and inside there is fine vaulting beneath it, installed as late as 1859. Other features that make this church worth visiting include a small north porch, a pleasantly shaped Norman tub font, and the Royal Arms of George III.

Walk eastwards from here beneath the edge to Saintbury ★, and onwards up to Dover's Hill ★, from where it is possible to walk to Chipping Campden ★.

Winchcombe (150,163) (SP 02-28) *6 mi. NE Cheltenham.* This surprisingly unspoilt town lies in a fold of the Cotswold edge and is sheltered on three sides by partly wooded hills. One of the seats of Mercian royalty, it was the capital of its own shire until it was incorporated into Gloucestershire in the early years of the 11th century. It prospered greatly in medieval times, due largely to the presence of the abbey founded here in 798 by King Kenulf of Mercia, and dedicated soon after to his martyred son, St Kenelm. Although this event is now believed to be the fabrication of a later period, it brought pilgrims to the shrine of St Kenelm in great

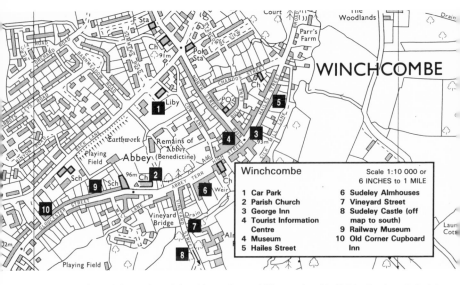

WINCHCOMBE

Winchcombe	Scale 1:10 000 or 6 INCHES to 1 MILE
1 Car Park	6 Sudeley Almshouses
2 Parish Church	7 Vineyard Street
3 George Inn	8 Sudeley Castle (off
4 Tourist Information	map to south)
Centre	9 Railway Museum
4 Museum	10 Old Corner Cupboard
5 Hailes Street	Inn

quantities, and stood the monks and the citizens of Winchcombe in good stead for several hundred years. A great Benedictine abbey was established here in the 13th century, and this continued to grow in power, thanks not only to the number of its pilgrims but also to the prosperity of its very extensive Cotswold sheep runs. The town must also have derived some benefit from its proximity to Sudeley Castle ★.

Our **Walk 2** starts from the *Car Park* behind the *Library (1)*, and this is probably also the best place from which to explore the town. It is only a short walk from here to the *Parish Church (2)*. This fine Perpendicular 'wool church' was built jointly by the

Winchcombe . . . a happy blend of half-timber and stone

parishioners, by Sir Ralph Boteler of Sudeley Castle, who provided the nave, and by the abbot, who provided the chancel. But despite this connection with the abbey, it survived the Dissolution entirely. Its fine west tower is in the best 'wool' tradition and is today crowned by the gilded weathercock which once graced the tower of St Mary Redcliffe, Bristol. Inside the broad, beautifully proportioned, but rather severely restored interior will be found a number of wooden 15th-century screens, an old door and floor tiles from the abbey, displayed on a wall, a 17th-century holy table, the Royal Arms of George III and a number of interesting monuments. These include a rather sad monument in the chancel with a lonely Sir Thomas Williams of Corndean kneeling at a prayer desk, opposite an empty space reserved for his widow — a lady who eventually remarried and who apparently had no wish to join the lonely effigy of her first husband.

Winchcombe's great abbey, unlike the church, did not survive the Dissolution. It was destroyed so thoroughly by Lord Seymour of Sudeley that no single trace remains above ground. The only reminder of its past glories is the medieval *George Inn (3)* in the High Street, which was once the abbey's hostel for pilgrims. Carved on its doorway are the arms of Richard Kidderminster, the 16th-century abbot, whose efforts on behalf of the abbey were so successful that it was claimed to have been 'equal to a little university'.

Almost opposite the George Inn is the *Tourist Information Centre (4)* (tel: (0242) 602925), which is housed in the old court room on the upper floor of the little *Town Hall (4)*, together with the *Simms Collection of Police Memorabilia*, while the adjoining Judge's Room houses the interesting *Winchcombe Folk Museum*. In the little fenced enclosure below are the town's old stocks.

There are several pleasant old houses, some timber-framed, in narrow *Hailes Street (5)*, but having walked down there, it is then best for visitors to retrace their steps, back past the George Inn, into Abbey Terrace. Here, extending to the left down Dent Terrace, will be found the pretty *Sudeley Almshouses (6)*. The work of Sir Giles Gilbert

Scott, they were built at the expense of Emma Dent of Sudeley Castle in 1865. Also to the left, a little further on and almost opposite the church, is **Vineyard Street (7)** which is lined with pollarded trees and a series of delightful cottages, each with its own rustic porch. Beyond the cottages there is an old stone bridge over the little River Isbourne, carrying a small road which leads to the historic **Sudeley Castle (8)** ★ *(off map to south).*

Beyond the turn to Vineyard Street visitors will again pass the **Parish Church (2)** and go beyond to explore the length of Gloucester Street, which contains a number of attractive old buildings. On the right, at No. 23, will be found the interesting little **Winchcombe Railway Museum (9)**, where visitors are encouraged to operate some of the working exhibits. *(Tel: (0242) 602257.)* Well beyond this, also on the right-hand side, is the pleasant 16th-century **Old Corner Cupboard Inn (10)**.

Windrush (163) (SP 19-13) *4 mi. W Burford.* Prettily sited above the Windrush meadows, this delightful village has a small triangular green around which are several pleasant houses and cottages. The green is also overlooked by the handsome Perpendicular tower of Windrush church — an attractive and most interesting building. Its outstanding feature is the beautiful Norman south

Norman south doorway at Windrush

doorway with its double row of grotesque beakheads — one of the finest in the Cotswolds. There is also a lovely 15th-century roof to the nave, a medieval screen, a fine Jacobean pulpit, a 15th-century font, some interesting medieval floor tiles and a charming little sheep's head above the arcading. The churchyard contains an impressive series of 18th-century table tombs.

Windrush was once noted for its stone quarries, or to be more precise its mines. These were driven up to a quarter of a mile in length, into the valley

slopes between the village and the line of the present A40, and were worked until the 1890s, when safety regulations became too stringent for them to continue profitably.

There are the earthworks of an Iron Age settlement, Windrush Camp, about a mile to the southwest of the village, beside a bridleway leading over open country beyond the A40. However, the best walks from Windrush are up the valley to Sherborne ★ or down to Little Barrington ★.

Winson (163) (SP 09-08) *2 mi. NW Bibury.* Situated on the lovely River Coln, this minute village has a handsome 18th-century manor house and a small Norman church. The latter stands in a neat churchyard with some 18th-century table tombs, and overlooks a fine group of farm buildings. It has a typical Cotswold-style bellcote and a Norman south doorway. Its simple interior contains a Norman chancel arch, a 15th-century stone pulpit (so ruthlessly restored that it looks more like a 19th-century reproduction) and some quaint Victorian wall-paintings in the chancel, with vine and honeysuckle in profusion.

There are pleasant walks up the Coln Valley to Coln Rogers ★, Coln St Dennis ★ and Fossebridge ★, or down to Ablington ★ and Bibury ★. It is also possible to walk southwards over the wolds to Barnsley ★, going through Barnsley Park.

Winstone (163) (SO 96-09) *6 mi. NW Cirencester. (See map on page 81.)* A rather scattered village with an unusually large number of farms, but little of special interest apart from its church. This is attractively situated at the eastern end of the village, looking south and east over open farmland. It has a saddleback tower, but it has been ruthlessly restored both inside and out, and tantalising glimpses of medieval wall-paintings on stonework show what the Victorian restorers must have scraped away. The blocked north doorway and the chancel arch, both with their massive jambs, are late Anglo-Saxon, but the south doorway is more Norman in character. It would therefore appear that much of this church was built at about the time of the Norman Conquest. Do not miss the base and broken shaft of a 14th-century churchyard cross near the south porch.

There is a good linear walk southwards to Duntisbourne Abbots ★, and down the Duntisbourne Valley towards Cirencester ★. Also use the **mini-walk** shown on the map on page 81 if you wish to walk across the deep Frome Valley to Miserden ★.

Witcombe Roman Villa (163) (SO 90-14) *4 mi. SE Gloucester. (Turn south off the A417 about ¼ mi. east of its intersection with A46 at roundabout — follow sign marked Droys Court — after ½ mi. bear left at Droys Court — after ½ mi. arrive at small car park on left — villa now only a short walk up farm road.)*

This is a large 1st-century Roman villa built around three sides of a courtyard. There is a small mosaic pavement with dolphins and sea-horses, and various items from the excavation are displayed in a small building on the site. It is situated on a terrace beneath high woodlands and there are fine views out over the Severn Plain — proving, as so often, how adept the Romans were in their choice of villa sites. This villa is on our **Walk 7**. *(In the care of English Heritage, it is open at any reasonable time.)*

Withington (163) (SP 03-15) *5 mi. W Northleach.* An exceptionally pretty village situated near the head of the Coln Valley, less than six miles below the river's source near Brockhampton ★. Its manorial rights were once held by the bishops of Worcester, and both the manor house and Halewell Close were once used by them. Both have 15th-century origins, but have been much altered and added to in the following centuries. There are several other very pleasant buildings including the hospitable Mill Inn, which has the River Coln flowing through its gardens.

However, the village is very much centred upon its stout-towered church. The tower itself is partly Norman and there is a blocked Norman north doorway, as well as a fine Norman south doorway still in use. The interior was ruthlessly scraped by the Victorians and lacks any great feeling of antiquity. However, there is a fine wall monument to Sir John and Lady Howe of nearby Cassey Compton ★, complete with their eight children, and several other interesting monuments. The east window of the south chapel is by Sir Ninian Comper, one of the 20th century's most capable church decorators.

There is no trace above ground of the large Roman villa which once stood to the south of the village (see map), but a mosaic pavement from here is in the British Museum. One of four known villas in this vicinity, its farm area must have amounted to about 4000 acres.

Our mapped **mini-walk** explores part of the village and goes south through the extensive Withington Woods. There is also a pleasant walk down the Coln Valley to Cassey Compton ★ and Chedworth Roman Villa ★, linking near the latter with our **Walk 11**.

Howe Monument in Withington Church

Withington   SCALE 1:25 000 or 2½ INCHES to 1 MILE

Witney (164) (SP 36-10) *7 mi. E Burford.* This pleasant old cloth town astride the River Windrush prospered from the days of Edward III through the making of blankets, an industry which is still very much alive today. Dr Plot, in his *Natural History of Oxfordshire* (published in 1677), claimed 'that no place yields blanketing so notoriously white as is made at Witney'. The coming of the Industrial Revolution, which removed most of the Cotswold woollen industry to Yorkshire, with its supplies of cheap coal for fuel, might have been expected to put an end to Witney's blanket weaving, but it continued to prosper because by then it had become noted throughout the trading world for the quality of its products. These were even popular with the Red Indians, who purchased their Witney blankets at the remote trading posts of the Hudson's Bay Company.

The mills here, which are certainly not cast in the 'dark Satanic' mould of William Blake, were founded by the Early family over three centuries ago. This family was part of a group of wealthy weavers who were granted a charter for their Company of Blanket Weavers in 1711 and who built the *Blanket Hall* in the High Street in 1721.

Witney's most attractive streets run south to the *Market Square*. Here are the quaint little 17th-century *Butter Cross*, with its clock turret beneath a cupola, and the 18th-century *Town Hall* which incorporates a *Tourist Information Centre*. *(Tel: (0993) 775802.)* Beyond the Market Square is Church Green, an unusually large tree-bordered green overlooked by lovely 17th- and 18th-century houses and, at the far end, by the massive tower and tall spire of Witney's mainly 13th-century **Parish Church**. Viewed from the green, the exterior is most impressive, but the interior was unfortunate enough to be restored by the over-enthusiastic Victorian architect, G.E. Street, and lacks the sense of antiquity that might have been expected. However, there is a wealth of interesting detail including several fine windows of the Decorated period and a number of monuments.

Woodgreen, on the north-eastern edge of the town, grew up in the 18th century, and there are many pleasant houses of this period looking out across its wide green. The 19th-century blanket mill on its south side has been turned into flats.

There is a fascinating **Farm Museum** at **Cogges Manor Farm**, to the immediate south-east of Witney, off the B4022. This is equipped as an Edwardian farm and is complete with period machinery and tools. There is also a working kitchen with a dairy, and some livestock. In addition there are nature and history walks beside the River Windrush, a cafeteria, bookshop and small **Tourist Information Centre**. *(Tel: (0993) 772602.)*

Walk north and west from Witney, up the Windrush Valley to Crawley and Minster Lovell ★ .

Woodchester (162) (SO 84-02) *2 mi. S Stroud.* Modest village on the steep western slopes of the Avon Valley between Stroud and Nailsworth, with several 18th- and 19th-century mills in the valley bottom. The new church of St Mary, designed by the talented Victorian architect, S.S. Teulon, contains a few monuments taken from the old church, which was abandoned in 1863. The remains of this building, situated to the north of the village, consist of a Norman chancel arch and north doorway and a Perpendicular window. However, its churchyard is the site of Woodchester's greatest treasure — the remains of a luxurious Roman villa, the principal feature of which is a splendid mosaic pavement featuring the myth of Orpheus, with Orpheus playing a lyre in its centre, surrounded by animals in two circles. First excavated systematically in 1796 by the Gloucestershire antiquary Samuel Lysons, it used to be uncovered every ten years in recent times. This is unlikely to occur again in the foreseeable future, but plans are afoot for a beautiful full-sized replica to be put on permanent display. *(Tel: (0453) 764252 for the latest information.)* The churchyard also contains monuments to the prosperous mill-owning Paul family, including the tomb of prison reformer, Sir George Onesiphorus Paul (see also Northleach ★ , Doughton ★ and Rodborough ★).

The ambitious mid-19th-century mansion of Woodchester Park, well to the west of the village (162) (SO 80-01), was designed by local architect Benjamin Bucknall, in a neo-Gothic style much influenced by the work of the great French architect, Viollet-le-Duc. Regrettably it was never completed although it still stands as a substantial ruin. It is possible to visit the mansion from the Coaley Peak Picnic Site ★ on the last Sunday in each month between April and October, and also on Bank Holiday Mondays. *(For further details, tel: (0453) 860531.)*

The best walk from Woodchester is westwards up onto the ridge occupied by the open spaces of Selsley Common ★ , and on through winding Stanley Wood, to Frocester Hill ★ .

Woodmancote (163) (SO 00-08) *5 mi. N Cirencester.* Substantial hamlet on a ridge to the north-west of North Cerney with a number of attractive 19th-century houses and cottages. There are two attractive walks from here — one south-westwards to Middle Duntisbourne ★ , and another southwards to Daglingworth ★ , both crossing the busy A417, the Romans' Ermin Way ★ .

Wood Stanway (150) (SP 06-31) *3 mi. NE Winchcombe.* This delightful hamlet beneath the steep Cotswold scarp has several beautiful houses and farms, and a number of fine walks. It is possible to walk over the fields to Hailes Abbey ★ , then up a track above the abbey, and back to Wood Stanway via Beckbury Camp ★ and Stumps Cross — making a fine circular walk. It is also possible to walk north over the fields to Stanway ★ , or south-eastwards up to Stumps Cross (150) (SP 07-30), both routes following the course of the Cotswold Way ★ .

Woodstock (164) (SP 44-16) *7 mi. NE Witney. (See maps on pages 31 and 120.)* This prosperous and beautiful little town was already a royal manor before the Norman Conquest. From these early times the story of the town is indivisible from that of the manor and the great park in which it stood. This was first enclosed by Henry I, in the early years of the 12th century, and he built a palace or hunting lodge here and even maintained a menagerie in the park, the contents of which included lynx, leopard, camel and even porcupine. It is not recorded whether or not these exotic beasts were kept for the purpose of hunting, but if replacements were

Park Street, Woodstock

available they would certainly have been released and pursued.

Henry I's grandson, Henry II, came here both for the hunting and for the company of his mistress, Rosamund Clifford — the 'Fair Rosamund' of many a legend. Henry II enlarged the palace and built the town of New Woodstock to house his court. The medieval palace of Woodstock was used by a succession of monarchs until the 17th century, when it was besieged and damaged beyond repair in the Civil War.

In 1704 the manor and its park were presented to John Churchill, first Duke of Marlborough, as a reward for his great victory at the Battle of Blenheim. The remains of the old royal palace were soon swept away and work commenced on the massive Blenheim Palace★. Ever since then the town's prosperity has been greatly influenced by the affairs of the palace and its great estate. From medieval times it was also noted for its glove-making, but although this trade lasted well into the 20th century, tourism must now be Woodstock's most important activity.

If possible make use of the *Main Car Park (1)* off the Hensington Road, to the east of the A44, and then call at the adjoining *Tourist Information Centre (1)*, which is in the Library. *(Tel: (0993) 811038.)* Now cross the very busy Oxford Street, the A34, and walk up the High Street, passing the wonderful assortment of 17th- and 18th-century houses, shops, restaurants, hotels and inns, towards the dignified *Town Hall (2)*. This was built by Sir William Chambers in 1766 at the Duke of Marlborough's expense, and makes a perfect foil to the cosier charms of the much older *Bear Hotel (3)*, which is on the left at the beginning of Park Street. *St Mary Magdalen's Church (4)*, also on the left and not far beyond the Bear, has a splendid tower, built in the classical style in 1785, which stands above a church medieval in origin, but almost entirely rebuilt about ninety years after the tower's construction. The interior is not of great interest, largely because this church was until the 18th century only a chapel of ease under the parish of Bladon★ (where Sir Winston Churchill lies in the churchyard), and the Marlboroughs have been buried in their own magnificent chapel at Blenheim.

Opposite the church, behind the Town Stocks, is *Fletcher's House (5)*, a 16th-century merchant's house in which is the Oxford City and County Museum. This contains a series of very interesting displays depicting life and work in Oxfordshire. The museum has pleasant gardens, a coffee bar and a bookshop. *(Tel: (0993) 811456.)* At the far end of Park Street is Nicholas Hawksmoor's massive Triumphal Arch, known as the *Woodstock Gate (6)*, and the best pedestrian entrance to the park from the town. The view of the park and its great lake from a point just beyond the Woodstock Gate should on no account be missed (see Blenheim Palace and its accompanying map★). Much of the park is open to pedestrians for 364 days a year on payment of a modest fee, which also includes entry to a butterfly house and a play area in the summer. *(If in doubt, tel: (0993) 811325.)*

It is suggested that on their return to the main car park, visitors fork left by the Town Hall and go down Market Street, before turning right onto Oxford Street (A44), and then left into Hensington Road. A glance at the plan of Woodstock will reveal several other little streets which are also well worth exploring.

Wotton-under-Edge (162) (ST 76-93) *3 mi. S Dursley.* This was burnt to the ground in the reign of King John by the king's mercenaries, who were bitter enemies of the Berkeley family of nearby Berkeley Castle★. However, it was soon rebuilt and became a borough in 1253. Now an attractive little market town, it still shows signs of its prosperity as a cloth centre in the 17th and 18th centuries, and in recent years it appears to have come alive again after a long sleep. See especially the little Tolsey House in Market Street, the 17th-century Hugh Perry's Almshouses in Church Street and, of course, the imposing church of St Mary the Virgin. This has a fine Perpendicular tower and a large over-restored interior, the contents of which include several interesting monuments and the splendid late 14th-century brass of Lord and Lady Berkeley. This is not normally viewable, but there is an excellent glass fibre replica on display.

The Cotswold Way★ passes through the town and this can be used for walks northwards to Dursley★, passing the Tyndale Monument★ and Stinchcombe Hill, or southwards to the Somerset Monument★ and Horton★. There is also an attractive walk north-eastwards up the wooded Tyley Bottom.

Wroxton (151) (SP 41-41) *3 mi. W Banbury.* This is a delightful village, much of it around a sloping green with a pretty pond usually lively with ducks. Here are many of the thatched stone cottages so typical of the Oxfordshire Cotswolds, where the local ironstone is less suitable for splitting into tiles than the true Cotswold stone further to the south and west. Each roofing method has its own merits, but how attractive these cottages look with their climbing roses and small trim gardens. There are two lively inns here, the White Horse and the Lord North, and a pleasant hotel and restaurant, the Wroxton House Hotel.

An Augustinian priory was founded here in the early 13th century, but only fragments of this remain in the present Wroxton Abbey, a fine 17th-century mansion with 18th- and 19th-century modifications. The 17th-century house was built by Sir William Pope, but it passed to the North family soon after. Many improvements were made in the 18th century by Lord North, Prime Minister during the time England lost her North American colonies. He appears to have been not only a client, but also a great friend, of Sanderson Miller, the architect-

Woodstock — Scale 1:10 000 or 6 INCHES TO 1 MILE

1 Main Car Park
1 Tourist Information Centre
2 Town Hall
3 Bear Hotel
4 Parish Church
5 Fletcher's House (Oxford City & County Museum)
6 Woodstock Gate (Blenheim Park)

squire of Radway (151) (SP 36-48), and Miller carried out work for him not only on the house, the chapel and the park, but also on the village church. Wroxton Abbey is now a college for students of Farleigh Dickinson University, New Jersey, and is only infrequently open to the public. *(Tel: (0295) 730551.)* However, the lovely gardens and park, with their sweeping lawns, rich woodlands and series of lakes, are now once again open regularly, having been extensively renovated in recent years. Do not miss a visit to the early 18th-century ice-house and the octagonal dovecot, nor the distant views of the Gothic arch on a wooded ridge to the east. These features are probably also the work of Sanderson Miller.

The largely 14th-century church has a west tower designed by the same architect, and built in 1748. See the series of elaborate tombs to various inhabitants of Wroxton Abbey, especially the beautifully canopied tomb of the builder of Wroxton, William Pope, Earl of Downe, and his wife; and the handsome monument to George III's Prime Minister, Lord North, by the brilliant sculptor, John Flaxman. Thomas Coutts, the founder of the famous private bank still bearing his name, is also buried here.

Wychwood Forest (164) (SP 33-17) *To immediate SW Charlbury.* From as early as Saxon times this was a royal forest, with the royal hunting lodge at Woodstock★ and its great woodlands extending from the Glyme Valley near Enstone (164) (SP 37-24) southwards to the Thames near Stanton Harcourt (164) (SP 41-05), and from Taynton★ in the west to the Cherwell Valley in the east. Every English king from Ethelred the Unready to James I is said to have visited the forest, and even as late as the 17th century Charles I started to build a wall round the whole forest — a process completed by Cromwell in 1655. The area was subject to the extremely harsh Forest Law, but although it was sometimes said that Oxford gaol was built largely to house those caught stealing game from here, this does not seem to have deterred the more determined poachers. Burford's reputation for great meals, known locally as 'Burford bait', appears to have been based on the ability of its citizens to acquire large quantities of venison — certainly not all the result of their one day's permitted hunting per year and the town's ancient right to two bucks.

Although this state of affairs did not wholly cease until as late as 1856, several great parks had by then been carved out of the forest — Ditchley★, Blenheim★, Cornbury★ and Eynsham (164) (SP 42-09) — and most of the remainder had been cleared for farming. Wychwood is therefore now confined to a modest triangle between Charlbury, Finstock and Leafield, and most of this is part of the strictly preserved Cornbury Estate. The road south from Ranger's Lodge (164) (SP 33-19) to Leafield (164) (SP 32-15) has great woodlands on its east side for almost three miles and is very pleasant. There is an attractive footpath running south-eastwards from a point on this road (SP 33-18) through the forest to Finstock (SP 35-16). For a detailed account of Wychwood Forest and its history, read Josceline Finberg's excellent book, *The Cotswolds.*

Wyck Rissington (163) (SP 19-21) *1½ mi. NE Bourton-on-the-Water.* This unspoilt little village has a wide rough green, complete with Victorian drinking fountain, about which are situated several attractive houses and cottages, the most pleasing of which is a substantial farmhouse fronting on to a well stocked duckpond. The delightful road sign on the green asking motorists to 'beware of the ducks' should of course be heeded at all times.

The church of St Laurence, which once belonged to the monks of Eynsham Abbey in Oxfordshire, has a squat 13th-century tower and a chancel of the same period with two unusual lancet windows at its east end. There was once a strange maze, with religious significance, in the old vicarage garden close to the church. Although this has now been cleared away its creator, Canon Harry Cheales, who died in 1984, is fittingly remembered with a well lettered wall-tablet, beneath which is a reproduction of the maze itself in a beautifully designed mosaic. See also the colourful fragments of 14th-century stained glass and an interesting series of 16th-century wooden plaques, which are believed to be Flemish in origin. The composer Gustav Holst was organist here in 1892 at the early age of seventeen. In the lovingly tended churchyard will be found the grave of 'James Loveridge, Gypsy — of no fixed abode' — a travelling man whose final journey ended at Wyck Rissington.

This village is astride the Oxfordshire Way★, and it is possible to use part of this long footpath to walk eastwards over Wyck Beacon to Bledington★ in the Evenlode Valley.

Yanworth (163) (SP 07-13) *2 mi. W Northleach.* This modest village overlooks the beautifully

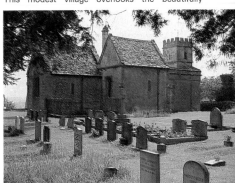

Yanworth's small Norman church

wooded Coln Valley, where Yanworth Mill, an attractive group of buildings, marks the beginning of our **Walk 11**. The small Norman church stands among a fine group of farm buildings to the east of the village. It has a Norman south doorway with chevron moulding, a Norman chancel arch and a stout tub font of the same period. From a much later period, probably the late 16th century, there is a wall-painting of Father Time complete with his scythe.

Apart from our **Walk 11** (see above) there are two good walks from here, one north-eastwards to Hampnett★, and the other north-westwards to Compton Abdale★.

Motor and Cycle Tours

Tour 1
Broadway and the Northern Cotswolds

60 miles. *This, the longest of our five tours, passes through the classic tourist centres of Broadway, Chipping Campden and Moreton-in-Marsh, and explores the hills and vales on the northern fringes of the Cotswolds before heading over some of its finest wold country — that lying between Moreton and Winchcombe. After dropping down to delightful Hailes Abbey, it climbs yet again onto the wolds, passing the source of the lovely River Windrush, before returning via Snowshill to Broadway.*

This tour provides a number of challenges for the cyclist, including the long Fish Hill out of Broadway, but the toil involved should be well worth while.

Start from the ever-popular village of **Broadway** (which is also the start of our **Walk 1**), heading up the High Street (A44) to climb the first part of **Fish Hill**. Fish Inn is on right beyond top of hill. Turn left at X-rds just beyond (Sign — Saintbury) (but turn right if you wish to visit **Broadway Tower Country Park**, on right after ½ mi). On main route, the 12-acre Fish Hill Picnic Area is on left with toilets and topograph. Route now follows course of the Roman **Ryknild Street** for a short time. Bear right at small X-rds (Sign — Chipping Campden), and then bear right at Y-junction beyond quarries on left. After about ¾ mi, the **Kiftsgate Stone** is in woods to left, but not very easy to spot.

Turn right at X-rds (Sign — Chipping Campden) and at bottom of hill bear left into the outstandingly beautiful town of **Chipping Campden**. Our route heads straight through the town, passing the Market Hall on left, and the turn to the almshouses and church up to the right. Keep straight out of the town on B4035 (Sign — Evesham) and after ½ mi bear right at Y-junction onto B4081, then almost immediately fork right onto minor road (Sign — Hidcote Garden). After ½ mi pass a tree-clad embankment, the spoil heaps created in about 1850 by the builders of the **Campden Railway Tunnel**. Turn left at X-rds (Sign — Hidcote Bartrim), and go straight, not right, at edge of **Hidcote Boyce**. Pass beautiful 17th-century Hidcote House on right. Go straight not left at T-junction (Sign — Hidcote Bartrim), and after ¼ mi

pass turn to **Hidcote Manor Garden** and **Hidcote Bartrim** village on right **(Mini-walk from here)**, and entrance to **Kiftsgate Court Garden** on left. Try to visit both of these delightful gardens. Fine views ahead before dropping down long hill.

(A) Now keep right at all junctions until reaching the village of **Ilmington**, attractively sited below the northernmost Cotswold edge. Turn right at entry to **Ilmington**, pass church on left, and bear left at T-junction. Bear left by war memorial on green, and sharp right up hill by village hall. **(Mini-walk from here.)** Climb steep hill and beyond top, fine views over to left and good walking opportunities using Landranger Sheet 151. Keep straight for 2 mi, turn right beyond gate in **Charingworth** hamlet and almost immediately turn left.

Down hill, turn right onto B4035 and almost immediately turn left onto B4479 (Sign — Blockley). After 1 mi turn sharp left onto minor road and go 2½ mi before turning right with care onto A429, the **Foss Way**. Almost immediately turn left (Sign — Todenham). Go over the little Knee Brook, and just beyond is the course of the long-vanished **Stratford and Moreton Tramway**. Turn right and almost immediately left at entry to **Todenham**. (But turn left to visit village — 14th-century church with fine spire and interesting interior, plus an inn of considerable character.) Turn right at entry to **Great Wolford** and go straight over small X-rds near tall-spired church. Keep straight beyond village and go straight, not left, at entry to **Barton-on-the-Heath**, with its attractive green and small church with Anglo-Danish origins.

Turn left beyond green (Sign — Little Compton) and after 1½ mi turn right beyond entry to **Little Compton**. Turn right beyond church and lovely manor house on right. At end of village turn left onto A44, and soon turn right onto minor road (Sign — Chastleton. Bear left at entry to small village of **Chastleton**, and pass enchanting 17th-century Chastleton House on left, noting dovecot over to right. Bear right at top of hill, and after ½ mi Iron Age **Chastleton Barrow** is over to left. Turn left with care onto A436 and after ¼ mi turn right onto narrow road.

(B) Turn sharp right by phone box in **Cornwell**, a delightful village restored by Clough Williams-Ellis, the creator of Portmeirion. (But walk back left for a glimpse of the manor house.) Go straight over X-rds, then bear left onto A436 and almost immediately turn right onto minor road (Sign — Adlestrop). Bear left into quiet village of **Adlestrop** (the start of our **Walk 5**), right near church and then left by bus shelter with old station sign.

Bear right twice (Signs — Evenlode), and

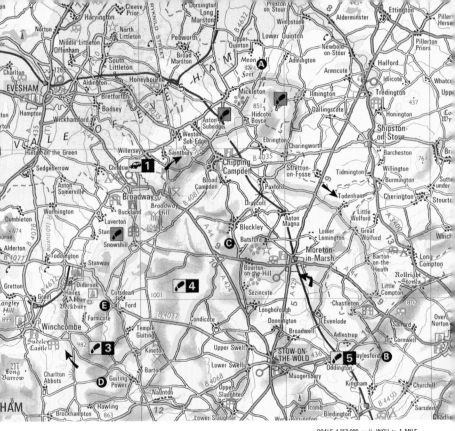

bear left at entry to widespread village of **Evenlode**. Pass interesting church on left and bear left at end of village. Bear right near entry to woodlands and turn left onto A44, with the **Four Shire Stone** soon on right. Keep on A44 through the pleasant old town of **Moreton-in-Marsh**, turning left and then right to cross the A429 (**Foss Way**). After 1½ mi pass a turn on right to **Batsford Park Arboretum** and, opposite, a turn on left to **Sezincote**, with its lovely garden and exotic 18th-century mansion. Climb up through attractive **Bourton-on-the-Hill**.

(C) After 1 mi bear left off A44, and soon go straight over X-rds crossing A424. After 2 mi, go straight not left in beautifully sited **Hinchwick** hamlet, which is the start of our **Walk 4**. Go along pleasant tree-lined road, over X-rds crossing B4077 and after 2 mi bear right by quarries and almost immediately right at X-rds (Sign — Snowshill). Entrance to the fascinating **Cotswold Farm Park** is on left, fine views over to right, and after ½ mi, turn left (Sign — Kineton). Down narrow road, fork left before fording the infant River Windrush, and turn right into **Kineton** hamlet. Turn left beyond the Half Way House Inn and through ford before going over X-rds by small car park on left (which is the start of our **Walk 3**)'.

(D) Turn right at X-rds (Sign — Winch-

combe), bear right well beyond woods, and almost immediately bear right again. Turn left at T-junction and almost immediately turn right onto small road eventually leading down hill. This is Salter's Lane and is on the course of the medieval **Salt Way**. Bear left at Y-junction (but turn right to visit **Hailes Abbey**), turn right onto B4632 and immediately turn right again, off B4632 (Sign — Didbrook). Turn left beyond **Didbrook** and then turn right at X-rds, by attractive war memorial, onto B4077. (But turn left if you wish to visit the **Gloucestershire Warwickshire Railway** at Toddington, or go over X-rds if you wish to visit **Stanway**). Now climb tree-lined Stanway Hill.

(E) Turn left at X-rds ½ mi beyond top of Stanway Hill, and soon bear left at next X-rds (Sign — Snowshill). Through **Taddington** hamlet (source of the River Windrush near Field Barn in valley over to right) and after 1¼ mi turn left to go through lovely village of **Snowshill**. **(Mini-walk from here.)** Bear left in village and use car park at far end on left to visit the National Trust's enchanting Snowshill Manor. Now go down long hill, past Broadway's interesting 'old church' on left and the 'new church' some way beyond on right, to return to **Broadway**, thus completing Tour 1.

Tour 2
The Upper Windrush Valley and the Central Wolds

50 miles. Our route takes us first from Stow-on-the-Wold to ever-popular Bourton-on-the-Water (try to avoid peak times) before heading south-eastwards through quiet country to lovely Burford. It now turns westwards, first up the delicious Windrush Valley, and then over the hills to Northleach. From this small wool town it moves further west to pass the Chedworth Roman Villa before heading north over the wolds, and eventually down to the charming old town of Winchcombe and the neighbouring Sudeley Castle. Now up onto the wold country again to run eastwards through a series of delightful villages — Guiting Power, Naunton, the Slaughters and the Swells — before returning to Stow-on-the-Wold.

Cyclists will have a relatively easy run down to Burford, up beside the Windrush and then across to the Churn Valley near the Chedworth Roman Villa. From here the going gets tougher, but it's grand country, and well worth the effort!

Head southwards from the charming old market town of **Stow-on-the-Wold** on the A429, **Foss Way**. Fork right at bottom of hill keeping on the A429, and after 2¼ mi turn left to enter popular tourist village of **Bourton-on-the-Water**. Bear left in village centre, and main car park is soon on right. Well beyond village turn right (Sign — Great Rissington), and after 2 mi bear right at entry to **Great Rissington**. Bear right again and on reaching the well restored church turn about and bear right to climb out of the village.

(A) Turn right well beyond Great Rissington and after 2½ mi turn left in the charming village of **Great Barrington**. **(Mini-walk from here.)** (But go straight ahead if you wish to visit church.) Now drive through **Taynton**, with its distant memories of stone quarried for London's St Paul's Cathedral and many of the Oxford colleges, and fork right beyond village before joining the A424 and A361 to go over the Windrush and into the highly attractive main street of **Burford**. Half-way up the street turn right by the little Tolsey Museum (identified by projecting clock-face), and after ½ mi turn right by small post-box onto smaller road (No sign). Route now runs along the Windrush valley before entering **Little Barrington**. **(Mini-walk from here.)** Turn right after passing church, and fork left beyond village (Sign — Windrush) where the Fox Inn is

SCALE 1:250 000 or ¼ INCH to 1 MILE

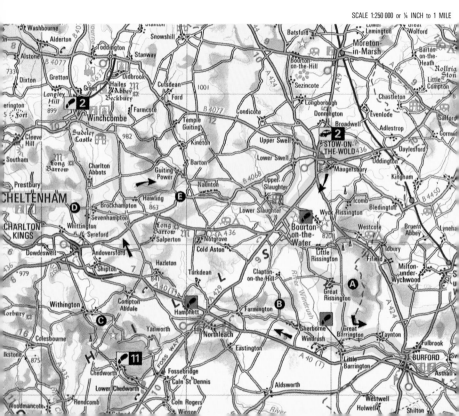

visible down to right. Fork right by the interesting church in **Windrush** and after 1 ¼ mi, fork right, by cottage with Norman arch, at entry to lovely village of **Sherborne** (Sign — Farmington). Soon turn left in village, and Sherborne Park (house) and church are on left, parkland on right.

(B) Go over X-rds at end of **Sherborne**. Now on quiet road up valley to the unspoilt village of **Farmington** where we turn left by green and then fork left to cross a deep valley. Beyond this we go under the busy Northleach bypass, and then turn right into the main street of the old wool town of **Northleach** with its splendid church. **(Mini-walk from here.)** At the end of the town turn left at X-rds onto the A429 (**Foss Way**) near the interesting **Cotswold Countryside Collection**.

Soon turn right off the A429, then go over X-rds through belt of trees, and after ¾ mi pass driveway on left to fascinating **Stowell** church (pedestrians only). Down steep hill, fork right (Sign — Yanworth), and pass road to Norman Yanworth church on right. Turn left in little **Yanworth** village, and then go straight, not left, just beyond. (But turn left for Yanworth Mill if you wish to go to the start of **Walk 11** — ½ mi ahead, beyond mill.) After 1 ¼ mi turn right in valley to follow course of the infant River Coln. (But go straight ahead to visit **Chedworth Roman Villa** — do not miss this.)

(C) Bear right at diagonal X-rds south of **Cassey Compton** hamlet (Sign — Compton Abdale), climb out of valley and then drop down into sleepy **Compton Abdale**. Go over offset X-rds in **Compton Abdale**, up onto the wolds to cross the busy A40, and after 2 mi cross the A436. Now follow signs to **Brockhampton**, a hamlet not far from the source of the south-flowing River Coln.

(D) Turn right at 2nd X-rds in **Brockhampton** (Sign — Winchcombe), go over X-rds, pass turn on right for **Charlton Abbots**, and after 1 ½ mi pass path on left leading to the fascinating **Belas Knap** long barrow. Turn right not far beyond and go steeply down to eventually turn right onto the B4632 at the entry to the charming little town of **Winchcombe**, which is the start of our **Walk 2**. Church is on left and immediately on right is a road to the fine **Sudeley Castle**.

Turn right in **Winchcombe** by the White Hart, down Castle street, and ½ mi beyond private entry to **Sudeley Castle** keep straight, not left, on steep hill. At top of hill bear right and then fork right, joining the course of the medieval **Salt Way**. Our route soon coincides for a short time with the course of our **Walk 2** and there are fine views over to the right. Go over X-rds at **Roel Gate**, and bear left twice to pass through the attractive little village of **Hawling**. Go over offset X-rds at end of village and drop gently down to quiet valley, passing Hawling Lodge.

(E) Bear left well beyond Hawling Lodge and eventually bear left at entry to trim **Guiting Power** (but turn right to visit church), and sharp right by green. Cross River Windrush beyond village, turn right and almost immediately fork left up hill. Take two turns to the right and drop down into the village of **Naunton**, attractively situated in the valley of the Windrush. Turn left in village and follow the valley before eventually turning left onto the B4068. Go over X-rds beyond top of hill and after ¼ mi turn right onto minor road. Pass turn on left to enchanting village of **Upper Slaughter**. **(Mini-walk from here.)** Do not miss a visit here, but if you come by car try to choose a quiet time. To continue on route turn left at next junction and go with care into equally enchanting, but even better known, **Lower Slaughter**.

Turn left in centre of **Lower Slaughter (Mini-walk from here)**, and bear right twice before turning right onto B4068 in **Lower Swell**. Almost immediately go straight beyond war memorial, leaving B4068 where it curves to the right. Lower Swell church is soon on right, and after ¾ mi turn sharp right onto B4077, to go through minute and attractive village of **Upper Swell** (walk back to visit this from lay-by beyond), and climb out of valley to return to **Stow-on-the-Wold**, thus completing Tour 2.

The little River Isbourne at Winchcombe

125

Tour 3
Mighty Blenheim and the Oxfordshire Cotswolds

48 miles. *Our route heads south and then south-east from the busy market town of Chipping Norton, over wold country to delightful little Charlbury, on the edge of Wychwood Forest. It now runs eastwards to Woodstock passing the northern confines of Blenheim Park. After visiting handsome Woodstock and the fabulous palace of Blenheim, the route turns south-westwards to pass Bladon, Sir Winston Churchill's last resting place. Now it goes up beside the River Evenlode to visit the North Leigh Roman Villa, and then westwards again, to the Windrush Valley. It continues through Minster Lovell, with its fine medieval manor hall and dovecot, and up the valley to Asthall and Swinbrook, both beloved by the 'Mitford Girls', and still enchantingly beautiful. The route now passes Burford, perhaps the loveliest of Cotswold towns, before heading northwards over the wolds to the Evenlode Valley villages of Shipton-under-Wychwood and Kingham, finally returning to Chipping Norton.*

This valley country is ideal for cyclists. Hills

Burford High Street

are small and not too frequent and the roads (apart from that between Burford and Shipton-under-Wychwood) are usually quiet.

Set out southwards from the lively market town of **Chipping Norton** on the A361, initially following signs to Burford. After 2 mi fork left off A361 (Sign — Chadlington), and turn left at X-rds in centre of the extensive village of **Chadlington**. Follow road out of village with church on right and turn right onto B4026 in **Spelsbury**. (Do not miss splendid Lee family monuments in the church.) Keep straight into the centre of the delightful country town of **Charlbury**, situated on the edge of **Wychwood Forest**, and leave on the B4437 following signs to Woodstock.

(A) After 5 mi pass the Ditchley Gate (the northernmost gate of Blenheim Park) and soon turn right with great care onto the busy A44 to drive to the elegant little town of **Woodstock**. Explore the town with its pleasant shops, restaurants and hotels, and then visit glorious **Blenheim Palace**, with its memories of Sir Winston Churchill and his ancestor the 1st Duke of Marlborough, and its splendid park landscaped by Capability Brown. (Entrance is on right of A44 at far end of the town.) Bear right at roundabout onto A4095 (Sign — Witney) and through **Bladon**, where Sir Winston Churchill's simple tombstone stands in the churchyard.

(B) After 3 ¼ mi, having passed through Long Hanborough, turn right off A4095 (Sign — Finstock) and almost immediately turn right again (Sign — East End). After ½ mi pass Leather Bottle Inn on left, and ½ mi beyond is path on right to pleasantly sited **North Leigh Roman Villa** with its interesting mosaics. Go over three X-rds, passing through the delightful hamlet of Wilcote, and then entering equally attractive **Delly End**. Bear right in Delly End and then turn right onto B4022, but almost immediately turn left off B4022. Follow signs to Minster Lovell, going over offset X-rds and then straight, not right, leaving wider road. Route now runs down to the valley of the lovely River Windrush. Enter the attractive village of **Minster Lovell**, passing small car park on left for medieval Minster Lovell Hall and its nearby dovecot (do not miss either).

(C) Turn right beyond Minster Lovell's Swan Hotel **(mini-walk from here)**, then fork left (Sign — Asthall Leigh) and turn left in Asthall Leigh. Take second turn left (Sign — Asthall), over bridge crossing River Windrush, and bear right three times in the minute village of **Asthall**, home of the Mitfords for six years before they moved into their new house north of Swinbrook (see below).

Go over X-rds well beyond village (Sign — Burford). (But turn right and go over River Windrush to visit the beautiful village of Swinbrook, with its fine church and its memories of the Mitford family, who lived here during the 1930s.) **(Mini-walk from here.)** After ½ mi pass turning to right to the interesting **Widford** church, with its floor incorporating part of a Roman mosaic pavement. Go beside the Windrush into the lovely old town of **Burford**, and turn right with care onto the main street. Do not miss a visit to its fine church, nor a look round some of its pleasant shops. Leave town on the A361, bearing right at mini-roundabout beyond bridge (Sign — Chipping Norton).

(D) Pass through large village of **Fulbrook** keeping on A361, and into attractive **Shipton-under-Wychwood** — the Lamb Inn and the Shaven Crown are both worth visiting. Near end of village, where A361 turns right, turn left and eventually bear right in **Milton-under-Wychwood**. Keep straight out of village and eventually bear right by woodlands, and pass **Bruern Abbey** on right before crossing railway line. Now turn left twice and follow the B4450 for ¾ mi, before turning right to go through the pleasant village of **Kingham** — spare a glance for the lovely Old Rectory on left near our entry to the village.

(E) Turn right at end of village, and bear left onto B4450 in **Churchill**. (But turn right if you wish to visit church.) Now follow B4450 into **Chipping Norton**, thus completing Tour 3.

SCALE 1:250 000 or ¼ INCH to 1 MILE

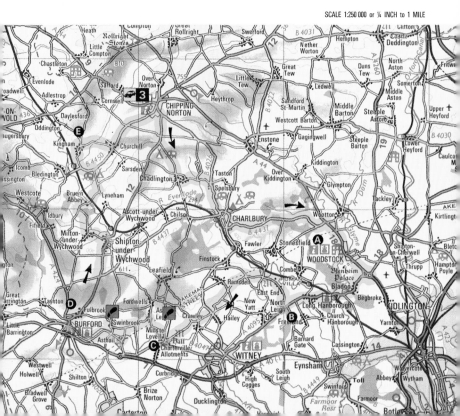

Tour 4

Cirencester, the Duntisbournes and the Coln Valley

45 miles. *Our route heads north-west from busy Cirencester, soon following the valley of the little Dunt stream, through Daglingworth and the Duntisbournes, before crossing over the dangerously fast Ermin Way to Elkstone. Now it goes across the Churn Valley at Colesbourne and over wooded hills into attractive Withington, astride the infant Coln. After passing Chedworth village the route rejoins the River Coln at Fossebridge and follows its course through a series of enchanting villages, including much-visited Bibury, before heading further east to the lovely Eastleaches. From here it turns west, over the Coln again, this time at Quenington, before heading past the Ampneys to return to Cirencester.*

Cyclists have a few hills to tackle in the early part of this tour, but once into the Coln Valley they will have a reasonably easy time.

Set out from **Cirencester**, prosperous market town and undisputed centre of the southern Cotswolds, heading north-westwards on the A417, the Roman **Ermin Way** (Signs — Gloucester). After 1½ mi fork left off A417 by war memorial in **Stratton** village (Sign — Daglingworth). Go over small X-rds in pretty village of **Daglingworth**. (But turn left to visit church with Saxon origins.) Turn right at end of village (Sign — The Duntisbournes). After ¾ mi pass path to delightful **Duntisbourne Rouse** church on right. Now follow signs to **Duntisbourne Abbots**, bearing right twice near entry to this trim village, and then bearing left by church.

(A) After climbing out of valley, turn left with great care onto the busy A417 (**Ermin Way**) and pass inn on right. Go over X-rds and after ¾ mi fork right off A417 at 2nd X-rds, and almost immediately straight, not right (Signs — Elkstone). Go over small X-rds in village of **Elkstone** — do not miss its exceptionally interesting Norman church — and turn right at 2nd X-rds beyond church. At small X-rds bear left and immediately left again, down hill into small village of **Colesbourne**. Bear right at entry and keep straight through to bear right with care onto the A435. Pass turning on left to **Colesbourne** church, situated in pleasantly wooded Colesbourne Park, and soon turn left off A435 onto minor road (Sign — Withington). Lake is soon just visible through trees down to left. Then climb steep hill, and after 1 mi bear right at Y-junction and drop down into attractive village of **Withington**. **(Mini-walk from here.)** Go straight, not right, at entry to village, turn right near large church, over little River Coln by the popular Mill Inn on left, go straight not right and soon turn up to right leaving village (Sign — Roman Villa).

(B) After 1 mi pass **Cassey Compton** Manor House and Farm on left, and turn right at diagonal X-rds just beyond, joining the course of the Roman **White Way**. (But go straight over if you wish to visit **Chedworth Roman Villa**, 1 mi ahead.) Go up through woods and over disused airfield, then turn left and fork left to enter the widespread village of **Chedworth**, with its interesting late Norman church. Keep straight through village (but turn down left to visit church and inn), and go well beyond, following all signs to Fossebridge.

Bear left near Denfurlong Farm (Sign — Fossebridge) (but turn right for **Denfurlong Farm Trail** which is just beyond on left). Turn left with great care onto A429 (**The Foss Way**) and drop steeply into valley at **Fossebridge**. Cross River Coln beyond hotel on left and immediately turn right with great care onto minor road leading to the trim village of **Coln St Dennis**. Bear right by the tall-towered Norman church, over River Coln, and follow valley road to equally enchanting **Coln Rogers**, first passing its attractive, partly Saxon church on left.

Bear left at far end of **Coln Rogers** and over River Coln, but soon turn right by mill house and re-cross Coln near entry to delightful little **Winson**. (All these Coln valley villages are quite remarkably beautiful.) First bear left in Winson, then bear left by small church and head down the valley. Turn left at entry to **Ablington**, the village of J. Arthur Gibbs, the author of that classic description of country life, *A Cotswold Village*. Now cross over the Coln once again, passing fine old barns and Gibbs's old home, the Manor House, on right, and then bear right onto road leading slightly above the valley to the outstandingly beautiful and much-visited village of **Bibury**.

Eastleach Martin Church . . . a view from Eastleach Turville

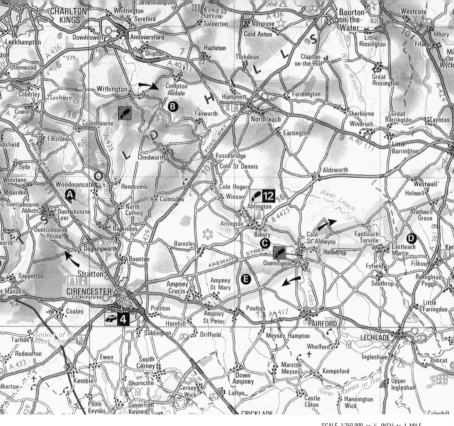

SCALE 1:250 000 or ¼ INCH to 1 MILE

Pass Bibury Trout Farm on left and then go straight, not right, joining the B4425 by the Swan Hotel. If possible park beyond the bridge (our **Walk 12** starts from here) or by the riverside, to walk back and over the bridge to visit the Arlington Mill Museum and the Trout Farm. Walk back via Rack Isle and the lovely Arlington Row, both in the care of the National Trust. While still on foot try also to visit the church by turning right after crossing the footbridge beyond Arlington Row.

(C) Bear left on B4425 and, ignoring road to the church, soon turn right onto minor road near end of village (Sign — Coln St Aldwyns). Turn right at entry to lovely **Coln St Aldwyns** and then bear left in centre. **(Mini-walk from here.)** (But walk to right to visit church, or straight ahead to visit New Inn or to cross bridge over the Coln.) Pass entry to Hatherop Castle on right, then pass lychgate on right (walk down long path to **Hatherop** church — do not miss the monument to Lady de Mauley) and soon turn left at end of village. After 1 mi bear half right joining the course of the Roman **Akeman Street**. Fork left down steep hill, and bear left, over infant River Leach. Course of **Akeman Street** visible in valley field to left. Now go up steep hill through woods and in 1 ¼ mi turn right at X-rds (Sign — Fyfield).

(D) After 1 ½ mi turn right at X-rds (Sign —

Eastleach). (But turn left if you wish to visit the **Cotswold Wildlife Park** — only 3 mi to NW.) Bear right at X-rds by **Eastleach Martin** church, and cross over River Leach into **Eastleach Turville**, noting church up to right and attractive footbridge to left — linger here if at all possible. Go straight, not left, near end of village (Sign — Hatherop) and soon turn left (Sign — Fairford) and then right (Sign — Hatherop) to head back towards **Hatherop**.

Turn left just before entering **Hatherop** (Sign — Fairford), then sharp right by gate pillars (Sign — Quenington) and soon go over bridge crossing River Coln. Turn left and then keep straight into charming village of **Quenington**. Bear right up small hill, and then bear second right. (But temporarily turn down to left to visit small church with its fine Norman doorways and the nearby medieval gateway of Quenington Court.) Now go up small hill passing the Earl Grey Inn and the Keepers' Arms. Fork left at large green and go over X-rds at end of village (Sign — Cirencester).

(E) Now keep straight on this road for 4 mi, going over three X-rds before bearing right with care onto the A417. Keep on A417 through **Ampney St Peter** and **Ampney Crucis** (interesting church is up road to right), before returning to **Cirencester**, thus completing Tour 4.

129

Tour 5
Secret Watershed Country between the Thames and Severn

50 miles. *Our route first heads south from Cirencester, almost to the borders of the Cotswold Water Park, and then turns westwards to visit the source of the Thames near Tarlton. It now follows as closely as possible the course of the long-vanished Thames and Severn Canal and also passes the western end of the splendid Cirencester Park. It continues north-westwards over hills and deep wooded valleys, through delightful little Bisley and Slad to elegant Painswick. Beyond here the route soon swings north-eastwards to follow some of the most dramatic 'edge country', before going over quiet country behind the edge, to Seven Springs. Then south through deep woodlands to Withington, and returning through North Cerney and Bagendon to Cirencester.*

The early stages of this route are temptingly easy, but once beyond the Thames-Severn watershed at Sapperton cyclists may find their physical energy being sapped at a rate perhaps only exceeded by that of the leggers who once propelled barges through the long tunnel beneath the hills!

Leave the centre of the bustling market town of **Cirencester** by heading south-westwards down Castle Street. Bear left at end of Castle Street (Sign — Somerford Keynes) and over bridge crossing ring road. (If you wish to visit the Roman Amphitheatre, turn right immediately beyond bridge, and it is soon on right.) Go over X-rds (Sign — Somerford Keynes) and after 2¼ mi turn right at X-rds (Sign — Ewen). (But turn left and go second right if you wish to visit **The Cotswold Water Park**.) Enter Ewen with welcoming Wild Duck Inn on left.

Turn right in quiet village of **Ewen** and immediately fork left. After ¾ mi turn right with care onto A429 and very soon turn left onto minor road by Smerrill Farm. Turn left with care onto the busy A433 (**Foss Way**), and soon cross course of **Thames and Severn Canal** at Thames Head Bridge, a canal bridge on lay-by to right. Go under narrow railway bridge with care and Thames Head Inn is on right. (It is possible to walk to the source of the Thames from here.)

(A) Soon turn right off A433 (Sign — Tarlton), and after 1¼ mi turn right in small village of **Tarlton**. After ¾ mi go over bridge crossing the course of the **Thames and Severn Canal**. (Path on right follows south

bank of canal course to the source of the Thames.) Just beyond the bridge, there is a roadway on the left to the **Tunnel House Inn**, which stands near the southern end of the tunnel which carried the **Thames and Severn Canal** beneath the Cotswold watershed. **(Mini-walk from here.)** Back on the main route and just beyond this diversion, there is a charming little canal 'round house' on right. Turn left at entry to wide-spread village of **Coates**, turn right by church, and then soon turn left up pretty tree-lined road.

Bear left in woodlands onto A419 and soon fork right onto minor road (Sign — Sapperton). Turn right at X-rds and soon left, opening an open space to right where **Cirencester Park's** Broad Ride crosses the road (fine gates are just visible from road). Soon enter the attractive village of **Sapperton** with its memories of Ernest Gimson and the Barnsley brothers. Turn left above the church, with its stylish interior (our **Walk 10** starts from here), and then bear right to drop down through woods to **Daneway**, and the Daneway Inn. Bear left by the inn, climb steeply up through woods and down to sheltered **Tunley** hamlet, to fork left and then bear right to widespread **Waterlane**. Now follow signs to the large but wholly delightful village of **Bisley**. Go over small X-rds beyond village entry, turn right and then left beyond church, passing village lock-up on right and the Bear Inn on left.

(B) After ¾ mi bear left and then right (sign — Anstead's Farm), eventually down hill through woods, past Swift's Hill Nature Reserve. Bear right, and then turn sharp right with great care onto B4070, and soon enter the village of **Slad** — immortalised in Laurie Lee's book, *Cider with Rosie*. 1 mi beyond Slad, turn left off B4070 at Bulls Cross (our **Walk 8** starts from here), and follow signs to Painswick.

Enter the elegant 17th- and 18th-century town of **Painswick**, first bearing right, then left at the Cross, and right beyond bow-fronted shop. Turn left onto A46 just beyond beautifully spired church and turn right onto Edge Road opposite lychgate. Bear right beyond bridge in valley bottom, left at T-junction on slope and bear right twice in **Edge** onto A4173 (Sign — Gloucester). (But go over small X-rds crossing A4173 with great care, soon turn left, bear right after 1 mi and then fork left, if you wish to move to the start of **Walk 6**.)

On main route, soon fork right off A4173 (watch for this with care), after ¾ mi bear left (Sign — Upton) and after ¼ mi go straight, not right (Sign — Upton). (But turn right and eventually right again onto B4073 if you wish to visit the delightful Painswick (★) Rococo Garden — ¼ mi.) Note fine views over to left from Cud Hill, and soon turn right onto B4073

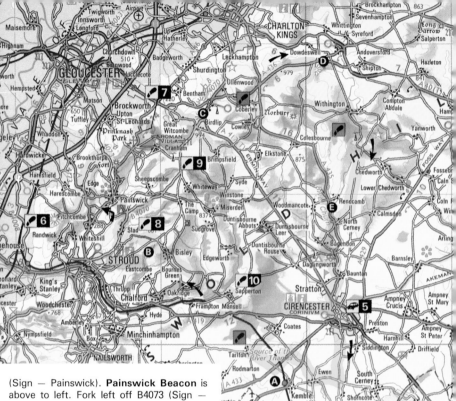

SCALE 1:250 000 or ¼ INCH to 1 MILE

(Sign — Painswick). **Painswick Beacon** is above to left. Fork left off B4073 (Sign — Painswick Beacon) and then turn left onto A46 (Sign — Cheltenham). Keep on A46 into lovely **Cranham Woods**, and after 1 mi, fork right onto minor road (Sign — Cranham). (But keep on A46 for ½ mi and then turn left if you wish to visit **Prinknash Abbey**, or go beyond on A46 past the Prinknash turn for another ¼ mi if you wish to start **Walk 7** from Fiddler's Elbow Car Park.) Immediately, go straight, not right (Sign — Birdlip), and soon bear left in woods onto B4070.

(C) Turn right with care near entry to **Birdlip**. (But bear left and down steep hill if you wish to visit **Witcombe Roman Villa** — turn on left after 2 mi.) Go straight, not left, in **Birdlip**, but almost immediately turn right in village onto minor road (Sign — Brimpsfield). Follow signs to **Brimpsfield** (our **Walk 9** starts from a point just beyond village), turn left in village, pass path to church on right and after 1 mi cross the A417 (**Ermin Way**) with great care. Go through woods and past parkland to enter the attractive village of **Cowley**. Bear right in village, pass church on right and cross bridge with lake on left. Turn left with great care onto A435 and after 1¼ mi turn right at X-rds onto A436 near **Seven Springs**. (Turn left onto A436 for lay-by soon on right, if you wish to view this rather unexciting birthplace of the little River Churn. However, there is a **mini-walk from here**.)

(D) After 3 mi turn sharp right off the A436 with great care, near to the Kilkenny Viewpoint Car Park, and head south through quiet woodlands before turning left at X-rds (Sign — Withington). Cross the Hilcot Brook with pool on left and after 1½ mi go straight, not right, before dropping down to the attractive village of **Withington**. (**Mini-walk from here.**) Turn right and right again, unless you wish to visit village, and eventually climb up through pleasant woodlands. Bear right at small road junction near deserted airfield, joining the Roman **White Way**. Head straight along this for 2½ mi before forking right (Sign — North Cerney), and drop down into pleasant village of **North Cerney**.

(E) Bear right at Y-junction by large sycamore tree in **North Cerney** and go over offset X-rds beyond the Bathurst Arms, crossing the A435 (Sign — Bagendon). Pass North Cerney's beautifully restored Norman church on left. Go over X-rds (Sign — Bagendon) and bear left by war memorial at entry to minute village of **Bagendon**, with interesting little church soon on left. After ½ mi turn right at T-junction (Sign — Perrott's Brook), and then go over X-rds (Sign — Cirencester) — this is on the southern boundary of the pre-Roman capital of the Iron Age tribe, the Dobunni (see **Bagendon**). Bear right with care onto A435 and after 1 mi go over X-rds. (But turn left and keep left if you wish to visit interesting **Baunton** church. After 1 mi bear left onto A417 and soon enter **Cirencester**, thus completing Tour 5.

131

Walks

Walk 1
Broadway Tower and some Cotswold Edge Country

Approximately 7 miles. Allow 4½ hours

This walk climbs steeply out of the busy village of Broadway to visit the famous landmark of Broadway Tower, which is perched on the very edge of the Cotswolds. From here to the delightful village of Snowshill public roads are used, but if you wish to avoid these, and return more directly across country to Broadway, our map reveals several interesting rights of way dropping back into the vale. However, those who follow our route to Snowshill will be rewarded in several ways — a visit to the National Trust's Snowshill Manor, a call at the friendly Snowshill Arms and a fine return walk to Broadway along the partly wooded ridge running northwards between Buckland and Broadway.

(A) Start walk from **Broadway** which is on **Tour 1**. Use the car park just to the east of the B4632, near its junction with the main A44 road which runs through the village (see plan on page 35). Leave car park by path leading behind toilets, via narrow passage to the High Street. Turn left up High Street, and soon turn right by Pear Tree House (sign — Broadway Tower). You are now on the **Cotswold Way**, which is normally waymarked with a yellow arrow and a white dot. Climb over two stiles, and go through gate at top of field, beyond stream. Climb over stile and bear diagonally left, now starting to climb more steeply.

Follow sunken track up next field almost straight up hill, and through gate, bearing slightly to left. Now follow sunken trackway keeping slightly to right, heading for top right of field by National Trust sign indicating 'Clump Farm'. Take right-hand of two gates into right-hand field, and then head up field with hedge to immediate left and old quarry workings to right. Ignore bridleway forking to right. Look back for fine views of Bredon Hill and the Malverns. Climb over a series of stiles keeping hedge or wall to immediate left, and following well defined path heading straight for **Broadway Tower**. Pass clump of beech trees to left and go through gate into field below **Broadway Tower**, which is part of a country park and well worth visiting, both for its interesting contents and for the dramatic panoramas from its windy roof.

(B) Keep to left of tower and then head to right, behind it (Cotswold Way leads away to left at this point). Walk to gate at end of 'tower field' and join public road. Go to right if you wish to visit the rest of **Broadway Tower Country Park**, but main route now follows the public road southwards (this section is known as **Buckle Street**). The walk will now be on public roads as far as **Snowshill**, but these should be reasonably quiet except at peak holiday times. Bear right at T-junction by entry to Spring Hill Estate, keeping on public road (sign — Snowshill). Point-to-Point course is over to left.

(C) Fork right at Y-junction, keeping on public road (sign — Snowshill). Pass timber yard in old quarry to right, and then go through farmstead of Hill Barn Farm. Bear right at diagonal crossroads keeping on public road (sign — Snowshill).

(D) Now drop down past Snowshill entry sign, go over small crossroads and walk steeply down into delightful little village of **Snowshill**. Fork left by church. (But fork right if you wish to visit the National Trust's fascinating Snowshill Manor or the hospitable Snowshill Arms.) Bear left on main route past the church and follow out of village up small wooded hill beyond Oat Hill Cottages.

(E) At top of hill fork right off 'through road' onto surfaced road (signed — 'No Through Road'). Turn right at T-junction beyond house onto surfaced farm road. Go down hill and eventually fork left onto track leading behind Great Brockhampton Farm. Keep along this track with extensive coniferous woodlands to left. Ignore track to right leading to Little Brockhampton Farm and soon go through gate into fields with woods to left, keeping on the same general line. There are good views to right across valley to Middle Hill (mansion) and Broadway Tower.

(F) At end of field bear left through gate between two woods and go down field to the start of a straight farm road. The walk now follows the course of the **Cotswold Way** back to **Broadway**. You are now on a miniature plateau heading due north on a good farm road. Field with gallops and modern stud farm is over to left, with fine views of Bredon Hill and the Malverns beyond.

(G) Turn right and almost immediately left by small wooden buildings where farm road leaves our route, bending to left and down to **Buckland**. Now continue northwards on same general line with hedge line on immediate right. Go through gate at end of field and steeply down to right through Broadway Coppice for a short distance. Go straight down field and (unless waymarking has

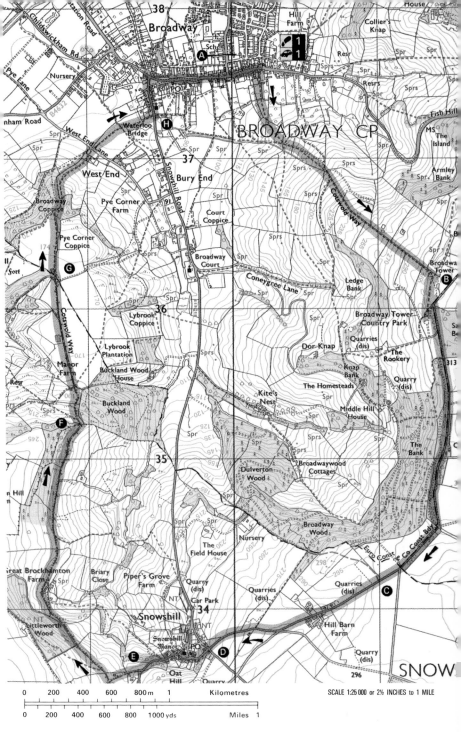

changed slightly) cross two small paddocks to cross public road just to left of house and small outbuildings. Beyond road, follow path heading directly towards the tall tower of Broadway's 'new church'. Go over small wooden bridge crossing the Badsey Brook.

(H) Soon turn left onto public road near church, entering **Broadway**. Pass the church and the attractive Crown and Trumpet Inn, and then turn right to walk up much of Broadway's fine High Street. Turn left onto the B4632, and almost immediately turn right into the starting car park **(A)**, thus completing Walk 1.

Walk 2
Winchcombe, Sudeley Castle and a 'Roman Valley'

Approximately 8 miles. Allow 4½ — 5 hours

This walk starts from the delightful old town of Winchcombe and soon passes the splendid castle of Sudeley before heading up a broad valley once occupied by the castle's great deer park, and across fields to Sudeley Lodge. Once past this handsome Georgian house, we start to climb out of the valley. On the hill ridge above the valley we follow a road along the line of the medieval Salt Way. We now go back down into the valley, and eventually through dense woodlands that shelter the remains of the fine Spoonley Roman villa. Largely along farm roads, we head across the valley and climb its western slopes, eventually joining the line of the Cotswold Way, near a small wood that shelters the site of another Roman villa. Finally we return to Winchcombe on the well marked Cotswold Way, passing the entrance to Sudeley Castle not far from the town.

If possible park in the Free Car Park behind the library at **Winchcombe**, which is on **Tour 2**. If this is full there is a car park in the centre of the town and several roadside opportunities not far from the centre.

(A) Start walk from the Free Car Park behind the library by going to the right down Cowl Lane following footpath sign (Town Centre). Turn left into the High Street, cross this and almost immediately turn right down Castle Street. Go over bridge crossing little River Isbourne and turn right immediately beyond Sudeley Castle Holiday Cottages, following footpath sign. Head diagonally across field in direction just to right of **Sudeley Castle**. Go through metal farm gate below oak tree, heading in same direction, with car park well over to left. (Apply at ticket kiosk if you wish to visit the castle.) Cross surfaced road following waymark over stile, and head for kissing gate beyond 'play area'. Go through gate and keep to immediate right of fence, with good views of **Sudeley Castle** beyond to left. Go through 2nd kissing gate and bear diagonally left across the Home Parks. Climb over stile in wire fence not shown on map, and continue on same line, heading for trees in far corner of the Home Parks.

(B) Go over small stream and stile just beyond. Almost immediately turn left and go

over stile, following left-hand waymark. Now follow to immediate right of hedge line, and turn right at top of field following waymark, still keeping to right of hedge line. Just beyond coloured pipeline marker turn left, go over stile following waymark and continue up field to right of hedge line. Go through hunting gate at top of field and turn right onto surfaced private road. Keep on private road to immediate left of handsome 18th-century Sudeley Lodge, noting stone plaque stating that George III visited here in 1788 while on his way from Sudeley Castle to Brockhampton Park.

(C) Turn left near end of road just beyond Sudeley Lodge (bridleway signed) and up farm road between barns. Follow surfaced farm road up hill, bearing right near top of rise which is overlooked from the left by the woodlands of Limekiln Plantation. Keep on farm road through gate and after a few minutes note fine views back to Sudeley Lodge, Sudeley Castle and Winchcombe. Go through gate into Parks Farm farmyard but immediately fork left on higher road keeping buildings below to right. At end of farmyard turn up to left opposite farm cottages and follow track up hill. Bear right through wooden farm gate keeping on track into edge of woodlands, which are largely up to left.

(D) Go through hunting gate and turn right onto surfaced minor road, following the course of the medieval **Salt Way**. Keep on this road through two areas of woodland and after dropping down beyond the 2nd wooded area, turn sharp right onto a farm road with the name 'Spoonley Farm' carved on a stone in the wall, and a concrete footpath sign nearby. Continue down farm road passing small quarry on right and Spoonley Farm on left.

(E) Well beyond Spoonley Farm go through gateway and almost immediately turn sharp right off main track, through a metal farm gate and onto a less used track. Keep on track heading for gap between Spoonley Wood and Limehill Wood. At this gap turn left off track and over stile onto path leading down through Spoonley Wood. Follow reasonably well defined path through wood, first bearing slightly to left, then turning right and soon bearing left, maintaining a generally north-western direction. With luck the scanty and overgrown remains of **Spoonley Roman Villa** will be encountered, but any walls seen will almost certainly be those reconstructed by the Victorian excavators. Go over small stream and stile leaving wood, and turn left to continue to immediate right of its edge.

(F) Bear diagonally left at end of field and down track over causeway crossing small stream. Now head diagonally across field aiming for Waterhatch farm buildings. Keep to left of first barn at Waterhatch and turn right beyond its end to go down farm road between 'Atcost' barn and old barn with brick arches. Well beyond Waterhatch fork right, keeping on better farm road with stream and trees on right. Bend round to left and then to right, keeping on farm road as far as Newmeadow Farm. Turn left at Newmeadow Farm onto public road optimistically signed 'Andoversford 5'. Immediately afterwards pass through gate with sign beyond indicating with some justification 'Unsuitable for Motor Vehicles', as the 'road' is now a grass-grown track.

(G) After steep climb up track turn sharp right just below wood and walk on track along its edge. Just beyond Humblebee Cottages bear right down track which forms part of the **Cotswold Way** (this long-distance footpath will now be used for the return to Winchcombe and its waymarks should be followed). Small conifer plantation up to left is the site of the **Wadfield Roman Villa** (do not trespass). Walk down track to Wadfield Farm and, leaving track, keep to immediate right of farm buildings and fine early 18th-century farmhouse. Climb over stile beside farm gate beyond house and start to drop down field keeping hedge line on immediate right. Go over stile by metal gate; there are pleasant views of **Sudeley Castle** in valley straight ahead. Follow down field with hedge on immediate right, bear left at corner and pass an oak tree with waymark.

(H) Soon turn right, go over stile and turn left, now keeping hedge line on left. Turn right at end of field and immediately turn left to cross small wooden bridge and stile. Now follow waymarks over fields in the general direction of Winchcombe church and eventually bear left onto quiet public road. Follow this road past the entrance to **Sudeley Castle** and over bridge crossing the River Isbourne to enter **Winchcombe**. Walk up pretty Vineyard Street and turn right into the High Street, before turning left to Cowl Lane to return to the starting car park (A), thus completing Walk 2.

SCALE 1:25 000 or 2½ INCHES to 1 MILE

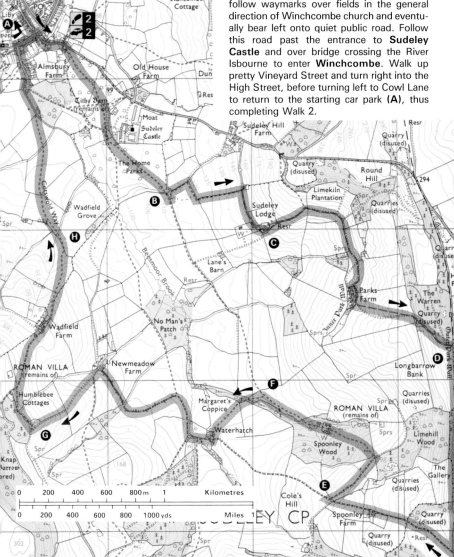

Walk 3
Guiting Woods and the Castlett Valley

Approximately 6 miles. Allow 3 hours

This walk starts from delightful miniature parkland overlooked by a fine manor house, and soon heads across the southern side of the great Guiting Wood. Turning northwards at quaintly titled Deadmanbury Gate, it then follows a medieval trackway known as Campden Lane over open country to Lynes Barn. This is watershed country, with a small stream not far away flowing south-east towards the distant Thames, while the western edge of the Cotswolds is only a few hundred yards beyond our road, with fine views out over the Avon and Severn Valleys. The walk now follows a small road before plunging down to a sunken tree-shaded path leading to the site of a long-vanished medie-

val village. Beyond here, the route crosses the little Castlett Stream not far from its source, and then again heads over open country before dropping down once more to run parallel with the Castlett, now flowing through the eastern fringes of the highly attractive Guiting Wood. Only too soon, the walk emerges from the wood and ends at the car park from which it commenced.

(A) Start walk from the small car park (but beware, this can be very muddy in the depths of winter) which is situated to the left of minute crossroads (163) (SP 08-25) about a mile south-west of **Kineton**, and which is on **Tour 1**. Walk out of car park and over crossroads onto minor public road keeping to the left of the handsome manor house. Pass through gateway beneath trees and turn right up private drive (signed — Public Footpath). Turn left immediately before drive enters private grounds at the rear of the Manor House, and follow to immediate left of fence line at top of field. Bear round to right near top of field and through gap at its end. Now

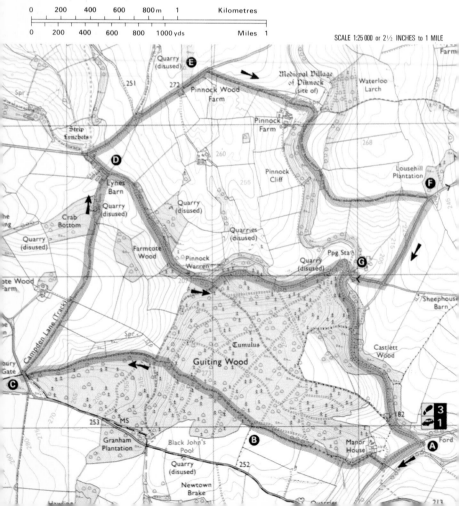

go across next field keeping to the immediate left of the edge of the wood (part of **Guiting Wood**). Pass through gap into next field still keeping to immediate left of the edge of woods.

(B) Just before next hedge gap, turn right onto path into woods, following yellow waymark. Immediately bear diagonally left in woods following second yellow waymark, and keep to reasonably well defined path, which follows intermittently-used track. Woodlands here are an attractive blend of hard- and softwoods. Follow a third yellow waymark heading straight across a well defined track, and start to drop gently down towards valley. Now drop down more steeply and go straight over 'crossroads' of paths in valley bottom, following one of three yellow waymarks. Soon start to climb gently out of valley keeping just within the right-hand edge of the wood.

(C) Eventually turn right onto minor road at Deadmanbury Gate, but immediately fork right off this onto a signed bridleway, with blue waymark a little further on. This bridleway is known as **Campden Lane** and was almost certainly a medieval trackway used by traders with pack animals, carrying wool from **Chipping Campden** and probably salt from Droitwich. This theory would appear to be strengthened by the fact that for part of the way this narrow track has hedges either side of it. Farmcote Wood Farm is visible over to left. Pass cottage to immediate left and keep straight on, now following to immediate right of hedge and wall to left. There are now good views over to the right.

Route now starts to drop down, with good views ahead. Pass through gate at end of field following blue waymark just beyond start of small coppice to left. Continue to follow down left-hand edge of next field. Lynes Barn farm buildings are soon visible ahead. Bear round to right following blue waymark, and pass first farm buildings to left.

(D) Bear left at corner of Lynes Barn farm buildings onto minor public road. (But turn right and walk down road to Point **(G)** if you wish to make a shorter walk through **Guiting Wood**. Road is usually very quiet and therefore suitable for walking.) On main route, turn right at T-junction beyond bungalow on right (signed — Ford), onto slightly busier minor road. There are fine views down on left to Alderton Hill. Road now climbs gently out of valley. Bear right at Y-junction, still keeping on public road (signed — Ford). (But bear left if you wish to visit **Farmcote** and possibly go down beyond to **Hailes Abbey**, linking with the **Cotswold Way**.) Pass farm on right.

(E) About 20 yards **before** hedge line comes down to the road from a radio mast on

In Guiting Wood

left, turn right and cross stile onto sunken, tree-shaded path (signed 'footpath' on low concrete marker). Go down sunken path which is sometimes overgrown. Its depth below the surrounding country probably indicates its great age, and it must certainly have been used by the inhabitants of the lost medieval village of Pinnock. Climb over small stile at end of bushy trees, but path is still sunken beyond. Go through wooden farm gate, over surfaced farm road, with farm up to right, and through gate onto track immediately opposite. Only very slight indications of Pinnock medieval village site remain — in the form of scooped platforms on the banks above the track.

Follow track as it curves to right in valley, crosses the head of the little Castlett Stream (a tributary of the Windrush, and also, therefore, of the Thames) and climbs bank with stream and woods down to right. Follow track across more open country with woods still visible down to right. Track now curves fairly steeply up to left and eventually there are fine views to right over **Guiting Wood**. Keep heading in same direction when track peters out, and then over stile to left of last gate where track becomes better defined again, with Lousehill Plantation on left.

(F) Turn right onto minor public road by small beech-wood on opposite side of road. Walk down road, turn right at 'crossroads' where tracks meet, and drop steeply down public road. In bottom of valley cross the Castlett Stream on the edge of Guiting Wood.

(G) Immediately turn sharp left onto less used public road. (Walkers taking the short cut from Point **(D)** will rejoin the main route here.) Now follow this quiet public road along, but inside, the delightful eastern edge of the great **Guiting Wood** with the Castlett Stream running close to the left for most of the way. Pass through gate at end of woodlands and continue on public road through unspoilt parkland, with views of manor house up to right. Soon arrive at small crossroads and the starting car park **(A)** just beyond, thus completing Walk 3.

Walk 4
Hinchwick and Ryknild Street

Approximately 4½ miles. Allow 2½ hours

This walk explores a remote valley once busy with Roman traffic heading northwards on Ryknild Street. Why not add an extra dimension to your walk by trying (without trespassing away from the paths shown) to trace the line of this long-vanished road, much of whose course is still shown on the map as only conjectural. The valley through which it partly runs is streamless, grassy and usually grazed by sheep — so please ensure that dogs are kept on a lead at all times. There are fine views of the rolling country in which the valley lies, especially from the higher ground crossed on the return southwards.

Park somewhere in the vicinity of the hamlet of **Hinchwick** (151) (SP 14-30), which is on our **Tour 1**. There is no formal car parking, but there are several small places where at least one car can be parked. If in doubt we suggest that you ask locally.

(A) Start walk from the Hinchwick T-junction where there is a signpost for motorists, but at the time of writing no footpath sign. Now walk north through gate on surfaced farm road and immediately fork half right diagonally across the field, heading for a gate in the broad valley bottom to the right of the woods ahead. Go through farm gate and continue up valley bottom. Beyond second farm gate start bearing to the left, keeping in valley. Go through third gateway and bear gently to the right, still keeping in broad valley bottom.

(B) At the end of this field go through small hunting gate to immediate right of large farm gate, and beyond it keep close to the wall on right. Our path curves round to the left, still following line of wall. Pass beginning of small wood up bank to left. If you look carefully to the right near this point it should be possible to spot slight signs of the Roman **Ryknild Street** zig-zagging up the bank (see map).

(C) Pass through farm gate at end of field and immediately turn right through hunting gate with helpful footpath sign, stating very politely, 'Landowners welcome careful walkers.' Now immediately turn left continuing up main valley, with fence line now to our left. Enter small wood with hazelnut trees and a few oaks, part of a belt of trees coming down slope to our left. Go through farm gate into a hazelnut coppice with fence and dilapidated wall still to our left. Walk up a steep little pitch still in coppice with wall line still to left.

(D) Turn right up through coppice when you reach a wall coming down from the right, following blue waymark about 20 yards ahead. (Only go straight ahead if you wish to link on to public road which is only three minutes away and which would provide an alternative starting point, this being identified on the roadside by a stone signed 'Bridle Way'.) Back on main route at **(D)** — climb up through coppice and emerge into open scrub country with views of quarry over to left. Continue up slight rise along left-hand edge of field with wall line to left. Bourton Far Hill Farm is soon visible over to left. Turn left and through metal farm gate following yellow waymarks and keeping wall line and then farm buildings to left.

Course of the Roman **Ryknild Street** first runs parallel with our route, and then crosses it in the corner of the field by the farm buildings to left. Near the far corner of the field look back (southwards) along its line (a very slight rise in the field) and on the far horizon you will see the minor road running towards **Condicote**, which exactly follows the Roman road's course.

(E) Turn left through metal farm gate in corner following blue waymark, and immediately turn right through second metal farm gate following yellow waymark, thereby avoiding the farm roadway. Now head up field with wall and telephone line on immediate left. The mansion of Spring Hill House is soon visible well over to left in front of extensive woodlands. Go through another metal farm gate still keeping wall and telephone line on immediate left. Start dropping gently down hill, through metal farm gate following yellow waymark, and drop down more steeply towards minor road in valley.

Go through wooden farm gate and turn right with care onto minor road with fine woodlands now up to our left. Pass Spring Hill drive entrance on left, pond on left, letterbox on post on right and farm road to Far Upton Wold on left. Note the neat little sign on left reading: 'Let no one say, and say it to your shame, that all was beauty until you came. Please no litter.'

(F) Immediately beyond letterbox on right, turn right off minor road and through metal farm gate following bridleway sign. (This could make another useful starting point.) Now walk up field with valley bottom well to left and fence line (not marked on map) to immediate right. Soon turn right through metal farm gate following blue waymark. Go up through small scrubby area and follow yellow waymark round to left, keeping fence line on immediate left for some time, with

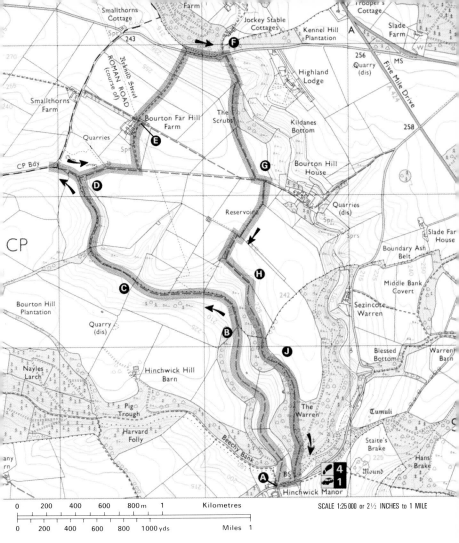

woodland to left (marked 'The Scrubs' on map). Pass through metal farm gate and immediately turn right, keeping to immediate left of fence line to top of field. Soon turn left and keep to immediate left of hedge line along top of field. Note fine rolling wold views over to left.

(G) Follow blue waymark through wooden hunting gate by power line, turning left onto a farm track and keeping wall and power line on immediate left. Soon turn right onto another track following blue waymark, keeping line of conifer trees on left. Bear slightly right keeping on track beyond trees. Turn right on track following blue waymark, and almost immediately turn left through double farm gate and down by hedge line on immediate right, soon using a sunken track. Through wooden farm gate, immediately turn left and keep along top of field with fence line on immediate left.

(H) Arrive at wooden post on left with blue waymark. Fork half right to cross field diagonally heading for left-hand edge of the dense woodland. There is a good view down to right — of the valley up which we walked much earlier. Preferably (but not essen-tially) pick up line of path across fields, keep- ing above most of the scrubby bushes on the bank dropping down to the right. Go through wooden hunting gate at entry to woods, following blue waymark. Head through attractive woodlands on a path which soon becomes a track. The track soon starts to curve round to the left and there are pleasant views down on right to the valley, through handsome beech-trees.

(J) Cross the course of another track near the left-hand edge of woods. Keep on track for some distance. Bear right onto a more frequently used track and keep on down hill. Turn right onto minor road and walk along this a short distance to join the starting point at the **Hinchwick** T-junction **(A)**, thus com-pleting Walk 4.

Walk 5
Warren Hastings Country

Approximately 4½ miles. Allow 2½ hours

This walk starts from the unspoilt village of Adlestrop, once well loved by Jane Austen, and much later widely remembered from Edward Thomas's haunting poem, Adlestrop. Passing largely through wooded country, the walk skirts around three sides of the estate created by Warren Hastings, the great Governor General of India, who was impeached at the Bar of the House of Lords. The mansion which he had built is, with its oriental dome, only just visible from the later part of the walk. Beyond Daylesford church, where Hastings lies buried, the walk crosses the little River Evenlode before passing the delightfully unspoilt old church outside Oddington. Beyond Oddington's quiet streets, a short stretch of main road takes us across the railway line close to the point where Edward Thomas's train stopped so 'briefly one hot afternoon in late June'. From here a short stroll across Adlestrop's park brings us back to our starting point near the church.

Park as near as possible to the church in the small village of **Adlestrop** (163) (SP 24-

27), which is on our **Tour 1**. There is no formal car parking, and if space is tight (perhaps when a church service is in progress) please park outside the village.

(A) Start from **Adlestrop** church, walking northwards along surfaced public road, and soon turn right up smaller road. At the end of the village turn right onto wider minor road and follow this road around to the right before eventually turning left with care onto the busy A436 (sign — Chipping Norton).

(B) Almost immediately cross A436 and go through farm gate on right into woods (following sign which should be here by time of publication). This gate is between the entrance to the Daylesford estate and the public road heading off A436 to Cornwell. Go through small wood and climb over fence. Now follow grass path to left between edge of wood and post and rail fence, and then turn right down grass path between two fences, before turning left at bottom and heading along track to gate at edge of woods.

(C) Pass through gate below large lime-tree at entrance to woods and proceed along track, first going over 'bridge' with low stone walls (no sign of stream). Follow well defined track through woods, soon going over small crossroads onto better surfaced farm road. Now walk through well kept farmyard (Daylesford Hill Farm) with Dutch barn on left and stone barns on right.

(D) Turn right near the far end of farmyard,

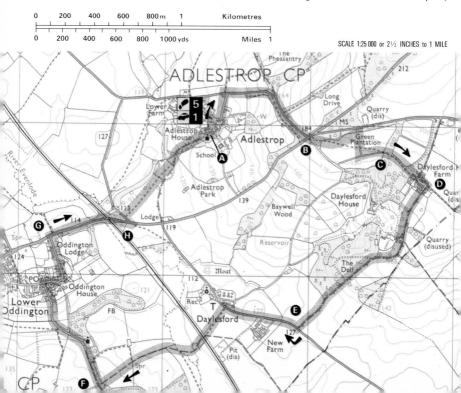

Cottages at Adlestrop

passing farm cottage on left. Keep straight on down track passing electricity transformer on poles to left. Gardens of **Daylesford House** lie over to right, but house is not visible from here. Uneven ground to left is all that remains of a disused quarry. There is a house with gates in a high stone wall to right; soon after pass yellow waymarks on left confirming our route. Bear right, keeping to track beside high wall to immediate right (do not follow bridleway arrows to left). Start to gradually drop down hill with fine views across the Evenlode Valley to Icomb Hill and Wyck Beacon on the skyline beyond. Wall to right ends, but is replaced by a post and rail fence, with pleasant beech-woods to right beyond (the Dell). Keep on track down hill to public road.

(E) Turn right onto surfaced public road, soon passing New Farm on left. **Daylesford House**, still not visible, is over to right. At the entry to **Daylesford** village turn left (footpath sign — Oddington) through metal farm gate. (But keep on road if you wish to visit **Daylesford** church — burial place of Warren Hastings.) Keep to immediate left of fence and hedge line. Daylesford church is just to right, and **Churchill** church tower is visible on skyline to left (this was Warren Hastings's native village). Soon cross bridge over the London to Worcester railway line and go down short track beyond before going through metal farm gate and heading half right to a wooden gate.

Go through gate and over small footbridge crossing the little River Evenlode, and head diagonally, slightly right, across field to next gate. Pass through gate and start to climb gently to immediate left of hedge line. At top of field go through gap in hedge and head straight across next field (but go round edge to right to avoid damaging possible crops). Look back for view of **Daylesford House**,

with its oriental dome normally just visible in trees across valley to north-east. **Adlestrop Park** (house) is also visible, to north. Walk through narrow belt of woodland.

(F) Turn right onto track, and **Oddington** old church is soon on right. Do not miss a visit to this unspoilt building with its extensive 'Doom' wall-paintings. Follow the now well surfaced road into attractive **Oddington** village and turn right by Post Office Stores. Bear left by the little Fox Inn.

(G) Turn right onto the busy A436 using footpath on right (sign — Chipping Norton). At end of path cross with great care to left-hand side of A436 and go over railway bridge. Look left to railway line where once stood Adlestrop Station, immortalised by Edward Thomas (see **Adlestrop**).

(H) Just beyond railway bridge, turn left onto minor road (sign — Adlestrop) and almost immediately turn right off road and go carefully over broad, slatted hunting gap (no footpath sign). (Fields between here and Adlestrop are part of a stud farm — do not disturb horses, especially mares and foals.) Go straight across park, first aiming slightly to left of Adlestrop Park; beyond slight rise, head for stile in fence surrounding cricket field. Right of way on map appears to head straight across cricket field, but we suggest that you go over stile and then keep to left, passing in front of pavilion, and go through metal farm gate at end of cricket field. Keep to left of the main field, turn left through wicket gate and immediately turn right to go up right-hand side of field, with belt of woodland to right. Handsome Adlestrop House, ahead left, used to be visited regularly by Jane Austen, when her uncle, Theophilus Leigh, was rector here. Go through wicket gate and up track into village to start point near **Adlestrop** church **(A)**, thus completing Walk 5.

Walk 6
National Trust Country on the Cotswold Edge

Approximately 4 miles. Allow 2¼ hours

This walk, much easier than most others on this end of the Cotswolds, follows two lengths of the Cotswold Way, and provides a mouth-watering introduction to the joys of this splendid long-distance footpath. There are pleasant sections of well managed woodland, open grassy stretches and a number of superb views out over the Severn Vale to the distant skylines beyond. The finest viewpoints are at the end of the walk — the Iron Age earthworks of Haresfield Beacon and the fascinating topograph at Shortwood. Most of the area covered by this walk is in the care of the National Trust. Do please support the Trust by leaving a contribution in the Shortwood Car Park's collecting box.

The Shortwood Topograph . . . close to the end of this walk

(A) Start walk from the National Trust's Shortwood Car Park (162) (SO 83-08), which is reached by a short diversion from **Edge**, and which is beyond **Painswick**, on our **Tour 5**. Leave car park eastwards through gap in wall close to the entrance, following yellow waymark with white dot, and go into Standish Wood. The white dot indicates that we are on the **Cotswold Way**, the course of which will be followed for most of this walk. Almost immediately fork left on highest of three tracks, following yellow waymark with white dot. From good path through woods there are fine views of distant Severn Estuary, to right through gap in trees. Pass through gap to left of hunting gate in woodlands, following yellow waymark with white dot. Take left-hand of three tracks, following yellow waymark (but no white dot, as we leave the **Cotswold Way** here). At end of Standish Wood, go through two gaps and turn left onto surfaced public road at Bird in Hand hamlet. Walk along wide verge to left and bear left onto busier public road (sign — Haresfield).

(B) Soon turn right through gap in wall with stile, following footpath sign just beyond last house and just before bus stop. Now head diagonally across large field aiming for post above wall line, well to left of woods on right. Arrive at post (now clearly a footpath sign), climb over stile and turn right with care onto surfaced public road. Almost immediately turn left off road, following footpath sign, into National Trust's Stockend Wood (not signed here). Soon fork left in

woods, go diagonally over track and start steep descent.

(C) Turn very sharp left at bottom of woods, joining the **Cotswold Way** (which will now be followed almost exactly for the rest of the walk), and proceed on surfaced farm drive. Soon go straight ahead onto track where farm drive turns to right. Route is now relatively level inside the wood, first along its bottom edge and then further into it. Keep on wide main track with some short uphill stretches. Sign indicates the end of the National Trust's Stockend Wood, but woods continue. Pass blue waymark on tree to right (this indicates that we are on a bridle path).

(D) Now climb up to small parking area and bear right onto surfaced public road. Walk down beside road keeping to small path on verge to right. Soon turn up to left off surfaced road (footpath sign — Haresfield Beacon) by Cliff Well and Cliffwell Cottages. The little well-house on left complete with blocked shaft is dated 1870. Within can be seen a verse which appears to read:

Who'er the bucketful upwindeth
Let him blefs God, who water findeth
Yet water here that shall availeth
Go seek that well which never faileth

Continue up surfaced path, soon passing the Cromwell Siege Stone on right, on a bend to the left. Reasons for its location here are not clear, but it was erected in the 19th century to commemorate the raising of the Royalist siege of Gloucester on 5 September 1643, following the capture of Cheltenham by

Roundhead troops under the Earl of Essex. The stone is not very inspiring, but there are fine views from it. Route is now below the steep slopes of Haresfield Hill which is up to left. Keep on main track where narrower path forks up to left.

(E) Turn left up steep public road by Ringhill Farm and almost immediately turn right (footpath sign — Haresfield Beacon) following Cotswold Way waymarks. Go over stile with farmyard to right, ensuring that dogs are on lead, and up steep farm track. Keep to right of farm gate and up steep bank with scrub down to right. Climb over stile, follow path over field to left of fence line, aiming for centre of bushes ahead, and enter the earthworks of the Iron Age promontory fort of **Haresfield Beacon**. Now bear slightly left to arrive at the 'trig point' (an Ordnance Survey Triangulation Station) on the western extremity of **Haresfield Beacon**. There are outstanding views out over the Severn Vale and south-westwards along the Cotswold Edge.

(F) Turn very sharp left and walk along the top of the southern ramparts of the Beacon. Drop down to right and go through gap following **Cotswold Way** waymarks. Fence line is now to immediate left with scrubby trees to right. Bear right and cross the lower, eastern end of the Beacon's wooded eastern ramparts. Path curves round to left and soon goes through gap to right of hunting gate, following Cotswold Way waymark, and turning right in parking area beside public road (a useful alternative starting point for this walk).

(G) Bear right (sign ⸱— Cotswold Way) by this Haresfield Beacon parking area and go down steep, step-cut path. Bear left at bottom of steps, and soon bear left again onto better surfaced path going slightly uphill, with wall and woods to left and fence to right. Go over stile onto track in woodlands, soon climbing fairly steeply. At end of woods bear well to the right following less defined track across fields, heading towards the Shortwood Topograph, a direction indicator with an interesting relief map cast in bronze. There are splendid views of the curving and ever-widening Severn Estuary from here. Amongst the many points shown on the topograph's perimeter are: the Tyndale Monument — 9½ miles, Mendips — 38 miles, Dunkery Beacon — 71 miles, and the Wyndcliff — 20 miles. All these and many more objects on the distant skyline are visible from here, but most of them only on a really clear day. Now turn sharp left and head across field to the Shortwood Car Park **(A)**, thus completing Walk 6.

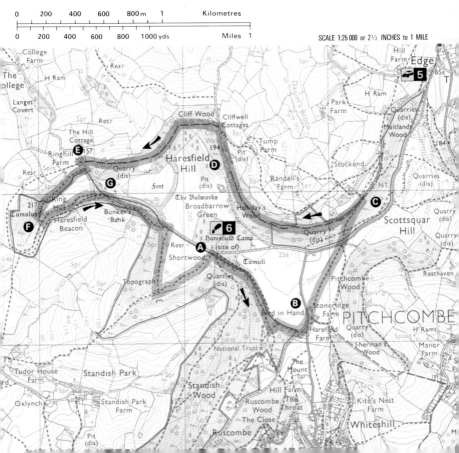

Walk 7
Wooded Edge Country and the Cheese Rolling Slope

Approximately 6 miles. Allow 4½ — 5 hours

This walk explores some of the classic Cotswold edge country, passing the foot of Cooper's Hill, scene each year of the famous Cheese Rolling Races. It then visits the interesting Witcombe Roman Villa before dropping down to Witcombe Reservoirs, with their interesting birdlife and ever-patient fly-fishermen. From here, after passing through the secluded village of Great Witcombe, it starts a long steep climb back to the woods below Birdlip and Cranham. After a well earned rest at the top, possibly in one of Birdlip's several inns, walkers will have an easy stroll through great woodlands before climbing once again, up over the southern slopes of Cooper's Hill to return to the start.

(A) Start walk from the Fiddler's Elbow Car Park (162) (SO 88-13) on the A46 between Cheltenham and Painswick. This point can be reached by diverting for three quarters of a mile from our **Tour 5** some way beyond Painswick Beacon. Walk to the immediate left of toilet block up into Upton Wood, following early stages of the official Cooper's Hill Walk and Nature Trail. Almost immed-iately turn right (sign — Nature Trail) and bear left steeply up through woods, partly up wide steps. Turn left at top of steps and soon pass sign relating to coppicing. Fork right following 'green route' (post with green band), and then bear right over small stile, into short 'hedged corridor' between two fields which connects two parts of the Cooper's Hill Nature Reserve's woodlands.

(B) Climb over second stile and turn left, following combined yellow and red way-marks, and keeping on wide main track through woods. Bear slightly left downwards at fork, ignoring yellow waymark, and almost immediately fork right onto path going level along hillside. Soon bear round to right keeping on lower path, with good views down left to Brockworth, and drop steeply down path. Go through small gate, following yellow waymark with white dot (this signifies that our route has now coincided with the **Cooper's Way**) into the hamlet of **Cooper's Hill**, where there is a tea-garden open in the summer. The Cheese Rolling Slope (see Cooper's Hill★) is up to the immediate right, with minute car park just beyond. Bear right onto small surfaced road by Primrose Cottage, and keep on this road until it ends (still on **Cotswold Way**). Go through hunting gate at end of road onto track passing Woodcot Cottage, with woods up to right and views of reservoirs soon down to left. Continue to follow bottom of woods on the **Cotswold Way**.

(C) Now turn very sharp left off the **Cotswold Way**. Pass through metal farm gate at end of wood, head along top of field and climb stile beside farm gate. Now head to

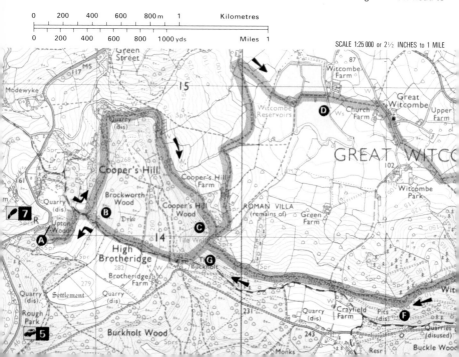

SCALE 1:25 000 or 2½ INCHES to 1 MILE

immediate right of Cooper's Hill Farm buildings, onto surfaced farm road. Turn right off road just beyond farm if you wish to visit the interesting **Witcombe Roman Villa**, then go down farm road passing small car park for villa visitors on right-hand bend. Continue down farm road for about 800 yards and then, following sign, turn sharp right off road across field towards stile in hedge ahead. Go over stile following yellow waymark, and along well defined path to pass through small metal gate into reservoir area. Walk to immediate right of 1st reservoir, go in front of cottage, turn left and almost immediately bear right to follow road between 2nd and 3rd reservoirs.

(D) Immediately beyond reservoirs turn right over stile, following yellow waymark across field and heading in general direction of church tower. Pass through small wooden gate and go diagonally left across field (but keep to left-hand edge to avoid damaging growing crops). Go through metal farm gate and turn right onto public road in village of **Great Witcombe**. Pass interesting, partly Norman church on left, and the neo-Gothic Witcombe School (now a private house) on right. Turn left into field, following footpath sign, where road bends to right in small valley just before reaching Brook Cottage. Keep up field with hedge to immediate left, and near end of field bear left through metal gate following yellow waymark. Now start long steep climb diagonally left up field heading first for a yellow-tipped post, and then for a stile by gate at edge of wood, with yellow waymark. Climb over stile, go across track and head diagonally right up steep path into woods. Cross another track and continue to climb steeply up through woods.

The Cheese Rolling Slope, Cooper's Hill

(E) Turn right and (with considerable relief) head along reasonably level and better surfaced woodland track. (Turn left here if you wish to walk up into **Birdlip** for refreshment — ¼ mile.) Yellow waymarks with white dot now indicate that we have again joined the **Cotswold Way** which we shall follow for almost two miles. Go over small crossroads of tracks by small quarry to left. Bear left at Y-junction beyond pheasant-rearing enclosure to right, and soon start to climb by conifer trees and old park wall on right. Old stone gateposts to right once marked the upper entrance to Witcombe Park.

(F) Soon bear right twice at two forks, keeping on main track (still on **Cotswold Way**). Go straight not left, ignoring yellow and green waymark up to left. Witcombe Roman Villa eventually becomes just visible ahead right. Now watch carefully for the next path up to the left, but only after the villa is visible and the long belt of trees stretching northwards has been passed (see map).

(G) Now bear diagonally left up hill on a non-waymarked path leading off the track. Climb steeply up path through woods, and just beyond the top, pass sawmill and the entry to Buckholt Wood Nature Reserve on immediate left. Turn right and follow track up inside the left-hand edge of the wood. Bear slightly left beyond wall line following yellow waymark, eventually pass highest point and start to drop down the far side of Brockworth Wood. Pass through special gap in fence and bear left over stile into hedged corridor at Point **B**, thus completing a full circle. Now go over stile at end of hedged corridor, turn left and eventually walk down steps to right, following our original path back to the start point at Fiddler's Elbow Car Park **(A)**, thus completing Walk 7.

WALKS

Walk 8
Rosie's Countryside

Approximately 6 miles. Allow 4½ hours

This walk explores some of the deep, lushly wooded valleys that lie to the north and north-east of the village of Slad — the village where Laurie Lee spent his early years. These times are described in his great classic, Cider with Rosie, *and walking through the beech-woods here in late spring or early summer, we can perhaps recapture some of this haunting book's flavour of times past. Echoes of even earlier years come from some of the farmhouses in the valleys here. With their handsome Queen Anne and Georgian features they reflect the prosperity of the district's clothiers in their 18th-century heyday.*

(A) Start walk from one of the parking areas at Bulls Cross, which is on **Tour 5**, on the B4070 just beyond and to the north of **Slad** (SO 87-08). Walk south-westwards from the vicinity of the bus stop and follow blue waymark into Frith Wood, which is part of a Nature Reserve. Follow track well up into woods and fork left in small clearing onto another track, starting to go slightly downwards. Fork left again following blue way-mark and walk along lower edge of wood with back gardens beyond wall to left. At end of woods turn left and follow surfaced road down hill. Go over crossroads with care crossing B4070 by Slad War Memorial. (But turn right if you wish to walk into **Slad**.) Continue down narrow, winding road, turning sharp left at bottom of hill. You are now heading eastwards on road down valley, but beyond Steanbridge, where there was once a cloth mill, turn right beyond a long low barn to right, onto a track with pool now to left. Soon go over stile following yellow waymark and up right-hand edge of field. Go over stile at top of field and go up path into woodlands following yellow waymark.

(B) Turn left near top of wood, draw breath (!) and continue to climb up following path through attractive beech-woods with wall to right. Turn right up sunken trackway and after about 200 yards turn sharp left onto track along top of Redding Wood. Soon fork left, following yellow waymark on lower of two tracks into heart of Redding Wood. Track now goes slightly downwards to the lower edge of Catswood, with valley fields soon to left. Follow track for some way and at gentle bend fork left on lower path following yellow waymark.

(C) At end of wood, do not go through metal gate, but fork left going steeply down sunken, stream-eroded path. Go over main stream in valley bottom and up steep path. Turn right onto surfaced track by two small

Valley country above Slad . . . on the early stages of this walk

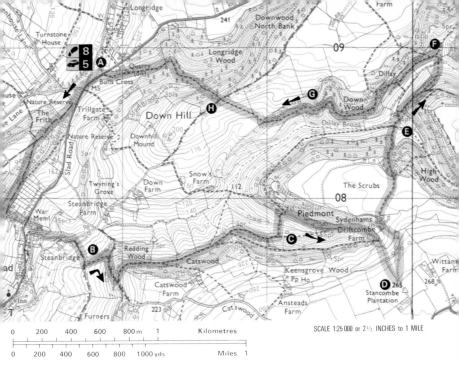

garages, following yellow waymark. Fork left near end of track up narrow path behind and above house on right, following yellow waymark. Continue up path near edge of wood with valley field down to right. Bear right, up path at end of woods and through two hunting gates, still following yellow waymarks.

(D) At end of triangular field turn sharp left onto surfaced road. Follow road down past house on right, fork left by low building, pass through stone gate posts and follow surfaced road to right, with lovely Sydenham's Farm to left. Where road bends to left, go straight ahead following footpath sign. Walk over large field known as 'The Scrubs', with wall to immediate right. Go through hunting gate into woods, and immediately over a Y-junction of tracks and down small path, keeping straight down hill. Fork right half-way down hill, down steep path. (Do not go through wooden gate to left.) Bear left at bottom of valley, over line of stream, and pass cottage on left.

(E) Now climb up inside edge of wood and after some time bear left onto wider track, still following left-hand edge of wood. Fork left following lower of two paths in the vicinity of a house up to the right, and soon fork left again. Keep going down in same general direction if path's course is not clear, and eventually arrive at fence line at bottom end of wood. Cross this fence at stile. (Walk to left or right if stile's position is not immediately located.) Following yellow waymark, go to the right down across field and head for gap in fence line.

(F) Turn left onto track following yellow waymark and go through metal farm gate in valley bottom. Now head diagonally left up slope following yellow waymark and soon bear left onto farm track. Keep on track to Dillay Farm, turn right just beyond farmhouse and immediately left up track through woods. Take first turn left down track, soon going through metal gate by 'Fire Danger' sign.

(G) After about a third of a mile, where track turns sharp right into a zig-zag climb, go straight ahead onto a very narrow path through bushes. (Watch for this with care.) Follow path, first down through bushy country and then up again through small wooden gate into Nature Reserve. Continue to climb steadily and follow path to the very end of the wood. Where old track comes up from left, turn right and go up field with hedge line to right. After 100 yards head diagonally left across field. (But follow wall line if crops could be damaged.)

(H) Beyond field go up path across scrubby bank and over stone stile in wall into woodlands. Go slightly left across track and head very steeply down through woods, hopefully keeping to ill defined path. Go over track in valley bottom and keep to immediate left of a pool formed by the damming of the Slad Brook. Climb better defined path beyond pool and soon turn left onto woodland track. Follow this track up through woods, and then scrub country, and eventually turn left with care onto the B4070. Go down this a few yards to return to the start point at Bulls Cross **(A)**, thus completing Walk 8.

Walk 9
Secret Valleys of the Upper Frome Country

Approximately 5 miles. Allow 3 hours

This walk explores the richly wooded valley of the infant River Frome, southwards from Brimpsfield, near its source, to the two delightful hamlets of Syde and Caudle Green. These look at each other across the deep valley, and at any season of the year they must surely provide the town-dweller with dreams of an idyllic country life. From here the walk heads north up a tributary valley, eventually to return over a short stretch of windy, open country to Brimpsfield.

(A) Start walk from a point just to the north of the village of **Brimpsfield** (which is on **Tour 5**), where there should be space to park two or three cars on the grass verge (SO 93-12). Do not obstruct gateways. If there is no space here, park further away from village. Now walk down road towards centre of village and turn left nearly opposite war memorial, up concrete path towards church. But when earthworks of medieval castle are on immediate right, bear left off path and head across field for stile with yellow waymark. (Small barn to left of churchyard possibly incorporates scanty remains of a 12th-century priory once belonging to the abbey of Fontenay in Burgundy.) Go straight

Quiet Caudle Green

ahead, however, if you wish to visit the interesting church and look over the fence at the castle earthworks; otherwise climb stile with yellow waymark and head diagonally across field to cross another stile with yellow waymark. Turn right onto public road and go down hill ignoring stile on left. Pool visible in valley down to left is very close to the source of the River Frome.

(B) Near bottom of hill bear right, following footpath sign, onto track leading just to right of, and above, cottage. You are now heading down the valley of the infant River Frome. Immediately beyond house on right, go down small footpath and through gate, following yellow waymark. Drop steeply down into wood, and follow well defined path with yellow waymarks in valley with little River Frome on immediate left. Path (very muddy in winter) then leads through coniferous woods with stream still on left. Bear right following yellow waymark and ignoring wooden farm gate ahead. Stream is still on left. Soon cross stile into more coniferous woodlands. Earthworks of a second medieval castle are somewhere above valley to right, but they are not visible from path and are on private land (see **Brimpsfield**).

(C) Climb over stile at end of wood, turn left onto track following yellow waymark, go over the Frome and bear right through wooden gate following track leading down the valley, although slightly uphill at first. First of two lakes in valley is now seen to right with substantial house (Brimpsfield Park) on bank beyond. When track peters out follow same general line, aiming for stile at end of field. Climb over stile following yellow waymark and follow round right-hand edge of field. At end of field, go over stile following yellow waymark, and over two small wooden bridges below dam of first lake, with second lake to left. Turn left onto track and follow down valley to right of second lake. Keep on down track at end of second lake, following two blue waymarks (this is a bridleway). Pass sign on left indicating 'Squirrel Clump — Planted 27th April 1986'. Go through wooden farm gate, almost immediately turn right and head for wood in valley bottom with yellow waymark on gatepost. Pass through this gateway and follow down wooded valley — this area is known as Poston Wood. River Frome is now on right. Where track comes down hill from left, curve slightly round to right following yellow waymark. Bear left where side valley joins from the right and go over small wooden bridge crossing the Frome.

(D) Soon bear left through gate at end of woodlands, following yellow waymark, and into open field. Follow along right-hand edge of field in valley with fence and Ostrich Wood to right and the Frome over to left. Keep straight down narrow field in valley, heading for farm gate. Go through farm gate following yellow waymark into next field, head slightly right up rise and then down again, back towards the Frome. Cross stone 'bridge' and keep heading for stile at end of field with the Frome now on right. Climb over stile following yellow waymark and keep in valley with small plantation on bank up to left. Keep to left of fence line with Frome just beyond it.

(E) Bear left by yellow waymark on post in field and go diagonally up bank heading just to right of a beech-tree. Bear left round corner of a wall, with pool becoming visible over wall just beyond. Now go through metal gate into often muddy farmyard, aiming for yellow waymark at end of yard. Pass through gate and bear left onto public road in delightful hamlet of **Syde**. Now bear round to right and again right, onto public road (sign — 'To the Church'). Pass entry to Syde's interesting early Norman church, which has a fine tithe barn to its south. (Now keep on public road as far as Caudle Green hamlet.) Follow road down into valley, passing Haycroft, a cottage on the right with buttresses, 14th-century windows and an arched stone doorway. This may possibly have been a chantry chapel founded in 1344 by Sir Thomas Berkeley.

(F) Turn right at first T-junction in valley (sign — Caudle Green), cross River Frome and fork left up hill (sign — Caudle Green). Climb quite steeply up into **Caudle Green**, passing road coming in from right just before entry to hamlet. There are good views back to Syde. Telephone box is on left and post box on right at entry to open green. Go up driveway towards handsome 18th-century house on right for about ten yards, and then bear right following modest footpath sign. Soon go over stones forming rudimentary stile in wall, following yellow waymark. Now go steeply down through small coppice and bear slightly to left in valley bottom.

(G) Go through hunting gate in valley by the Rudge Bottom Plantation, immediately cross stream and turn left through gate following yellow waymark. There are no waymarks beyond this point. Route is now up grassy valley with woods on both sides and with stream to left — this is a tributary of the River Frome. Go over small stone 'bridge' — stream is now on right. Pass through metal farm gate and continue to follow track up valley, ignoring well defined track up through woods to right. Stoneyhill Farm is briefly visible up valley to left. Bear right, keeping in flat bottomed, ever narrowing valley with woods still on either side.

(H) Branch right at end of last field and go over small stile to left of wooden farm gate. Climb out of valley with woods and fence to immediate left, and keep same general line beyond wood, aiming for wooden farm gate at top of field. Go through this gate and keep in same general line, with hedge now to immediate left. Pass through metal farm gate and go straight ahead, joining public road at entry to **Brimpsfield**. Go straight, not left (sign — Birdlip), and soon arrive at village centre with war memorial on left. Go straight, not left (sign — Cirencester), and pass path to church on right, which is on the early course of the walk. Head out of village and soon arrive back at parking space **(A)**, thus completing Walk 9.

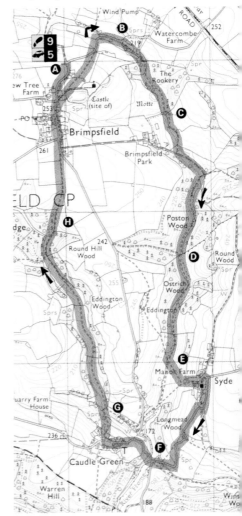

SCALE 1:25 000 or 2½ INCHES to 1 MILE

| 0 | 200 | 400 | 600 | 800 m | 1 | Kilometres |
| 0 | 200 | 400 | 600 | 800 | 1000 yds | Miles 1 |

Walk 10
Through a Country of Navigators and Craftsmen

About 6½ miles. Allow 4 hours

Starting from lovely Sapperton, this walk first follows the course of the old Thames and Severn Canal. It then climbs up into high country, dropping down briefly to visit Edgeworth, before heading southwards, again over the open wolds. Turning eastwards it drops down into the beautifully wooded Frome Valley. After crossing the river, it climbs up past the exquisite house and garden of Pinbury Park. Now it goes

back into the Frome Valley, to ford the river and heads down through woodlands, to return after a short steep climb to Sapperton.

If possible start this walk from **Sapperton** (SO 94-03) which is on **Tour 5**. There is limited parking space just beyond the church. Alternatively if you wish to eat or drink at the attractive Daneway Inn (also on **Tour 5**) it may be possible to obtain the landlord's permission to use his car park (see **(B)** below).

(A) Starting from just beyond Sapperton church, walk back just above it and then turn right at corner of its churchyard. Turn left at end of churchyard onto small road and take first turn right, just beyond third cottage on right. Now go down hill on path with scrubby woodland to left, and into large sloping field. Go diagonally down across field and over stile

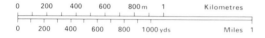

```
0    200   400   600   800 m   1
|----|-----|-----|-----|-----|        Kilometres

0    200   400   600   800   1000 yds
|----|-----|-----|-----|-----|        Miles   1
```

SCALE 1:25 000 or 2½ INCHES to 1 MILE

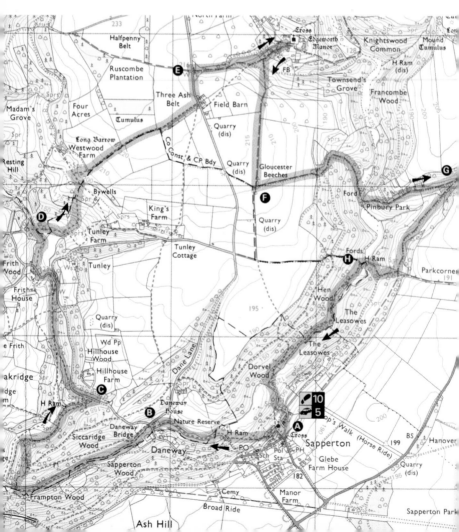

into wooded area. Immediately cross over the top of the west portal of the **Thames and Severn Canal's** Sapperton Tunnel, and turn right just beyond to follow its old towpath for over half a mile to **Daneway**. Now pass the Daneway Inn and its car park to right.

(B) Turn right onto public road in **Daneway** hamlet just beyond Daneway Inn's car park, go over bridge crossing canal bed and immediately turn left onto old towpath along right-hand side of canal bed (sign — Chalford). Now pass five old lock chambers, cross small bridge to left-hand side of canal bed and pass another old lock. Turn right to cross brick canal bridge and enter the Siccaridge Wood Nature Reserve. Keep straight up through woods following yellow waymark, and start to climb steep bank. After about 200 yards turn left off this well used bridleway and onto smaller path, soon going down into valley. Turn right at bottom of hill and follow path up valley, going along edge of wood with fence and stream on immediate left. Ignore small hunting gate to left and start climb into woodlands, with path soon becoming a wider track. Go through wooden farm gate and walk up track to pass house in trees to left.

(C) Turn sharp left onto public road by entrance drive to house, and walk along tree-shaded road for about 200 yards before forking left onto an unsigned track down through woods. Go through wooden farm gate at end of wood and bear slightly left into field, heading between wood on right and stream bed on left, and soon climb over small wooden stile into woodland. Follow well defined path up valley with woods up to right and a few trees to left. Pass pool over to left, and turn left onto public road at the entry to the scattered hamlet of **Tunley**. Bear left at junction (sign — Waterlane), follow public road with post box on left and go up slight rise. Turn right through wooden farm gate opposite Frith House (no footpath sign) and head diagonally left across field to bottom right-hand corner, aiming for the right-hand of the two electric supply poles, and wooded area beyond. Go through hunting gate in valley bottom at end of field and keep on path for about 100 yards.

(D) Now turn right to follow along left-hand edge of a triangular plantation, and go through hunting gate into large field. Climb this field, first aiming for gap between a succession of bushes with line of electric supply poles close by, but then veering well to left to arrive at the top left-hand end of field. Go over double stile following yellow waymark, head for electric supply pole and turn right at pole, following one of two yellow waymarks. Continue up rest of hill with Westwood Farm visible over to left, and through metal farm gate onto well surfaced track, following yellow waymark. You are

now on open wold country. Pass battered earthworks of a Stone Age long barrow on left and keep on track, before turning left onto public road near Field Barn Farm.

(E) After about 250 yards turn right through stone gate pillars between two lodges onto old driveway, following first a concrete bridleway sign and then a blue waymark. After about another 250 yards bear right through wooden farm gate, following blue waymark, and head down field towards wooden farm gate to immediate right of cottage. Turn very sharp right at gate (but go through farm gate if you wish to visit **Edgeworth** church which is 250 yards beyond). Now aim for top right-hand end of field to go over a small stile. Route is now on top of open wold country. Go along edge of small field with metal fence on immediate left, through wooden farm gate, and follow metal fence on immediate left. Pass through hunting gate and keep in same (southern) direction with fence line to left.

(F) Cross stile at Gloucester Beeches and turn left onto track leading to immediate right of fragmentary wall and hedge line. Soon drop down from high wold country, and just beyond ruined buildings to left, go through wooden farm gate at end of field. Almost immediately bend round to left on well used bridle track through woodlands, then bend to right and start to descend steeply to wooden farm gate at end of wood. Now cross small field in valley bottom and go over wooden footbridge crossing the River Frome just to right of ford. Turn right beyond bridge and climb steeply up bank on well defined, surfaced track. Now pass in front of the lovely garden and house of Pinbury Park (see **Edgeworth**), once the home of Ernest Gimson and the Barnsley brothers.

(G) Beyond pool on right, turn sharp right off driveway and around head of pool. Pass through wooden farm gate and head across field, following slight track along contour, and heading to immediate right of a clump of trees. Once over the brow by the clump, head for farm gate at edge of large wood. Go through this gate and turn right down track in wood, following one of three yellow waymarks. Go round one bend to right and down track into valley.

(H) Cross the little River Frome, bear left up track into woods and then fork left. Down valley through woods with the River Frome to the left. Eventually fork left following downhill track, and go over causeway, recrossing the River Frome, and start to climb track out of valley. Climb sunken trackway passing house on the left and bear right onto surfaced road. Bear right at road junction beyond first cottage in **Sapperton** and head up road to limited parking space on left **(A)**, which is the end of Walk 10.

Walk 11
The Coln Valley and a Roman Villa

Approximately 6 ½ miles. Allow 3 ½ — 4 hours

This walk explores one of the most beautiful stretches of the little River Coln, where its valley and surrounding woodlands are teeming with game birds and an abundance of wildlife. For this reason alone, walkers are particularly asked to keep to the rights of way indicated on the map and in the directions below, especially when passing through Chedworth Woods. The Romans knew this idyllic valley well, and indeed our walk passes Chedworth Roman Villa, which has been excavated and wonderfully preserved. This is in the care of the National Trust and should on no account be passed by. Our walk also passes two pleasant inns, one on the Foss Way at Fossebridge, and one in the attractive village of Chedworth. If walking this way in winter or after wet weather at any season, wellies would be preferable to all but the stoutest of walking boots.

(A) Start walk from the wide grass verge just short of Coulsty Barn, on the right about 50 yards beyond Yanworth Mill (163) (SP 07-13), which is reached from **Yanworth** on **Tour 2**. Now walk back along road to Yanworth Mill and opposite it, turn right off road through hunting gate (no footpath sign), heading down Coln Valley. Follow along bottom of field keeping hedge on immediate right. At end of field go through gap in end hedge and keep in same direction with hedge line to right. **Stowell Park** (mansion) is visible ahead left, and River Coln is in field to right. Pass through gap in next hedge and keep wall to immediate right.

(B) Go through farm gate onto corner of public road, but then turn right to go through second farm gate into next field. Now head diagonally across field, aiming just to left of Stowell Mill. Cross stone stile and turn right onto public road to pass Stowell Mill. Cross River Coln by mill, and turn left through gap in wall well beyond house on left, onto farm road (no footpath sign). Almost immediately go through hunting gate and turn right to follow along right-hand edge of field with bluebell woods up to right. There are good views of Stowell Park back to left. You are now heading down Coln Valley again with stream to left. Go through farm gate, but still keep to right-hand edge of next field.

(C) At end of wood still keep hedge line on immediate right, but when hedge turns to right keep straight on, heading for gap between River Coln on left and the hedge on right. There is an attractive meandering, willow-bordered stretch of stream here. Cross stone stile and aim just to the right of a road signpost visible ahead. Go through hunting gate and turn left onto public road. Almost immediately go straight, not right, at road junction (sign — Fossebridge). Now keep on public road for half a mile, passing houses on right and, beyond small valley, a signed footpath forking left to the hospitable Fossebridge Hotel at **Fossebridge** (bar snacks available).

(D) Turn right with great care onto the **Foss Way**, keeping on grass verge on right, and immediately turn right onto modest driveway beside the first and only house on right (no footpath sign). Walk up driveway and continue along right-hand edge of field with back gardens to immediate right. Bear left at corner of field and keep thick hedge to immediate right. Go through gate and along 'terrace' to the upper left-hand side of pleasant valley — this is Hedgley Bottom. Wall line is on immediate left. Climb over modern wooden stile and continue up valley with stream over to right. Pass small pool on right and after some time turn right beyond modern stile onto public road.

(E) Cross stream and soon fork left by post-box up smaller road, through the delightful hillside hamlet of Pancakehill. Follow this road up from the valley and at end of hamlet fork right off surfaced road, to immediate right of entrance to Greenhill Farm. Walk up tree-shaded track and at its end turn left onto well used farm track with fences on both sides. Go straight over crossroads of tracks near a footpath sign pointing right (but do not follow it). Pass two tracks heading down to left and then pass small line of pine trees in field to left.

(F) Turn left just beyond this line of trees, cross stile and go down field keeping hedge line to immediate right. Soon cross second stile, drop even more steeply down and go through wooden farm gate over small lawn (with care), before joining surfaced road in Calveshill hamlet. Walk down surfaced road into valley and immediately after crossing small stream, turn right and go over low stone stile. Now follow path up valley, crossing five stiles before heading to top left of last full field. Cross stile in corner of field and turn sharp left to climb old railway embankment. Cross stile beyond embankment, turn sharp right and go over another stile. Now head diagonally across field, aiming for Chedworth church tower.

Cross stile at top left-hand end of field and turn right into the attractive village of **Chedworth**. Pass the welcoming Seven Tuns Inn

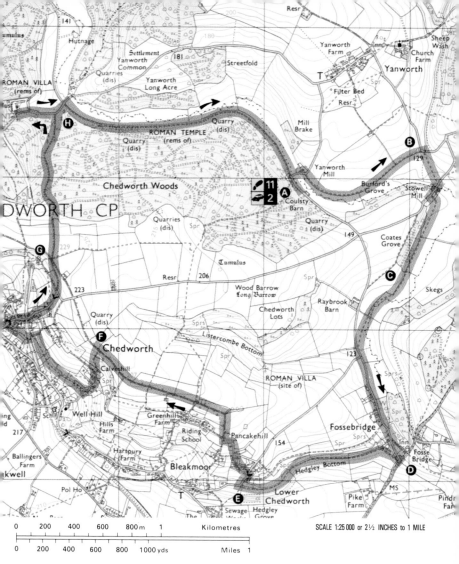

0	200	400	600	800 m	1		Kilometres
0	200	400	600	800	1000 yds		Miles 1

SCALE 1:25 000 or 2½ INCHES to 1 MILE

on right, with pretty spring in garden opposite and path up to the interesting church beside it. Walk down village street (now rid of the large railway viaduct which used to overshadow it) and climb steeply out of valley using public road. Where road turns sharply to the right, walk straight ahead through hunting gate to the immediate right of the Hartshill private drive. Rest at top of steep pitch for fine views back to Chedworth. Now continue to follow fence line to immediate left to reach a metal farm gate.

(G) Go through gate and bear slightly right to follow left-hand side of wall line on the right. Soon start to drop down towards Chedworth Woods. There are fine views ahead with **Cleeve Hill** on the horizon slightly to the left of walk's direction. Now enter attractive mixed woodlands of Chedworth Woods, but this section of descending bridle road is narrow in parts and can be very muddy in winter. Bear right onto better surfaced track near bottom of hill and soon go through hunting gate beside wooden farm gate, leaving Chedworth Woods.

(H) Now turn right onto well surfaced road on edge of woods; but turn left if you wish to visit the most interesting **Chedworth Roman Villa** which is about 250 yards away (entrance fee payable). Follow main route down road beside wood and turn right at small crossroads onto surfaced private road (signed — pedestrians only). Route now follows private road which runs between the woodlands of Chedworth Wood and the River Coln. These woodlands are private and it is not possible to look at the remains of the small Roman temple indicated on the map. Eventually rejoin the public road near Yanworth Mill and walk straight on to return almost at once to the starting point **(A)**, thus completing Walk 11.

153

Walk 12
Bibury, the Coln Valley and a Medieval Trackway

Approximately 5 miles. Allow 3 hours

This walk starts from the delightful village of Bibury with its clear stream, watermill and trout farm. It soon heads north-westwards, parallel with the River Coln, across fields to the smaller but equally entrancing village of Ablington, before heading north-eastwards over open wold country. After about a mile it turns again, this time to follow the ancient Salt Way, once used by pack animals carrying salt from Droitwich to the head of the navigable Thames. It then heads over more wold country, back towards the lovely Coln Valley. Here it passes beyond the lawns of splendid Bibury Court Hotel, crossing the Coln by old mill buildings just beyond, before climbing the opposite bank. The return to Bibury heads between cricket field and fine beech-woods before a woodland path leads finally to its world-famous cottages — Arlington Row.

Use small car park to immediate south-west of the bridge over the River Coln by the Swan Hotel, **Bibury** (163) (SP 11-06), which is on our **Tour 4**. Space is limited here, so in summer an early start is recommended!

(A) Set out south-westwards up the main B4425, passing the Trout Farm and Arlington Mill on right. Road is very busy, so keep to the path. Pass the Village Stores on right and the Catherine Wheel Inn on left. Turn right off B4425 opposite phone-box and just beyond small shop. Soon pass footpath sign ('To Ablington') and bear left along a surfaced driveway following sign ('Public Footpath'). Beyond the last building on the right go over stone stile to right of farm gate. Go through gap into second field,

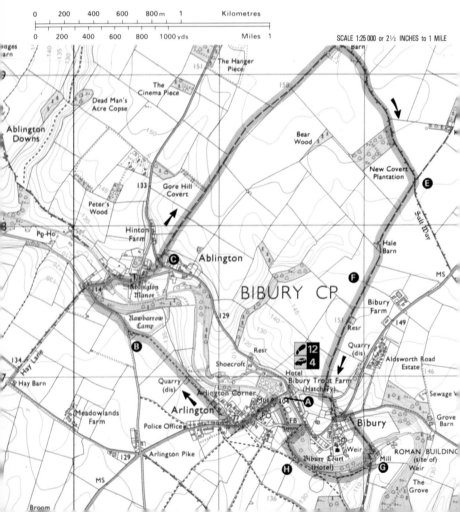

and head straight towards gate into third field. Now head straight towards double gate, but then veer to immediate left of it and keep along left of fence line. Low earthworks of Iron Age Rowbarrow Camp are just visible in field to right. Go through gate to immediate right of house.

(B) Keep to path just to right of house, and at end of garden bear right onto public road (house name now revealed as 'Upper Severalls'). Walk down attractive road with woodlands to right, and turn right at T-junction near entry to **Ablington**. Go over bridge crossing the clear waters of the River Coln and bear right by small drinking fountain with plaque remembering those who fell in the 1914-18 War. Pass lovely gabled manor house on right (once home of J. Arthur Gibbs, author of *A Cotswold Village*). Go straight, not left, at T-junction by a phonebox and a stone bus-shelter, but almost immediately turn up a very small road with Bank House soon on the right.

(C) Bear left by a large lime tree and cross road with great care to go onto a track to the immediate right of Hinton Cottage. After 50 yards go straight, not right, onto a less used track, gradually going up onto more open country. Go through farm gate into field, and keep hedge line to immediate right. Go through second farm gate, keeping fence line to immediate right, then through third, with line of woodlands (Gore Hill Covert) running at right-angles down to left. There are fine open views of rolling wold country over to left. Pass through a gap into the next field, with fence line to left. Go through gate onto a track with a fence on both sides, and through another gate to cross old airfield dispersalpoint, heading for a gateway at the far side.

(D) Turn right onto a track just beyond gateway at 'Saltway Barn', a collection of dilapidated low farm buildings over to the left. This track now follows the course of the medieval **Salt Way**, which ran from the salt-producing town of Droitwich to the head of the navigable Thames near Lechlade. Keep on the gently curving Salt Way which runs to the left of a tall hedge, with open views to left being rather spoilt by power lines. Go through two successive farm gates and then pass New Covert Plantation on right, with pleasant old barns visible well over to left.

(E) Go through farm gate, immediately turn right leaving the Salt Way and go through a second gate. Now keep up field with wall line to immediate right, and then pass the stone Hale Barn on right. Pass through gap between wall on right and fence to small pool on left, and go through gate keeping on track with wall line to right. Impressive buildings of Bibury Farm are well over to the left.

(F) Beyond farm gate go straight, not left,

Arlington Mill, near the start of this walk

onto surfaced farm road and through second gate with wall now on left, soon passing a grass-covered reservoir on left. Surfaced road ends but continue on track in the same direction, gradually starting to descend. Go over stile to immediate left of farm gate, and soon pass house on left (the effective re-entry to **Bibury**). Proceed onto part-concrete driveway and follow this down to main B4425 road, passing old circular dovecot on right. Turn left with care onto B4425, cross to path on other side and soon fork right onto minor road (sign — Coln St Aldwyns). After 50 yards turn right down a private road (also a public bridleway) to Bibury Court Farm. Do not miss the fine views of Bibury Court Hotel across lawns to right, before crossing the River Coln and passing old mill buildings. Keep on surfaced road up hill.

(G) At top of hill turn right following sign ('Public Footpath'). (Bridleway straight ahead leads to **Coln St Aldwyns** and makes a pleasant alternative walk, partly beside the River Coln.) Keep on track with wall and woodlands to right, and fine views of wooded Coln Valley over to left. Go through gate and head for gap between a small cricket pavilion to left and wall line to right. There are fine beech-woods to left and also at far end of field.

(H) Go over a stone stile at far right-hand end of field and through woodlands. Turn right by remains of old stone stile and walk down small hill, to pass gardens on left at back of Bibury's famous Arlington Row, now in the care of the National Trust. Bear left at end of cottages, go over stone stile and then bear left again onto path in front of Arlington Row. Bear right at end of row and go along path which follows the left-hand edge of Rack Isle, once used for drying cloth on racks after it had been worked by the weavers of Arlington Row, and now a wildfowl refuge also in the care of the National Trust. At the end of path turn right with care onto B4425 and arrive in a few yards at the starting car park (A), thus completing **Walk 12**.

CONVENTIONAL SIGNS   1:250 000 or 1 INCH to 4 MILES

ROADS
Not necessarily rights of way

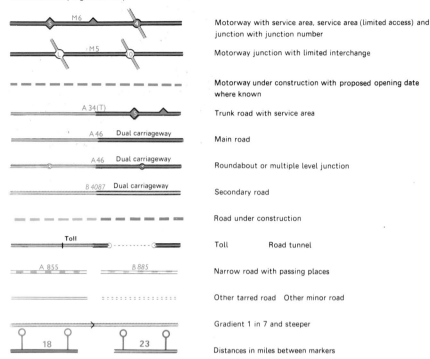

Motorway with service area, service area (limited access) and junction with junction number

Motorway junction with limited interchange

Motorway under construction with proposed opening date where known

Trunk road with service area

Main road

Roundabout or multiple level junction

Secondary road

Road under construction

Toll   Road tunnel

Narrow road with passing places

Other tarred road   Other minor road

Gradient 1 in 7 and steeper

Distances in miles between markers

The representation of a road is no evidence of the existence of a right of way

PRIMARY ROUTES
These form a national network of recommended through routes which complement the motorway system.
Selected places of major traffic importance are known as Primary Route Destinations and are shown thus **STROUD**
Distances and directions to such destinations are repeated on traffic signs which, on primary routes, have a green background or, on motorways, have a blue background.
To continue on a primary route through or past a place which has appeared as a destination on previous signs, follow the directions to the next primary destination shown on the green-backed signs.

RAILWAYS

Standard gauge track

Narrow gauge track

Tunnel

Road crossing under or over

Level crossing

Station

WATER FEATURES

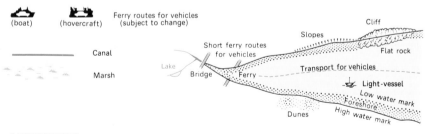

(boat)   (hovercraft)   Ferry routes for vehicles (subject to change)

Canal

Marsh

Lake   Bridge   Ferry

Short ferry routes for vehicles

Cliff

Slopes

Flat rock

Transport for vehicles

Light-vessel

Low water mark

Foreshore

High water mark

Dunes

ANTIQUITIES

✳ Native fortress   ⚔ Site of battle (with date)   ------ Roman road (course of)   CANOVIUM .   Roman antiquity

Castle ·   Other antiquities

卅   Ancient Monuments and Historic Buildings in the care of the Secretaries of State for the Environment, for Scotland and for Wales and that are open to the public.

BOUNDARIES

 National

– – – – – – – { County, Region or Islands Area

GENERAL FEATURES

 Buildings

 Wood

⚓ Lighthouse (in use)   ⚓ Lighthouse (disused)

⚓ Windmill   ⚓ Radio or TV mast

▲ Youth hostel

⊕ Civil aerodrome { with Customs facilities
⊹   { without Customs facilities

Ⓗ Heliport

☎ Public telephone

☎ Motoring organisation telephone

+ Intersection, latitude & longitude at 30' intervals (not shown where it confuses important detail)

TOURIST INFORMATION

✝ Abbey, Cathedral, Priory	❀ Garden	☆ Other tourist feature
🐟 Aquarium	⚑ Golf course or links	✕ Picnic site
Å Camp site	⌂ Historic house	Preserved railway
🚐 Caravan site	🅸 Information centre	Racecourse
Castle	Motor racing	Skiing
Cave	Museum	Viewpoint
Country park	! Nature or forest trail	Wildlife park
Craft centre	🦆 Nature reserve	🐘 Zoo

WALKS, CYCLE & MOTOR TOURS
Applicable to all scales

 Start point of walk

➡ Route of walk

 Featured walk

 Start point of tour

➡ Route of tour

Featured tour

 Start point of mini-walk

Featured mini-walk

FOLLOW THE COUNTRY CODE
Enjoy the countryside and respect its life and work

Guard against all risk of fire

Fasten all gates

Keep your dogs under close control

Keep to public paths across farmland

Leave livestock, crops and machinery alone

Use gates and stiles to cross fences, hedges and walls

Take your litter home

Help to keep all water clean

Protect wildlife, plants and trees

Take special care on country roads

Make no unnecessary noise

CONVENTIONAL SIGNS 1:25 000 or 2½ INCHES to 1 MILE

ROADS AND PATHS

Not necessarily rights of way

M1 or A6(M)	M1 or A6(M)	Motorway
A31(T)	A31(T)	Trunk road
A35	A35	Main road
B3074	B3074	Secondary road
A35	A35	Dual carriageway
		Road generally more than 4m wide
		Road generally less than 4m wide
		Other road, drive or track

Narrow roads with passing places are annotated

Unfenced roads and tracks are shown by pecked lines

.... Path

PUBLIC RIGHTS OF WAY

Public rights of way may not be evident on the ground

- - - - - - - } Public paths { Footpath
- - - - - - - Bridleway

+ + + + + Byway open to all traffic
- - - - - Road used as a public path

The indication of a towpath in this book does not necessarily imply a public right of way
The representation of any other road, track or path is no evidence of the existence of a right of way

RAILWAYS

	Multiple track } Standard gauge
	Single track
	Narrow gauge
	Siding
	Cutting
	Embankment
	Tunnel
	Road over & under
	Level crossing; station

DANGER AREA

MOD ranges in the area
Danger!
Observe warning notices

⊕ Mountain Rescue Post

BOUNDARIES

— · — · — County (England and Wales)
— — — — District
-⋄-⋄-⋄-⋄- London Borough
· · · · · · · · Civil Parish (England)* Community (Wales)
— — — — — Constituency (County, Borough, Burgh or European Assembly)

} Coincident boundaries are shown by the first appropriate symbol

*For Ordnance Survey purposes County Boundary is deemed to be the limit of the parish structure whether or not a parish area adjoins

SYMBOLS

Church or chapel { with tower	with tower
	with spire
+	without tower or spire
Glasshouse; youth hostel
Bus or coach station
Lighthouse; lightship; beacon
△ Triangulation station
Triangulation point on { church or chapel	lighthouse, beacon	building; chimney
pylon pole Electricity transmission line

VILLA Roman antiquity (AD 43 to AD 420)
Castle Other antiquities
✢ Site of antiquity
⚔ 1066 Site of battle (with date)
Gravel pit
Sand pit
Chalk pit, clay pit or quarry
Refuse or slag heap
Sloping wall

	Water			Mud
	Sand; sand & shingle
	National Park or Forest Park Boundary
NT	National Trust always open
NT	National Trust opening restricted
FC	Forestry Commission

VEGETATION

Limits of vegetation are defined by positioning of the symbols but may be delineated also by pecks or dots

Coniferous trees
Non-coniferous trees
Coppice
Orchard

Scrub
Bracken, rough grassland
In some areas bracken (⚲) and rough grassland (≈≈≈) are shown separately } Shown collectively as rough grassland on some sheets
Heath

Reeds
Marsh
Saltings

HEIGHTS AND ROCK FEATURES

50 ·
285 · } Determined by { ground survey | air survey

Surface heights are to the nearest metre above mean sea level. Heights shown close to a triangulation pillar refer to the station height at ground level and not necessarily to the summit

Vertical face

Loose rock Boulders Outcrop Scree

Contours are at 5 metres vertical interval

ABBREVIATIONS 1:25 000 or 2½ INCHES to 1 MILE also 1:10 000/1:10 560 or 6 INCHES to 1 MILE

BP,BS	Boundary Post or Stone	P	Post Office	A,R	Telephone, AA or RAC
CH	Club House	Pol Sta	Police Station	TH	Town Hall
F V	Ferry Foot or Vehicle	PC	Public Convenience	Twr	Tower
FB	Foot Bridge	PH	Public House	W	Well
HO	House	Sch	School	Wd Pp	Wind Pump
MP,MS	Mile Post or Stone	Spr	Spring		
Mon	Monument	T	Telephone, public		

Abbreviations applicable only to 1:10 000/1:10 560 or 6 INCHES to 1 MILE

Ch	Church	GP	Guide Post	TCB	Telephone Call Box
F Sta	Fire Station	P	Pole or Post	TCP	Telephone Call Post
Fn	Fountain	S	Stone	Y	Youth Hostel

Maps and Mapping

Most early maps of the area covered by this guide were published on a county basis, and if you wish to follow their development in detail R. V. Tooley's *Maps and Map Makers* will be found most useful. The first significant county maps were produced by Christopher Saxton in the 1570s, the whole of England and Wales being covered in only six years. Although he did not cover the whole country, John Norden, working at the end of the 16th century, was the first map-maker to show roads. In 1611-12 John Speed, making use of Saxton's and Norden's pioneer work, produced his *'Theatre of the Empire of Great Britaine'*, adding excellent town plans, battle scenes, and magnificent coats of arms. The next great English map-maker was John Ogilby, and in 1675 he published *Britannia, Volume I*, in which all the roads of England and Wales were engraved on a scale of one inch to the mile, in a massive series of strip maps. From this time onwards, no map was published without roads, and throughout the 18th century, steady progress was made in accuracy, if not always in the beauty of presentation.

The first Ordnance Survey maps came about as a result of Bonnie Prince Charlie's Jacobite rebellion of 1745. It was, however, in 1791, following the successful completion of the military survey of Scotland by General Roy, that the Ordnance Survey was formally established. The threat of invasion by Napoleon in the early 19th century accelerated the demand for accurate and detailed mapping for military purposes, and to meet this need the first Ordnance Survey one-inch map, covering part of Essex, was published in 1805 in a single colour. This was the first numbered sheet in the First Series of one-inch maps.

Over the next seventy years the one-inch map was extended to cover the whole of Great Britain. Reprints of some of these First Series maps, incorporating various later 19th-century amendments, have been published by David & Charles. The reprinted sheets covering most of our area are Numbers 51, 52, 60 and 61.

The Ordnance Survey's one-inch maps evolved through a number of 'Series' and 'Editions', to the Seventh Series which was replaced in 1972 by the metric 1:50 000 scale Landranger Series. Between the First Series one-inch and the current Landranger maps many changes in style, format, content and purpose have taken place. Colour, for example, first appeared with the timid use of light brown for hill shading on the 1889 one-inch sheets. By 1892 as many as five colours were being used for this scale and at one stage the Seventh Series was being printed in no fewer than ten colours. Recent developments in 'process printing' — a technique in which four basic colours produce almost any required tint — are now used to produce Ordnance Survey Landranger and other map series. Through the years the one-inch series has gradually turned away from its military origins and has developed to meet a wider demand. The modern detailed full-colour Landranger maps at 1:50 000 scale incorporate Rights of Way and Tourist Information and are much used for both leisure and business purposes. To compare the old and new approaches to changing demand, see the two map extracts of Stow-on-the-Wold on the following pages.

Modern Ordnance Survey Maps of the Area.

The Cotswolds are covered by Ordnance Survey 1:50 000 scale (1 ¼ inches to 1 mile) **Landranger** map sheets 150, 151, 162, 163 and 164. These all-purpose maps are packed full of information to help you explore the area. Viewpoints, picnic sites, places of interest, caravan and camping sites are shown, as is information on public rights of way such as footpaths and bridleways. The area is also largely covered by a single map in the Ordnance Survey **Touring Map** series at 1 inch to 1 mile scale. To look at the area surrounding the Cotswolds and to help you plan and follow your route there, the Ordnance Survey 1 inch to 4 miles scale **Routemaster** series — Sheet 7 (Wales and West Midlands), Sheet 8 (South West England and South Wales) and Sheet 9 (South East England) — will prove most useful. An alternative will be found in the form of the **OS Motoring Atlas** of Great Britain at the larger scale of 1 inch to 3 miles.

To examine the Cotswolds in more detail and especially if you are planning walks, Ordnance Survey 1:25 000 scale (2 ½ inches to 1 mile) **Pathfinder** maps, which include public rights of way information, are ideal.

To place the area in a historical context the following Ordnance Survey **Historical Maps** will also be found useful: **Ancient Britain** and **Roman Britain**.

Ordnance Survey maps are available from officially appointed agents (local agents are shown on page 21, under 'Useful Addresses'), and from most booksellers, stationers and newsagents.

See following pages for map extracts relating to the Stow-on-the-Wold area taken from a First Series One-inch map, and a recent Landranger map.

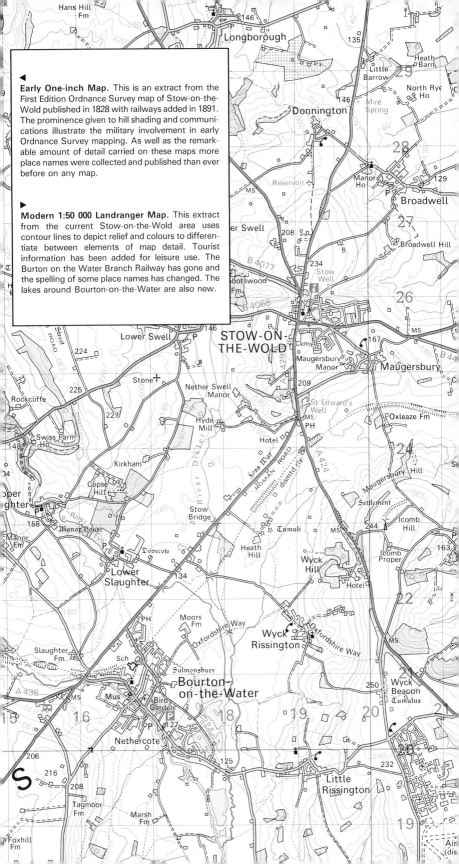

Early One-inch Map. This is an extract from the First Edition Ordnance Survey map of Stow-on-the-Wold published in 1828 with railways added in 1891. The prominence given to hill shading and communications illustrate the military involvement in early Ordnance Survey mapping. As well as the remarkable amount of detail carried on these maps more place names were collected and published than ever before on any map.

Modern 1:50 000 Landranger Map. This extract from the current Stow-on-the-Wold area uses contour lines to depict relief and colours to differentiate between elements of map detail. Tourist information has been added for leisure use. The Burton on the Water Branch Railway has gone and the spelling of some place names has changed. The lakes around Bourton-on-the-Water are also new.

Index

INDEX

Further Reading . . .
A List of Books

General
Beckinsale, R. & M. *The English Heartland.* Duckworth
Brill, E. *Cotswold Crafts.* Batsford
Brill, E. *Cotswold Ways.* Hale
Brill, E. *Life and Tradition on the Cotswolds.* Dent
Brill, E. *Old Cotswold.* David & Charles
Brill, E. *Portrait of the Cotswolds.* Hale
Brill, E. & Turner, P. *The Minor Pleasures of Cotswold.* Dent
Brooks, J.A. *Ghosts and Witches of the Cotswolds.* Jarrold
Crosher, G.R. *Along the Cotswold Ways.* Pan
Emery, F. *The Oxfordshire Landscape.* Hodder & Stoughton
Evans, H.A. *Highways and Byways in Oxford & the Cotswolds.* Macmillan
Finberg, J. *The Cotswolds.* Eyre Methuen
Finberg, H.P.R. *The Gloucestershire Landscape.* Hodder & Stoughton
Gibbs, J.A. *A Cotswold Village.* Murray
Hadfield, C. & M. *The Cotswolds.* Batsford
Henderson, P. *William Morris, his life, work and friends.* Thames & Hudson
Hoskins, W.G. *The Making of the English Landscape.* Pelican
Massingham, H.J. *Cotswold Country.* Batsford
Massingham, H.J. *Wold without End.* Cobden-Sanderson (1932)
Mee, A. *Gloucestershire (King's England Series).* Hodder & Stoughton
Mee, A. *Oxfordshire (King's England Series).* Hodder & Stoughton
Mee, A. *Warwickshire (King's England Series).* Hodder & Stoughton
Piper, J. *Shell Guide to Oxfordshire.* Faber
Smith, B. *The Cotswolds.* Batsford
Verey, D. *Shell Guide to Gloucestershire.* Faber
Warren, C.H. *A Cotswold Year.* Alan Sutton
Waters, B. *Thirteen Rivers to the Thames.* Dent
Witts, F.E. *The Diary of a Cotswold Parson.* Alan Sutton

Art, Architecture & History
Arkell, W.J. *Oxford Stone.* Faber
Atkyns, R. *The Ancient and Present State of Gloucestershire.* (1776)
Beecham, K.J. *A History of Cirencester: The Roman Corinium.* Alan Sutton
Beresford, M. *The Lost Villages of England.* Alan Sutton
Clifford, E.M. *Bagendon: A Belgic Oppidum.* Heffer
Cobbett, W. *Rural Rides.* Penguin
Crawford, O.G.S. *The Long Barrows of the Cotswolds.* (1925)
Derrick, F. *Cotswold Stone.* Chapman & Hall
Dyer, J. *Prehistoric England & Wales.* Penguin
Hart, G. *A History of Cheltenham.* Alan Sutton
Hawkes, J. *Guide to Prehistoric & Roman Monuments in England and Wales.* Cardinal

Jewson, N. *By Chance I Did Rove.* Earle & Ludlow
Johnson, J. *Stow-on-the-Wold.* Alan Sutton
Johnson, J. *Tudor Gloucestershire.* Alan Sutton
Lees-Milne, J. *Some Cotswold Country Houses.* Dovecote Press
McWhirr, A. *Roman Gloucestershire.* Alan Sutton
Margary, I.D. *Roman Roads in Britain.* Phoenix House
Morris, J. (Ed.) *Domesday Book: Gloucestershire.* Phillimore
Morris, J. (Ed.) *Domesday Book: Oxfordshire.* Phillimore
Morris, J. (Ed.) *Domesday Book: Warwickshire.* Phillimore
Playne, A.T. *Minchinhampton and Avening.* Alan Sutton
Plot, N. *The Natural History of Oxfordshire.* (1677)
Powell, G. *The Book of Campden.* Barracuda
Richard, M. & Carpenter, H. *A Thames Companion.* Oxford
Rudder, S. *A New History of Gloucestershire.* (1779) Reprinted by Alan Sutton
Sherwood, J. *Oxfordshire (Buildings of England Series).* Penguin
Tann, J. *Gloucestershire Woollen Mills.* David & Charles
Tooley, R.V. *Maps and Map-Makers.* Batsford
Verey, D. *Gloucestershire: The Cotswolds (Buildings of England Series).* Penguin
Wood, E.S. *Field Guide to Archaeology in Britain.* Collins

Canals and Docks
Conway-Jones, A.H. *A History of Gloucester Docks.* Alan Sutton
Handford, M. *The Stroudwater Canal.* Alan Sutton
Handford, M. & Viner, D. *Stroudwater & Thames and Severn Canals Towpath Guide.* Alan Sutton
Household, H. *The Thames and Severn Canal.* Alan Sutton

Literary Interest and Early Travellers
Defoe, D. *A Tour Through England and Wales.* Penguin
Guinness, J. & C. *The House of Mitford.* Fontana
Mitford, J. *Hons and Rebels.* Penguin
Morris, C. (Ed.) *The Journeys of Celia Fiennes.* Macdonald

Railways
Coleman, T. *The Railway Navvies.* Penguin
Household, H. *Gloucestershire Railways in the Twenties.* Alan Sutton
MacDermot, E.T. *History of the Great Western Railway.* Ian Allen
Maggs, C. *Railways of the Cotswolds.* Peter Nicholson
Norris, J. *The Stratford & Moreton Tramway.* Railway & Canal Historical Society
Rolt, L.T.C. *Isambard Kingdom Brunel.* Penguin

Walks and Walking
Conduit, B. and Brooks, J. *Cotswold Walks Pathfinder Guide.* Ordnance Survey/Jarrold Publishing
Lewis, J. *Walking the Cotswold Way.* David & Charles
Oxfordshire County Council *The Oxfordshire Way Guide.*
Sale, R. *A Guide to the Cotswold Way.* Constable